Orlando Deaths
Oct 22, 1922 - April 30, 1929

Transcribed from "Register of Deaths"
Orlando (Florida) Health Department

Compiled and edited by Betty Jo Stockton
Data extraction and entry by Eva Buchanan

Table of Contents

Abbreviations

Race: B or C = black / colored; W = white; Cu = Cuban
Marital statue: S = single; M = married; D = divorced; W = widowed; Inf = infant
Age or length of residence: yr = year; mo or m = months; da or d = days
                               h or hr = hours; mi = minutes
Other: SB = stillborn; DK = don't know; HW = housewife

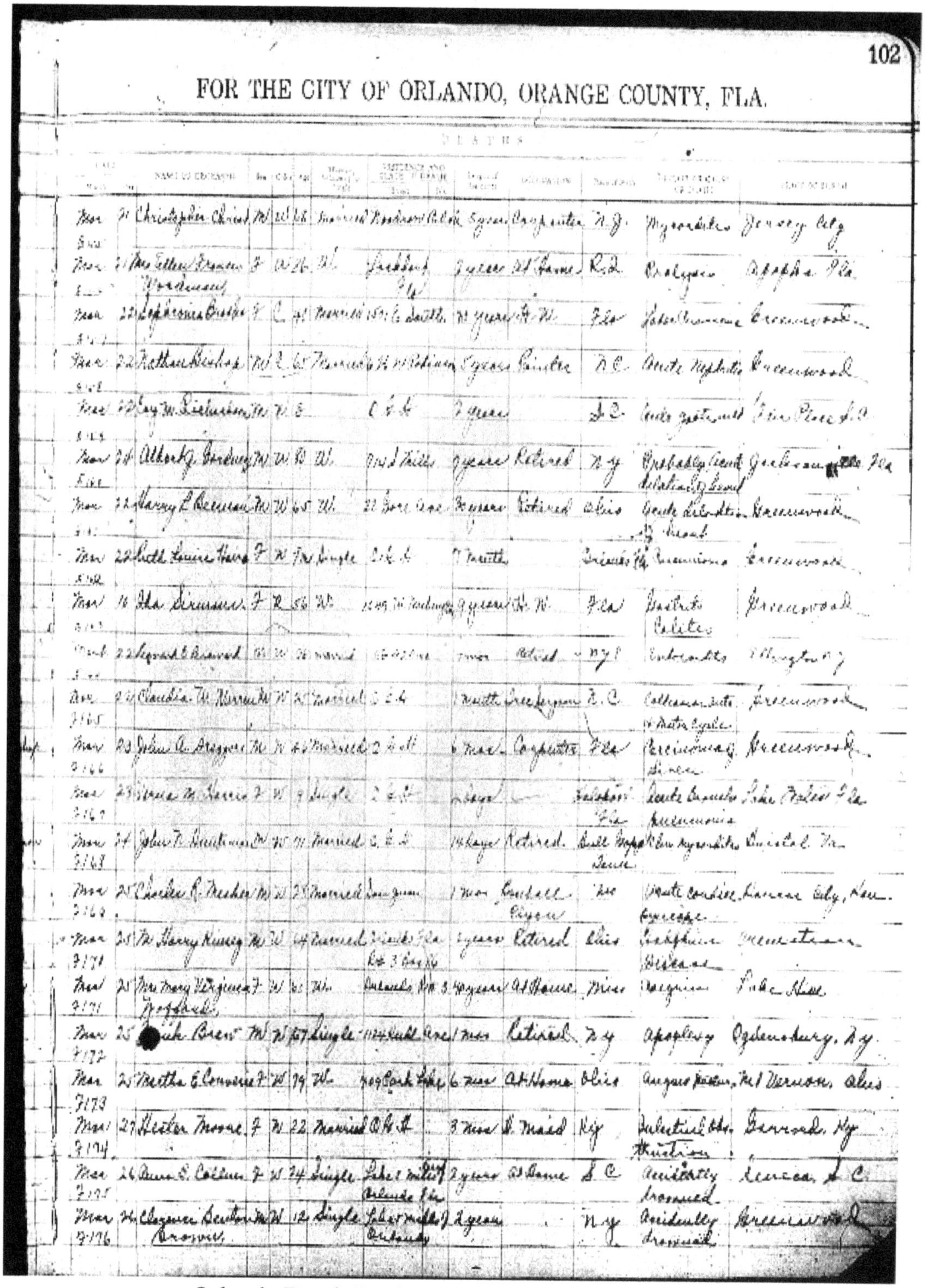

102

FOR THE CITY OF ORLANDO, ORANGE COUNTY, FLA.

DEATHS

Date / No.	Day	Name of Deceased	Sex	Color	Age	Marital	Residence	Length of Residence	Occupation	Nativity	Cause of Death	Place of Burial
Mar [illegible]	21	Christopher Christ	M	W	68	Married	[illegible]	5 years	Carpenter	N.J.	Myocarditis	Jersey City
Mar [illegible]	21	Mrs Ellen Frances Woodman	F	W	76	W.	[illegible] Fla	7 years	At Home	R.I.	Paralysis	Apopka Fla
Mar [illegible]	22	Sophronia Bishop	F	C	45	Married	[illegible]	10 years	H. W.	Fla	[illegible]	Greenwood
Mar [illegible]	22	Nathan Bishop	M	C	65	Married	[illegible]	5 years	Painter	N.C.	Acute Nephritis	Greenwood
Mar [illegible]	22	Guy W. [illegible]	M	W	8		O.H.A.	7 years		S.C.	Acute gastritis	[illegible] S.C.
Mar [illegible]	24	Albert G. [illegible]	M	W	80	W.	[illegible]	9 years	Retired	N.Y.	Probably Acute dilatation of heart	Jacksonville Fla
Mar [illegible]	22	Harry L. [illegible]	M	W	65	W.	[illegible]	3 years	Retired	Ohio	Acute dilatation of heart	Greenwood
Mar [illegible]	22	Ruth Louise [illegible]	F	W	[illegible]	Single	O.H.A.	7 months		[illegible]	Pneumonia	Greenwood
Mar [illegible]	16	Ida Simmons	F	R	56	W.	[illegible]	9 years	H. W.	Fla	Diabetes Colitis	Greenwood
Mar [illegible]	22	[illegible]	M	W	[illegible]	Married	[illegible]	[illegible]	Retired	N.Y.	[illegible]	[illegible] N.Y.
Mar 7165	24	Claudia W. [illegible]	M	W	25	Married	O.H.A.	1 month	[illegible]	N.C.	Collision auto & motor cycle	Greenwood
Mar 7166	23	John A. [illegible]	M	W	44	Married	[illegible]	6 mos.	Carpenter	Fla	[illegible]	Greenwood
Mar 7167	23	[illegible] M. Harris	F	W	9	Single	O.H.A.	[illegible] days		[illegible] Fla	Acute [illegible] pneumonia	Lake Wales Fla
Mar 7168	24	John W. [illegible]	M	W	71	Married	O.H.A.	14 days	Retired.	[illegible] Tenn	[illegible]	Bristol Va.
Mar 7169	25	Charles R. [illegible]	M	W	28	Married	[illegible]	1 mo.	[illegible]	[illegible]	[illegible]	Kansas City, Kan.
Mar 7170	25	Mr Harry [illegible]	M	W	64	Married	[illegible] Fla	2 years	Retired	Ohio	[illegible] Disease	[illegible]
Mar 7171	25	Mrs Mary Virginia [illegible]	F	W	60	W.	Orlando [illegible]	4 years	At Home	Miss	[illegible]	Lake View
Mar 7172	25	[illegible] Brew	M	W	67	Single	[illegible] Ave	1 mo.	Retired	N.Y.	Apoplexy	Ogdensburg, N.Y.
Mar 7173	25	Bertha E. Converse	F	W	74	W.	[illegible]	6 mos.	At Home	Ohio	[illegible]	Mt Vernon, Ohio
Mar 7174	27	Hester Moore	F	W	22	Married	O.H.A.	3 mos.	H. Maid	Ky	[illegible]	[illegible], Ky
Mar 7175	26	Anna E. Collins	F	W	24	Single	[illegible] Orlando Fla	2 years	At Home	S.C.	Accidentally drowned	Seneca, S.C.
Mar 7176	26	Clarence Benton Brown	M	W	12	Single	[illegible] Orlando	2 years		N.Y.	Accidentally drowned	Greenwood

Orlando Death Register 1922-1929, p. 102 [1927]

Introduction

The city of Orlando maintained a Register of Deaths within the city during the period of 1910-October 20, 1929. These were kept in large ledger books by the Orlando City Department of Health. These were moved to the Florida State Office of Vital Statistics in Jacksonville and are only available for viewing by appointment.

The first volume, which recorded both births and deaths from January 1910 to Oct 20, 1922 was microfilmed in 1998 and the film placed in the Orlando Public Library. The second volume recorded only deaths and included those from October 22, 1922 until April 30, 1929. This was microfilmed by the Family History Library and is available through local Family History Centers as film #2110368, Items 7-8. It is also on permanent loan at the Orlando Family History Center. To the best of our knowledge, these records are not available anywhere else.

The Central Florida Genealogical Society has published two books, *Orlando Births 1910-1922* and *Orlando Deaths 1910-1922*, covering the records in Volume 1 of the Death Register. These are available through the CFGS website at <www.cfgs.org>. This book covers deaths from October 22, 1922 to April 30, 1929. The ledgers were not continued after that date.

Florida Sanitarium (now Florida Hospital) opened in 1908; Orange General Hospital (now Orlando Health) opened in late 1918. These attracted patients from all of central Florida, as well as many visitors to the area. Thus the records of Orlando deaths include many who were not from Orlando, but died here. This volume gives name, date of death, residence, occupation, place of death, length of time in Orlando, cause of death and burial place.

Where writing was legible, names are listed exactly as they were spelled in the ledger. Many were barely legible, so, for those, we made a "best guess" effort to record the name as written. In those instances where we could determine the correct name from other sources, we included the name as written along with the corrected name following in brackets i.e. Smith [Smythe].

Transcribing cause of death presents a real challenge. Many of the entries were totally illegible. Others refer to diseases and conditions unknown to the abstractor. We made a guess or included the letters that we were able to read along with ___ to show illegible ones. Where there were guesses, they were marked with a question mark.

During the period that this book was in progress, other records have gone online that expand the information found here. The Family History Library has released *Florida Deaths 1877-1939*, which can be found at <www.familysearch.org>. The Central Florida Memory Project includes the early records of Carey Hand Funeral Home in Orlando. Carey Hand was the undertaker for many Orlandoans, mostly caucasian or those who died at the Orange County Home. These may be found at <www.cfmemory.org/Collection/CareyHand>. Those persons who are in Carey Hand records are marked with an *. Since each source included slightly different information, using all three gives a more complete picture of those who died in Orlando during this time period.

Date	Name of Deceased	Sex	Race	Age	Marital Status	Residence & Place of Death	Orlando Resident	Occupation	Place of Birth	Cause of Death	Place of Burial
22-Oct	*John G. Walker	M	W	69	M	E. Amelia Ave	35 yr	Engineer	Ga	Carcinoma of Liver	Greenwood
20-Oct	J. R. Rowes	M	W	54	M	244 Rosalind	10 yr	Lawyer	Waverly, Ala	Acute Cardiac Dilitation	Catholic Cemetery
25-Oct	*Frank M. Banter	M	W	79	M	Orlando		Druggist	Steuben Co., N.Y.	Shock following Operation	Minn., Minn
29-Oct	*Mrs. Mollie Marshall	F	W	50	M	31½ W. Church	3 yrs	At Home	Roanoke, Ala	Chronic Eczema & Progressive Anemia	Greenwood
29-Oct	John Clay	M	C	56	M	Orlando	11 m	Farmer	Ga	Acute Nephritis	Ashburn, Ga
31-Oct	Victor Greenwood [Greenmore?]	M	C	Inf	S	Orlando			Orlando	Eph____?	Geo. Greenmore
1-Nov	*Oliver Smith	M	W	57		Orlando	3 da	Naval Officer	Denholm, Scotland	Ruptured Cardiac A____?	Washington, D.C.
3-Nov	Geo. Greenmore	M	W	5½ d	S	Pine Castle Rural	5 da	Infant	Orange Co.	Inmature Infant	Greenwood
1-Nov	*Susan P. Jacobs	F	C	53	D	Orlando	1 mo 10 d	House Work	Valdosta, Ga	M____? Cerebral Abscess	Valdosta, Ga
7-Nov	*Mrs. Lobbie [Lottie] D. Ray	F	W	41	W	W. Pine	8 mo	At Home	Thomas? Co, Ga	Pneumonia	St. Petersburg, Fla
8-Nov	*Master Harry N. Dickson	M	W	4	S	166 E. Amelia			Orlando, Fla	Colitis	Greenwood
7-Nov	*Hugh B. Russell	M	W	39	M	W. Kaley Ave	2 yrs	Painter	Carrolton, Ga	Perforated Duodenal Ulcers?	Carrolton, Ga
8-Nov	William Rigsbee	M	C		S	Orlando		Baby	Orlando, Fla	Pneumonia	Greenwood
8-Nov	Tomme [Tommie] Willis	F	C	46	M	Orlando	1 yr	House wife	Ga	Pneumonia	Greenwood
14-Nov	Infant of Mr & Mrs C. J. Davis		W		S				C. J. Davis	Stillborn	Greenwood
14-Nov	*Emma Eletha [Aletha] Proctor	F	W	3	S				Summerfield, Fla	Dyphtheria	Oxford, Fla
10-Nov	*Infant of Mr & Mrs V. Martina	F	W		S		1 yr		Orlando, Fla	Born Dead	Catholic Cemetery
12-Nov	*Wm Edmond Cleary	M	W	49	M	Orlando	3 mo	Real Estate	Westfield, Mass	Asthma & Cardiac Failure	Catholic Cemetery
16-Nov	Eddie Lee Anderson	M	C	7 ds	S	Orlando	7 ds		Orange Co.	____? Colon	Greenwood
17-Nov	*Monroe Maxwell	M	C	85	W	Orlando	35 yrs	Labor	Ga	Gangrene in Foot Rt. Leg	Winter Park
19-Nov	*Myrtice Dorthy Dickson?	F	W	7 mo	S	166 E. Amelia			Orlando, Fla	Acute Bacillary? Dysentery	Greenwood
18-Nov	*Odis Kendrick	M	C	35	S	Orange Co.	1 mo	Day Labor	P. ?. Thompson	Killed by Train	Greenwood
16-Nov	*M. H. Nelson	M	W	60	W	Orlando		Day Labor	No Relatives	Erysipelatous? Of Face	Greenwood
19-Nov	*Dortha Isabel Davis	F	W	15	S	Lockhart	10 ds	In School	America?, N.Y.	Acute Poliomyelitis	Greenwood
21-Nov	*Joe Tierney	M	W	55	M	Orlando	12 ds	Hotel Employee	Not Known	Pulmonary T. B.	New York City
24-Nov	*Wilson Forsaith	M	W	80	W	Orlando	7 ds	Retired Banker	Leving?, N. H.	Heart Disease	Hillboro, N. H.
19-Nov	*Robt. James Cromartie?	M	C	50	M	606 Wash.	35 yrs	Day Labor	Fla	Cirrhosis of Liver?	Greenwood

1922	Name of Deceased	Sex	Race	Age	Marital Status	Residence & Place of Death	Orlando Resident	Occupation	Place of Birth	Cause of Death	Place of Burial
29-Nov	Mrs. Martha Geiger	F	W	67	W	Orlando	15 ds	None	Marion Co., Fla	Pylo-nephritis	Apopka, Fla
29-Nov	*Wm Crawford Morris	M	W	92	M	579 Cathcart	4 yrs	Section? Foreman	Ga	Pneumonia	Maitland, Fla
3-Dec	*Edwin S. Gilbert	M	W	66	M	Orlando	3 ds	Machin-ist?	Augusta, Maine	Asthma & Cardiac Failure	Philadelphia
1-Dec	*James M. Earp	M	W	71	W	Orlando	2 yrs	Merchant	Wilks? Co., N.C.	Organic Heart Disease	Greenwood
5-Dec	*Mr. Angus Campbell	M	W	75	M	Orlando	10 yrs	Farming	Quebec, Canada	Senility; Chro-nic Nephritis	Kissimmee
7-Dec	Maury? Baylarion?	F	W	60	W	Orlando	9 yrs		Gesoria? Romania	Cerebral Hemorrhage	Greenwood
9-Dec	*Mr. Wm T. Williams	M	W	64	W	Orlando		Fruit Grower	Wales	Carcinoma of Face	Greenwood
9-Dec	*Corine Wesson	F	W	2	S	Orlando	2 yrs		Orlando, Fla	Acute Gastroenteritis	Winter Park
10-Dec	*William Peterson	M	W	13	S	Orlando			Ludlow, Pa	Dyphtheria	Greenwood
11-Dec	*Mrs Katie Gresham	F	W	54	M	Orlando	2 ds	At Home	Fla	Pylo-nephritis	Geneva, Fla
12-Dec	*Mary Eliza. Deull	F	W	42	M	Orlando	1 da	At Home	Maitland, Fla	Pneumonia	Maitland, Fla
13-Dec	*Fredic. Berk [Berke]	M	W	24	M	421 Ruth St.	10 yrs	Clerical Work	W Hobo-kin, N.J.	Broncho Pneumonia	Catholic Cemetery
14-Dec	Clara Parrish	F	C		S	Kentucky Ave.		None	Orlando, Fla	Stillborn	Greenwood
15-Dec	*Raymond F. Haskill	M	W	45	S	Orlando	2 da	Piedmont Directory Co.	Manches-ter, Mass	Chronic Asthma	Ashville, N.C.
14-Dec	Mannie Hamish [Harrish?]	F	C	57	M	Orlando	4 da	Cook	Ga	Broncho Pneumonia	Taft, Fla
15-Dec	Christian Byson	M	W	80	M	222 Ridge-wood			Denmark	Carcinoma of Stomach	Algona? Iowa
14-Dec	*Lwaynda [Lucynda?] Sanders	F	C	75	W	433 Holden St.		House Work	Tallahassee, Fla	Chronic Nephritis	Greenwood
18-Dec	*Infant of W. J. Campbell & Wife	M	W		S	Orlando	Par-ents 3 mo		Orlando	Premature 28 weeks	Greenwood
16-Dec	*Robt Louis Crouse	M	W	3 da	S	E. Mark St.			Orlando	Hemorrhage	Greenwood
16-Dec	*Egbert Martin Carver	M	W	84	M	14 N. Hughey	8 yrs	Banker	Vermont	Cardio-Nephritis	
18-Dec	*Taft Hall	M	W	14	S	Orlando		Day Labor	Moultrie?, Ga	Pulmonary Em-boli Following Flu	Winter Park
18-Dec	*Lubish [Lutish?] Williams	F	C	35	M	30 W. Robinson	2 yrs	Domestic	S.C.	Hemorrhage from Wound	County Home
20-Dec	Hanson King	M	C	23	S	Orlando		Laborer	Leon Co	Incipient T.B.	Greenwood
19-Dec	*Wm Henry Baughman	M	W	72	W	Orlando		Farming	Canada	Pleurisy with Myocarditis	Greenwood
20-Dec	*Lebbie [Lettie] Austin	F	C	42	M	140 W. Livingston	8 yrs 11 m	At Home	Lord? Co, Fla	Acute Gastric Indigestion	Greenwood
23-Dec	*Dr. Mathew Wilton	M	W	87	M	207 Liberty St.	6 yrs	Medical M.D.	New York City	Chronic Interstitial Nephritis	Greensbury, Ind

Date	Name of Deceased	Sex	Race	Age	Marital Status	Residence & Place of Death	Orlando Resident	Occupation	Place of Birth	Cause of Death	Place of Burial
24-Dec	*Elmer Elsworth Williams	M	W	22	S	Orlando	6 mos	Core? Maker	Pittsburgh, Pa	Diabetes	Greenwood
25-Dec	Johnnie Williams	M	C	18	S	Orlando	2 yrs	Labor	Lord?, Fla	Pneumonia	Greenwood
25-Dec	*Miss Mary Helen Ingram	F	W	72	S	Orlando	3 ds	Teacher	Cincinnati	Uremia	Spring Valley, Ohio
26-Dec	*Marian C. Wilson	F	W	22	M	Orlando	5 ds	At Home	Astatula	Pueperal Septicemia	Astatula, Fla
24-Dec	*Georgia Lucile Mack	F	W	3 mo	S	Orlando	12 ds		Orlando	Pneumonia	Greenwood
24-Dec	*John L. Allen	M	W	73	M	Orlando	1 yr 6 mo	Retired Banker	Bainbridge, Ga.	Cirrhosis of Liver?	Greenwood
26-Dec	*Miss Sarah A. Green	F	W	69	W	145 E. Amelia	15 yrs	At Home	Epp Eng.	Acute Indigestion	Greenwood
27-Dec	*Tallie [Lillie] May Haddox	F	W	2	S	Orlando	2 yrs		Orlando, Fla	Double Pneumonia	Apopka, Fla
28-Dec	*Wilmot Eaton Carpenter	M	W	83	W	Orlando	1 mo 14 ds	Retired Farmer	Tunkhan-nock, Pa	Chronic Nephritis	Tunkhannock, Pa
28-Dec	*Milton T. [J?] Merideth	M	W	9	S	Orlando	1 da		Ala	Malaria	Greenwood
31-Dec	*Annie Blanch Wettengel	F	W	58	M	Orlando	3 wks	At Home	Pittsburgh, Pa	Gangrene Colon	Pittsburgh, Pa

1923	Name of Deceased	Sex	Race	Age	Marital	Residence & Place of Death	Resid	Occupation	Place of Birth	Cause of Death	Place of Burial
1-Jan	*James T. Steed	M	W	70	W	Pine Castle	2 mos	Retired Farmer	Lincoln, Ga	Heart Disease	Floral City, Fla
2-Jan	Wesley Bullock	M	C	88	W	Chasham? St.	6 mos	None	Ga	Paralysis	Greenwood
1-Jan	Infant Jackson	F	C		S	Washing-ton			Orlando	Stillborn	County Home
1-Jan	Infant Jackson	M	C		S	Washington			Orlando	Stillborn	County Home
3-Jan	*Chester E. Thomas, Jr.	M	C	2	S	609 Gore Ave	2 years		Orlando	Septic Tonsilitis	Greenwood
5-Jan	Infant Davis	M	C		S	Orlando		Babe	Orlando	Stillborn	Greenwood
5-Jan	Anne Bivens	F	C	27	M	Orlando	37	Housewife	Orlando	Malaria Fever	Greenwood
6-Jan	*Infant Mr & Mrs H. M. Starbird	M	W		S	Orlando	1 day		Orlando	Stillborn - premature	Apopka, Fla
6-Jan	*Miss Lilla McDonald Keldrain	F	W	74	W	Orlando	3 mo	At Home	Blooming ton	Myocarditis	Indianapolis, Ind
7-Jan	Ruth Williams	F	C	19	S	Orlando		Cook	Madison, Fla	Child Birth & Plural? Convulsion	Live Oak, Fla
8-Jan	Willie Bronth	M	C	1 d	S	Terry Ave			Orlando	Stillborn	Greenwood
10-Jan	*Chas. W. Ripley	M	W	75	M	Orlando		Hotel Business	Boston, Mass	T.B. of Lungs	Wareham, Mass
9-Jan	*Jesse Sellins (Sellers)	M	W	73	M	Orlando		Farmer	Penn	Opr. Enlarged prostate; carcinoma	Mt. Vernon, Ohio
13-Jan	*Wm C. Yartman (Zartman)	M	W	83	M	Orlando	4 ½ da	Carpenter	Ohio	Cerebral Hemorrhage	Lowell, Ind
15-Jan	*Mary B. Schubart	F	W		W	Trenton, Ohio	7 days	At Home	Martins Ferry, OH	Broncho-Pneu monia	Ironton, Ohio
14-Jan	*Howard S. Graham	M	W	58	M	Orlando		Retired Farmer	Mt. Ver-non, Ohio		Mt. Vernon, Ohio
16-Jan	*Sarah Eugenia Walters	F	W	34	M	Orlando	4 yrs	At Home	Houston Co., Ga	Pulmonary T. B.	Greenwood
18-Jan	*Aaron Brown	M	W	51	M	Orlando	11 days	Flour & Feed Business	Exeter, Pa	Chronic Myocarditis	Tunkhannock, Pa
18-Jan	*Mr. Maurice R. Cohen	M	W	63	M	Orlando	1 day	Traveling Salesman		Dropped dead	Jacksonville, Fla
17-Jan	Seebren Cannon	F	W	18	M	Orlando	5 da		Fla	Peritonitis	Worthington Springs, Fla
19-Jan	Sam Ward	M	C	47		408 Wash-ington		Labor	Ga	Broncho Pneumonia	Greenwood
22-Jan	*Miss Helen Nye White	F	W	74	S	Orlando		At Home	Pittsburgh Pa	Secondary Anemia	Sewickley, Pa
20-Jan	*Harvey Kildinger	M	W	11 mo	S	Orlando	abt 3 wks		Witwau-kee, Wis	Iliocolitis	Greenwood
21-Jan	Thomas Deadwiler	M	C	38	M	208 Parramore		Labor		Arterio-sclerosis	Greenwood
21-Jan	Sarah A Pervat [Prevat]	F	W	56	W	Orlando		Housewife	Sumter Co., Ga	_elam?	Shingle Creek Cemetery
24-Jan	*Hirmon (Hiram) H. Ramsey (Ranney)	M	W	80	M	Orlando	7 days	Merchant Retired	Mohawk, N.Y.	Septic Pros-tatitis & Cys_	Herkimer, N.Y.
23-Jan	Mrs Margaret Schnarr	F	W	53	M	Orlando	10 yrs		Harmon?, Pa	Toxemia	Catholic Cemetery

10

1923	Name of Deceased	Sex	Race	Age	Marital	Residence & Place of Death	Resid	Occupation	Place of Birth	Cause of Death	Place of Burial
23Jan1 4	Louise Homer	F	C	12	S	Orlando			Jackson-ville	Mitral Insufficiency	Greenwood
24-Jan	*Henry H. Merritt	M	W	57	M	Orlando	1 mo	Lumber Merchant	Hartland, Vt.	Peritonitis	Claremont, N.H.
26-Jan	*Mr John Irvin Marshall	M	W	58	M	Orlando	14 days	Mfgr	Watertown N.Y.	Apoplexy	Chicago
27-Jan	*Gerald Crook (Crooks)	M	W		S	Fern Creek Road			Orlando	Mucous Colitis	Cincinnati, Ohio
27-Jan	*Jona (Jammie) Francis Davis	F	W	1	S	826 W. Church	1 yr 3 mo		Sanders-ville, Ga	Inb__? Colitis	Greenwood
29-Jan	*Anthony Victor Batulis	M	W	28	S	Orlando	1 mo	Public Account	Patton, Pa	Pulmonary T.B.	Philadelphia
29-Jan	Verincen Armstrong	F	C	2	S	Orlando			Orlando	Burns; Scalded	Greenwood
30-Jan	*Infant of Mr.& Mrs Chas. Adams	F	W		S	Orlando			Orlando	?	Lake Alfred
31-Jan	*Elizabeth Farris Keller	F	W	53	M	Lucerne Court	15 yrs	At Home	Danville, Ky	Chronic Nephritis	Greenwood
28-Jan	*John A. Hopper	M	W	62	M	308 W. Church	5 yrs	Merchant	Tenn	Pneumonia & Complications	Greenwood Cemetery
28-Jan	Joseph Fenton	M	C	57	W	Washing-ton	11 yrs	Merchant	S.C.	Renal Hemorrhage	Greenwood
30-Jan	*Gus C. Noyes	M	W	70	M	307 E. Robinson	6 yrs	Stockman	Augusta, Maine	Pneumonia	Fort Worth, Tex
2-Feb	*John Emory Buxton	M	W	83	W	Orlando	4 mo	Mine Operator	Middle-town Sprs, Vt	Chronic Myocarditis	Middletown Springs, Vt
01Feb1 4	*Mr Ward Tompkin (Lampkin)	M	W	59	M	Formosa	2 mo 14 ds	Farmer & Book-keeping	Kings Ferry, N.Y	Malnutrition	In Vault
1-Feb	*Amelia Hillman	F	W	67	M	Orlando	3 mos	At Home	Denmark	Apoplexy	Patterson, N. Y.
4-Feb	*Chas. B. Becker	M	W	1	S	1000 S. Hughey	1 yr 1 mo		Orlando	Acute Lef__?	County Home
4-Feb	*Calla Abical? Liflink (Lillivick)	F	W	34	M	Orlando	2? y 9 mo	At Home	Iowa	Pulmonary T.B.	Greenwood
4-Feb	*Mrs Ettie May Whitfield	F	W	27	M	Orlando/ O.G.H.	2	At Home	Plains-ville, Ala	Toxemia of Pregnancy	In Vault at present
6-Feb	James Griffen	M	C	24	M	408 Division/ Orlando		Labor	Ga	Gangrene of Penis & Scrotum	Greenwood
8-Feb	Baby Price	M	C	0	S	Orlando			Orlando	Stillborn	Greenwood
7-Feb	*John T. Horseman	M	W	90	W	628 E. Washington Orlando	10 yrs	Farmer Retired	Fairfax Co., Va	Pulmonary Odemia	Greenwood
9-Feb	John Mumford	M	Co l	78	S	Orlando		Labor	Ga	Mitral Spenosis?	Greenwood
13-Feb	*Mrs Lizzie Elwell Read	F	W	40	M	3 Green-leaf Ave/ Medford, Mass (Maine?)		At Home	N. Pen-obscot, Maine	Infuenza	Winter Park
10-Feb	*Sidney A. Dunaway	M	W	74	W	Orlando/ Orlando		Farming Retired	Wood-berry, Ga	Cerebral Hemorrhage	Apopka

1923	Name of Deceased	Sex	Race	Age	Marital	Residence & Place of Death	Resid	Occupation	Place of Birth	Cause of Death	Place of Burial
11-Feb	*Mrs Mae Jones	F	W	37	M	8 mi E Orlando/ O.G.H.	5 ds	At Home	York-town, Canada	Infected Embolis	Greenwood
12-Feb	*Edward Estle Baldwin	M	W	77	M	Parsippany N.J./OGH.	1 mo 15 ds	Farmer Retired	Parsip-pany, N.J.	Acute Nephritis	Parsippany, N.J.
15-Feb	Sarrah Jones	F	C		S	225Division / Orlando			Orlando	Stillborn	Greenwood
16-Feb	*Myron H. Ray	M	W	67	M	Bellows Falls, Vt/ Fairgrounds	3 mos	Lumber Dealer	Heiniken N.H.	Apoplexy	Bellows Falls, Vt
14-Feb	*John Frederick Wm. Lersch	M	W	41	D	Orlando/ Fern Creek Drive	3 yrs	Builder Self	Talion, Ohio	Sarcoma	Greenwood
16-Feb	Caroline Connor	F	C			422 Jack-son/ Orl			Orlando	Stillborn	Greenwood
14-Feb	Ellerby Brooks	F	C	7	S	South St./ Orlando		None	Jackson-ville	Hemorrhage	Greenwood
21-Feb	*Ethel Bell Wilkerson	F	W	25	M	Winter Garden/ O.G.H.	10 ds	At Home	Long Creek, S.C.	Ecluptice?	Clayton, Ga
20-Feb	*Mr. Jacob Kleinman	M	W	49	M	Orlando	6 yrs	Merchant Fruit	Russia	Acute Nephritis	Pittsburg, Pa
20-Feb	*Richard Harding	M	W	1	S	Washington, D.C./OGH.	21 days		Washing-ton, D.C.	Septic Meningitis	Greenwood
16-Feb	*Mrs Carolina G. Gore	F	W	79	W	211 Lucerne Circle	17 yrs	At Home	Germany	La Grippe & Acute Myocarditis	Sioux City, Iowa
21-Feb	*Albert Boulice	M	W	45	M	East Bane, Vt/ Howell Sanitarium	1 mo	Stone Cuttter	Canada	Pulmonary Eadema (Edema)	East Bane, Vt
23-Feb	*Maurice K. Reynolds	M	W	56	M	Fall River, Mass/ 621 E. Wash-ington		Cont. Apron & Towel Supply Co	Fall River, Mass	Chronic Nephritis; Cardiac Insufficency	Fall River, Mass
21-Feb	*Mrs Emma Govantist	F	W	60	W	Orlando, Fla/ O.G.H.	9 yrs			Cardio-Renal Insufficiency	Greenwood
20-Feb	*John Bates (Baltes)	M	W	61	M	Cor. Wood-ward & Shine/ Orlando	8 mos	Clothing Cutter Retired	Kanoska, Wis	Cerebral Hemorrhage	New York City
22-Feb	*C. C. High	M	W	69	M	Dutton, Kalamazoo, Mich/ Orlando		Clerk		Cardo Nephritis	Kalamazoo, Mich
no date	Rudolph V. Partiss	M	W	2 mo	S	842 S. Hughey/ Orlando	2 mo 7 ds		Orlando	Pneumonia; Malnutrition	Greenwood
23-Feb	*John W. Wheeler	M	W	66	W	Charlotte, N.C.	6 mos	Carpenter	Meni-town, Pa	Apoplexy	Union Town, Pa
23-Feb	*Henry Revanue	M	C	35	S	County Home	6 mos	Labor		Acute Pul-monary T.B.	Greenwood
26-Feb	*Elma A. Carpenter	F	W	75	S	Pontiac, Mich/ 441 S. Main	4 mos	At Home	Mich	Cerebral Hemorrhage	Pontiac, Mich

12

1923	Name of Deceased	Sex	Race	Age	Marital	Residence & Place of Death	Resid	Occupation	Place of Birth	Cause of Death	Place of Burial
25-Feb	Augustus M. Dawson	M	W	76	W	1401 Lakeview/ 1401 Lakeview		Retired	Columbia Co, Ohio	Acute Nephritis	Belleview, Kansas
27-Feb	*Mary N. Richeson	F	W	78	W	Greenville, Ohio/ OGH.	3 mos	At Home	Ohio	Myocarditis; Acute Delerium	Greenville, Ohio
28-Feb	*Mrs. Florence May Barker	F	W	40	M	640 W. Pine	2 yrs	At Home	Parkersburg, Wva	Chronic Interstitial Nephritis	Greenwood
1-Mar	Mrs. Floria Everleth? (Eveleth)	F	W	76	W	24 E. Church	Sev Yrs	At Home	Lockhart, N.Y.	Cerebral Hemorrhage	Kansas City, Mo.
1-Mar	*Geo. S. Griffin	M	W	16	S	Orlando/ 433 Ruth St.	4 yrs	School Student	Americus, Ga	Chronic Nephritis	Greenwood
1-Mar	*Miss Mary J. Martin	F	W	62	S	Crawfordville, Ind/ O.G.H.	2 mos	At Home	Crawfordville, Ind	Influenza	Crawfordville, Ind.
1-Mar	Jaminin? Culbreth?	F	C	38	M	/ Orlando	9 yrs	Housewife	Ga	Ovarian Cyst	Greenwood
2-Mar	Ellen Butler	F	C	49	W	515 Jefferson/ Orlando	20 yrs	Cook	Fla	Nephritis Complicated Uremia	Greenwood
2-Mar	*Thomas J. Mathers	M	W	26	W	Orlando/ O.G.H.	5 ds	Farming & Fruit Grower	Madison Co, Fla	Acute Dilation of Heart	Lake Howell, Fla
2-Mar	Infant Mr & Mrs Edw. Prokap?	F			S	Orlando			Orlando, Fla	Prematurity	Greenwood
3-Mar	*Merritt B. Hayes	M	W	60	M	Plattsburg, NY/ Park Ave	3 mos.	Janitor	Champlain, N.Y.	Senile Degeneration of the Brain	Plattsburg, N.Y.
3-Mar	*Clance (Clarence) H. Faxon	M	W	60	D	Orlando/ O.G.H.	6 yrs	Comm. Agt C & O. RR.	Chicago, Ill	Paralysis Agitans	Greenwood
4-Mar	*Bara Masie (Marie) Jewell	F	W	3	S	Granville, Mich/ E Colonial		Granville, Mich		Pyelitis	Granville, Mich
5-Mar	*Marion Ward Chandler	F	W	69	S	S. Lancaster, Mass	4 mos	At Home	S. Lancaster, Mass	Organic Disease of Heart	So. Lancaster, Mass
6-Mar	*Mrs. Macey A. Bushefield	F	W	64	W	Toronto, Ohio; O.G.H.	2 mo 14 ds	At Home	Waiterville, Oh	Pulmonary Tubercuslosis	Toronto, Ohio
6-Mar	*Fillman (Freeman) Mason	M	C	22	S	Winter Garden/ O.G.H.	2 ds	Day Labor	Washington Co, Ga	Gun Shot Wound (Homicidal)	Tenille? , Ga
8-Mar	*Frank Reinsch	M	W	73	M	Orlando; 1 mi S of City	26 yrs	Gardener & Orange Growing	Germany	Pulmonary Aedemia & Carcinoma of Liver	Catholic Cemetery
8-Mar	*Mrs. Bessie T. Roumillat	F	W	55	W	16 N. Summerlin/16 N. Summerlin	6 mo		Charleston, S.C.	Carcinoma Uterus	Catholic Cemetery
9-Mar	Samie? Lee? Williams	F	C	6 d	S	900 South, Orlando	6 ds	None	Ga	Bronchitis	Greenwood
6-Mar	Susie Dieheart Murphy	F	C	25	W	706 Long, Orlando	25 yrs	Laundress	Jacksonville	Miscarriage	Greenwood

1923	Name of Deceased	Sex	Race	Age	Marital	Residence & Place of Death	Resid	Occupation	Place of Birth	Cause of Death	Place of Burial
8-Mar	Neal E. Phillips	M	W	30	M	Clermont, Fla/ Orlando		Farmer	Ga	Fracture	Webster
8-Mar	*Sylvester L. Sears	M	W	75	M	Chicago, Ill/ N Orange	3 mos	Foreman in Shop	Rome, Mass	Abscess of Liver	W. Pullman, Chicago, Ill
9-Mar	Baby Gaven	F	C	4	S	415 Parramore	4 mos	None	Orlando	Ileocolitis	Greenwood
8-Mar	*Frank Aiken (Akin)	M	C	64	W	Tallahassee/ E S Orlando	7 mos	Labor	Tallahassee, Fla	Brights Disease	Greenwood
8-Mar	James Corbett	M	C	47	M	Jackson St., Orlando	6 yrs	Cement Worker	N.C.	Acute Myocarditis	Greenwood
8-Mar	*Mary J. Wright	F	W	76	W	427 S. Lake	4 mos	At Home	England	Chronic Interstitial Nephritis	Providence, R.I.
11-Mar	Mr. Wm. M. Cason	M	W	43	M	Nichols, Ga / Orlando	1 m 1da	Day Labor		Cerebral Hemorrhage	Nichols, Ga
12-Mar	*Wm. L. Lemmon	M	W	77	W	2 mi. S. of City		Contractor	Wamf-fedine?, Scotland	Pneumonia	Greenwood
10-Mar	Jane Hester Ann McDemitt	F	W		W	11 Washington	4 mos	None	Garden & Orange Farming	Malignant Disease of Gall Bladder	Kissimmee Cemetery
12-Mar	*Earnest Godwin	M	W	21	S	Orlando/ O.G.H.	5 mos		Duval Co., Fla	Intestinal Obstruction	Bristol, Ga
14-Mar	*Andrew Edward Benke (Burke)	M	W	68	M	Orlando/ O.G.H.	3 yrs	Book-keeper	Bridge-port, Conn	Chronic Nephritis	Bridge Port, Conn
13-Mar	Infant of Mr. & Mrs. T. M. Holman	F	W		S	Fla Sanitarium			Orlando	Stillborn	Greenwood Cemetery
16-Mar	Baby Bryon	F	C	5 mo	S	1015 Livingston	5 mos		Orlando	Diarrhea	Greenwood
17-Mar	*Maryan Haye	F	W	18	M	715 Division/Orlando	2 yrs	At Home	Jefferson Co., Fla	Septicemia, Post Partum Infection?	Lake Howell Cemetery
18-Mar	*Sarah Montes Warren	F	W	80	W	Providence R.I./ Orlando	4 mos	At Home	Long Plane?, Mass	Broncho pneumonia	Providence, R.I.
19-Mar	*Chas J. Megargee	M	W	33	M	Scranton, Pa/ O.G.H.	1 d	Salesman	Scranton, Pa	Is__? Rectal	Scranton, Pa
6-Mar	Elizabeth Jameson	F	W	79	W	414 Magnolia	2 mos	At Home	Ohio	Aortic ___? Abdominal	Plandome, L.I., N.Y.
19-Mar	Samuel Aikens	M	C	40	M	Orlando/ 912 Bentley	4 yrs	Com. Labor	Fla	Acute Miliary T.B.	Orange Spring, Fla
16-Mar	*Mrs. Jesse Mae Murray	F	W	46	M	206 W South/ 206 W South	2 yrs	At Home	Connerssville, Ind?	Uremia	Connersville, Ind
17-Mar	*John S. Hicks	M	W	81	W	S. Haven, Mich/ 132 E Church	1 yr	Retired	N.Y.	Senile Dysentery	S. Haven, Mich
20-Mar	*Carl B. Robinson	M	W	43	M	Orlando/ 2 Gore Ave	28 yrs	Attorney at Law	Zellwood, Fla	Abscess of Liver	Greenwood
21-Mar	*Annie E. Mallory	F	W	81	W	614 S. Lake			Elmira, N.Y.	Senility; Toxemia	Greenwood

1923	Name of Deceased	Sex	Race	Age	Marital	Residence & Place of Death	Resid	Occupation	Place of Birth	Cause of Death	Place of Burial
21-Mar	*Thomas Lang Bruce	M	W	42	M	Orlando/ Marks & Mills	7 mos	Foreman in Shop	Dooly Co., Ga	Pulmonary Tuberculosis	Greenwood
19-Mar	*Francis Robinson	M	C	40	W	Orlando/ E South	6 yrs	Laundry Work	Montgomery, Ala	Myocarditis	Greenwood
22-Mar	Steven E. Abbott	M	W	73	M	617 Franklin/ Orlando	1 yr 6 mo	Retired Farmer	Andover, Mass	Shock following RR Accident	Andover, Mass
22-Mar	*Miss Perscilla Marsh	F	W	10	S	E. Washington/ OGH.	8 yrs	In School	Brooklyn, N.Y.	Gen'l Peritonitis	Greenwood
25-Mar	*Frank E. McMillan, Jr.	M	W	1	S	Idlewild Park			Orlando, Fla	Acute Gastroenteritis	Greenwood
25-Mar	Able Hill Crawford	M	W	79	M	222 S. Main/ Orlando	2 mo 15 ds	Retired	Cotton Valley, Ala	Pneumonia, Lobar	Linsoha?, Ala
29-Mar	*Wm. Walter Campbell	M	W	75	M	Chantaugia, N.Y./ E Washington	6 mos	Wholesale Grain & Feed Co	N.Y.	Concussion of Brain & Internal Injuries	Jamestown, N.Y.
30-Mar	Jas. Jones	M	C	46	S	W. Gore Ave/ Orlando	3 mos	Laborer	Ga	Infection, Some Unknown Organism	Greenwood
1-Apr	*Ruben J. Roberts	M	W	83	M	Knoxville, Tenn/ 100 Summerlin Place	4 yrs	Real Estate	N.Y.	Chronic Bright's Disease	Knoxville, Tenn
5-Apr	*Mrs. Jennie Cartland	F	W	60	M	Dover, N.H/ O.G.H.	3 mo	At Home	Windham Center, Maine	Chronic Myocarditis	Dover, N.H.
5-Apr	*Chas H. Turner	M	W	60	M	?/ 626 N. Garland	4 mos	Farming	Stuben Co., Ind	Chronic Bronchitis	Orland, Ind
6-Apr	*Miss Mary Ellen Thayer	F	W	83	S	Orlando/ O.G.H.	5 yrs 6 mo	At Home	Madina Co, Ohio	Nephritis; Senility	Greenwood
6-Apr	Olivia James	F	C	3 mo	S	523 South/ Orlando	3 mos	None	Lloyd, Fla	Diarrhea	Greenwood
6-Apr	*Geo. David Ghent	M	W	74	M	Holden Ave/ O.G.H.	12 yrs	Fruit Grower	Frankfort, Ind	Thrombus From Wound in Bladder Following prostecto__?	Greenwood
9-Apr	*Ephraim H. Norris	M	W	27	S	Glenn Falls, N.Y/ 410 N. Orange	3 mo 7 da	Manufacturer	Shoe Maker from PA	Chronic Nephritis	Glenn Falls, N.Y.
7-Apr	Wm C. Hickman	M	W	75	M	Clarksburg, Wva/ Orlando	5 mos. 13 da	Farmer	W.Va	Abscess of Liver	Clarksburg, Wva.
10-Apr	*Henry Hall	M	W	1	S	Orlando/ 1 3/ 4 mi S.E. Orlando	12 yrs 6 mos		Orlando	IleoColitis	Greenwood
9-Apr	*John H. Bentley	M	W	69	M	Orlando/ O.G.H.	3 mos	Silk Manufacturer	England	Acute Dilation of Heart	Patterson, N.J.
11-Apr	Infant Mr & Mrs. Leo Curcia	M				210 S. Garland/ Orlando			Orlando	Stillborn	Catholic Cemetery
10-Apr	*Simon D. Hatch	M	W	29	M	S of City/ S of City	1 yr	Mechanic	Belmont, Mass	Diabetes	Greenwood

1923	Name of Deceased	Sex	Race	Age	Marital	Residence & Place of Death	Resid	Occupation	Place of Birth	Cause of Death	Place of Burial
15-Apr	*Rev. J. H. Reynart	M	W	80	S	Orlando/ Orlando	12 yrs	Retired Priest	Belgium	Senility	Catholic Cemetery
14-Apr	*Carrie X. Burkett	F	W	47	M	Altamonte Springs, Fla/ O.G.H.	7 ds	At Home	Macon Co., Ga	Acidosis	Conway Cemetery
16-Apr	*Vincent H. Green	M	W	35	M	515 Lexington/ Orlando	12 yrs	Civil Engineer	Tampa, Fla	Carcinoma of Face	Tampa, Fla
17-Apr	*Fred Malby Warner	M	W	58	M	Farmington, Mich/ Orlando	1 mo	Banker & Manufacturer	Hickling, Eng	Interstitial Nephritis; Acute Exacerbation	Farmington, Mich
16-Apr	*Infant of Mr & Mrs O. O. Hamilton	F	W		S	Tavares/ Orlando			Orlando	Stillborn	Greenwood
17-Apr	J. H. Higdon	M	C	55	S	Orlando/ O.G.H.	20 yrs	Labor	Ga	Typhoid Fever	Greenwood
19-Apr	*Mrs Martha A. Stephens	F	W	75	M	Atlanta, Ga/ Orlando	1 mo	At Home	Cherokee Co., Ala	Tuberculosis	Greenwood
19-Apr	*Wm R. Webster	M	W	78	M	1313 N. Summerlin/ Orlando	4 yrs	Druggist	West India	Senility	Worchester, Ohio
19-Apr	*Hugh Wing	M	W	17	S	Winter Garden/ O.G.H.	1 d		Lyons, Ga	Carcinoma of Utim?	Calahan, Fla
21-Apr	Florida Bateman	F	C	45	M	600 Douglas/ Orlando		Cook	Tallahassee Fla	Cancer of Uterus	Greenwood
23-Apr	*Wm M. Harper	M	W	53	M	425 Boone/ Fla San	17 yrs	Physician	Loganville, Ky	Surgical Shock	Catholic Cemetery
22-Apr	*Mrs Anna F. Taylor	F	W	56	W	W Church/ W Church	5 yrs	At Home	Elmira, N.Y.	Cerebral Hemorrhage	Umatilla
21-Apr	Minnie Potter	F	C	25	S	Carter/ Orlando	6 mos	Housework	S.C.	Tuberculosis	Greenwood
22-Apr	*Clarence H. Bibbens	M	W	63	M	211 Liberty St/ Fla San	5 mo 10 ds	Journalist	Weedsport, N.Y.	Pulmonary Edema; Uremia	Syracuse, N.Y.
25-Apr	Will Lee	M	C	13 ds	S	219 Division/ Orlando	15 ds		Orlando	Malnutrition; Premature	Greenwood
23-Apr	*Mrs. Gladys T. P. Eaton	F	W	29	M	/ Formosa	6 mo	At Home	Orange, Mass	Pulmonary Tuberculosis	Waltham, Mass
28-Apr	Earnest Geo. Savage	M	W	6	S	/ O.G.H.	2 wks		Maine	Typhoid Fever	Greenwood
27-Apr	*Mrs Stella Simms	F	W	53	M	Ocoee/ O.G.H.	7 ds	At Home	Texas	Carcinoma of Bladder	Ocoee Cemetery
30-Apr	*Mrs. Mary V. Ipsen	F	W	35	M	Piedmont, Fla/ O.G.H.	2 ds	At Home	Sweden	Carcinoma of Kidney	Apopka
28-Apr	*Mary Krenzina	F	W	74	W	526 E East/ Orlando	3 yrs	At Home	Albany, N.Y.	Heart Disease	Catholic Cemetery
no date	*Mrs Helen E. Clark Ratts	F	W	54	M	Orlando	1 mo 21 ds	At Home	Canton, Ohio	Cerebral Hemorrhage	Canton, Ohio
3-May	*Miss Mary Branson Church	F	W	71	S	Albany NY/ Formosa	4 mo 3 ds	Teacher	Albany, N.Y.	Carcinoma of Liver and Stomach	Albany, N.Y.

1923	Name of Deceased	Sex	Race	Age	Marital	Residence & Place of Death	Resid	Occupation	Place of Birth	Cause of Death	Place of Burial
No date	*Lenora Lucile Harris	F	W	8	S	Orlando	1 d	In School	Orange Co., Fla	Injuries Caused by Auto Collision	Lenox, Ga
4-May	*Donald E. Seaman	M	W	1	S	Orlando	5 mos		Drumond, Mich	Acute Toxemia	Tampa, Fla
5-May	*Mr. James W. Taylor	M	W	75	D	932 W Church/ Orlando	5 yrs	Retired Engineer		Intestinal Toxemia?	Greenwood
2-May	Chas. Alexander	M	C	53	S	Parramore/ Orlando	12 Yrs	Cook	Dawson, Ga	Apoplexy	Greenwood
13-May	*Mary C. West	F	W	15	S	271 Hughey/ Orlando	9 yrs	In School	Ind.	Gen. Peritonitis	Greenwood
13-May	*Mrs. Matilda Thomas	F	W	82	W	Orlando/ OGH	8 yrs	At Home	Camden, N.J.	Broncho-pneumonia	Camden, N.J.
15-May	Queen Esther Mitchell	F	C	5		1005 Livingston	6 wks		Ga	Acute Gastritis	Greenwood
16-May	Wm. King	M	C	45		271 Long/ Orlando		Labor	Raleigh, N.C.	Broncho-pneumonia	Greenwood
16-May	*Milton A. Dovell	M	W	54	M	S. of city/ Orlando		Agent	Luray, Va	Acute Heart Disease	Greenwood
17-May	Coral Morse	F	W	38	S	/ O.G.H.	2 ds		Belvidere, Kan.	Pneumonia	Mt. Dora, Fla
10-May	*Mrs. Anna G. Smith	F	W	82	W	Orlando	5 mo	At Home	Lockhart, N.Y.	Intestinal & Heart Disease	Lockhart, N.Y.
16-May	Infant (Found) at Garbage Plant in City of Orlando, Fla										County Home
19-May	Cora Davenport	F	C	25	M	Parramore/ Orlando	21 ds	Housewife	Ga	Acute Salpingitis	Sylvester, Ga
24-May	*Mrs. Mattie Depault (De Vault)	F	W	44	M	Winter Park/ O.G.H.	5 ds	At Home	KY	Nephritis	Winter Park
24-May	*Wm. Clark	M	W	65	M	Fairvilla		Labor		Lightning	
23-May	*Beatrice M. Hancock	F	W	24	M	Oviedo/ O.G.H.		At Home	Riverview, Fla	Operation	Oviedo
25-May	*Mrs. Jerama Peters	F	W	73	W	/ Orlando	40 yrs	At Home	Alexander City, Ala	Acute Myocarditis	Conway Cemetery
26-May	*W. R. Hamer (Horner)	M	W	67	M	Maryville, Tenn/OGH.	7 mo	Minister	Morris-town Tenn	Pneumonia	Whitesburg, Tenn
25-May	D. E. Lilly	M	W	50	S	Orlando	4 mos			Asthma	Manhattan, Kan
27-May	*Infant of Mr & Mrs F. (S.) L. Sheppard	F	W		S	335 Carter/ O.G.H.			Orlando	Stillborn	Greenwood
27-May	*Child of Mr & Mrs Henry (Harry) James	F	W	22d	S	279 Palmer/ O.G.H.			Orlando	Gastroenteritis	Greenwood
23-May	*Richard Cowhig	M	W	41	S	Lynchburg, Va/ O.G.H.	7 mos	Plumber	Lynch-burg	Acute Nephritis	Lynchburg, Va
25-May	Ida Marshall Williams	F	C	50	S	/ Orlando	4 yrs 10 m.	Cook	Sumline, SC	Tetanus	Greenwood
2-Jun	*Infant of John Washington	F	C	2ds	S	318 Lime/ 318 Lime	2 ds		Orlando	Premature Birth	Greenwood
2-Jun	*Clinton Hewett	M	W	6 mos	S	Orlando/ O.G.H.	1 mo		Wayne Co., Ga	Coletis, Etiology Unknown	Greenwood

17

1923	Name of Deceased	Sex	Race	Age	Marital	Residence & Place of Death	Resid	Occupation	Place of Birth	Cause of Death	Place of Burial
3-Jun	*Mrs. Clara M. Lawrence	F	W	40	M	Orlando/ O.G.H.	9 mos	At Home	Cincinnati, Ohio	Thrombus Cerebral Artery	Greenwood
4-Jun	Lizzie Lee	F	C	60	S	Orlando/ County Home	1 mo.	Servant	N.C.	Pneumonia	County Home
5-Jun	Pearl Starke	F	C	27	D	947 Bentley/ Orlando	1 yr	Cook	Fla	Pneumonia	Greenwood
6-Jun	*Nancy Blance	F	W	80	W	711 E. South	40 yrs	At Home	Columbia, S.C.	Gastric Dyspepsia, Weak Heart	Greenwood
1-Jun	Child of Mr & Mrs Mable Quaide	F	W	2 hrs	S	306 E. South			Orlando	Leongent? Malformation of Heart	Catholic
8-Jun	*Joseph M. Griffith	M	W	73	M	404 E. Hughey	3 yrs	Painter	Spring-field, Ohio	Carcinoma of Lower Jaw & Tongue	Greenwood
1-Jun	David Fort Anderson	M	W	93	M	106 S. Delaney/ Orlando	15 years	Physician	Phoenix-ville, Pa	Senility	Conway
12-Jun	Ellen Clemon	F	C	4	S	148 Jefferson/ Orlando			Swu, Fla	Spasms	Greenwood
14-Jun	Haynes Branson	M	W	4 mo	S	Orlando/ O.G.H.	4 ds		Kissimmee	Whooping Cough	Valdosta, Ga
15-Jun	*Sadie Wells	F	W	70	M	517 Lexington	12 yrs	At Home	Gaylord, Ohio	Pernicious Anemia	Greenwood
no date	*J. P. A. Herman	M	W	66	M	Pine Castle Rural	12 yrs	Farming	Penn	Mitral Regurgitation	Oak Ridge
19-Jun	Infant of B. G. F. Moore	F	C			1004 Wash-ington/ Orlando			Orlando	Stillborn	Greenwood
18-Jun	*Mendel (Wendel) S. Padgett	M	W	11	S	Pine Castle Rural	4 yrs		Millriff, Penn	Tubercular Meningitis	Greenwood
20-Jun	*Infant of Chester & Charlott Jones	M	C		S	E. Orlando			E. Orlando	Stillborn	Greenwood
18-Jun	Wilson Serls	M	W	65	W	Apopka Road/ O.G.H.	8 yrs	Carpenter	Canada	Carcinoma of Sigmoid	Leesburg, Fla
22-Jun	*Buck Fralick	M	W	16	S	High Springs/ O.G.H.	2 ds	Daywork	High Springs, Fla	Crushed Chest	High Springs
21-Jun	*Margaret C. Rice	F	W	86	W	229 Ridgewood	3 yrs 6 mo	At Home	Orlando	Cancer of Liver	Orleans, Ind
22-Jun	Hampton Robinson	M	C	60	M	1000 Division		Labor	N.C.	Parenchymatis ? Nephritis	Greenwood
23-Jun	*Thomton (Juanita) M. Hayes	F	W	3 mo	S	555 High/ Orlando	3 mo 16 ds		Orlando	Broncho-pneumonia	Lake Howell
26-Jun	*Mr Edward H. Ray	M	W	57	M	Taft/ O.G.H.		Merchant	Salem, Ill	Pulmonia Oedemia	Jacksonville, Fla
30-Jun	Elijah Parnell Nixon			73		308 Mariposa/ Orlando	12 mos	Dr.M.D.	Palmetto, Ga	Heart Disease	Palmetto, Ga
28-Jun	Wam Blackman	M	C	45	S	220 South/ Orlando	12 yrs	Labor	Va	Acute Indigestion	Greenwood

1923	Name of Deceased	Sex	Race	Age	Marital	Residence & Place of Death	Resid	Occupation	Place of Birth	Cause of Death	Place of Burial
3-Jul	*James Stanley Butts	M	W	13 mos	S	O.G.H./ Orlando	1 d.		Orlando	Accidentally burned	Sylacanga, Ala
1-Jul	*Cashus Boone Jernigan	M	W	32	W	Orlando/ County Home	1 mo.		Orlando	Pulmonary T.B.	Powell Cem
6-Jul	Infant ___	F	C			12 Bryant/ Orlando			Orlando	Stillborn	Greenwood
6-Jul	*Mrs. Ida Carver	F	W	22	M	Orlando/ O.G.H.	1 d.	At Home	Murray Co., Ga	Septicemia	
9-Jul	Eddie J. Harris	M	C	22	S	273 Gore Ave/ Orlando	3 yrs	Labor	Ga	Typhoid Fever	Greenwood
7-Jul	*Mrs Ruth Stephens	F	W	75	M	720 Grand Ave	5 yrs	At Home	New York	Gangrene of Back and Hips	Greenwood
9-Jul	*Harley Brown	M	W	10 mos	S	Orlando/ O.G.H.	1 d.		Monroe, Mich	Uremia, Coma	Greenwood
6-Jul	Wm. H. Irvin	M	W	78	W	Rosewood Ave/ Orlando	1 yr	Retired Farmer	Ala	Comatose Condition When Seen	Greenwood
11-Jul	Kattie Polite	F	C	40	M	Orlando/ O.G.H.	10 yrs	Cook	Fla	Uremia	Haines City
no date	Lamar Franklin Barnett	M	W	36	M	Orlando	2 yrs	Telegraph Operator	Hampton, Ga	Diabetic Coma	Hogan, Ga
11-Jul	Infant of Mr & Mrs J. E. Trotter	F	W	2 hrs	S	Formosa/ Winter Park			Formosa	Born Still	Winter Park
12-Jul	*Franklin W. Dunham	M	W	76	M	Formosa/ Formosa	2 yrs 9 mo.	Salesman	Loraine Co., Ohio	Cardiac Failure; Pulmonary Oedemia	Winter Park
17-Jul	John James Elizah Byrd	M	W	56	W	208 Grace?/ Orlando	10 yrs		Ga.	Chronic Myocarditis	Boxley, Ga
22-Jul	*Child of Susie & B. F. Griffin	M	W		S	Groveland/ O.G.H.				Stillborn	Greenwood
22-Jul	*Susie Griffin (Mrs)	F	W	37	M	Groveland/ O.G.H.	5 ds.	At Home	Ga	Ruptured Appendix with gen. Peritonitis	Greenwood
24-Jul	Sam Weaver	M	C	1 d	S	Orlando	2 yrs		Orlando	Prematurity 7 mos. Baby	Greenwood
27Jul14	*Infant of Mr & Mrs Gordon Doss	M	W	1 d	S	O.G.H/ Orlando	1 d		Orlando	Atelectasis	Crescent City, Fla
23-Jul	*Mrs Mamie Gaines	F	W	30	M	O.G.H/ Orlando	8 yrs	At Home	Georgia	Cardiac Depression	Gainesville, Fla
26-Jul	*Child of Mr & Mrs A. M. Ellis	F	W	6 ds	S	Orlando			Orlando	Hemophilia	Patrick Cem
28-Jul	Maggie Gallon	F	C	20	M	39 Bryant/ Orlando	5 mos	Cook	Tallahassee, Leon Co.	Apoplexy of Brain	Tallahassee, Fla
22-Jul	Jennie B. Bailey	F	W	33	M	Winter Haven/ O.G.H.	22 yrs	Housewife	E. Liverpool, Ohio		Winter Haven
21-Jul	*Mary Elizabeth Dolive	F	W	79	W	Orlando	35 yrs	At Home	Baldwin Co., Ala	Pulmonary Edema; Uremia	Greenwood

1923	Name of Deceased	Sex	Race	Age	Marital	Residence & Place of Death	Resid	Occupation	Place of Birth	Cause of Death	Place of Burial
Aug	*Helen Rose Simmons	F	W	10 mos	S	1018 Pine Crest/ Orlando			Orlando	Pyelitis & EnteroCitis	Wauchula
2-Aug	Vermill Joyner	F	C	25	M	308 S. Bryant/ Orlando	10 yrs	Laundress	Lee Co., S.C.	Eclampsia	Greenwood
4-Aug	*Mrs. Julia Ward	F	W	45	W	Orlando/ Jail			Willing- ton, N.C.	Found Dead in Cell in Jail	Greenwood
2-Aug	*Mr. Berry Lee Partin	M	W	29	S	Conway	29 yr 3 mo 19 d	Farming		Acute Endocaditis	Conway Cemetery
5-Aug	Jim Sneed	M	C	54	M	Orlando		Labor	Ga	Intestinal Obstruction	Greenwood Cemetery
6-Aug	*John Wm Tedford	M	W	7	S	1110 Kuhl Ave/ Orlando	7 yrs 1 mo 21 ds		Hunting- ton, Pa	Hemophilia	Greenwood
5-Aug	*Mrs. Leila Topliff	F	W	57	M	206 W. Churchill/ Orlando		At Home	Taberton, Ga	Cancer of Pelvis / Metastases From Former Necro_? Of Uterus Greenwood	
6-Aug	*Fannie Lee Berry	F	W	2 yrs	S	523 Ohio Ave/ Orlando			Orlando	Acute Nephritis	Oak Ridge
	*Thomas Y. Haggerty	M	W	41	M	Pine Castle	3 mos	Electrician	Huntington Long Island, N.Y.	Injury Sustained In Fall Thru Elevator Shaft, Fracture of Base of Skull, Broken Neck, Fracture humerus	Burial not given
8-Aug	*Jewell Hobby	F	W	17	S	Winter Park/ O.G. Hospital	3 da	At Home	Dakoha, Ga	Typhoid Fever	Winter Park
9-Aug	*John E. Lafler	M	W	79	W	718 W. Church	2 yrs	Retired	Cumbus, Ohio	Senility	Greenwood
10-Aug	*Eugene Caldwell	M	W	1 yr	S	806 S. Hughey	1 yr 10 mos		Orlando	Diphtheria	Greenwood
8-Aug	Dora Harris	F	C	54	M		1 da	Housewife	Georgia	Ac. Myocarditis	Eustis, Fla
9-Aug	*Rose Lee Nutting	F	W	abt 35	M	Orlando	abt 20 yrs	At Home	Ky	Respiration Paralysis Due to an Overdose of Bromide Taken by Herself. Found Dead in Room Greenwood	
9-Aug	Henry Robinson	M	C	1 da			1 da		Orange	Congenital Syphilis	Greenwood
10-Aug	*Luther J. Durrence	M	W	26y 6m 28d	M	Winter Park/ O.G.H.	2 da	Labor	Tatnal Co., Ga	Pyemia	Glenville, Ga
11-Aug	*Frances Dudley	F	W	3 y, 2 m 5 d	S	Sanford, Fla	8 da		Bay City, Mich	Malaria	Greenwood
12-Aug	*Chester Lee Hullinger	M	W	abt 70 yrs	M	Jacksonville /Fla Sanitarium		Retired	Ind.	Apoplexy	Jacksonville, Fla
14-Aug	Sarah Peterson	F	C	22 yrs	S	107 W Livingston	15 yrs	Domestic	Jasper, Fla	Carcinoma of Peritoneum	Greenwood
16-Aug	*Wm Henry Waterhouse	M	W	81y 6 m 5 d	M	Maitland, Fl	40 yrs	Fruit Grower	Greenport, N.Y.	Angina Pectoris	Maitland Cem

1923	Name of Deceased	Sex	Race	Age	Marital	Residence & Place of Death	Resid	Occupation	Place of Birth	Cause of Death	Place of Burial
17-Aug	*Payson Branch	M	W	36 y 8 mo	S	N.Orange Ave/ Orlando		Musician	Parker, S.D.	Pellagra	Greenwood
18-Aug	*Wm A. Carpenter	M	W	65 yrs 8 mo	W	Island Lake, Mich/ 310 E. Colonial Drive	10 mos	Farming	Island Lake, Mich	Mitral Regurgitation	Pontiac, Mich
26-Aug	Joseph Johnson	M	C	30 y 11m 12 d	S	1103 Jefferson	10 ds	Express-man	Lake City	Acute indigestion -death occurred before mo---ial examination	Lake City
26-Aug	*David Lockhart	M	W	59y 5m 7d	M	127 E. Livingston/ O.G.H	40 yrs	Lumber Barron & Cattle Business	Red Plains, Ga	Shock Following Operation for Intestinal Obstruction	Greenwood
27-Aug	*Child of Mr & Mrs F. L. Hewes	M	W	3 ds	S	Virginia Ct/ O.G.H/ Winter Park, Fla	2 ½ ds		Orlando	Atelectosis	In Vault
29-Aug	*Infant of Mr & Mrs W. B. Caldwell	F	W		S	Winter Haven, Fla/ O.G.H.			Orlando	Atelectosis	Greenwood
30-Aug	*Infant of Mr & Mrs Joe Scott	M	W	9 ds	S	300 S. Hughey St/ O.G.H.			Orlando	Serosis meonatorum?	Conway Cemetery
30-Aug	*Henry L. Powers (Power)	M	W	72 yrs 7 ds	S	Winder-mere, Fla/ O.G.H.	1 mo	Postal Service, Retired	New York	Carcinoma of Omenta	Fort Dodge, Iowa
30-Aug	Hannah Green	F	C	50y rs	W	W Wash-ington	15 yrs	Domestic	Georgia	Chronic Nephritis	Greenwood
31-Aug	*Joseph Harry Knowles	M	W	50y 5 m	M	Orlando	8 mos	Actor with Moving Picture Co.	England	Listian? Malaria	Brooklyn, NY
3-Sep	*Helen Allen	F	W	1 yr 9 m	S	N.W. Part of City	1 yr 9 mo		Orlando, Fla	Acute IleoColitis	Powell Cemetery
4-Sep	*Durward P. McKay	M	W	27 yrs	M	O.G.H/ Rosewood Ave	12 yrs	Clerk Dry Goods	Georgia	Acute Peritonitis Following Gangrene Neptine?? Appendix	Greenwood
5-Sep	*Philander Stout	M	W	67	M	O.G.H/ Bridge-port, Wva	7 ds	Farming Retired	Bridge-port, Wva	Intestinal Illness present at time of operation for gangrous appendix & resutent? gall	Bridgeport, W. Va
5-Sep	*Mrs Ann E. Everingham	F	W	64	M	144 N. Roselind	12 yrs	At Home	Ripley, N.Y.	Diabetes Mellitus	Greenwood
8-Sep	*Willie Williams	W	M	22	S	Ocoee, Fla/ O.G.H	6 wks	Day Work	Newton, Ala	Typhoid Fever	Newton, Ala
9-Sep	*Madeline Agnes McKnight	F	W	14	S	410 E Colonial	1 yr 11 m	At Home	Blanchard, Iowa	Ostio Sarcoma Right Shoulder abt 6 mo	Greenwood
14-Sep	*Arthur Browning	M	W	43	M	Illahaw	2 das	Day Worker	Hellena, Ga	Acute Alcoholism	Scotland, Ga
14-Sep	Cary Rozier	M	C	40	M		2 yrs	Laborer	Ga	Basal Skull Fracture	Empire, Ga
16-Sep	Willie Gaston	M	C	14d	S				Orlando	Dysentary	Greenwood
16-Sep	*Mrs Margaret Webb	F	W	53	M	628 E. Washington	10 yrs	At Home	Fairfield Co., Ohio	Carcinoma Gall Bladder & Possibly Head of Pancreas	burial not given

1923	Name of Deceased	Sex	Race	Age	Marital	Residence & Place of Death	Resid	Occupation	Place of Birth	Cause of Death	Place of Burial
16-Sep	*Mrs. Ellen R. Newell	F	W	80	W	Pine Castle	15 yrs	At Home	Ashtabula, Ohio	Cerebral Hemorrhage	Ashtabula, Ohio
17-Sep	*Sarah Jane Hall	F	W	75	W	421 W. Amelia	9 mos	At Home	White Co., Ind	Internal Tumor with Inflammation of Bowels	Grove (Lowes) Chapel, Ky
16-Sep	*Miss Lula Edith McDonald	F	W	45	S	Sioux City, Iowa/ 3810 Orlean? Ave	20 ds	At Home	Wyoming	Infection of Gall Bladder	Sioux City, Iowa
21-Sep	Ben Williams	M	C	32	S		4 yrs	Labor	Waldo, Fla	Shock, Hemorrhage, Accident - Left Arm Pulled Off, Partial Muscle Opening Chest Cavity Pulled Off, Partial Muscle Opening Chest Cavity So Heart Could Be Seen Beating	Hampton, Fla
22-Sep	*Mrs. Jolena King	F	W	33	M	Zellwood, Fla/ O.G. Hospital	21 ds	At Home	Maury	Tetany Following Acute Tonsilitis	Tangerine
21-Sep	Infant Mullin	M	C		M [sic]	1120 W. Jefferson S.W.				Stillborn	Greenwood
25-Sep	*Child of Mr & Mrs E. E. Culver (Culvert)	M	W	4 hrs	S	Corner of City			Orlando, Fla	Premature	Patrick Cemetery
26-Sep	*Child of Mr & Mrs E. P. Neid	M	W		S	Kissimmee/ O.G.H.	1 da		Orlando, Fla	Stillborn	Kissimmee
25-Sep	Idella Johnson	F	C	42	M	702 S. Parramore		Housewife	Fla	Child Birth	Greenwood
26-Sep	*Chas Greenwood	M	W	67	M	409 Highland Ave /O.G.H	7 mos	Electric Sign Mfr	Gallitfield, Ohio	Pernicious Anemia	Knoxville, Tenn
2-Sep	Ethel Saunders	F	C	25	M	E. Orlando	3 yrs	Domestic	Valdosta, Ga	Acute Nephritis	Greenwood
29-Sep	Johnnie F. Hollie	F	C			Orlando			Orlando	Convulsion	Greenwood
27-Sep	Isabell Mary Winch (Mrs E. P. Neill?)	F	W	22	M	Orlando/ O.G.H		Housewife	Java N.Y.	Eclampsia	Rose Hill Cemetery
29-Sep	Infant Son of Mr & Mrs J. J. Quinn	M	W		S	621 W. Pine St			Orlando	Premature	Catholic Cemetery
30-Sep	Infant of Solomon Williams	F	C			607 Parramore			Orlando	Croupious	Greenwood
28-Sep	*Guy P. Dodge	M	W	49	M	New York City/ Fla Sanitarium	1 yr	Broker, Retired	New York City	Suicide - Paroldehyde	Simsbury Con
3-Oct	Ryal Small	M	C	abt 48	M	Jackson		Laborer	Charleston, S.C.	Accident Struck in Stomach by Lever While Moving House	Kissimmee
6-Oct	Jasper Scott	M	N	33	W	John		Brick Layer	Milledgeville, Ga	Mitral Stenosis	Greenwood
6-Oct	*Richard Kasper	M	W	14	S	Winter Garden/ O.G.H.	21 ds	In School	St. Louis, Mo	Acute Infection Endocarditis	Greenwood
8-Oct	Infant of Frank & Flosy Massie	M	N	5ds	Infant	110 W. Hoskin	5 ds	Infant	Orlando	Tetanus Neonatorum	Greenwood
8-Oct	Willie Buia	M	C	35	M	523 W. Pine	4 mos	Labor	Fla	Septicemia Following Extraction of Teeth	Greenwood

1923	Name of Deceased	Sex	Race	Age	Marital	Residence & Place of Death	Resid	Occupation	Place of Birth	Cause of Death	Place of Burial
9-Oct	Wright Williams	M	C	30	M	407 Division		Cook	Layad Jefferson?	Stroke, Paralysis	Lloyd, Fla
10-Oct	Mrs. Mattie Lee	F	W	18	M	Ocoee/ O.G.H.	7 ds	At Home	Ga	Prenicious Vomiting of Pregnancy	Ocoee Cemetery
10-Oct	Theodore Demps	M	C	10d	Infant	31 S. Bryant		Infant	Orlando	Unknown Born Dead	Greenwood
12-Oct	*Mrs. Ida Diggett	F	W	61	M	611 N. Parramore	1 y 3 mo	At Home	England	Cancer of Stomach	Greenwood
13-Oct	*Mrs Anna Huffman	F	W	abt 45	M	412 ½ W. Church/ O.G.H.	1 yr 1 mo	At Home	Ireland	Carcinoma of Stomach	Greenwood
13-Oct	*Jennie R. Irving	F	W	71	M	New York City/ 335 E. Amelia	3 mos	At Home	New York City	Acute Dilation of Heart	New York City
13-Oct	*Townsend Hand	M	W	65	W	38 W Pine	8 yrs	Inventor	Shelby-ville, Ind.	Acute Nephritis	Greenwood
14-Oct	*William Sherman Reynolds	M	W	57	M	Wichita, Kansas/ 211 E. Jackson	3 days	Merchant	Wilmath-ville?, MO	Carcinoma of Stomach	St. Cloud, Fla
12-Oct	Hanson Williams	M	C	31	D	552 Long	15 yrs	Painter	Tallahassee Fla	Lobar Pneumonia?	Greenwood
16-Oct	*Mrs. Katherine A. Livingston	F	W	48	W	Orlando/ O.G.H.	1 mo	At Home	Dodge Co., Ga	Acute Septic Endocarditis	Eldorado, Ga
15-Oct	*Mrs. Harriett Ann Rowe	F	W	74	M	Chattanooga Tenn/ 509 W. Central	3 yrs	At Home	Myrth, Ont. Canada	Chronic Pulmonary TB	Greenwood
16-Oct	Daphney Battey	F	C	21	M	702 S. Parramore	2 yr 1 mo	Domestic	Bradford, Fla	Septic Infection from Pelvic Abscess	Greenwood
16-Oct	*Bessie Nickels	F	W	42	W	28 N. Reed	12 yrs	At Home	Putman Co., Ga	Acute Malaria & Cholecystitis	Greenwood
19-Oct	*Mrs Endora Jane Chamberlin	F	W	75	W	Crawford-ville, Ind; O.G.H.	5 yrs	At Home	Crawford-ville, Ind	Chronic Interstitial Nephritis	Crawfordville, Ind.
17-Oct	*Wm. Ledford	M	W	24	S	Prentis, N. Carolina/ Lake Side Park	1 da	Western Union Telegraph Co		Acute Alcoholism	Prentiss, N.C.
19-Oct	Rachil Hudson	F	C	75		612 S. South	30 yrs	Housewife	S.C.	Apoplexy	Greenwood
20-Oct	Nathaniel Prince	F	C	3 hrs		1017 South	5 mos	None	Orlando	Stillborn	Greenwood
20-Oct	George Green	M	C			843 Redford	5 yrs		Orlando	Stillborn	Greenwood
19-Oct	*Chas. A. Reinthaler	M	W	62	M	Morristown, N.J/ O.G.H	21 ds	Farmer	New York City	Chr. Nephritis Acute	Morristown, N.J.
19-Oct	*Mrs. Pearle Cooley	F	W	42	D	118 S. Orange/ O.G.H	4 yrs	Restaurant	Odesa, Mo	Uremia & Pulmonary Edema	Greenwood
21-Oct	*Anna Alderman Newton	F	W	31	M	223 S Rosalind	1 yr 3 mos	At Home	Hope Mill, N.C.	Eclampsia - 8 mos Pregnant Had Double Pu__ Kidneys	Fayetteville, NC

1923	Name of Deceased	Sex	Race	Age	Marital	Residence & Place of Death	Resid	Occupation	Place of Birth	Cause of Death	Place of Burial
22-Oct	*Mrs Ida H. Grant	F	W	56	M	Birdsbroro, Penn/ O.G.H	20 ds	At Home	Birdsboro, Penn	Acute Dilalrtion of Heart Following Acute indigestion	Birdsboro, Penn
22-Oct	Henry Johnson	M	C			Hospital		None	Orlando	Stillborn-Dystocia	Greenwood
21-Oct	*Laban J. Dollins	M	W	72	M	Kissimmee/ O.G.H.	9 ds	Real Estate	Franklin Co, Tenn	Carcinoma of Stomach, Metastasis in Liver	Greenwood
25-Oct	*Leander W. Dance	M	W	55	M	Orlando, S. W. Corner of City	18 ds	Farming	Putman Co., Ga	Acute Meningitis from Dengue Fever working in sun with high fever	Eatonton, GA
25-Oct	Mabel Johnson	F	C	38	M	hospital		Housewife	Savannah, Ga	Dystonic Labor Co_n? Section	Greenwood
24-Oct	*Sarah C. Shepard	F	W	18	M	Orlando, Fla/ O.G.H.	2 ds	At Home	Dublin, Ga	Acute Dilatation of Heart	Oakland
29-Oct	*Mary A. Dykeman	F	W	51	M	Lake Wales/ O.G.H.	15 ds	At Home	Pine Co., Minn	Cholecystectomy with Adhesions -Appendectomy, Rectocele with Adhesions, Cholamia? From Jaundice Gall Stones	Lake Wales, Fla
29-Oct	*Miss Marie K.? Rice	F	W	53	S	229 Ridgewood	4 yrs	At Home	Crawford Co., Ind	Uremia	Orlean, Indiana
29-Oct	Marget Johnson	F	C	2 hrs					Orlando	Stillborn	Greenwood
29-Oct	West Barnes	M	C	48	M	503 Lee		Labor	Rome, Ga	Mitral Regurgitation	Greenwood
31-Oct	*James Carroll Reeves, Jr.	M	W	3	S	Ft. Christmas	1 ds		Ft. Christmas	Uremia; Convulsions	Chuluota, Fla
31-Oct	Rose Lee Frank	F	W	58	M	St. Cloud, Fla	2 yrs	Housewife		Carcinoma of Liver & Pancreas	St. Cloud, Fla
31-Oct	Infant of Chester Turner?	F	C	st		609 Gore Ave			609 Gore	Stillborn	Greenwood
2-Nov	*David D. Awde	M	W	61	M	203 S. Roslind	13 years	Salesman	Waynes-boro, Va	Locomotor Ataxia	Greenwood
5-Nov	*Mae Willie Thorp	F	C			900 W. Jefferson			Orlando, Fla	Stillborn	Greenwood
30-Oct	Albert Smith	M	C	22	S	418 Holden		Laborer	Unknown	Automobile Accident, Accidental	Greenwood
17-Oct	Dorrey Dewitt Dunn	M	W	7	S	Winter Haven/ O.G.H.	1 da		Bacon Co., Ga	Intestional Hemorrhage, Possibly Typhoid Fever	Oakland
6-Nov	*Aubrey Smith	M	W	62	M	910 W. Central	42 yrs	Dairy Business	Cobb Co., Ga	Hypostatic Pneumonia	Greenwood
7-Nov	*Thomas N. Rhodes	M	W	2 m 10d	S	2 miles West of Orlando	2 mos		Orlando	Pneumonia	Patrick Cemetery
8-Nov	*Charles L. Haskill	M	W	42	M	Okeecho-bee, Fla/ O.G.H.	1 mo 12 ds	Carpenter	Nevada	Fracture of Spine	OReechobee, Fla

24

1923	Name of Deceased	Sex	Race	Age	Marital	Residence & Place of Death	Resid	Occupation	Place of Birth	Cause of Death	Place of Burial
6-Nov	Eva Jennings	F	C	40	M	17 N. East St.		Cook	Gutman, Ga	Cardiac Failure;Pulmonary Oedemia	Greenwood
9-Nov	*Lula Levenson	F	W	28	M	Apopka Road/ Orlando, Fla	1 yr 1 mo	At Home	Montgomery, Ala	Carcinoma of Uterus	Tampa, Fla
10-Nov	*Louisa Burton	F	W	67	M	936 W. Jackson	40 yrs	At Home	Dry Ridge, Ky	Heart Disease	Greenwood
13-Nov	*Lillia Hicks	F	W	2	S	Taft, Fla/ O.G.Hl	2 days		Taft, Fla	Acute Burns Legs, Face & Arms	Oak Ridge, Taft
13-Nov	*Edward M. Yoder	M	W	70	M	Orlando, County Home	2 yrs 10 mos	Retired	Indiana, Brown Co.	General Debility Incidental to Old Age with a Severe Laryngitis, Probably Tubercular	Greenwood
13-Nov	*I. C. Perkins	M	W	abt 40	M	Ludowici Ga/ O.B.H	1 da	Stone Mason	Not Known	Accident Caused from Fall, Fractured Skull	Ludowici, Ga
11-Nov	*Henry Carroll	M	W	86	M	224 Park Ave	6 yrs	Mechanic, Retired	Union City, Penn	Carcinoma of Bladder	In Vault (Carey Hand)
12-Nov	*Anna Harrington	F	C	abt 44	S	Jonestown, East Orlando	1 yr	House work	S. Carolina	Broncho-pneumonia	Greenwood
13-Nov	Infant M. H. Poe	M	W		S	Orlando/ Fl Sanitarium			Florida	Stillborn, Probably Dead for Several Hours	Greenwood
13-Nov	Henry Calhoun	M	C	57	M	1010 W. Robinson/ Orlando		Worked for City	D.K.(Don't Know)	Bronchial Asthma & Intestinal Paresis	Greenwood Cemetery
15-Nov	*David Magoon	M	W	81	M	Orlando/ Fla Sanitarium	2 mos	Farmer, Retired	N.Y.	Asthma & Senility	Greenwood Carey Hand
16-Nov	*John W. Wilson	M	W	47	M	735 W. Central/ Fla Sanitarium	8 yrs	Mechanic, Orlando Gas. Co.	Clio, S.C.	Nephritis	Greenwood Carey Hand
18-Nov	*Arthur F. Glines	M	W	66	M	Salem, N.Y/ 403 W Concord	2 ds	Potato Business	Hebron, N.Y.	Sudden Death, Probably due to Thrombosis of Coronary Artery	Salem, NY / Carey Hand
16-Nov	*Jessie Mallory O'Neal	F	W	60	M	614 S. Lake St.			Naperville, Ill.	Illness post operation	Greenwood
16-Nov	*Charles Krause	M	W	73	M	901 E. Washington	6 yrs	Farming, Retired	Germany	Uremia	Greenwood Carey Hand
17-Nov	*George W. Sharpe	M	W	75	M	Jamestown, N.Y/ O.G.H	1 day	Dry Goods Merchant	West Chester, Ohio	Acute Dilation of Heart	In Vault -Jamestown, N.Y. Carey Hand
17-Nov	*Vessie Whitaker	F	W	28	M	Ocoee/ O.G.H	8 ds	At Home	Conyer, Ga	Hyperermear Grandeum?	Ocoee Cem Carey Hand
12-Nov	Eunice Lester	F	C	14	S	Drennen		School Girl	Drennen	Scarlet Fever	Greenwood

1923	Name of Deceased	Sex	Race	Age	Marital	Residence & Place of Death	Resid	Occupation	Place of Birth	Cause of Death	Place of Burial
17-Nov	*Wm Graham	M	C	Abt 46	S	County Home/ Orlando		Day Laborer	Unknown	Chronic Valvular Heart Disease	County Home
19-Nov	*Natalie Golden	F	W	3	S	10 W. Livingston/ O.G.H	1 yr		New York City	Acute Widening of Larynx	Greenwood
20-Nov	*Stella Gertrude Bouton	F	W	22	S	W Church St. in Cumberland near Delaney		At Home	Greenwich, Conn	Pulmonary Tuberculosis	Greenwood
22-Nov	Infant Rollins	F	C			1204 South St.			1204 South St.	Stillborn	Greenwood
22-Nov	Willie J. White	M	C	26	S	201 N. Bryant		Manager Pool Room	Tallahassee, Fla	Pulmonary Tuberculosis	Greenwood
21-Nov	Lynn Getch	M	W	37	M	Altoona, Fla/ O.G.H	14 da	Farmer	Altoona, Fla	Anemia	Umatilla, Fla
21-Nov	Walter Routhford	M	C	Abt 40	S	Osceola, Fla/ O.G.H.	2 ds	Day Laborer	Ga	Acute Peritonitis Following Gunshot Wound	County Home
23-Nov	*John Ivey	M	W	89	M	3 1/2 M. W.of Orlando	60 yrs	Farming	Hamilton Co., Fla	Senility	Lake Hill Cemetery
23-Nov	*Infant Mr & Mrs A. R. Barber	F	W		S	309 N. Main St/ O.G.H.	1 da		Orlando, Fla	Stillborn	Greenwood
24-Nov	Jade Mongumry	M	C	65	S	Hospital		Labor	Ga	Strangulated Hernia; General Peritonitis	Greenwood
24-Nov	*Mrs. Gabrella Curry Griffin	F	W	55	M	Greenville, S.C/ 136 E. Concord Ave	7 ds	At Home	Fairview Township, S.C.	Acute Cariac Dilation	Greenville, S.C.
25-Nov	*Henry Finny	M	C	Abt 50	M	Camilla	12 ds	Brick Mason	Jones Co, Ga	Ruptured Left Kidney Run Operational Abscess	Camilla
20-Nov	Milligan Stevenson	M	W	14	S	Mt. Dora, Fla/ Fla Sanitarium	2 ds	None	Clearwater, Fla	Surgical Shock Following Operation for Osteomyelitis of OsCner? Necrotic Condition TB	Mt. Dora, Fla
23-Nov	*Ruth G. Shelverton	F	W	1	S	317 E Pine / O.G.H.	2 mo 4 ds		Eustus, Fla	Pyelitis	In Vault
25-Nov	Hezakiah Bovie	M	C	22	M	820 Rutherford		Plasterer	Quincy	Paralysis of Spine	Quincy, Fla
26-Nov	Abram Peaterson	M	C	abt 80	W	107 W Livingston		taking Care Yards	S.C.	Stroke, Paralysis	Greenwood
26-Nov	*Infant of Mr & Mrs Wallace J. Hill	M	W		S	Winter Park, Fla/ Fl Sanitarium	2 ds in San		Fla Sanitarium	Prematurity of Birth	Greenwood
28-Nov	Wm L. Hill	M	W	3 ds	S	South Road near Pine Castle, Fla			Country, south of Pine Castle	Spina Bifida	Greenwood

1923	Name of Deceased	Sex	Race	Age	Marital	Residence & Place of Death	Resid	Occupation	Place of Birth	Cause of Death	Place of Burial
Found Dec 21, 1922	*Alexander P. Boyer	M		24	M	Fruitland Park		Small Truck Farm	Delaware	Skeleton of Human Body Found Dec 21, 1922, ? Said had been there several mo. from evidence produced the skeleton was that of Alexander P. Bayer. Supposed to have been murdered.	In Vault at Sheriff's Office
29-Nov	*Mrs Mary Anyonette Wait	F	W	Abt 80	W	Hudson Falls, N.Y.	1 mo 17 da	At Home	Amster-dam, N.Y.	Apoplexy	Hudson Falls, N.Y.
4-Dec	*Mrs. Emma D. Snow	F	W	68	W	LeRays-ville, Penn.	1 mo 7 ds	At Home	Waverly, N.Y.	Angina Pect__?	Wyaluning, Penn
1-Dec	F C. Baumman	M	W	76	M	Winter Home, Fl/ County Home	1 mo	Merchant & Postmaster some yrs ago	Germany	Apoplexy	County Home
6-Dec	*Albert L. Johnson	M	W	63	M	Alliance, Ohio/ 211 Hillman St.	2 mo	Oil Operator	Wesley, Pa	Acute Dilitation	In Vault
6-Dec	*Miss Elizabeth Giles	F	W	14	S	O.G.Hosp	5 da		Orlando	Pneumonia, Meningitis	Winter Park
8-Dec	---	F	B		Infant	108 Bryant St			108 Bryant St	Stillborn	Greenwood
5-Dec	*Thos. T. Stephenson	M	W	52	M	Leoma, Tenn/ Fla Sanitarium	18 ds	Farming	Terra Haute, Ind	Tubercular Bone Meningitis	Leoma, Tenn
3-Dec	*Joe Brown	M	C	56	D	415 S. Parramore	2 yrs	Day Labor	Ga	Pulmonary Hemorrhage	Greenwood
5-Dec	*Sims T. Stallings	M	W	45	M	614 S. Hughey	9 yrs	Day Labor	Polk Co., Fla	Bronchial Pneumonia	Greenwood
8-Dec	*Agnes Cornett	F	W	55	S	N. Scituate, Mass/ O.G.H.	1 da	At Home	Madison, Ind	Shock, Burns All Over Body	Boston, Mass
8-Dec	Nixon Jones	M	C	20	S	406 Rober-son Ave	20 yrs	Labor	Tallahassee	Tuberculosis Rehmantic?	Greenwood
9-Dec	Ernestine Ginlock	F	C	12	S	48 Robinson	12 yrs	None	Orlando	Cerebral Spinal Meningitis (Streptococcus)	Greenwood
10-Dec	*Henry Karg	M	W	62	W	Westerville, Ohio/ Fla Sanitarium	1 mo 12 ds	Contractor & Builder	Leesville, Ohio	Syphilis	Westerville, Ohio
10-Dec	Lee Demps	M	C	76	M	620 Indiana Ave		Common Labor	Fla	Hyper Cirrhosis of Liver	Greenwood
11-Dec	*Jay Nye	M	W	73	W	512 E. Anderson	14 yrs	Fruit Broker	McCon Co, Mich	Carcinoma	Seffner, Ala
10-Dec	George Neal	M	C	58	M	901 Roberson	10 yrs	Common Labor	Fla	Bright's Disease	Greenwood
12-Dec	*Infant of Mr & Mrs John Quilling	M	W		S	Orlando			Orlando	Separation of Placenta at 6 mo of pregnancy and death was in utero	Bought coffin and done their own work
13-Dec	*Eliza A. Meriman	F	W	91	W	700 W. Amelia	4 yrs	At Home	Vermont	Broncho Pneumonia	In Vault, Later to be Shipped to Kansas

1923	Name of Deceased	Sex	Race	Age	Marital	Residence & Place of Death	Resid	Occupation	Place of Birth	Cause of Death	Place of Burial
14-Dec	Andrew Robinson	M	C	51	M	Pine	14 yr	Labor	S.C.	Apoplexy	Greenwood
14-Dec	*Nancy French	M	C	20	D	436 Parra-more/ OGH.	1 yr	Domestic	Leesburg, Ga	Pelvic Peritonitis	Leesburg, Ga
15-Dec	Rosa McGregor	F	C	30	M	434 S. Parramore	1 yr	Housewife	S.C.	Broncho Pneumonia	Greenwood
15-Dec	George August Meyers	M	W	60	M	E. Central Ave	1 yr 9 mos	Carpenter	Ft. Wayne, Ind	Pulmonary Edema; Uremia	Greenwood Cemetery
14-Dec	*Mary Ellen Ames	F	W	66	M	Pontiac, Mich/ O.G.H.	1 mo 4 ds	At Home	Comb Co, Mich	Acute Dilation of Heart Following Influenza	Rochester, Mich
20-Dec	*Mrs Lucy Whitall Erwin	F	W	49	M	Gross Ite,		At Home	Humbolt, Tenn	Genl Peritonitis, anemea? & Heart Failure	Detroit, Mich
21-Dec	Dorothia Brooks	F	W	4 m	S	Winter Garden/ O.G.H.			Alabama	Broncho Pneumonia	Goodwater. Ala
24-Dec	Infant of Mr & Mrs G. W. Hinson	M	W		S	102 W. Washington			Orlando	Stillborn	Greenwood
22-Dec	Edward Moore	M	C	7 ds	Infant	611 Jefferson		Infant	Orlando	Convulstion	Greenwood
22-Dec	Will K. Hale	M	W	61	M	Mayer St on Lake Shine		Orange Grower	New York State	Dead on Arrival, presumably Angina Pectoris	Catskill, Green Co., N.Y.
23-Dec	*Infant Mr & Mrs Earle Dukes	F	W			206 Anderson/ O.G.H.			Orlando	Born Dead, Breach Presentation incarorated?; death due to pressure on cord by after coming head?	Greenwood
25-Dec	*Mrs Catherine Ann Snyder	F	W	74	W	Maquoketa, Iowa/ 701 N Orange	1 mo 14 ds	At Home	German-town, Pa	Acute Nephritis	Maquoketa, Iowa
25-Dec	*Martin H. Bennett	M	W	88	W	436 S. Summerlin	8 yrs	Grain Business	New York	Aortic Abdominal Aneurysm	In Vault, Toledo, Ohio
25-Dec	*Mrs Ellen A. Howe	F	W	66	M	Dover, N.H./ Fern Creek Road Orlando	1 mo 9 ds	At Home	Dover, N.H.	Acute Dilation of Heart	Greenwood
24-Dec	*Miss Emily P. Sherman	F	W	65	S	435 S. Main	3 mo	None	L. I., N.Y.	Asphyxiation from Gas	Greenwood
25-Dec	*Mrs Ruby M. Tinker	F	W	40	M	437 Ruth St.	3 yrs	At Home	St. Louis, Mo	Gun Shot Wound Head	Greenwood
26-Dec	*Mrs Martha Ann Malloy	F	W	57	M	Valdosta, Ga/ 214 S. Rosalind	2 mos	At Home	Lumber Bridge, N.C.	Acute Oedema of Lung	Lumber Bridge, N.C.
No date	*Clara E. Hoogland	F	W	57	M	1301 Rosewood Ave	1 yr 2 mo	At Home	Erin, N.Y.	Organic Disease of the Heart	Greenwood
28-Dec	*Herman G. Hennig	M	W	74	W	Ky Ave	10 yrs	Merchant , Grocery, Retired	Hamberg, Germany	Carcinoma of Stomach	Greenwood
28-Dec	*David C. Roney	M	W	68	M	222 E. Jackson	11 yrs	Md	Kiattan-ning [Pa]	Acute Cadiac Dilitation	Greenwood

1923	Name of Deceased	Sex	Race	Age	Marital	Residence & Place of Death	Resid	Occupation	Place of Birth	Cause of Death	Place of Burial
30-Dec	*Charles Henry Goodenough	M	W	76	M	Seventh St. at Clermont, Fla	39 yrs	Banker	Heddens Cornore?, N.J.	Acute Dilitation of Heart in Aortic Stenosis following apoplexy	Asbury Park, N.J.
31-Dec	*Alexandra B. Hall	F	W	68	W	106 James St/ Fla Sanitarium	7 yrs	At Home	Bowling Green, Ky	Broncho Pneumonia	Greenwood

1924	Name of Deceased	Sex	Race	Age	Marital	Residence & Place of Death	Orlando Resident	Occupation	Place of Birth	Cause of Death	Place of Burial
4-Jan	*W. T. Brooks	M	W	2	S	Haines City, Fla/O.G. Hosp	6 ds		Orlando	General Septicemia	Lake Alford, Fla
5-Jan	*Nicklos Billinger	M	W	54	M	Cincinnati, Oh / 225 Palmetto	1 mo	Merchant, Retired	Cincinnati, Ohio	Cirrhosis of Liver	Cincinnati, Ohio
4-Jan	Laura Jane Taylor	F	C	42	W	519 W. Pine St/ 519 W. Pine St	10 yrs	Domestic	Florida	Epileptic Convulsion	Greenwood
5-Jan	*Avril Estell Saxon	F	W	29	M	Maitland, Fla/ O.G.H.	2 ds	At Home	Good-water, Clay Co, Ala	Typhoid Fever	Goodwater, Ala
6-Jan	*Eulah Louise Turlington	F	W	1	S	429 E Livingston	1 yr 4 mo		Orlando	Ileum Colitis, sceclosa?	Greenwood
6-Jan	*Henry N. Morris	M	W	54	M	Roanoke, Va/ 711 N. Summerland	2 mo	Telegraph Operator	Maysville, Ky	Cerebral Apoplexy; patient was dead when I arrived	Greenwood
3-Jan	Stillborn	F	C			96 South St.			Orlando	Stillborn	Greenwod
11-Jan	*Mary Frances Touchton	F	W	19	S	Trilby, Fla/ O.G.H.	3 yrs	Nurse	Valdosta, Ga	Acidosis Due to Neurosis	Trilby, Fla
10-Jan	George Leeds Zell	M	W	51	M	Mt.Dora, Fla/ O.G.H.	22 ds	Retired	Baltimore, Md	Bronchial Asthma	Mt. Dora, Fla
10-Jan	Ethel House	F	C	23	M	602 Parramore	5 mo	House wife	Decatur, Ga	Acute Nephritis	Quincey, Fla
14-Jan	*Rosetta Giles	F	W	10 m	S	Bartow, Fla/ O.G.Hosp.	1 da		Winter Park	Entero? Citis	Winter Park
14-Jan	Elizabeth Hall	F	C	35	M	106 Division	3 yrs	House wife	Fla	Chronic Malaria	Greenwood
16-Jan	Clarence Z. Lord	M	W	53	S	207 W. South St.		Painter	Jefferson Co., Fla	Cardiac p__?	Greenwood
16-Jan	*Mary Ellen Fairchild	F	W	77	W	406 Grace St.	7 yrs	At Home	Zanesville, Ohio	Broncho Pneumonia	Morrow, Ohio
16-Jan	*Edith Dixon	F	W	79	W	Blackshear	11 mos	At Home	Pierce Co, Ga	Apoplexy	Waycross, Ga
18-Jan	Abraham P. Patterson	M	C	40	M	710 Jackson	18 yrs	Carpenter	Madison, Fla	Killed in Auto Wreck, Car Overturn	Greenwood
18-Jan	Dann Prince	M	C	22	M	1017 W.South St.	4 yrs	Common Labor	Fla		Madison, Fla

1924	Name of Deceased	Sex	Race	Age	Marital	Residence & Place of Death	Orlando Resident	Occupation	Place of Birth	Cause of Death	Place of Burial
18-Jan	*Anna J. Tindle	F	W	79	W	Otter Creek, Fla/ 118 Hughey	22 ds	At Home	S.C.	Senility	Otter Creek, Fla
18-Jan	*William Henry Baldenton	M	W	47	M	Trenton, N.J./ 312 N. Summerlin	2 mo	Farming	Bucks Co, Pa	Broncho pneumonia	Trenton, N.J.
28-Jan	*James David Smethers	M	W	63	M	Versailles, Ky/ Wissahichan?	5 mo	Farming	Ky	Chronic Nephritis	Lexington, Ky (In Vault)
20-Jan	*James Howell	M	W	86	M	Holapaw, Fla/ O.G.H.	7 da	Planter	Ga	Carcinoma of Bladder	Greenwood
21-Jan	*Edward William Goez	M	W	60		/ O.G.H.	1 da			Angina Pectoris	Webster Grove, St.Louis,Mo
20-Jan	*Mrs Lucy Anderson	F	W	66	W	Franklin, WVa/ 215 Main St.	a 1 mo	At Home	Franklin, W. Va.	Chronic Valvular Heart Disease	Franklin, W Va
22-Jan	Isiah Jenkins	M	C	2 ds	Infant	/ 511 W. Washington	2 ds	Infant	Orlando	Umbilical Hemorrhage	Greenwood
22-Jan	Henry Bell Campbell, Jr	M	C	4 mo	M	6 Osey? St	7 yrs		Fla	Pneumonia	Greenwood
22-Jan	*Lamar Newton Hunt	M	W	2 mos	S	Orlando/ 400 N. Parramore	2 mos		Orlando	Broncho Pneumonia	Greenwood
22-Jan	*Harry M Dearborn	M	W	51	S	St. Johns, New Brunswick, Can/ OGH	1 mo 14 days	Book keeper	Summerville, Mass	Chronic Nephritis	St John., New Brunswick, Canada
23-Jan	Melvin James Crittenden	M	W	2 ds	S	Pine Castle/ O.G.H.	2 ds		Orlando	Acute Dilation	Greewood
23-Jan	*Charles Henry Baker	M	W	76	W	Zellwood, Fla/ O.G.H.	7 ds	Citrus Fruit	Philadelphia, Pa	Possible Malignant	Zellwood
24-Jan	Infant F. R. Miller	M	C			McFall St.			Orlando	Stillborn	Greenwood
28-Jan	*Mrs. Nettie M. Leinhart	F	W	76	W	Oviedo/ Fla San	25 ds	At Home	New York	Carcinoma of Stomach, Liver & Pancreas	Catholic
28-Jan	January Burke	M	C	85	S	Orlando/ County Home	5 yrs	Day Labor	Fla	Apoplexy	County Home

1924	Name of Deceased	Sex	Race	Age	Marital	Residence & Place of Death	Orlando Resident	Occupation	Place of Birth	Cause of Death	Place of Burial
29-Jan	*Frank A. Taber	M	W	72	M	Grand Ledge, Mich?/ 121 Summerlin	1 mo	Manu-facturer	Eaton Co., Mich	Chronic Interstitial Nephritis	Grand Ledge, Mich
29-Jan	*Mrs Margaret E. Graham	F	W	75	W	2 Gore Ave	10 yrs	At Home	Peter-burg, Va	Shis? Myocarditis	Greenwood
29-Jan	Henry Archey	M	C	69	W	1029 W. Bentley	3 mo	Wood Chopper	Virginia	Parenchymato us Nephritis	Greenwood
3-Feb	Robert Donahue	M	W	84	M	2 miles S. E. of Orlando	3 yrs	Farming	London-derry, Ireland	Chronic Citis	Greenwood
4-Feb	Lena Brooks	F	C	22	M	40 Holden	3 yrs	House wife	Ga	Acute Paren-chymatous Nephritis	Tifton, Ga
29-Jan	*George J. Munsell	M	W	65	M	Detroit, Mich/ O.G.Hosp	4 mos	Adver-tising Business	Chardon, Ohio	Bullet Wound Through Rt Cheek Bone & Orbit? To __? Was 3 wounds St. Louis	
29-Jan	*Mrs Nettie H. Smith	F	W	21	M	Winter Park/ O.G.H.	1 da	At Home	N. Carolina	Puerperal Septicemia	Kings Mountain, N.C.
30-Jan	*David D. Davison	M	W	73	M	Carnegie, Okla/ Fairvilla	30 ds	Book keeper	Clarksburg W Va	Drowned	Greenwood
31-Jan	*David H. Thornton	M	W	80	M	414 W. Central	6 yrs	Merchant	Danville, Pa	Uremia	Greenwood
1-Feb	*Richard E. Daniels	M	W	54	M	Westboro, Mass	4 mos	Insurance Agt	Dickson City, Penn	Aortic Regurgitation	Greenwood
2-Feb	*Chas Lenard Richardson	M	W	58	M	Avon by the Sea, N.J./ 224 E Concord	3 mos	With the Standard Oil Co. in NY	Brooklyn, NY	Cerebron Spinal Luci?	Avon by the Sea (In Vault)
3-Feb	*David Polland	M	W	87	W		Sev Yrs			Apoplexy	County Home
4-Feb	*Elmer David Iverson (Alverson)	M	W	52	M	Kenova, W Va/ O.G.H.	6 ds	Mechan-ical Engineer	Gailsburg, Ill	Carcinoma of Stomach	Kenova, W Va
6-Feb	*Michael Senseman	M	W	77	W	Mechanicsburg, Pa / Fla San	1 mo	Farming	New Kingston, Pa	Bronchial Ashtma	Mechanicsburg, Pa
28-Jan	Addie Thomas	F	C	27	M	609 Gore Ave		House wife	Orlando	Acute Nephritis	Greenwood

1924	Name of Deceased	Sex	Race	Age	Marital	Residence & Place of Death	Orlando Resident	Occupation	Place of Birth	Cause of Death	Place of Burial
7-Feb	Gordon Brown Lawson	M	W	59	M	Kissimmee/ O.G.H.	31 yr 1 da	Farmer	Chattahoochee, Co., Ga	Fracture Base of Skull	Kissimmee
9-Feb	*Herbert J. Hartwell	M	W	47	M	Plattsburg,	1 mo 7 ds	Grocer Business	Crown Point, N.Y.	Organic Heart Disease/ Mitral Insufficiency w/ Dilatation Plattsburg, NY	
11-Feb	*Smith D. Barnum	M	W	82	W	1/ 2 m South of City	5 mos	Mill Owner, Retired	Schohora Co, NY	Organic disease of heart	In Vault Waverley, N.Y.
11-Feb	*Ernest Millett Holden	M	W	68	M	326 N. Magnolia	45?	Laundry, Retired	Sweeden, Main	Chronic Interstitial Nephritis, arteocelerus? & myocarditis Greenwood	
11-Feb	*Mrs Rosa Lee Roberson	F	W	27	M	W. Church		At Home	Orlando, Fla	Cancer Cervix, vagina, & gestation?	Patrick Cemetery
12-Feb	Lugene Penenton	M	C	6m		418 Parramore	14 mos	None	Orlando	Diphtheria membraneous	Greenwood
4-Feb	Louis Reed	M	W	45	S	Nicholsville, Ky/ O.G.H.	2 mos	At Fairgrounds with Race Horse as Labor	Ky	Chronic myocarditis	Greenwood
13-Feb	*Infant of Mr & Mrs Joe Kelly	F	W	1d	S	Fairvilla/ OGH.	1 da		Fairvilla	Premature Birth	Patrick Cemetery
14-Feb	*Infant of Mr & Mrs O. B. Canada	M	W	12 da	S	519 Ohio Ave/ O.G.H.	12 ds		Orlando	Intro Cranial Hemorrhage	Draughty Cemetery
13-Feb	*Mrs Florence Anna Michael	F	W	41	M	Orlando/ Apopka Road	2 yrs	At Home	Buffalo, N.Y.	Uremia (Suicidal Intent)	Boggie Creek
16-Feb	Josephene Lampe	F	C	23	M	436 Holden	6 yrs	Waitress	Mt. Gomery, Ala	Chronic Pulmonary Tuberculosis	Greenwood
18-Feb	Robert M. Rathbun	M	W	3 mo	S	Westerly R.I./ Fla San	5 ds		Westerly, R.I.	Delayed Asphyxia	Westerly, Rhode Island
19-Feb	*Fredrick L. Coes	M	W	74	W	Worcester, Mass/ O.G.Hosp	1 mo	Retired	W. Mass	Chronic Glanular	Worcester, Mass
19-Feb	*Edward B. Hafertelfen	M	W	54	M	317 W-84th St., N.Y.C./ 126 Concord Ave	3 mos	Traveling Salesman, Shoes	Hamilton, Ohio	Organic Heart Disease	New York

1924	Name of Deceased	Sex	Race	Age	Marital	Residence & Place of Death	Orlando Resident	Occupation	Place of Birth	Cause of Death	Place of Burial
22-Feb	Lois Helen Davies	F	W	61	W	St. Johns, Mich/ Fla San	1 mo 6 das	None	St. Johns	Apoplexy	Mt. Dora, Fla
19-Feb	*Dewitt Clinton Hurd	M	W	83	M	Utica, N.Y./ Wyoming Hotel	3 mos	Manufacturer, Retired	Monteumer, N.Y.	Cardiac Asthma	Utica, N.Y.
20-Feb	*Mrs Nellie Fuller	F	W	60	M	523 W. Central	13 yrs	At Home	Lake City, Minn	Acute Nephritis	Catholic
20-Feb	*Lydia B. Railsback	F	W	1	S	1632 N. Mill	1 yr 9		Orlando	Uremia	Greenwood
20-Feb	*Mrs Emma L. Sadler	F	W	67	M	Syracuse, N.Y/ 208 Hillman	3 mo	At Home	Cicero?	Myocarditis	Syracuse, N.Y.
22-Feb	Yorkster King Meeks	M	C	68	M	522 W. Pine	5 yrs	Jewelry-man	Block-shear	Apoplexy	Greenwood
22-Feb	*Lewis L. Goolsby	M	W	44	S	Lake Gem, Fla/ O.G.H	6 ds	Engineer	Orange Co., Fla	Hemorrhage	McDonald Cemetery
22-Feb	Adolphus Jackson	M	C	37	M	County Home	Sev Mos	Day Loborer	Jacksonville, Fla	Aortic & Mitral Insufficiency	County Home
24-Feb	*Mrs Clara Jones	F	W	60	W	Formosa	2 yrs 6 mo	At Home	Sweden	Dropsy & Myocarditis	Kane, Penn
24-Feb	*Mrs. Mary B. Roberts	F	W	81	W	Knoxville, Tenn/ Fla San	1 mo 23	At Home	Oswego, NY	Myocarditis	Knoxville, Tenn
25-Feb	*Michel (Michael) J. McCarey	M	W	60	M	Portsville	6 mos	Physician	Pa	Pulmonary Edema	Olean, N.Y.
26-Feb	*Howard E. Williams	M	W	65	W	Richmond, Ind/ O.G.H.	3 mos	Implement Dealer	Wayne Co., Ind	Chronic Myocarditis	Richmond, Ind
25-Feb	*Nancy I. Pettingill	F	W	82	W	Asbury Park, N.J./ O.G.H.	5 mos	At Home	Birming-ham, Iowa	Apoplexy	Asbury Park, N.J.
26-Feb	Mrs Ollie Olivia Bowles	F	W	30	M	Bithlo, Fla/ O.G.H.	1 ds		Nassau Co., Fla	Lobar Pneumonia?	Hilliard, Fla
27-Feb	*Chas Irvin Rogers	M	W	65	M	Portland, Mich/ O.G.H.	14 ds	Contrac-tor	Eden Rapids, Mich	Myocarditis, Acute Dilitation	Portland, Mich
29-Feb	*Chas J. Garett	M	W	39	S	924 Kuhl Ave	9 yrs	County Warden	Milledge-ville, Ga	Pulmonary Tuberculosis	Greenwood
3-Mar	Meyer Benson	M	W	46	M	Shreveport, La/ O.G.H.	1 mo 14 ds	Merchant	Russia	Acute Myocarditis, Acute Pericarditis, Acute Endocarditis	Shreveport, La

1924	Name of Deceased	Sex	Race	Age	Marital	Residence & Place of Death	Orlando Resident	Occupation	Place of Birth	Cause of Death	Place of Burial
29-Feb	*Eva Kyle	F	W	66	M	616 S. Hyer	4 yrs	At Home	London, Ontario, Canada	Chr. Bronchitis	Greenwood
29-Feb	*Willis Wilkinson	M	W	84	S	Charleston, S.C./ O.G.H.	5 mo	Fruit Grower	Charleston, S.C.	Uremia	Charleston, S.C.
27-Feb	Mattie White	F	C	43	M	Furgeson, SC / 806 Rutherford	13 mos	Cook	Frog-moore	Lobar Pneumonia	Greenwood
27-Feb	*Mrs. Ida Marie Stoly Simms	F	W	46	M	155 Clifton Ave, Clifton, N.J / 500 E. Jackson	3 mo	At Home	Patterson, N.J.	Pulmonary Edema	Paterson, N.J.
1-Mar	*Theodore F. Daniels	M	W	79	W	Fern Creek Ave	18 yrs	Banker	Kaledonia, N.Y.	Pergonic (Organic) Heart Tissue	Greenwood
3-Mar	Clearance H. Adams	M	C	20	S	1029 W. Livingston	11 mo	Laborer	Highey, Lake Co.	Pulmonary Tuberculosis	Greenwood
4-Mar	*Geo. W. Hinson	M	W	21	M	102 W. Washington	abt 3 yrs	Stationary Engineer	Coffee Co., Ala	Acute Brights Disease (Nephritis)	Greenwood
5-Mar	*Mollie P. Young	F	W	68	M	Ocala, Fla/ O.G.H.	1 da	At Home	Miss	Carcinoma of Liver	Ocala, Fla
5-Mar	*John Franklin McKee	M	W	51	M	Carter St/ O.G.H.	35 yrs	Gardner	Georgia	Accidentally Hit by Auto & Died Instantly	Greenwood
5-Mar	Joe Causey Mobley	M	C	23	M	Hospital	1 da	Labor	Ga	Fracture of Cervical Vertebrae	Valdosta, Ga
1-Mar	Earl Inslock	M	W	2	S	abt Fern Creek/ O.G.H.	abt 1 yr		Perry, Fla	Scalded by Falling into Tub of Water	Whigham, GA
6-Mar	*Henry V. D. Vorhies	M	W	68	M	Orlando/ 606 E Hillcrest	15 yrs	Lumber Business	Brooklyn, N.Y.	Carcinoma of Bowels	Brooklyn, N.Y.
7-Mar	Calvin Otho Germeinhardt	M	W	2 ds	S	Winter Garden Road	2 ds		Orlando	Premature	Patrick Cemetery
7-Mar	*Patrick J. Moran	M	W	48	M	Cincinnati, Ohio/ O.G.H.	6 ds	Baseball Manager	Fitchburg, Mass	Uremia, Acute Nephritis	Fitchburg, Mass
6-Mar	*Frederick A. Lewter	M	W	69	M	811 N. Orange	41 yrs	Real Estate	Halifax N.C.	Chronic Myocarditis	Greenwood
7-Mar	Rawan Walker	M	C	68	M	502 W. Pine	20 yrs	Laborer	Mt. Pleasant, Gadson	Mitral Stenosis	Greenwood

1924	Name of Deceased	Sex	Race	Age	Marital	Residence & Place of Death	Orlando Resident	Occupation	Place of Birth	Cause of Death	Place of Burial
8-Mar	*Samuel G. Garvin	M	W	73	M	28 E. Concord	2 yrs	Supt Steel Mill	Portsmouth, Oh	Mitral Regurgitation; Chr. Nephritis	Greenwood
8-Mar	*Roy John Kuntz	M	W	29	M	Johnstown, Pa/ Fla San	abt 6 mos	Whole-sale Coal	Johns-town, Pa	Mitral Re-gurgitation	Johnstown, Pa
8-Mar	*Addie V. Markey	F	W	53	M	51 Palmer Ave., Detroit/ Lucerne Hotel	1 mo 7 ds	At Home	Embro, Ont., Canada	Pyelitis with acute abcess kidneys	Detroit, Mich
9-Mar	*Alfred Leonidus Baker	M	W	63	M	521 Oak Park Ave, Chicago/ Hotel Villa	1 mo	Publisher	Illinois	Lobar Pneumonia Left Lung	Chicago, Ill
11-Mar	*Miss Elaine Chase Williamson	F	W	21	S	1517 E. 65 St, Chicago/ Jefferson Court	4 mos		Chicago, Ill	Endocarditis, Rheumatic	Chicago, Ill
11-Mar	*Murdock Lee Dunaway	M	W	a 16	S	Lake Hamilton, Fla./ O.G.H.	1 da	Boxmaker W. E. Lee & Co.	Bartow, Fla	Some Form of Meningitis	Haines City, Fla
11-Mar	Tom Brown	M	C	70	S	710 Washington	1 mo	Labor	Fla	Diabetes Mellitus	Greenwood
11-Mar	Alex Brooks	M	C	41	M	537 W. Church	3 yrs	Labor	Brunswick, Ga	Mitral Valvular Insufficiency, Ascites	Greenwood
12-Mar	Rufus Joffer	M	C	24	S	S. E. Of Orlando	4 mos	Labor	S.C.	Probably Chronic Myocarditis	Greenwood
12-Mar	*Mrs Lena Einstein	F	W	66	W	Cleveland, Ohio/ San Juan Hotel	3 mos	At Home	Cleveland, Ohio	Morbus Cardiac Valvulation, Etc.	Cleveland, Ohio
13-Mar	*Mrs Sarah B. Butterfield	F	W	52	M	Chicago, Ill/ St. Charles Hotel	1 mo 14 da	At Home	Vir__, Wis	Vincintis Angina	Chicago, Ill
4-Mar	Mrs Anna McDonald	F	W	33	D	Melrose Highland, Mass/ 1014 N. Reel	a 2 yr	at Home	Scotland	Murdered	Greenwood
10-Mar	Geo. H. Foote	M	W	a79	W	Farnum	abt 5 mos			Acute Cardiac Dilitation	Farnum, Neb
13-Mar	Stillborn of J. B. Williams	M	C		Inf	1009 W. South			Orlando	Stillborn	Greenwood

1924	Name of Deceased	Sex	Race	Age	Marital	Residence & Place of Death	Orlando Resident	Occupation	Place of Birth	Cause of Death	Place of Burial
20-Feb	Mrs Jennette Irvin?	F	W	73	M	St. Cloud, Fla/ O.G.H.	1 da	House wife	Ohio	Acite Dilitation Heart	Mt Peace Cemetery
12-Mar	*Mrs Lula A. Wattenscheidt	F	W	59	M	139 Court St/ O.G.H.	20 yrs	At Home	Baltimore MD	Intestinal Ileus	In Vault
15-Mar	*S. Joseph	M	W	a50	M	629 W Church/ O.G.H.	9 yrs	Merchant	Syria	Asthma	Greenwood
16-Mar	*Emma Letzing	F	W	64	M	Palmetto, Fla/ Fla San	7 ds	At Home	Milwaukee, Wis	Surgical Shock	St. Petersburg
16-Mar	*Anna Bell Heaton	F	W	83	W	Salem, Ohio/ 211 S. Rosalind Ave		None	Steubenville, Ohio	Angina Pectoris	Salem, Ohio
19-Mar	John Davis	M	C	31	M	106 N. Bryant/ O.G.H.	14 yrs	Cleaning Clothes	Virginia	Fracture & Dislocation of 3rd Cervical Vertebra. Probable Severe Concussion & Laceration of Spinal Cord	Greenwood
17-Mar	*Ola Lee Hildreth Allen	F	W	22	M	Formosa, Fl/ Fla San	abt 3	Clerk	Enterprise, Ala	Auto Accident; Fractured Base of Skull, Legs Broken & Neck	burial not given
18-Mar	*Mrs. Jennie F. Irvine	F	W	74	M	111 E. Church St	42	At Home	Georgia	Morbus Cardis Valvulam?	Greenwood
19-Mar	*Arren (Anen) D. Simmons	M	W	36	M	Indiana Ave	1 yr 1 mo	Farming	Benen Co., (Berrien?) Ga	Acute Hodgkin's Disease	Greenwood
19-Mar	*Joseph A. Kraen	M	W	46	M	Jacksonville/ Orlando Hotel	Sev mos	Contractor	San Francisco, Cal	Chonic Myocarditis	Daytona
20-Mar	*Rev Jacob Bowman Holley	M	W	57	M	Winter Park/ Fla San	2 mos	Minister	Edgefield S.C.	Apoplexy	Bennetsville
19-Mar	James Robinson	M	C	60	W	605 Gore Ave	35 yrs	Wood chopper	Wilmington, N.C.	Chronic Pareg___? Nephritis	Greenwood
19-Mar	*Infant of Mr & Mrs T. L. Hinsey	M	W		S	112 1/2 W. Church/ OGH			Orlando	Stillborn	Greenwood
17-Mar	*Lydia R. Joles	F	W	67	M	Formosa/ Fla San	13 yrs	At Home	Sherbian, N.Y. ?	Apoplexy	(Vault) Shurburne, N.Y.
17 Mar	*Mrs. Ada Green	F	W	47	M	Orlando/ O.G.H.	1 mo 7 da	At Home	Hamilton Co., Fla	Carcinoma of Uterus & Sigmoid	Patrick

1924	Name of Deceased	Sex	Race	Age	Marital	Residence & Place of Death	Orlando Resident	Occupation	Place of Birth	Cause of Death	Place of Burial
21-Mar	*Earnest Harrison Williams	M	W	1	S	204? Grace	abt 1 yr		St. Cloud, Fla	Acute EnteroCitis	Greenwood
23-Mar	*J. C. Johnson	M	W	85	W	County Home	5 yrs	Machinist in mill	Indiana	Uremia	County Home
20-Mar	*Edward K. Stone	M	W	54	M	812 S Hughey	4 yrs	Merchant	Lumberton N.C.	Influenza-Pneumonia, Broncho	Greenwood
20-Mar	*Mrs Martha Elizabeth Starling?	F	W	65	W	Windermere, Fla / OGH	14 ds	At Home	Liberty Co., Ga	Acute Peritonitis	Patrick
20-Mar	*Mrs. Irene May Allen	F	W	31	M	Mark St/ Fla San	12 yrs	At Home	Lockwood, Fla	Intestinal Obstruction	Iron Bridge Cemetery
24-Mar	*Mrs. Josephine F. Rathbun	F	W	58	M	Union, N.Y./ Fla San	6 mos	At Home	Penn	General Peritonitis, Acute	Union, N.Y.
25-Mar	*Mrs Margaret S. Jenks	F	W	65	M	Detroit, Mich/ O.G.H.	1 mos	At Home	Ohio	Morbis Cardiac Valbulane?	Detroit, Mich
26-Mar	*James A. Lee	M	W	63	M	Leesburg, Fla/ O.G.H.	5 hrs	Truck Farmer	Leesburg, Fla	Perforated Gastric Ulcer	Leesburg, Fla
15-Jan	Infant Duey Hobson Smith	F	W		S	Fern Creek Drive			Orange Co.	Stillbirth	Conway Cemetery
22-Mar	Willard Wellington Wells	M	W	72	W	302 Broadway	14 yrs	Jeweler	Jackson, Ohio	Organic Heart Disease	Greenwood
28-Mar	*Mary Honor Burdick	F	W	73	M	201	2 mos	House wife	Bradford, R.I.	Angina Pectoris	New York, N.Y.
28-Mar	*Mrs. Susie Mae Kasel (Kasell)	F	W	22	M	Chuluota/ O.G.H.	abt 3 wks	At Home	Ocala, Fla	Puerperal	Ocala, Fla
29-Mar	*Thos B. Sutherlan	M	W	12	S	McMinnville, Tenn/ O.G.H.	6 ds		McMinn-ville, Tn	Meningitis	McMinnville, Tenn
29-Mar	*John A. Lebarge	M	W	60		Holyoke, Mass/ Fla San				Surgical Shock	Holyoke, Mass
29-Mar	*Joe L. Lindsey	M	C	80	M	Eatonville, Fla/ O.G.H.	Abt 1 mos	Day Work	Lake City, Fla	Nephritis, Acute Peritonitis	County Home
29-Mar	*William A. Jennings	M	W	51	M	Chicago, Ill/ O.G.H.	10 mos	Lawyer	Arkansas	Chr. Myocarditis	Chicago, Ill

1924	Name of Deceased	Sex	Race	Age	Marital	Residence & Place of Death	Orlando Resident	Occupation	Place of Birth	Cause of Death	Place of Burial
31-Mar	*Madora Lincoln	F	W	67	W	Lockhart	4 mos	At Home	Howard Mills, NY	Organic Heart Disease	Greenwood
31-Mar	*Miss Edna Mae Ulery	F	W	25	S	Michigan Ave	2 mos	At Home	Galena , Kan.	Nephritis	Galena, Kan
30-Mar	Fannie L. Proctor	F	C	51	W	111		School Teacher	Atlanta, Ga	Heart Failure	Greenwood
31-Mar	Edward Phillip Moody Brown	M	W	6 ds	S	W Pine St.	6 ds		Orlando	Prematurity	Greenwood
2-Apr	*Amelia R. C. Rogers	F	W	73	M	Middletown, N.Y./ Duke Hall	2 mos 14 ds	At Home	Lambert-ville, N.J.	Cerebral Hemorrahage	Middletown, N.Y.
4-Apr	*Maggie Benefield	F	W	2	S	Fern Creek Road			Alabama	Broncho Pneumonia	Patrick
4-Apr	*Clarendon W. Barron	M	W	51	M	Columbus, S.C./ O.G.H.	2 mos	Practicing Physician	Maning, S.C.	Chronic Myocarditis	Cumbus, S.C.
28-Feb	Wm Roy Harris	M	W	25	M	Near Pine Castle		Express Agt	Orange Co.	Tuberculosis of Lungs	Greenwood
6-Apr	*Riley Davis	M	W	a46	M	Warrens? Mill/ O.G.H.	11 ds	Day Laborer	Ga	Peritonitis	Oviedo
6-Apr	*Walter E. Cobb	M	W	36	M	Pine Lock Ave	6 yrs	Real Estate	New Jersey	Apoplexy	Greenwood
6-Apr	*Minot Ellis	M	W	83	W	Lake Mary, Fl/ Howell San	3 ds	Mechanic	Keene, N.H.	Apoplexy	Greenfield, Mass
7-Apr	Mattie Porter	F	C	14	S	432 Holden	5yrs	School Girl	Ahart? S.C.	Acute Pneumonia	Greenwood
8-Apr	*Mrs Martha E. Hathoway	F	W	61	W	120 McKee Ave/ O.G.H.	9 mos	At Home	Milbury, Mass	Septicemia, Infected Throat	Fall River, Mass
8-Apr	*John H. Newell	M	W	77	W	Wisconsin/ O.G.H.	2 yrs	Carpenter	Pitsfield, N.H.	Shock following Suprapic? Operation	Oshkosh, Wis
9-Apr	*Mrs. Edith A. Power	F	W	69	M	Longwood/ O.G.H.	18 m 1 da	At Home	Brokville, Ontario, Can	Acute Cardiac Dilitation	Kingston, Ontario
10-Apr	Lillie Gaimer [Garner?]	F	C.	36	M	O.G.H.	14 days	House wife	Waynes-boro, Ga	Coma, Diabetic	Midville, Ga
4-Apr	Mrs Alice McClelland	F	W	80	M	O.G.H.	2 ds	House wife	Hudson, N.Y.	Shock, Auto Accident	Eustis, Fla

1924	Name of Deceased	Sex	Race	Age	Marital	Residence & Place of Death	Orlando Resident	Occupation	Place of Birth	Cause of Death	Place of Burial
31-Mar	Gallus Metz	M	W	83	M	Conway Road	42 yrs	Farming, Retired	Switzer-land	Bronchial Pneumonia	Greenwood
12-Apr	*Chas C. Cox	M	W	50	M	Forest City	14 yrs	Farming	Texas	Hypertension	Winter Park
13-Apr	*Mrs Sue Borden Douglas	F	W	51	W	Jacksonville, Fla/ Fla Sanitarium	10 or 12 ds	At Home	Golds-boro, N.C.	Myocarditis	Goldsboro, N.C.
14-Apr	*Adolphus F. Bell	M	W	66	M	Sanford/ Howell Sanitarium	1 mos	Merchant	Rome, Ga	Gangrene of Feet and Legs	Ocoee Cemetery
14-Apr	Marie Winner	F	C	11 mo	Inf	439 S. Division	9 mos		Palm Beach	Broncho pneumonia	Greenwood
15-Apr	*Ransom J. Sawyer	M	W	76	W	Bee Ridge, Fla/ O.G.H.	2 ds	Druggist	Wiscon-sin	Carcinoma of Stomach	Menomiville?, Mich
16-Apr	*Mrs Bertha M. Patton	F	W	56	M	512 N. Gar-land/ Fla San	3 yrs	At Home	Muncie, Ind	Myocarditis	Greenwood
16-Apr	*Mrs Grace M. May	F	W	47	M	Grays Lake, Ill/ O.G.H.	10 ds	At Home	Aven?, Ill	Fever-type unknown	Grays Lake, Ill
1-Apr	Mary Reeves	F	C			145 Parramore			Orlando	Stillborn	Greenwood
18-Apr	John Withingham	M	C	48	M	1100 South St	6 mos	Labor	Camilla, Ga	Acute Nephritis	Camilla, Ga
19-Apr	Mrs. Emma M. Crowl	F	W	71	M	418 E. Pine	2 yrs		Welle-ville, Oh	Cerebral Hemorrhage	Marshall Town, Iowa
21-Apr	*Howard Burton Tucker	M	W	1m 25d	S	Ft.Christmas/ 422 E. Central Ave	1 day		Ft. Christ-mas, Fla	Broncho Pneumonia	Ft. Christmas, Fla
22-Apr	Sallie Barnes	F	C			503 Lee			Orlando	Stilborn, Asphyxiation	Greenwood
22-Apr	Clara S. MacGlashan	F	W	52	M	Eustis, Fla/ O.G.H.	3 mos 3 ds	House wife	Swickley, Pa	Emphysemia	Eustis, Fla
19-Apr	*Eugene H. Stowe	M	W	55	M	322 E. South	3 yrs	Wood Carver		Cerebral Hemorrhage	Greenwood
20-Apr	Henry Monroe	M	C	35	M	W. Church St./ O.G.H.	2 yrs	Day Labor	Brant-wood, Ga	Gunshot Wound of Abdomen & Peritonitis	County Home
25-Apr	*Martin E. Williams	M	W	79	M	432 S. Lake St/ Revana, Ky	7 mos	Oil Operator	N.Y.	Acute Dilatation of Heart	Hamburg, N.Y.
30-Apr	Mary Taylor	F	C	4m	S	717 Long St.	4 mos		Orlando	Don't Know	Greenwood

1924	Name of Deceased	Sex	Race	Age	Marital	Residence & Place of Death	Orlando Resident	Occupation	Place of Birth	Cause of Death	Place of Burial
28-Apr	William Banks	M	C	83	M	325 W Washington	36 yrs	Laborer	Jackson	Chronic Interstitial Nephritis	Greenwood
1-May	Milton Mann Allen	M	W	60	M	3 yrs	3 yrs	Retired	Chester, Pa	Myocarditis	Mt. Dora, Fla
1-May	Nell Spencer Smith	M	W	42	M	707 S. Division	1 yr 2 mos	Lineman Bell Tel.	Ky	Drowned	Providence, Ky
2-May	Infant of J. O. Turner, Jr.	M	C			207 N. Terry			Orlando	Stillborn	Greenwood
2-May	*Miss Annie Johnson Graham	F	W	76	S	Orlando/ Fla Sanitarium	7 yrs 1 mo 21 ds	Deaconess Episcopal Church	Philadelphia	Myocarditis	Philadelphia
4-May	*Infant of Mr & Mrs John Goolsby	M	W			Mt. Dora/ Fla San	1 da		Orlando	Stillborn	Mt Dora, Fla
4-May	Leroy Williams	M	C	1m 2d		Robinson & Div.	1 mo		Orlando	Cata___? Dysentery	Greenwood
1-May	*Cyrus E. Kittell	M	W	68	M	Prinston, Ill/ 308 E. Livingston	8 mos	Farmer, Retired	Sabbona, Ill	Chronic Myocarditis	Prinston, Ill
5-May	Henry Parker	M	B	40	S	404 Robinson	25 mos	Labor	Fla	Organic Heart Disease	Greenwood
7-May	Vernon Moore	M	C	40	S	Hospital	3 ds	Taylor [Tailor?]	Valdosta, Ga	Acute Dilation of Heart	Melbourne, Fla
9-May	George Rogen [Rogers]	M	C	20	S		3 mos	Laborer	Kissimmee	Heart Trouble	Kissimmee, Fla
11-May	*Henry A. Breinig	M	W	88	W	O.G.H.	1 yr	Mail Carrier	Brensville, Pa	Hyperstolic Pneumonia	Greenwood
13-May	Thomas Scott	M	C		S	61 Robinson Ave	4 yrs	None	Orlando	Si__? Of Lung	Greenwood
10-May	Julia Gammond	F	C	8 m	Infant	827 Bentley	8 mos		Orlando	Toxemia	Greenwood
13-May	*Mrs Riddell Wackym	F	W	43	W	Apopka Road	6 yrs	At Home	Georgia	General Septicemia Following Local Infection of Teeth burial not given	
13-May	Manda Williams	F	C	50	M	434 Randall	4 ds	Domestic	N.C.	Fibroid Tumor	Greenwood
17-May	Virginia R. Gaines	F	W	62	M	117 S. Lake	9 yrs	Teacher	Munfordville, Ky	Acute Nephritis	Munfordville, Ky

1924	Name of Deceased	Sex	Race	Age	Marital	Residence & Place of Death	Orlando Resident	Occupation	Place of Birth	Cause of Death	Place of Burial
17-May	*Ben A. Stevenson	M	W	39	M	304 S. Hughey St./ O.G.H.	5 mos	Auto Mechanic	Manatee Co,, Fla	Fracture of Base of Skull	Youmam? Fla
17-May	*Chas L. H. Bodine	M	W	63	M	Conway, Fla/ O.G.H.	3 yrs	Contractor, Paint & Paper Busines	Trenton, N.J.	Chronic Myocarditis	Greenwood
17-May	*Leslie L. Nicholson	M	W	28	M	618 S. Division St.	2 mos	Cashier, Am. Ry. Ex. Co.	Orlando, Fla	Pulmonary Tuberculosis	Greenwood
18-May	Thomas William Jones, Jr.	M	W	2	S	Rose Court/ O.G.H.	1 da		Sanford, Fla	Acute Nephritis	Sanford, Fla
14-May	Infant of Edward Keel	F	W		S	Clear Lake			Orlando	Stillborn	Greenwood Cemetery
18-May	*Henry Atterna?	M	W	35	S	Formosa/ Fair Grounds	8 yrs	Painter & Decorator	Holland	Bullet Wound Through Left Lung	Greenwood
19-May	Infant of Melton Hoyt	F	C	8 ds	S	214 Robinson			Orlando	Measles & LaGrippe	Greenwood Cemetery
21-May	*Mrs. Pauline Berg	F	W	56	M	920 W. Concord/ O.G.H.	9 mos	At Home	Germany	Carcinoma of Liver and Gallbladder	Catholic Cemetery
23-May	Jake Williams	M	C	59	M	E South St.	5 mos	Insurance Agt	Live Oak, Fla	Apoplexy	Greenwood Cemetery
23-May	*Mrs. Mettie G. Haywood	F	W	60	M	Holden	15 yrs	At Home	Evans-ville, Ind	Arteriosclerosis; Chronic Cardiac Valvular Disease	Ripon, Wis
26-May	*Will Norteman	M	W	73	W	Gatlin Ave/ O.G.H.	4 yrs	Merchant	Hanover, Mass	Angina Pectoris	Quincy, Mass
27-May	Edna Ellis	F	W	5		Tampa Ave	1 yr 10 ds		Benton, Ala	Acute IleoColitis	Patrick Cemetery
27-May	Guerethen Colen?	F	C		S	818 South St.		None	Orlando	Stillborn	Greenwood
25-May	*Mrs Fran-cis Barnes	F	W	80	W	414 W Central Ave	abt 2 yrs	At Home	Berwick, Penn	Oedema of Lungs	Berwidk, Penn
27-May	James Bacon	M	C	35	S	Ga	Don't know	Day Labor	Ga	General Peri-tonitis, Acute	County Home
29-May	*Jason Range	M	C	60	S	Va/ 110 Beggs St/ O.G.H.	39 yrs		Va	Chronic Paren-chymatous Nephritis	Greenwood

1924	Name of Deceased	Sex	Race	Age	Marital	Residence & Place of Death	Orlando Resident	Occupation	Place of Birth	Cause of Death	Place of Burial
30-May	*Von A. Huffaker	M	W	56	M	Fairvilla/ Knoxville, Tenn	3 mos	Judge Circuit Court	Tenn	Cancer Of ?pine & Gallbladder	Knoxville, Tenn
1-Jun	*Laxton James Bush	M	W	25	S	Orlando/ RR Crossing	2 yrs 3 mos	Lineman	Ocilla, Ga	Ran Car into Freight Train	Scotland, Ga
30-May	*Julia McKinon	F	C	75	W	1020 W Washington	4 mos	At Home	Decatur, Ga	Dengue & Malaria	Greenwood
1-Jun	*Vera Lee Littlefield	F	W	2	S	420 W. Jackson	1 yr 9 mos		Deistin Co., Ga	Acute Intestinal Infection & General Toxemia	Greenwood
2-Jun	Cora Bowman	F	C	25	M	Jefferson	7 mos	Domestic	Ga	Acute Indigestion	Greenwood
2-Jun	*Carrie G. McCutcheon	F	W	50	M	Leesburg, Fla/ O.G.H.	5 ds	At Home	Nanpocer? Wis	Cerebral Hemorrhage	Clintonville, Wisc
3-Jun	Frank Battye	M	C	30	W	O.G.H	2 yrs	Laborer	Savannah, Ga	Fracture of Base of Skull from Injury Falling from Derrick Louisville, Ga	
3-Jun	*Franklin C. Branson	M	W	75	M	826 W Church	20 yrs	Merchant	Illinois	Probably Acute Dilitation of Heart burial not given	
4-Jun	Bennie Posey	M	C	23	S	Hospital		Labor	Ga	Appendicitis	Dawson, Ga
4-Jun	Joseph D. Johnson	M	W	29	M	Lake Alfred/ O.G.H.	14 ds	Mechanic	Concord, Ga	Splenomyogeneous Leukemia	Mashville, Ga
8-Jun	*Mrs Alice E. Rutherford	F	W	59	M	Harrisburg, Pa/ 20 High St	1 mo 6 ds	At Home	Iowa	Chronic Myocarditis	Harrisburg, Pa
10-Jun	*Everett Arnett	M	W	43	M	Apopka, Fla/ O.G.H	18 m 1 da	Painter	Ohio	Hemorrhage from Lung - Gunshot Wound	Apopka, Fla
11-Jun	Jessie E. Williams	M	C	29	M	606 Jefferson	2 wks	Laborer	Fla	Acute Gastritis	Leesburg, Fla
11-Jun	*Nathan Follett	W	M	75	M	Winter Park/ O.G.H.	1 mo 14 ds	Fruit Grower	Mich	Pulmonary Embolus	Pittsburgh, Pa
10-Jun	*Flora Turner	F	C	abt 9 or 10	S	Live Oak, Fla/ 316 W. Robinson	3 mos		Suwanee Co, Fla	Broncho Pneumonia	Live Oak, Fla
11-Jun	*Mrs Carrie Wood Temple	F	W	57	W	Bourne Hill/ Winter Park	22 mos	At Home	Marietta, Ohio	Gangrene of Right Lung	Winter Park, Fla
12-Jun	Mosetta Blackman	F	C	1 y 6m	S	Federal St/ O.G.H.	1 yr 6 mo	None	Orlando	Broncho Pneumonia	Longwood

1924	Name of Deceased	Sex	Race	Age	Marital	Residence & Place of Death	Orlando Resident	Occupation	Place of Birth	Cause of Death	Place of Burial
12-Jun	*Sylvester C. Stout	M	W	76	M	Plymouth/ O.G.H.	5 ds	Fruit Grower	Edge Hill, Penn	Complete Obstruction of Prostate Gland of Uretra? Uremia burial not given	
13-Jun	Rebecca Zinnerman	F	C	43	M	1000 South	4 yrs	House wife	Madison, Fla	Gastric Ulcer	Greenwood
13-Jun	Stillborn of C. B. McDowell	M	W		S	E. Washington/ O.G.H.			Orlando	Stillbirth	Conway Cemetery
12-Jun	Dan Hart	M	W	a55	S	County Home	21 yrs		Volusia Co., Fla	Pulmonary Tuberculosis	Conway Cemetery
14-Jun	Thelma Baker	F	C	4 h	S	424 Lee St	4 hrs	None	Orlando	Asphixiation	Greenwood
14-Jun	*Helen Sansbury	F	W	11m	S	Winter Garden/ O.G.H.	1 day		Winter Garden, Fla	Fever	Dalesville, Ala
16-Jun	Mamie Wooten	F	C	39	M	1 Hicks	21 yrs	House wife	Ga	Acute Nephritis	Greenwood
16-Jun	*Mrs Mamie Fillyaw	F	W	23	M	408 Virginia Dr.	5 yrs	At Home	Ga	Gastric Ulcer with Contracture of the Pylorus	Ray City, Ga
17-Jun	Rosa Ellick	F	C	22	M	415 S. Division	13 yrs	Laundress	Bishopville, S.C.	Acute Nephritis	Greenwood
17-Jun	*Infant of Robert F. Wilson		W		S	610 1/2 E. Washington			Orlando	Premature Birth (6 months)	Greenwood
21-Jun	Mary M. Hunter	F	W	34	M	Eustis, Fla/ O.G.H.	3 ds	House wife	Detroit, Mich	Perespinil? Septicemia	Eustis, Fla
18-Jun	Mrs Emma Agness Campbell	F	W	54	M	St. Louis, Mo/ Howell San	about 5 mos	At Home	St. Louis, Mo	Carcinoma of Bladder	Conway Cemetery
18-Jun	*William Thomas Donaldson	M	W	14	S	14 Ivanhoe Drive	2 yrs		Chester, Pa	Encephalitis Lethargias?	Chester, Penn
21-Jun	Georgia D. Hawkins	F	C	72	M	708 W. Robinson	5 mos	House wife	Canada	Mitral Regurgitation	Greenwood
22-Jun	Ralph Blackburn	M	W	17	S	Winter Garden/ O.G.H.	1 da	Farming	McDonough, Ga	Post Appendical Abscess w/ Intestinal Obstruction	McDonough, Ga
22-Jun	*James Washington	M	C	19	S	921 Division	abt 3 mos	Day Labor	Orangeburg, S.C.	Drowned	Greenwood

1924	Name of Deceased	Sex	Race	Age	Marital	Residence & Place of Death	Orlando Resident	Occupation	Place of Birth	Cause of Death	Place of Burial
22-Jun	*Mrs Delia Pritchett	F	W	30	M	Winter Garden/ O.G.H.	11 ds	At Home	Dublin, Ga	Toxemia of Pregnancy	Moore Station, Ga
21-Jun	*Carey Elwood Easom	M	W	39	M	RFD#3, Orlando/ O.G.H.	1 da	Lineman, So. Bell Tel.Co.	Laurel, Delaware	Hemorrhage of Cord	Greenwood
26-Jun	*William James Waddell	M	W	74	M	Winter Park/ O.G.H.	5 ds	Fruit Grower	Scotland	Pernicious Anemia	Winter Park Cemetery
26-Jun	Aron Daniels	M	C	47	M	906 Randell / O.G.H.	4 mos	Labor	Ga	Paralysis	Greenwood
25-Jun	*Madine Dryson	F	W	4 mos	S	Pine Castle, Fla	1 mo		Daytona, Fla	Colitis	Greenwood
28-Jun	*Mrs Marie Carson	F	W	53	M	O.G.H./ Orlando	1 da`	At Home	Viana, Australia	Acute Septicemia	Catholic
29-Jun	*Edward J. Newton	M	W	58	M	Astabula, Fla/ O.G.H.	3 ds	Sec. Foreman F & G RR	Conway, SC.	Streptocous Cellulitis of Face	Astabula, Fla
2-Jul	*David S. Bardo	M	W	84	W	RFD#2	9 mos	Farming, Retired	Avon, N.Y.	Septicemia	Flint, Mich
6-Jul	*Infant of Mr & Mrs W Prosser	M	W	2d	S	Orlando			Orlando	Premature Birth; Lack of Vitality	Greenwood
8-Jul	*Anna D. Frint	F	W	43	M	117 Earnestine	5 yrs	At Home	New Jersey	Carcinoma of Stomach	Elizabeth, N.J.
9-Jul	*Sarah Elizabeth Kerr	F	W	abt 76	S	Nashville, Tenn/ Duke Hall, Orlando	7 mos	At Home	Greensboro, Ala	Carcinoma, Pulmonary	Nashville, Tenn
10-Jul	*Infant of James Slade	F	W		S	14 Alexander Place/ Fla San			Orlando	Stillbirth	Greenwood
11-Jul	Infant of Doza L Frazer	F	C		S	Orlando			Orlando	Stillbirth	Greenwood
12-Jul	*Judson D. Wood	M	W	83	M	513 Trenton	3 yrs	Accountant Retired	Alliance, Ohio	Acute Indigestion	G.A.R., Greenwood
13-Jul	Julia Johnson	F	C	39	W	E South St.	6 ds	Domestic	Cuspid, Ga	Apoplexy	Greenwood
15-Jul	Agnes Brown	F	C	27	S	838 W. Jackson	3 yrs	Peritonitis	Quincy, Fla	Peritonitis	Greenwood
16-Jul	*Mrs May Beatty Patterson	F	W	67	W	19 Lucerne Circle	22 yrs	At Home	Steubenville, Ohio	Myocarditis	Greenwood

1924	Name of Deceased	Sex	Race	Age	Marital	Residence & Place of Death	Orlando Resident	Occupation	Place of Birth	Cause of Death	Place of Burial
17-Jul	Charlie Barnes	M	C	58	M	915 Division	24 yrs	Labor	Ga	Cerebral Apoplexy	Greenwood
18-Jul	*Mrs Nancy Jane Johnson	F	W	58	W	200 W. Amelia/ O.G.H.	3 yrs	At Home	Geneva, Ala	Carcinoma of ascending, etc.	Greenwood
20-Jul	*Geo Albert Storms	M	W	79	S	211 Liberty	4 yrs	Retired	Ann Arbor, Mich	Arterio-sclerosis	Clermont, Fla
21-Jul	*Mrs Joletta Bullard	F	W	48	M	519 N De Villa, Lockhart, Ala/ O.G.H.	1 mos	At Home	Millview, Fla	Lobar Pneumonia	PensaCa, Fla
22-Jul	*Rosa Irene Boyd	F	W	20 ds	S	Fern Creek Drive	20 ds		Orlando	Hemorrhage	Patrick
24-Jul	*Mrs Clarissa B. Taveau	F	W	64	M	327 E. Livingston	1 yr	At Home	Baltimore, Md	Broncho Pneumonia	Charleston, S.C.
25-Jul	*Franklin Marsh Soper	M	W	79	M	County Home	1 yr 3 mos	M.D., Retired	Canada	Dysentery	Greenwood
25-Jul	Harrell Warring	F	C	84	S	440 S. Parramore	1 yr	House wife	Ga	Chronic Nephritis	Greenwood
26-Jul	*Alvis Holt Hill	M	W	30	M	O.G.H.	1 da	Laborer	Ga	Fracture of Vertebra	Sylvester, Ga
27-Jul	*Mary D. White	F	C	44	M	O.G.H./ Jax, Fla	10 ds	At Home	Quincy, Fla	Myocarditis	Jacksonville, Fla
27-Jul	James N. Brown	M	W	26	M	Jax, Fla/ O.G.H.	7 ds	Traveling Salesman	East Lake, Ala	General Peritonitis	Jacksonville, Fla
29-Jul	*Austin D. Brigham	M	W	66	M	County Home	1 yr 6 mo	Painter	Maine	Apoplexy	Greenwood
27-Jul	*Geo Brownlee, Jr	M	W	27	S	634 Brook Haven Drive/ O.G.H.	27 ds		Orlando	Status Lymplaaticus	Greenwood
27-Jul	Pearl Moore	F	C	W	M	1137 W. Jefferson	7 mos	Domestic	Fla	Acute Gastritis	Greenwood
19-Jul	*Infant of S. J. Gillette	M	W		S	Wissahickon Drive/ ?O.G.H.	7 mos		Orlando	Prolapsed Cord	Gillette, Fla
31-Jul	Willema Robberson	F	C	8 yrs	S	Hospital		None	W. Garden	Accidently Killed, Truck Ran Over	Winter Garden
31-Jul	Frederick Kuhbach	M	W	45	S	Pine Castle	13 yrs		Germany	Acute Myocarditis	New York

1924	Name of Deceased	Sex	Race	Age	Marital	Residence & Place of Death	Orlando Resident	Occupation	Place of Birth	Cause of Death	Place of Burial
1-Aug	*Anna L. Pierce	F	W	63	M	Melbourne, Fla/ O.G.H	1 mo 14 ds	At Home	Elmore, Ohio	Acute Dilitation of Heart	Melbourne, Fla
31-Jul	*Unknown	M	C	a18		R R Crossing				Killed by A.C.L.	County Home
3-Aug	*Mary Ford	F	C	a16	S	8 mi S E of City	4 yrs	Domestic	Live Oak, Fla	Typhoid Fever	Gabriella?, Fla
no date	Clifford Alphonse Edmondson	M	C	46	M	19 Terry St.	12 yrs	Salesman	Unknown	Carcinoma of Stomach	Greenwood
5-Aug	*J. C. Sumner	M	W	abt 55	W	O.G.H/ 206 S. Hughey	sev yrs	Cigar maker	Dade City	Myocarditis	Dade City, Fla
6-Aug	*Mollie Sumerall	F	W	2	S	Orlando/ O.G.H.	2 mos		Polk Co., Fla	Meningitis	Greenwood
7-Aug	*Mrs Dell Shaw	F	W	33	M	Alachua, Fla/ O.G.H.	14 ds	At Home	Bradford Co., Fla	Acute Dilitation of Heart	Alachua, Fla
9-Aug	Isaac Schuller	M	C	2 ds	S	E Orlando	3 ds		Orlando	Unknown	Greenwood
8-Aug	*Henry W. Barksdale	M	W	60	S	Co Home	10 yrs	Merchant	Lynch-burg, Va	Apoplexy	Greenwood
8-Aug	*Edward R. Hotaling	M	W	70	M	9 E. Robinson/ OGH	18	Contrac-tor	Green Co, N.Y.	Acute Dilatation of Heart	Coxsackie, N.Y.
9-Aug	Harper Gerald Smith, Jr	M	W	6 hrs	S	Fla San/ 55 E Pine St	6 hrs		Orlando	Premature Birth	Greenwood
10-Aug	*Child of Ulus Rouse	F	W		S	1 mi E of Orlando/ O.G.H.	1 da		Orlando	Premature Delivery	Iron Bridge Cemetery
10-Aug	Allis Fain	F	C	29	M	O.G.H.	4 ds	Cook	Fla	Abscess of Pelvis	Tohapkee, Fla
1-Aug	Mardie Thomas	F	W	23	S	O.G.H./ Pittman, Fla	1 mo	House-keeper	Pittman, Fla	Chronic Parenchymatous Nephritis	Umatilla, Fla
13-Aug	Corean Johnson	F	C	S.B.	S	O.G.H.	1 da	None	Orlando	Asphyxiation of Lung	Portal, Ga
13-Aug	*Mrs. Matilda H. McQuaig	F	W	66	M	Mt. Verde, Fla/ O.G.H.	4 ds	At Home	Darien, Ga	Chronic Myocarditis	Mt. Verde
13-Aug	Corean Johnson	F	C	21	M	O.G.H.	1 da	Cook	Portal, Ga	Puerpie? Eclampsia	Portal, Ga

1924	Name of Deceased	Sex	Race	Age	Marital	Residence & Place of Death	Orlando Resident	Occupation	Place of Birth	Cause of Death	Place of Burial
14-Aug	Flora Durden	F	C	3	Inf	Lees Lane	4 ds	Infant	Swains-boro, Ga	Acute Incen_tion of Starvation	Greenwood
14-Aug	Irene Jefferson	F	C	17	S	921 W. South St.	13 m	Domestic	Gainesville Fla	Emphysema	Greenwood
15-Aug	*Paige Bell	M	C	47	M	O.G.H.	3 yrs	Day Labor	S.C.	Fractue of Base of Skull	Greenwood
20-Aug	Mary Holden	F	C	SB	S	114 Jefferson		None	Orlando	Stillborn	Greenwood
20-Aug	*Enoch Fetters	M	W	56	W	Orange City, Fla / W. Livingston	5 ds	Minister of Gospel, Retired	Wooster, Ohio	Gangrene of the Intestines	Plymouth, Ind
19-Aug	*John H. Earl	M	W	53	M	Cortland, N.Y./ 1301 Rosewood Ave	4 ds	RR Engineer	Erie, N.Y.	Chronic Heart Disease	Greenwood
20-Aug	*Clarence M. Phillips	M	W	63	M	719 W. Amelia	5 yrs	Farming	Clarence, Iowa	Mitral Re-gurgitation	Gentry, Arkansas
21-Aug	*Lorez S. Villenune	M	W	55	M	700 W Ch St/ Winter Garden Rd	15 yrs	Contrac-tor & Builder	Charles-ton, S.C.	Neck Broken, etc	Conway Cemetery
21-Aug	Albert H. Brown	M	W	71	M	1070 Greenwood Ave	8 mos	Toolmaker	North-field, Vt	Pernicious Anemia	Greenwood
22-Aug	Taylor Jerrett	M	C	55	M	America	9 ds	Laborer	S.C.	Arterio-sclerosis	Greenwood
22-Aug	Infant of Dock Young	F	C	SB	Inf	619 Parramore			Orlando	Stillborn	Greenwood
24-Aug	Charlie O'Neal	M	C	26	S	Division St.	4 mos	Labor	Fla	Unknown	Greenwood
27-Aug	Lillie Williams	F	C	SB	S	910 Edner			Orlando	Premature Birth	Greenwood
23-Aug	*Mrs Rebecca N. Lynch	F	W	84	W	716 Lucerne Terrace	27 yrs	At Home	Locust Hill, N.C.	Cerebral Hemorrhage	Greenwood
27-Aug	*Rachel A. Child	F	W	67	S	245 Ridgewood	15 yrs	At Home	Phila, Pa	Acute Dilation of Heart	Philadelphia, Pa
30-Aug	*Melton Middle-brooks	M	W	9	S	Haines City, Fla/ O.G.H.	2 ds		Jackson, Ga	Perforated Appendiceal Ulcer	Jackson, Ga
30-Aug	*Gladis Piner	F	C	20	M	730 S. Parramore		House wife	Dudley, Ga	Acute Dila-tion of Heart	Greenwood

48

1924	Name of Deceased	Sex	Race	Age	Marital	Residence & Place of Death	Orlando Resident	Occupation	Place of Birth	Cause of Death	Place of Burial
31-Aug	*Francis Harry Caldwell	F	W	31	M	Tampa, Fla / San Juan Hotel	4 ds	At Home	Charlotte, N.C.	Myocarditis	Greenboro, N.C.
31-Aug	Infant of James Williams	F	W	SB	S	Winter Park/ Fla San	1 da		Orlando	Stillborn	Winter Park
1-Sep	Child of James Harvey	F	W	SB	S	W Central Ave			Orlando	Stillborn	Greenwood
2-Sep	Venmel Joiner	F	C	1 yr	S	415 S. Division	1 yr		Orlando	Unknown	Greenwood
3-Sep	Henry E. Daniels	M	C	65	M	15 N. Bryant	28 yrs	Cook	Americus, Ga	Diabetic Coma	Greenwood
7-Sep	Infant of Wilson Holms	M	C	SB	S	600 McQuay St.			Orlando	Stillbirth	Greenwood
7-Sep	Marrie Watkins	F	C	17	S	OG.H./ Eustis, Fla	9 ds	House-keeper	Ga	Myocarditis	Eustis, Fla
6-Sep	*Mrs Louise Keigwin	F	W	56	M	Orlando/ O.G.H.	32 yrs	At Home	Baltimore Md	Apoplexy	Greenwood
9-Sep	*Mrs Susan Ann Small	F	W	80	W	Gatlin Ave	2 yrs	At Home	Davis Co., Ky	No Pathological Condition Manifested Except Senile Exhaustion	no burial given
9-Sep	*Nick Vukas	M	W	26	S	Bronx, N.Y./ County Home	2 mos	Day Laborer		Pulmonary Tuberculosis	New York City
10-Sep	William Fields	M	C	80	M	County Home	1 mo	Day Laborer	N.C.	Uremia	County Home
10-Sep	Lillie Bell Horten?	F	C	36	M	119 Butt	6 mos	Laundress	Eastman, Ga	Apoplexy	Greenwood
11-Sep	*Anna Ruth Kannon	F	W	2	S	Winter Garden/ O.G.H.	1 ds		Winter Garden, Fl	Laryngeal?	Oakland, Fla
13-Sep	Sam Johnson	M	C	75	M	E South St.	40 mos	Laborer	Valdosta, Ga	Chronic Intestinal?	Greenwood
13-Sep	*Edgar F. Pearson	M	W	2	S	Orlando/ OGH			Orlando	Acute Septic Infection	Dade City, Fla
14-Sep	Grant Huffman	M	C	50	M	Laughman/ O.G.H.	1 da	Laborer	Moultrie, Ga	Toxemia	Moultrie, Ga
14-Sep	*Willie Horace Davis	W	M	17	S	332 Long St/ O.G.H.		Labor Truck Driver	Orrington Maine	Accidental Fracture of Base of Skull	Greenwood

1924	Name of Deceased	Sex	Race	Age	Marital	Residence & Place of Death	Orlando Resident	Occupation	Place of Birth	Cause of Death	Place of Burial
14-Sep	*W. Edward Boddie	M	W	61	W	228 S. Main St.	Sev.1 yrs	Retired	N.C.	Chronic Nephritis	Greenwood
16-Sep	*Mrs Mary Hester	F	W	89	W	833 S. Division St.	10 yrs	At Home	Tenn	Senility	Boaz, Ky
16-Sep	Louis Robinson	M	C			419 W. Pine	2 mos		Orlando	Stillborn	Greenwood
17-Sep	*Mrs. Missouri Harvey	F	W	58	W	644 W Church	2 mos	At Home	Ga	Acute Cardiac Dilitation	Crystal River
19-Sep	*Aline Gouffman	F	W	85	S	720 Park Lake Ave	3 yrs	At Home	Switzerland	Senility	Knoxville, Tenn
22-Sep	*Mrs Loretta M. DeLong	F	W	23	M	O.G.H.	1 yr	At Home	Mass	Acute Cardiac Dilitation	Troy, N.Y.
22-Sep	*Mrs Katherine Clayton	F	W	82	W	108 E. Church	10 yrs	At Home	N.C.	Intestinal Obstruction	Greenwood
22-Sep	*Rufus S. Horne	M	W	55	M	802 N Summerlin	3 yrs	Salesman	Tenn	Apoplexy	Greenwood
24-Sep	*Mrs Vivia Amy Shipworth	F	W	56	M	Apopka/ O.G.H.	5 yrs 10 ds	At Home	England	Metastatic Carcinoma of Breast	Apopka
24-Sep	*Braxton Beacham	M	W	62	M	111 N. Orange	40 yrs	Realtor	Ga	Carcinoma of Bladder	Greenwood
24-Sep	Kattie Brown	F	C	48	S	924 W. Robinson	4 mos	House-wife	Fla	Toxemia	Greenwood
25-Sep	*Wm H. Walker, Jr	M	W	4	S	O.G.H.	2		Mt Verde, Fla	Thymic Death	Mt Verde, Fla
26-Sep	*Mrs Elizabeth Eunice Lee	F	W	83	W	242 E. Livingston	4 yrs	At Home	N.Y.	Intestinal Obstruction	Oxford, N.Y.
27-Sep	*Chas E. Paskswiete	M	W	73	M	724 E. Palmer	14 yrs	Standard Oil Co.	Germany	Uremia	Whiting, Ind
27-Sep	*Joe M. Doyle	M	W	41	M	Mulbery, Fla/ O.G.H.	4 ds	Steeple Jack	Wisconsin	Fracture of Kidneys, etc	Greenwood
29-Sep	*Martha E. Brown	F	W	40	S	Daytona, Fla/ Fla San	19 ds	English Teacher	Ohio	Nephritis	Daytona Beach, Fla
29-Sep	Child of Wm & Bulah Mobley	F	C		S	523 Long St.			Orlando	Premature	County Home

1924	Name of Deceased	Sex	Race	Age	Marital	Residence & Place of Death	Orlando Resident	Occupation	Place of Birth	Cause of Death	Place of Burial
29-Sep	Child of Wm & Bulah Mobley	F	C		S	523 Long St.			Orlando	Stillborn	County Home
19-Sep	Lara Rothrock	F	W	71	M	8 Penn/ Fla San	13 yrs	House-wife	Ill	Cancer of Uterus	St. Cloud, Fla
20-Sep	John Arthur McCarthy	M	W	52	M	Kentucky/ Fla San	12 yrs	Soldier	Mass	Pyonephritis	St. Cloud, Fla
1-Oct	*Revel E. Moragne	M	W	21	S	204 E. Concord/ O.G.H.	3 mos	College Student	Attala	Pneumonia	Greenwood
3-Oct	*Henry T. Butler	M	W	74	W	36 W. Gore Ave/ O.G.H.	15 yrs	Fruit Grower	Greenville, S.C.	Acute Dila-tion of Heart	Spartanburg, S.C.
5-Oct	C. A. Kirkland	M	W	48	M	Deer Park, Fla/ O.G.H.	1 da	Naval Stores Operator	Chatterton, Ga	Gangrene of Left Leg	Chatterton, Ga
6-Oct	Joe Wynn	M	C	30	S	523 W Church St.	4 mos	Labor	S.C.	Acute Nephritis	Greenwood
8-Oct	*Francis H. Enwright	M	W	58	M	Amherst Apts/ O.G.H.	1 da	Lumber, Coal & RR Operator	England	Strangulated Inguinal Hernia	Greenwood
11-Oct	*Mrs Helen Riley Heininger	F	W	37	M	21 Hyer St/ O.G.H.	11 yrs	At Home	Pittsburgh, Pa	Pulmonary Edema	Catholic
14-Oct	*Frederick A. Guile	M	W	55	M	25 Court/ O.G.H.	4 yrs	Furniture Salesman	Norwich	Glomerulitis	Greenwood
15-Oct	*Mrs Hattie T. Bass	F	W	40	M	338 Reel St	8 yrs	At Home	Kissimmee	Cancer of Uterus	Greenwood
15-Oct	*Infant of Mr & Mrs W.A. Pattishall	M	W		S	527 Park Lake			Orlando	Malforma-tion of heart	Greenwood
18-Oct	*Oren A. Sherwin	M	W	60	M	Keen, N.H./ O.G.H.	3 ds	Real Estate	Not Known	Lobar Pneumonia	Keen, N.H.
20-Oct	*Eugene Deyarlais	F	W	1	S	Orlando	9 mo		Rhode Island	Cholera Infantum	Catholic
20-Oct	Clarence Summerall	M	W	2	S	Kentucky Ave	4 mos		Polk Co., Fla	Bronchitis, Acute	Greenwood
20-Oct	*Nick Ray	M	W	65	W	O.G.H.	6 mos	Night Watchman	Green Co., Ga	Don't Know	Greenwood
23-Oct	William Fayson	M	C	23	S		2 mos	Labor	Ga	Acute Endocarditis	Greenwood Cemetery

1924	Name of Deceased	Sex	Race	Age	Marital	Residence & Place of Death	Orlando Resident	Occupation	Place of Birth	Cause of Death	Place of Burial
23-Oct	*Mrs. Jane Henson	F	W	80	W	Orlando	2 mos	At Home	Ohio	Mesenteric Thrombosis	Greenwood
24-Oct	Lavna Annette	F	C	59	M	320 N. Terry	30 yrs	House-wife	Quincy City, Fla	Nephritis	Greenwood
26-Oct	Thomas Henry Hancock	M	W	54	M	Bithlo/ Fla San	1 mo	Farmer	Polk Co., Fla	Cancer of Bladder	Fort Christmas
27-Oct	Stella James	F	C	35	M	917 W. South	3 yrs	House-wife	Macon, Ga	Acute Nephritis following Abortion	Greenwood
26-Oct	Martha Bray	F	C	65	W	812 Livingston	2 mos	Domestic	Ga	Acute Paren-chymous Nephritis	Greenwood
26-Oct	*Mrs Mary A. Friedland	F	W	69	W	124 N. Magnolia	5 yrs	At Home	Atlanta, Ga	Myocarditis	Scranton, Pa
28-Oct	Maryenia Rutherford	F	C	3 mo	S	815 Rutherford	3 ds		Orlando	Dengue?	Greenwood
28-Oct	*Ed Ponder	M	W	45	M	173 E. Amelia	1 yr 7 m	Foreman St. Dept	London, Ky	Cerebral Hemorrhage	Greenwood
28-Oct	*Arthur Reed	M	W	40	S	131 E. Amelia	12 yrs	Day Labor	Not Known	Acute Dilitation of Heart	Greenwood
30-Oct	Thomas Nash	M	C	45		County Home	1 yr	Day Labor	Not Known	Paresis	County Home
31-Oct	Claricy Richardson	F	C	98	W	523 Carter	27 yrs	Laundress	Not Known	Acute Gastritis	Greenwood
31-Oct	Ruth Ruthledge	F	W	21	M	O.G.H./ 103 S Conley	5 hrs	House-wife	Loughman	Tuberculosis of Throat	
31-Oct	Gary Harper	M	C	70	W	922 Livingston	8 mos	Laborer	Cuspid?, Ga	Ceptity?	Greenwood
1-Nov	*Hudson Albert Moore	M	W	42	M	O.G.H./ Lakeland, Fla	3 ds	Mechanic	Canada	Acute Anemia	Lakeland, Fla
1-Nov	*Mrs Rose Shader	F	W	63	M	RR#2	11 yrs	At Home	Russia	Cerebral Hemorrhage	Pittsburgh, Pa
2-Nov	*Child of Mr & Mrs E. S. Maddock	F	W		S	Fla Sant			Fla San/ Orlando	Stillborn	Greenwood
3-Nov	Infant Paine	F	C		S	14 N. Bryant			Orlando	Stillborn	Greenwood
3-Nov	*Mrs Anna Dominy	F	W	19	M	New Jersey	8 yrs	At Home	New Jersey	Acute Nephritis	Greenwood

1924	Name of Deceased	Sex	Race	Age	Marital	Residence & Place of Death	Orlando Resident	Occupation	Place of Birth	Cause of Death	Place of Burial
6-Nov	Isaac Nettler, Jr.	M	W	14	S	Kissimmee/ O.G.H.	1 mo		Osceola Co., Fla	Septicemia	Kissimmee
6-Nov	*Lucian E. Goodell	M	W	84	M	7 E. South	8 yrs	Farmer, Retired	N.Y.	Senility	Greenwood
6-Nov	Infant of Virginia Brown	F	C		S	406 Parramore St.			Orlando	Sepsis in Uterus	Greenwood
6-Nov	Louis E. Murry	M	C	64	M	914 W. Washington	10 m	Minister	Jacksonville	Acute Nephritis	Greenwood
8-Nov	Kelly Russell	M	W	70	W	810 Atlanta Ave/ O.G.H.	6 mos	Day Labor	D K	Chronic Nephritis	Greenwood
9-Nov	Willie Sims	M	C		S	611 McFallen			Orlando	Intrauterine Death	Greenwood
10-Nov	*David D. Eskerson	M	W	80	M	O.G.H..	2 yrs	Carpenter, Retired	Tomp...? Co., N.Y.	Chronic Nephritis	Greenwood
Nov	Annie Butler	F	C	30	M	826 W. Jackson	21 mos	Nurse	Cumbia, S.C.	Carcinoma of Uterus	Greenwood
12-Nov	Child of Mr & Mrs John H. Ceman	M	C		S	436 Holden St			Orlando	Stillborn	Greenwood
13-Nov	Frank Davis	M	C	37	S	706 Long streeet	7 mos	Barber	Ga	Pulmonary TB	Greenwood
13-Nov	Jessie Reed	F	C	28	M	15 America	1 yr	Housewife	Lumpkin, Ga	Apoplexy	Greenwood
14-Nov	Ula May Davis	F	C	1	S	1226 Jefferson St	1 mo	None	Brankford, Fla	Broncho Pneumonia	Greenwood
11-Nov	*Infant of Mr & Mrs D. D. Harrell	F	W	1	S	O.G..H./ Eustis, Fla	2		Orlando	Hemorrhage Mucous Membrane	Greenwood
13-Nov	*Infant of Mr & Mrs H. E. Morrison	M	W			Brown Street			Orlando	Still Birth	Cornell, Marion Co., Fla
13-Nov	*Mrs Vesta Abbie Revell	F	W	24	M	Moore Haven, Fla/ Fla San	4 ds	At Home	Summerfield, Fla	Acute Dilitation of Stomach	Wauchula, Fla
14-Nov	*Mrs Zordelphia Ross	F	W	70	W	207 W. Gore Ave	33 yrs	At Home	Ga	Acute Dilitation of Heart	Greenwood
14-Nov	*Mrs Mary Onsby	F	W	73	W	County Home	4 yrs	At Home	N.C.	Nephritis, Chronic Dysentery	Holly Spring, Ga

1924	Name of Deceased	Sex	Race	Age	Marital	Residence & Place of Death	Orlando Resident	Occupation	Place of Birth	Cause of Death	Place of Burial
17-Nov	*Mrs Nellie Hochslatter	F	W	52	M	O.G.H.	5 mos	At Home	Wisconsin	Cerebral Apoplexy	Andover, S.C.
17-Nov	James W. McCaskill	M	W	67	M	Winter Haven/ O.G.H.	10 ds	Day Labor	Ga	Uremia	Winter Haven
15-Nov	Jim Steverson	M	C	55	M	514 Conley	4 yrs	Labor	Ga	Cerebral Apoplexy of Brain	Valdosta, Ga
17-Nov	*Jessie W. Shoemaker	M	W	4	S	1149 Benson St.	8 mos		Tenn	Pneumonia	Johnson City, Tenn
17-Nov	Walter Kelly	M	C	42	M	903 W. Livingston	4 yrs	Brick Layer	S.C.	Chronic Myocarditis	Health Springs, S.C.
18-Nov	*Mrs Grace Griffin	F	W	20	M	Piedmont St/ O.G.H.	20 yrs	At Home	Orlando	Meningitis	Lake Howell
19-Nov	Weller Rankin	M	C	37	S	719 W. South	3 mos	Plaster	Petters? Ala	Acute Gastric Indigestion	Greenwood
21-Nov	*Vera Johnson	F	W	1	S	RFD#3/ O.G.H.	1 da		Orlando	Diphtheria	Greenwood
22-Nov	*Napoleon B. Broward	W	M	28	M	Orlando/ 414 Rosalind			Jacksonville, Fla	Gunshot	Jacksonville
22-Nov	*William H. Nichols	W	M	64	M	Orlando	12 yrs	Carpenter	Idaho	Embolism Coronary Vessels of Heart	Greenwood
22-Nov	*Alvirdia V. Whitted	F	W	23	M	E. Robinson Ave	3 yrs	At Home	Farmington, Mo	Streptococcus Septicemia	Greenwood
22-Nov	Lula Marshall	F	C	42	M	O.G.H.	1 da	H.W.	Goldsboro, S.C.	Shock Post Operation	Leesburg, Fla
22-Nov	*Luther Overstreet	M	W	27	S	5172 Jackson	4 yrs	Day Labor	Ga	Acute Intestional Obstruction	Greenwood
23-Nov	*Chas Russell Hodge	M	W	75	W	S. DeLong Street	2 yrs	Minister of Gospel	Oswego, N.Y.	Acute Bronchial Penumonia	Greenwood
23-Nov	Nettie Clutts	F	C	30	M	Church St San?	1 da	H W	Asheville, N.C.	Broncho Pneumonia	Cumbus, S.C.
25-Nov	*Henry W. Heffner	M	W	78	M	423 E. Pine St	8 yrs	Box Mfr	York, Pa	Acute Gastritis	Catholic
25-Nov	*Geo Tracy Flautt	M	W	3	S	S. Dixie Highway	3 yrs		Orlando, Fla	Diphtheria, Laryngeal	Greenwood

1924	Name of Deceased	Sex	Race	Age	Marital	Residence & Place of Death	Orlando Resident	Occupation	Place of Birth	Cause of Death	Place of Burial
27-Nov	*John Edward Tracy	M	W	78	M	437 E. Hilcrest / O.G.H.	14 yrs	Wood Working Shop	Richmond, Va	Uremia	Greenwood
28-Nov	K. D. C. Wilson, Jr.	M	W	12	S	Kissimmee/ O.G.H.	8 ds	School Boy	Shelbyville Ky	Endocarditis	Kissimmee, Fla
26-Nov	*Mrs Isobel C. Lynch	F	W	58	M	629 N.Orange Ave	1 yr	At Home	Alexander, Minn	Acute Cardiac Dilation	Greenwood
27-Nov	*John W. Spielman	M	W	67	M	824 W. Central Ave	8 yrs	Painter	Cincinnati, Ohio	Uremia & Endocarditis	Greenwood
28-Nov	*Helen S. Clatworthy	F	W	43	M	621 E. Wash/ Warrensville, Ohio	2 mos	At Home	Bedford, Ohio	Myocarditis	Warrensville, Ohio
29-Nov	Dora Jones	F	C	36	M	726 Carter/ O.G.H.	6 yrs	Housewife	S.C.	Gangrene	Greenwood
30-Nov	Ellen Huggins	F	C	20	M	716 Parramore	20 yrs	HW	Manning, S.C.	Pulmonary TB	Greenwood
1-Dec	*Mrs Emily Miller	F	W	83	W	Orlando Ave	25 yrs	At Home	Thomasville, Ga	Cardiac Renal Disease	Greenwood
2-Dec	Son of R A. Perry	M	W	11	S	O.G.H./ Eustis, Fla		None	Orlando	Trauma To Head in Birth	Eustis, Fla
3-Dec	*Mrs Ida Brown Lin	F	W	69	W	Apopka/ O.G.H.	14 ds	At Home	McDonough, Ga	Chronic Myocarditis	Apopka
26-Nov	Susie M. Williams	F	C	2 ds	S	915 Randall	2? ds		Orlando	Premature Birth	Greenwood
28-Nov	Katie Yates	F	W	a 50	W	711 E. South St	20 yrs	Housework		Cardiac Valvular Disease	Greenwood
3-Dec	Ada Ruth Workman	F	C	14	S	Hungerford School	2 ds	School Girl	Fruitland Park, Lake Co.	Cerebral Spinal Meningitis	Fruitland Park
5-Dec	Fannie Henrick	F	C	3 ds	S	932 Bentley	3 ds	None	Orlando	Emphysema of Lung	Greenwood
6-Dec	*Mrs Rosana A. Van Denbergh	F	W	67	M	O.G.H./ Victor, N.Y.	9 ds	At Home	Canandaigua, N.Y.	Malaria	Vicotr, N.Y.
7-Dec	*James J. Clark	M	W	84	M	625 N. Orange Ave.	14 yrs	Lawyer	Portage Co., Ohio	Cerebral Hemorrhage	Canton, Ohio
7-Dec	*Infant of Mr & Mrs Thos J. Eagan	W	M		S	20 Liberty St/ OGH			Orlando, Fla	Premature Birth	Greenwood

1924	Name of Deceased	Sex	Race	Age	Marital	Residence & Place of Death	Orlando Resident	Occupation	Place of Birth	Cause of Death	Place of Burial
8-Dec	*Dr. Thos. J. Foster	M	W	65	M	539 S. Lake St.	6 yrs	Doctor M.D., Retired	Ohio	Uremia	Greenwood
8-Dec	*Michael Burke	M	W	85	W	Ocoee/ O.G.H.	12 yrs	Merchant	Ireland	Chr Nephritis	In Vault (Thomaston, Me)
9-Dec	*Wilbur E. Richards	M	W	70	M	N. Mills St	8 yrs	Farmer	Indiana	Pernicious anemia	Sharpsville, Ind
28-Nov	Charles Warner Clark	M	W	75	M	St Cloud, Fla/ O.G.H.	2 yrs	Soldier, Retired	Virginia	Uremia following Prota---dory?	St. Cloud, Fla
1-Dec	Mrs Estella H. Wright	F	W	70	W	18 W. South St.	4	At Home		Acute Indigestion	Greenwood
7-Dec	*Francis E. Rice	M	W	29	M	Maitland, Fla/ Lake Lucerne	7	Labor	Ind	Drowning	Orleans
11-Dec	Nora Dean	F	C	39	M	Johns St.	3 yrs	Housewife	Macon, Ga	Acute Pneumonia	Greenwood
13-Dec	*Eugean G. Allen	M	W	63	M	O.G.H./ Orlando	4 yrs	Day Labor	Oxford, N.C.	Apoplexy	Live Oak, Fla
13-Dec	Child of Mr & Mrs A. O. McGuire	M	W		S	2½ mi E of O.	2		Orlando	Stillborn	Lake Monroe, Fla
13-Dec	*Frank Maruvio	M	W	40	S	Chicago Illl/ Orlando	1 da	Plumber	Chicago, Ill	Cerebral Hemorrhage	Chicago, Ill
14-Dec	*Joseph James	M	W	77	W	Boyonne, N.J./ 321 E. South	1 mo 7 ds	Master	Wales, Great Britain	Apoplexy	Bayonne, N.J.
16-Dec	*Homer L. Bosworth	M	W	90	M	Springfield, Mass/ Rock Lake	1 mo 3 ds	Manu-facturer	West Otis, Mass	Cerebral Apoplexy	Springfield, Mass
14-Dec	Brantly M. Jordan	F	C	42	M	32 N. Bryant	15 yrs	Housewife	Newbery	Diabetes	Greenwood
17-Dec	*Howard D. Von Norden	M	W	62	M	Sorento, Fla/ 15 W. Livingston	1 da	Real Es-tate Dealer	Nova Scotia	Obstruction of Stomach	Boston, Mass
18-Dec	*Joseph R. Hall	M	W	82	W	County Home	45 yrs	Day Laborer	Fla	Uremia	Fort Christmas
17-Dec	*Mrs Essie Mizelle	F	W	38	M	416 Grand Ave	4 yrs	At Home	Suwannee Co., Fla	Chr Myocarditis	Welborn, Fla
18-Dec	*Wm M. Browning	M	W	63	M	County Home	16 yrs	Day Work	Madison-ville, Ky	Uremia	Patrick

1924	Name of Deceased	Sex	Race	Age	Marital	Residence & Place of Death	Orlando Resident	Occupation	Place of Birth	Cause of Death	Place of Burial
18-Dec	*Bee Wesley Pullman	M	W	38	M	Kalamazoo, Mich/ 424	1 mo 20 da	Druggist	Boise, Idaho	Nephritis	Kalamazoo, Mich
18-Dec	*Horace De Los Burdick	M	W	77	W	526 Magnolia Ave/ OGH	2 yrs	Gov. Inspect. Union Stock Yds	Syracuse, N.Y.	Carcinoma of Bladder	Rome, N.Y.
20-Dec	Alberta Hurst	F	C	22	M	49 1/2 N. Bryant	4 yrs	H.W.	Newberry	Ruptured Tubal Pregnancy	Gainesville, Fla
22-Dec	*Mary Agnes Thurman	F	W	1	S	Welmont Ave	1 yr		Orlando	Diphtheria	Greenwood
22-Dec	*Frank Osborn	M	W	68	M	Miami, Fla/ Angebilt Hotel	17ds	Civil Engineer, Retired	Middletown, N.J.	Pneumonia	Red Bank, N.J.
27-Dec	Thomas Malishan	M	C	8 ds	S	116 Chadam St.	8 da	None	Orlando	Convulsions	Greenwood
27-Dec	Andrew Pruden	M	C		S	221 Division St.			Orlando	Born Dead	Greenwood
27-Dec	Ida May Ashbee	F	W	47	M	Kilgore Ave	1 yr 1 mo	H.W.	New Haven, Conn	Cerebral Apoplexy	Greenwood
28-Dec	Will H. Dodge	M	W	71	M	Tavares, Fla/ Fla San	10 ds	Retired Banker	Dodgeville, Ill	Fracture of Surgical Neck of Femur	Mt Dora, Fla
26-Dec	*Michal John Schaefer	M	W	77	W	Dayton, Ohio/ OGH	1 mo	Retired	Mudau, Germany	Pulmonary Edema	Dayton, Ohio
26-Dec	*Mrs May E Abbott	F	W	73	W	S Franklin	2 yrs	At Home	Andover, Mass	Myocarditis	Andover, Mass
27-Dec	*Wm E. Spruance	M	W	54	M	541 E. Ridgewood	5 yrs	Fruit Broker, Retired	Smyrna, Del	Infection Endocarditis	Philadelphia, Pa
29-Dec	*Gus P. Strickland	M	W	31	M	O.G.H.	3 mos	Tree Surgeon	Waycross Ga	Rupture of Left Kidney	Waycross, Ga
30-Dec	*Mrs May A. Wiles	F	W	25	M	Fla San/ Winter Garden	2 hrs	At Home	Orangeburg, S.C.	Inflammatory Rheumatism	Orangeburg, S.C.
28-Dec	*Edward Bosworth Jemison	M	W	62	M	208 N. Magnolia	6 yrs	Fruit Grower	Luthersburg, Penn	Myocarditis	Greenwood

1924	Name of Deceased	Sex	Race	Age	Marital	Residence & Place of Death	Orlando Resident	Occupation	Place of Birth	Cause of Death	Place of Burial
29-Dec	*Montferd Clifford Rerdell	M	W	73	M	W Lucerne Circle/ Fla San	12 yrs	Lawyer, Retired	Montgomery Co., Ala	Fracture of Surgical Neck of Right Femur	Greenwood
30-Dec	*William R. Bowman	M	W	74	M	Avonmore, Penn/ 426 W. Amelia	3 mos	Farming	Loyalhanna, Penn	Cerebral Hemorrhage	Avonmore, Penn
30-Dec	Joe Summerall	M	W	33	S	Sunset Park/ O.G.H.	3 yrs	Day Labor	Arcadia	Pneumonia, Lobar	Greenwood
31-Dec	*Mrs Susie Long	F	W	33	M	RR# 1/ O.G.H.	8 mos	At Home	Columbia City, Ind	Peritonitis	Cumbia City, Ind

	Name of Deceased	Sex	Race	Age	Marital	Residence/Place of Death	Orlando Resident	Occupation	Place of Birth	Cause of Death	Place of Burial
03Jan14	Joseph Calvert Decker	M	W	4m	S	Philadelphia/ OGH	abt 1 mo	-	Philadelphia	Marasmus	Catholic
3-Jan	*Lillian S. Holden	F	W	59	W	326 N. Magnolia	29 yrs	at home	Loudon, Va	Lymphatic leukemia	Greenwood
4-Jan	*Carrol Lamar Brown	M	W	8	S	Ocoee, Fla/ O.G.H.	8 days		Coffee Springs Lake, Ala	Lobar Pneumonia	Ocoee, Fla
5-Jan	Allie Jenkin	F	C	21	M	418 Parramore	3 mos	H.W.	Greenville, Fla	Embolism	Greenville, Fla
7-Jan	*James Bailey Magruder	M	W	65	M	618 E. Central/ O.G.H.	24 yrs	Real Estate	Thomasville, Ga	Renal Calculi	Greenwood
8-Jan	Laurinder Waters Ingram	F	W	80	W	Wellsville, Ohio/ O.G.H.	7 ds	H.W.	Hancock Co., W.Va	Cerebral Hemorrhage	Mt. Dora, Fla
8-Jan	*Bernice Dye	F	W	11	S	1210 S. Reel	abt 1 yr		Ala	Congenital Heart Defect	Greenwood
7-Jan	J. R. Ford	M	W	67	W	Clermont, Fla	2 yrs	Farmer, Retired	Allen Co., Ohio	Chronic Bright's Disease	Clermont Cemetery
9-Jan	*Mrs. Julia E. Burnett	F	W	50	D	O.G.H.	14 yrs	Seamstress	Ashville, N.C.	Acute Dilitation of Heart	Atlanta, Ga
9-Jan	*Mrs Nellie Conway	F	W	70	W	236 Rosalind Ave	14 yrs	At Home	Canada	Cachexia, Pulmonary Edema	Greenwood Cemetery
10-Jan	*Mrs Sophia Gazil	F	W	70 a	W	400 N Parramore	5 yrs	At Home	Syria	Chronic Myocarditis	Catholic
10-Jan	*Dr. Eleanor J. Pond	F	W	73	W	Blairstown, N.J./ O.G.H.	1 da	MD Retired	Philadelphia, Pa	Edema of Lungs	Philadelphia
11-Jan	*Ethel Garrett	F	W	19	S	Haines City/ O.G.H.	1 da		Midland, Fla	Encephalitis	Conway Cemetery
12-Jan	*Sim Tyner	M	W	85	W	Kentucky Ave	1 yr	Farming, Retired	Polk Co., Fla	Paralysis	Lock Cemetery near Taft
12-Jan	*Byron R. Brewster	M	W	79	M	223 W. Concord Ave	8 yrs	Farming/ Lumberman	North Elba, N.Y.	Myocarditis	Lake Placid, N.Y.
12-Jan	*Infant of Mr & Mrs Willis H. Butler	M	W		S	216 W. Church			Orlando	Stillborn	Greenwood
12-Jan	*Mrs Gabrilla C. Cates	F	W	58 a	M	Sanford, Fla/ O.G.H.	4 ds	At Home	Milleyeville, Ga	Angina Pectoris	Soperton, Ga
9-Jan	Josh Darlington	M	C	48 a	M	415 W Jackson	2 mos	Laborer	S.C.	Acute Myocarditis	Greenwood
10-Jan	Geo M. Cline	M	W	59	D	W. Winter Park	1 1/2 yrs	Carpenter	Mich	Nephritis	Greenwood
12-Jan	Tom Washington	M	C	65 a	M	603 S. Lee St.	2 yrs	Laborer	Madison, Fla	Acute Gastric Indigestion	Greenwood
13-Jan	*Geo. H. DeGolyer	M	W	79	M	530 N. Magnolia	6 yrs	Retired	N.Y.	Chronic Senility	Cincinnati, Ohio
13-Jan	*Mrs Francis E. Lee	F	W	71	M	Brookfield, Conn/ 710 E. Palmer	2 mos	At Home	Conn	Cerebral Hemorrhage	Danbury, Conn

1925	Name of Deceased	Sex	Race	Age	Marital	Residence/Place of Death	Orlando Resident	Occupation	Place of Birth	Cause of Death	Place of Burial
15-Jan	*Mrs Laura A. Shaw	F	W	62	M	45 E. Amelia Ave/ Fla San	2 yrs 4 mo	At Home	LeRoy, Ohio	Chronic Gastric Enteritis	Toledo, Ohio
16-Jan	*Mrs. Bell D. McEwan	F	W	45	M	Pittsburgh, Pa/ 152 Concord Ave	1 mo 14 ds	At Home	Penn	Acute Endocarditis	Punsan-towney, Pa
17-Jan	*Winifred N. Cox	F	W	14	S	219 W Concord	5 yrs		Vincenes, Ind	Influenza	Vincennes Ind
18-Jan	*Grace E. Braddock	F	W	1 tr	S	Altamonte Springs/ Fla San	18 ds		Altamonte, Fla	Pyelo-nephritis	Maitland Cemetery
16-Jan	Frank Milton	M	C	49 a	M	E. Orlando	20 mos	Laborer	Richmond, Va	Lobar Pneumonia Left Lung	Greenwood
20-Jan	*Samuel D. Yeargin	M	W	50	M	Orlando	5 yrs	Book-keeper	Commerce Ga	Pulmonary Hemor-rhage	Greenwood
21-Jan	Josephine Felton	F	C	41 a	W	519 W Pine	1 mo	Laundress	Tallahas-see, Fla	Aortic Re-gurgitation, Cardiac Dilitation	Greenwood
21-Jan	*Child of Mr & Mrs A. E. Smith	M	W		S	Orlando	Parents 1 yr		Orlando	Premature Delivery	Greenwood
22-Jan	Silas Gladden	M	C	46 a	S	422 W. Pine	1 yr	Laborer	Norfolk, Va	Don't Know	Greenwood
23-Jan	*Infant of Mr & Mrs Robert W. Case	M	W		S	Winter Park Hwy			Orlando	Stillborn	Greenwood
21-Jan	*John Cahill	M	W	?	?	O.G.H.	1 mo			Cerebral Hemor-rhage	Plainfield, Vt.
22-Jan	*Geo. W. Patterson	M	C	53	M	O.G.H.	17 ds	Laborer	Louisville, Ga	Chronic Myocarditis	Greenwood
23-Jan	*Joseph Thomas Tindall	M	W	67	M	533 Conroy Ave	3 mos	Farming	Gordon, Ga	Pneumonia & Mitral Insufficiency	Greenwood
23-Jan	*Fred C. Trimble	M	W	57	M	RFD Conway Rd	1 yr 2 mos	Whole-sale Produce	Canada	Cerebral Hemor-rhage	Greenwood
23-Jan	*Jenett Jackson	F	W	85	W	325 E. Livingston	12 yrs	At Home	Sampson Co., N.C.	Myocarditis	Dunn, N.C.
26-Jan	*Eloise May Lightfoot	F	W	6	S	O.G.H./ Lake Hamiton	7 Days		Prosser, Washington	Meningitis	Saint Cloud
28-Jan	*Joseph Todd	M	W	1m	S	Myrtle Heights	1 mo 18 d		Orlando	Whooping Cough	Greenwood
28-Jan	Mrs Lilla M. Nason	F	W	53	M	402 Putnam	7 yrs	HW	Lowell, Mass	Uremia	Greenwood Cem
29-Jan	*Frank L Cayll	M	W	48	M	O.G.H.	7 ds	Contrac-tor	Italy	Intestinal Obstruction	Winter Park
26-Jan	Hattie Riley	F	C	32	M	212 S. Mills St.	3 mos	Domestic	Gainesville, Fla	Cancer of Uterus	Greenwood

	Name of Deceased	Sex	Race	Age	Marital	Residence/Place of Death	Orlando Resident	Occupation	Place of Birth	Cause of Death	Place of Burial
27-Jan	*George H. Nehf	M	W	68	M	Melbourne, Fla/ 1219 E. Washington	2 mos	Real Estate Broker	Port Washington, Wis	Pyloric Obstruction Following Cirrhosis of the Liver	in Vault Washington, D.C.
30-Jan	*Bertha Caroline Dawson	F	W	59	M	420 S. Delong St.	35 yrs	At Home	Charleston, S.C.	Cerebral Hemorrhage	Greenwood
1-Feb	*Ramona Leonard	F	W		S	O.G.H./ Maitland			Orlando	Stillbirth	Greenwood
1-Feb	*Joseph E. Ricketson	M	W	68	W	W. Amelia Ave	7 y 1 mo 21 ds	Lawyer	Coffee Co, Ga	Chronic Interstitial Nephritis	Greenwood
1-Feb	Martha Davis	F	C	40	S	E. Orlando	3 yrs	Domestic	Ga	Pellagra	Greenwood
2-Feb	John Seymour Matthew	M	C	1m	S	2018 Mills	1 mo		Orlando	Broncho Pneumonia	Greenwood
2-Feb	Ellex Evrett	M	C	70	S	O.G.H.	1 mo	Labor	Fla	Cancer of Prostate	Center Hill, Fla
2-Feb	*Mrs Jessie B. Fish	F	W	61	M	O.G.H.	13 mos	At Home	Falmouth, Mass	Chronic Myocarditis	Greenwood
2-Feb	*Henry Allen Renfroe	M	W	63	M	146 E Concord	2 nda	Real Estate	Fla	Angina Pectoris	Jacksonville, Fla
2-Feb	*Troy Madison Mink	M	W	52	M	Winter Garden/ O.G.H.	7 ds	Farmer & Orange Grower	Grant, Va	Acute Angina	Oakland
3-Feb	Mrs A. J. Lossing	F	W	49	M	Sanford, Fla/ Herntz San		H.W.	Sioux Falls, S.D.	Influenza	Sanford, Fla
5-Feb	*Loyal A. Bigelow	M	W	79	W	Essex, N.Y./ Fla San	3 mos	Methodist Minister	Clintonville, N.Y.	Concussion of the Brain	Essex, N.Y.
8-Feb	Catherina Panella	F	W	70	W	901 W. Jackson	7 yrs	None	Italy	Gangrene of Leg	Catholic Cemetery
8-Feb	*Norman Raff	M	W	62	W	Canton, Ohio/ San Juan Hotel	1 mo	Real Estate	Canton, Ohio	Myocarditis	Canton, Ohio
9-Feb	*Benjamin F Greer	M	W	61	M	Grasmere, NH /403 W Concord	15 ds	Lumber Dealer	Grasmere, N.H.	Carcinoma of Colon	Manchester, N.H.
30-Jan	Lee Bradwill	M	C	6 ds	S	502 W. Jackson	6 ds	Infant	Orlando	Icterus Neonatorum	Greenwood
6-Feb	Richard Bailey	M	C	53	W	439 S. Division	1 mo	Laborer	Thomasville Ga	Cerebral Hemorrhage	Greenwood
9-Feb	*Wm Cassel	M	W	66	M	O.G.H./ Montrose, Co	4 ds	Clerical Work	Summerset, Ohio	Myocarditis	Greenwood
11-Feb	*Edith Sadler	F	W	17	M	Winter Garden/ O.G.H.	1 da	At Home	Pelham, Ga	Intestinal Obstruction	Beulah Cemetery
11-Feb	Joseph Armhein	M	W	57	M	Formosa/ O.G.H.	3 mos	Machinist	Germany	Abscess Brain	Brooklyn, N.Y.
11-Feb	*Martha Mobley	F	C	80	M	Oakland, Fla/ O.G.H.	6	Domestic	Montgomery, Ala	Hypostatic Pneumonia	Oakland Cemetery
12-Feb	Ellis Roger	M	C	8 mo	S	203 Reel St	8 mos		Orlando	Acute Gastritis	Greenwood
16-Feb	Mary Brantley	F	W	35	M	Mt Dora/ Fla San	28 days	H.W.	Chicago, Ill	Pancretitis	Mt. Dora, Fla
15-Feb	*Edwin Sampson	M	W	65	M	Toledo, Ohio/ Fla San	2 mo 10 ds	Retired	Palmyra, N.Y	Mitral Insufficiency	Palmyra, N.Y.

1925	Name of Deceased	Sex	Race	Age	Marital	Residence/Place of Death	Orlando Resident	Occupation	Place of Birth	Cause of Death	Place of Burial
15-Feb	*Infant of Carol Floyd	M	W		S	Orlando			Orlando	Premature Birth	Greenwood
15-Feb	Davidson Williams	M	C	30	M	416 W. Jackson	5 mos	Laborer	Quincy, Fla	Justifiable Homicide	Quincy, Fla
17-Feb	*Herman Albert Retsch	M	W	68	M	Atlanta, Ga/ O.G.H.	5 ds	Author	Germany	Lobar Pneumonia	Atlanta, Ga
19-Feb	*Adlumia D. Sterrett	F	W	77	W	Washington, D.C./ O.G.H.	2 ds	At Home	Washington, D.C.	Carcinoma Sena?	Washington, D.C.
19-Feb	*Joseph C. Johnson	M	W	25	M	Princeton Ave	40 yrs	Fruit Grower	Eaton, Ga	Angina Pectoris	Greenwood
19-Feb	*James Scanlon	M	W	60	S	Sanona, Ill/ N. Orange Ave	1 mo?	Engineer	Penn	Organic Heart Disease	Oregon, Wis
21-Feb	*Mrs Loise F. Smith	F	W	36	M	15 Eola Drive	1 mo	At Home	Texas	Acute Gastritis	Nocogdoches, Tex
22-Feb	*Edgar A. Morse	M	W	75	W	Brockton, Mass / O.G.H.	10 ds	Soldier	Mass	Fracture/ Neck of Femur	Berlin, Mass
22-Feb	*Julia Pratt Johnson	F	W	69	M	201 N. Main St.	45 yrs	At Home	Conn	Cerebral Hemorrhage	Greenwood
23-Feb	Moses Jenkins	M	C	2m	Inf	415 S. Parramore	2 mos	Infant	Orlando	Infantile Atrophy ?	Greenwood
23-Feb	*Agnes Grace Berner	F	W	31	S	Sanford, Fla / Orlando San	2 mos	Clerk in Bank	Palatka, Fla	Cerebral Apoplexy	Sanford, Fla
24-Feb	*Child of Geo Cartwright	M	W		S	11 E. Jackson			Orlando	Premature Birth	Greenwood
26-Feb	M. D. Spencer	M	C	10 mo	S	415 McFall St.	4 mos	None	Orlando	Otitis Media	Greenwood
24-Feb	*John Heist	M	W	62	M	O.G.H./ Lake Jem, Fla	23 ds	Fruit Grower	Peru, Ills	Chronic Myocarditis	Chicago, Ill
26-Feb	*Leslie O. Parrish	M	W	63	M	322 E. South	7 y 1 m 21 d	Salesman	Versailles, Ky	Pulmonary Abscess	Greenwood
28-Feb	Mary Powell	F	C	40	M	O.G.H.	4 mos	H W	Ala	Meningitis	Greenwood
28-Feb	*Harry E. Doty	M	W	57	M	Jefferson Court	3 yrs	Manager of Glen St Mary Nursery	Conn	Lobar Pneumonia	Cleveland, Ohio
28-Feb	*Julia Cookman	F	W	82	W	527 S. Osceola St.	4 yrs	At Home	W.Va	Mitral Insufficiency	Greenwood
28-Feb	Ed G. Peterson	M	C	55	M	Bentley Ave	10 yrs	Common Labor	Blakely, Ga	Valvulis? Of Intestine	Greenwood
2-Mar	Byron Hawley	M	W	8	W	O.G.H./ Woodstock, Ohio	4 mos	Farmer	Ohio	Pulmonary Embolus	Woodstock, Ohio
2-Mar	*Arthur E. Brundige	M	W	54	M	Lake Lancaster	1 yr	R.E. Development	Ohio	Accidental Drowning	Greenwood
3-Mar	Gertrude Choen	F	C	4m	S	905 W Long St.	4 mos	Infant	Orlando		Greenwood
4-Mar	W. B. Austin	M	C	40	M	206 Beg St.	8 yrs	Laborer	Kingston, S.C.	LaGrippe	Greenwood
5-Mar	*Andrew P. Heymann	M	W	69	M	9 N. Hyer	6 yrs	Retired	Brooklyn, N.Y.	Acute Cardiac Dilitation	Dayton, Ohio
6-Mar	L. J. Chisholm, Jr.	M	C	4m	S	918 S. Division	3 mos	Infant	Orlando	Broncho Pneumonia	Greenwood

1925	Name of Deceased	Sex	Race	Age	Marital	Residence/Place of Death	Orlando Resident	Occupation	Place of Birth	Cause of Death	Place of Burial
4-Mar	Calvin Siemer	M	W	10 mo	S	Kentucky Ave	10 mos		Orlando	Intestinal Obstruction	Lake Hill Cemetery
7-Mar	*John E. Escott	M	W	66	S	O.G.H./ Plymouth, Fla	4 ds	Farming	Louisville, Ky	Cerebral Embolism	Tangerine
8-Mar	*Harry L. Hashberger (Hasberger)	M	W	93	M	Pine Castle	3 yrs	Farmer	Ohio	Acute Dilitation of Heart	St. Cloud, Fla
12-Mar	Infant of Mr & Mrs J. L. Taylor	F?	W		S	Apopka, Fla/ O.G.H			Orlando	Still birth	Apopka Cemetery
5-Mar	George Hill	M	C	43	M	1030 W Robinson	4 yrs	Laborer	Crofeteville, Ga	Gangrene of Intestine	Greenwood
7-Mar	Christina Peterson	F	C	24	S	712 S. John	4 yrs		Jasper, Fla	Acute Nephritis	Greenwood
7-Mar	Priscilla Gifford	F	C	18	S	Dexter, Ga/ 442 S. Division	2 mo	Cook	Dexter, Ga	Typhoid Fever	Greendoow
7-Mar	*Mary Elizabeth Blakesley	F	W	69	M	201 N. Magnolia	7 yrs 1 m 21 d	At Home	Elgin, Iowa	Myocarditis	Greenwood
8-Mar	*Roy Dexter Jones	M	W		S	512 Broadway	4 mos		Hesperia, Mich	Acute Ileocolitis	Greenwood
8-Mar	*Mrs Elizabeth O. Styler	F	W	78	W	203 America	14 yrs	At Home	Ontario, Can.	Cerebral Hemorrhage	Greenwood
11-Mar	*Infant of Mr & Mrs Lyman Ange	M	W		S	O.G.H.			Orlando	Premature Birth	Greenwood
25-Feb	*Alfred Guffin (ashes of)								Framingham Mass	Broncho Pneumonia	Longwood, Fla
12-Mar	Francis Green	F	C	24	M	804 W. Robinson	1 mo	Domestic	Live Oak, Fla	Tuberculosis	Greenwood
11-Mar	*Dorothy Anderson	F	W	1	S	O.G.H.	1 yr 9 mos		Orlando	Acute Intestional	Greenwood
14-Mar	*Miss Lucy Williams	F	W	24	S	421 E. Anderson	3 yrs	Trained Nurse	Hagerstown, Ind	Pulmonary T.B.	Greenwood
15-Mar	Infant of James Toy	F	C		S	O.G.H.			Orlando	Stillbirth	Greenwood
16-Mar	Julia Babb	F	C	37	M	812 Edmer	5 yrs	H.W.	Barnesville, Ga	Post Operative Shock followed by LaGrippe	Greenwood
16-Mar	*Catherine Volf	F	W	35	M	O.G.H./ Canton St	5 yrs	At Home	Indianapolis, Ind	Acute Pneumonia	Greenwood
16-Mar	*Mrs Cora Lee Smith	F	W	25	M	O.G.H./ Plymouth, Fla	1 day	At Home	Dothan, Ala	Puerperal Septicemia	Apopka
16-Mar	*Infant of Mr & Mrs Emmett Peugh	M	W		S	325 W. Long St			Orlando	Premature Birth	Greenwood
17-Mar	K. P. Neal	M	C	60	W	830 W. Jackson	2 mos	Clergyman	Chears, Fla	Stone in Bladder	Tallahassee, Fla
18-Mar	*Geo Mayer	M	W	74	M	O.G.H./ Conway Road	4 yrs	Fruit Grower	Wis	General Edema & Broncho Pneumonia	Greenwood Cemetery
18-Mar	*Mrs Vera H. Kilgore	F	W	82	W	19 N.Eola Dr/ Portland, Maine	6 mos	At Home	Maine	Cerebral Hemorrhage	Portland, Maine

1925	Name of Deceased	Sex	Race	Age	Marital	Residence/Place of Death	Orlando Resident	Occupation	Place of Birth	Cause of Death	Place of Burial
19-Mar	*Mrs William (Wilmina) Thornton	F	W	77	W	Orlando	8 yrs	At Home	Berwick, Pa	Apoplexy	Greenwood
20-Mar	*Mrs Alice J. Kinney	F	W	79	M	O.G.H. Massena, N.Y.	2 ds	At Home	Massena, N. Y.	Secondary Anemia Due to Gallbladder Dis. Massena, N.Y.	
20-Mar	*John L. Riddell	M	W	25	M	O.G.H./ Cynthiana, Ky	2 yrs 6 mo	Labor	Cynthiana, Ky	Suicide	Cynthiana, Ky
21-Mar	*Silas McMillan	W	M	87	W	O.G.H./ Marketon, Pa	4 mos	Farmer	Penn	Strangulated Umbilical Hernia, etc.	Marketon, Pa
24-Mar	*Newton Hudson	W	M	64	M	109 W Hill St.	8 yrs	Painter/ Contractor	Walton, Ky	Pulmonary Tuberculosis	Umatilla, Fla
26-Mar	Marion Love	F	W	19	M	Kissimmee, Fla/ O.G.H.	3 y 12 d	House-wife	Carbondale, Ohio	General Peritonitis	Rose Hill Cemetery
19-Mar	*Adelbert M. Simmons	M	W	82	W	Orlando Sanitarium/ Chicago, Ill	abt 1 yr	Retired	Watertown, N.Y.	Cerebral Apoplexy	Chicago, Ill
25-Mar	*Andrew Trumbull	W	M	80	M	426 E. Jackson St/ Orlando Sanitarium	12 yrs	Retired	Scotland	Nephritis	Greenwood
27-Mar	Rosemere Henson	F	C	1	S	1036 Federal St.	7 mos		Quincy, Fla	Influenza	Greenwood
27-Mar	Lizzie Beth Johnson	F	C		S	Pine Castle, Fla			Pinecastle, Fla	Stillbirth	Taft, Fla
27-Mar	Memonia Coward	F	W	17	M	Ft. Christmas, Fla/ O.G.H.	5 ds	At Home	Ft. Christ-mas, Fla	Toxemia of Pregnancy	Ft. Christ-mas, Fla
27-Mar	*Clifton Sawyer	M	W	11	S	Fla San/ Virginia Drive	9 mos		Ala	Electrocu-tion, Fallen Wire	Greenwood
27-Mar	*John Thom-as Brannon	M	W	64	M	Orlando/ Pine Castle, Fla	1 yr	Farming	Ala	Train	Catholic Cemetery
28-Mar	*Geo Edwin Totman	M	W	33	M	Clarcona/ Lockhart	2 yrs	Gen carpenter	NY	Crushed by tractor	Greenwood
1-Apr	*Robert R Denbow	M	W	77	M	New Matmos, OH/ Pilgrim Hotel	3 mos	Oil operator	Louisville, Ohio	Bronchial Asthma	Friendly, W Va
2-Apr	*Mrs Evelyn H. Lothian	F	W	55	M	Albany, NH/ OGH	8 da	At home	Glouster, Mas	Myocarditis	Effingham Falls, NH
3-Apr	*Timothy R. McDonald	M	W	65	S	Clermont, Fla/ OGH	7 Days	Plumber	NY	Cerebral embolus	Rome NY
4-Apr	*Frank N. Quillen	M	W	68	M	Arcade Hotel	3 yrs	Painter & Decorator	Penn	Angina Pectoris	Chester, Penn
5-Apr	*Martha Jen-ness Lamphear	F	W	54	M	Orleans, Vt/ OGH	5 mos	At home	Browning-ton Vt	General septicimia	Orleans, Vt
5-Apr	*William Otterson	M	W	80	M	Red Bank, NJ/ 427 S Main St	2 m, 8 d	Real Estate	New Jersey	Angina Pectoris	Red Bank, NJ
6-Apr	*Geo Franklin Johns	M	W	82	W	County Home	10 yrs	Farmer	don't know	Cerebral Artermo-brosis?	Lake Hill Cemetery
5-Apr	Charlie Bellamy	M	C	24	M	Florence Villa, Fla / OGH	1 day	Laborer	Madison, Fla	Gunshot Wound	Greenwood
5-Apr	Jennie Butler	F	C	40	M	424 Long St	16 yr	House-wife	Fla	Pulmonary Tuberculosis	Greenwood

1925	Name of Deceased	Sex	Race	Age	Marital	Residence/Place of Death	Orlando Resident	Occupation	Place of Birth	Cause of Death	Place of Burial
4-Apr	*Mrs Jennie Hiddleson Andrews	F	W	76	W	Fla San	6 yrs	H W	Illinois	Neuralgia of Heart	Greenwood
7-Apr	*Mrs Anna C. Kuhl	F	W	81	W	Kuhl & Gore Ave	45 yrs	At home	Miss	Organic heart disease	Greenwood
8-Apr	*Francis Marion Bunn	M	W	70	M	Minneapolis, Minn/ Howell San	5 mos	Auto salesman	Illinois	Pulmonary tuberculosis	Greenwood
11-Apr	Mrs Mary Renick Mason	F	W	46	M	812 E. Anderson St	3 yrs	At home	Kan	Lobar Pneumonia	Jacksonville, Fla
12-Apr	*Mrs Emma Watson	F	W	83	W	S. Dixie Ave	11 yrs	At Home	Ky	Cerebral hemorrhage	Greenwood
13-Apr	*Walter Byron Bynum	M	W	58	M	Jacksonville, Fl/ OGH	1 da	Lumber Inspector	Ga	Fractured skull	Jacksonville, Fla
13-Apr	*Virgil M Prescott	M	W	2	S	Orlando/ OGH	1 da	-	Orlando	Intoxication	Greenwood
14-Apr	*Infant of Mr & Mrs Ben F. Hyer	M	W	-	S	Fla San	-	-	Orlando	Stillbirth	Winter Park
14-Apr	*W. A. Corvett Jr	M	W	3	S	St Cloud, Fla/ Pine Castle Rd	1 yr	-	St Cloud, FL	Acute Intestinal Intoxication	Wauchula, Fla
15-Apr	*Ilene Corvett	F	W	1	S	Pine Castle Rd	1 yr	-	Orlando	Acute Intestinal Intoxication	Wauchula, Fla
15-Apr	*Shelly Clark	M	W	28	M	Leesburg, FL/ OGH	1 da	Day laborer	Ala	Perforated duodenal ulcer	Leesburg, Fla
12-Apr	*Frank Ellis	M	W	20	M	Philadelphia, Pa/ 1242 E. Robinson Ave	5 mos	Retired	Philadelphia	Encordactis ? With ___	Philadelphia, Pa
14-Apr	*Morrison Oakes Kelley	M	W	80	W	23 W. Robinson Ave	7 yrs	Night Watchman	DK	Apoplexy	Spencer, Mass
14-Apr	*George Wilbert	M	C	45	M	O.G.H./ Orlando	3 mos	Day Labor	Ga	Aneurysm, Arch of Aorta	Greenwood
17-Apr	*Geo. Duvean Moffat	M	W	67	M	101 S Osceola	6 yrs	Mfg, Retired	Key West, Fla	Nephritis	Greenwood
11-Apr	Mrs Emma Adaline Henderson	F	W	57	M	W Pine St/ Orlando Sanitarium	2 yrs 3 mos	Salvation Army Worker	Ala	Broncho Pneumonia	Greenwood
16-Apr	James L. Canada	M	C	3	S	743 S. Parramore	2 mos		Starke, Fla	LaGrippe	Greenwood
17-Apr	*Levi Snyder	M	W	89	W	112 N.Mills St.	1 yr	Merchant, Retired	Pa	Chronic Myocarditis	Bethleham, Pa
18-Apr	Robert Ware	M	C		S	804 Edner St			Orlando	Stillborn	Greenwood
18-Apr	*Thos R. Levar	M	W	37	S	208 W. Jackson	3 yrs	Barber	Ga	Alcoholism	Cairo, Ga
21-Apr	*Luis D. Cavallera	M	W	19	S	Tampa, Fla/ Pine Castle	1da	Cigar-maker	Tampa, Fla	Auto Accident	Tampa, Fla
20-Apr	Minnie Mildred Hamilton	F	W	20	S	O.G.H./ Kissimmee	6 mos	School GIrl	Ga	Diffuse Cellulitis	St. Cloud, Fla

1925	Name of Deceased	Sex	Race	Age	Marital	Residence/Place of Death	Orlando Resident	Occupation	Place of Birth	Cause of Death	Place of Burial
21-Apr	*Frank Leon (*Cuban)	M	*	20	S	2 mi S of Pine Castle/ Tampa	1	Clerk	Tampa	Auto Accident	Tampa
25-Apr	Julia A. Chapman	F	W	81	W	Edgewood Park	1 yr	Retired	Canada	Intestinal Influenza	Lansing, Mich
23-Apr	*Ida Mae Ricketson	F	W	2m	S	1009 W Jackson	21 ds		Thomas-ville, Ga	Broncho Pneumonia	Greenwood
24-Apr	Fannie Graham	F	C	67	W	W. Central Ave	30 yrs	Laundress	Valdosta, Ga	Apoplexy	Greenwood
25-Apr	Annie M. Barnes	F	C	45	W	523 W. Jackson	1 yr	Laundress	Mariana, Fla	Acute Parenchymatous Nephritis	Greenwood
26-Apr	*Marie Cealia Werline	F	W	24	S	Cheney Drive 7 mi	8 mos	Stenog-rapher	Marion, Ind	Tuberculosis, Pulmonary	Catholic Cemetery
27-Apr	Arthur Cohoon Perkins	M	W	60	M	Bristol, Conn/ O.G.H.	19 ds	Coal Merchant	Vienna, Ohio	Cerebral Hemorrhage	Mt. Dora, Fla
27-Apr	*Chas Phillip Paddock, Jr	M	W	1 yr	S	400 Gore Ave	1 yr		Orlando	Acute Arcenical Poisoning	Greenwood
27-Apr	*William V. Clark	M	W	34	M	Cincinnati, Ohio/ O.G.H.	4 mos	Trucking	Masadonia, Bulgaria	Laceration through Upper Ilium; general peritonitis Powell Cemetery	
28-Apr	*Mary Eliz-abeth Fuller	F	W	4	S	936 W Church / O.G.H.	8 mos		Midland City, Ala	Auto Accident	Greenwood
30-Apr	*Frank V. Moore	M	W	64	M	524 Park Lake Ave	1 yr	Salesman	Calhoun, Ky	Apoplexy	Greenwood
30-Apr	*Wm Gill	M	W	95	W	24 Hyer St	30 yrs	Retired	England	Cerebral Hemorrhage	Greenwood
2-May	*John R. Duke	M	W	51	M	Hughey St bet Church & Pine	11 yrs	Farming	Parris, Ill	Apoplexy	Greenwood
3-May	*Pansy Grover	F	W	11 mo	S	RFD #3	11 mos		Orlando RR#3	Intero colitis	Lake Hill Cemetery
4-May	James Clark, Jr	M	C	5 yrs	S	426 S. Parramore	5 mos	None	Orlando, Fla	Bronchopne umonia	Greenwood
5-May	*James A. Compton	M	W	75	W	517 S. East St./ O.G.H.	5 yrs	Fruit Grower, Retired	West Union, Ohio	Mescutine? Thrombosis	Clermont, Fla
4-May	*Mary Alice Stewart	F	W	2	S	O.G.H. / Conway Dr	1 day		Ga	Cholera Infantum	Greenwood
5-May	James McDuffie	M	C	42	M	1140 W. Livingston	3 Yrs	Labor	S.C.	Acute Dili-tation / Heart	Greenwood
8-May	*Estel L. McLaughlin	F	W	76	W	RFD #3	3 yrs	At Home	Pa	Chronic Myocarditis	Pittsburgh, Pa
9-May	*Mrs Harriett S. Sleeper	F	W	65	M	Cincinnati, Oh/ Fla San	3 mos	At Home	R.I.	Surgical Shock	Newport, R.I.
10-May	Evelin Brown	F	C	45	M	E. Orlando	1 mo	Domestic	Ga	Intestinal? Nephritis	Greenwood
11-May	*Mrs Pauline B. Picken	F	W	36	M	Chaney Highway/ O.G.H.	2 yrs	At Home	Tenn	Post Operation Shock	Greenwood
12-May	Abner Lewis	M	C	21	M	Pine Castle	3 yrs	Laborer	Fla	Homocidle?	McClenny, Fla
15-May	*James T. Hackley	M	W	91	W	1114 S. Hughey St/ O.G.H.	2 mos	Farming, Retired	Ky	Hypostatic Penumonia	Stanford, Ky
8-May	Austin Wesley Eiselstein	M	W		S	O.G.H.			Orlando	Stillborn	St. Cloud

66

1925	Name of Deceased	Sex	Race	Age	Marital	Residence/Place of Death	Orlando Resident	Occupation	Place of Birth	Cause of Death	Place of Burial
11-May	Mary Eliza Allen	F	W	68	M	St Cloud/ Fla San.	6 mos	H.W.	St Johns, Newfoundland	Myocarditis	Mt. Peace Cemetery
13-May	Mrs Gertrude Eiselstein	F	W	35	M	St Cloud, Fla/ O.G.H.	6 yrs	H.W.	Jefferstown, Ky	Ruptured Uterus	St. Cloud, Fla
16-May	*August E. Liundgren	W	M	65 a	W	14 S. Hughey/ O.G.H.	25 yrs	Day Labor	Sweden	Septicemia	Greenwood
17-May	*Mrs Nettie F. Buckmaster	F	W	48	M	409 S. Rosalind	10 yrs	At Home	Kirksville, Mo	Myocarditis	Greenwood
17-May	*Miss Katherine Marvin Wingfield	F	W	63	S	437 Highland Ave	4 yrs	At Home	Elizabeth, N.J.	Outis? myelitis of sternum	Milford, Conn
17-May	*Child of Mr & Mrs S. F. Watts	F	W		S	Peppercorn Apts			Orlando	Asphyxia Neonatorum	Greenwood
18-May	*Samuel Smith Kimberly	M	W	71	M	Columbus, Ohio/ O.G.H.	14 ds	Comm. Traveler	Haron Co., Ohio	Chr. Myocarditis	Columbus, Ohio
18-May	Daniel F. Hall	M	C	64	W	914 Washington St.	15 mos	Minister	Quincy, Fla	Bright's Disease	Greenwood
18-May	*Infant of Mr & Mrs A. T. Fancloth	M	W		S	705 S. Main St., Leesburg, Fla/ O.G.H.	2 ds		Orlando	Stillborn	Greenwood
19-May	Joseph Gibbs Goggans	M	W	65	M	903 E. Robinson	5 yrs	Clerical Work, Retired	Newburg, SC	Pulmonary T B	Greenwood
20-May	*Roda M. Martin	F	W	a 1 mo	S	3 mi N.W. of City	about 1 mo		Orlando	Bronchopneumonia	Lake Hill Cemetery
20-May	*John N. Crotts	M	M	76	W	215 Palmetto	14 yrs	Retired	Pittsburgh, Pa	Senility	Greenwood
20-May	Mary Stewart	F	W	82	W	Angebilt Addi?		Housewife	N.Y.	Presumably Senile Debility	Mt. Peace Cemetery, St. Cloud
21-May	*Mary Alice Finley	F	W	4 hrs	S	Lockhart, Fla	1 mo		Lockhart, Fla	Premature	Greenwood
24-May	*Lucy Henson	F	W	9	S	O.G.H./ 400 S. Hughey St.	4 yrs		Bristol, Va	Cerebral Meningitis	Bristol, Va
23-May	*Child of Mr & Mrs Floyd E. Lott	M	W	4 hrs	S	S. Delaney St./ Fla San	4 hrs		Orlando	Premature Birth	Greenwood
24-May	Wm P Walker (Walter)	M	W	90 a	W	County Home	1 yr	Day Laborer		Cardio Vascular Renal Disease	County Home
25-May	*Child of Mr & Mrs Geo McLaughlin	F	W		S	Alexander Apt/ O.G.H.			Orlando	Stillborn	Greenwood
25-May	Mrs Florence May Hobson	F	W	67	W	110 N. Brown St.	2 yrs	Retired	St Johns, New Brunswick	Carcinoma of Liver & Duodenum	Titusville, Fla
23-May	Baby Ward	F	C	SB	S	814 W. South St.			Orlando	Premature Birth	Greenwood
23-May	Elick McAlester	M	C	21	S			Laborer	Brookfield, Ga	Tuberculosis, Pulmonary	Greenwood
4-Feb	Stephen R. Satchell	M	W	74	M	425 W Concord	1 yr 4 mo	Traveling Salesman	Iowa	Perichondritis & Hepatic Carcinoma	Grinnell, Iowa

67

1925	Name of Deceased	Sex	Race	Age	Marital	Residence/Place of Death	Orlando Resident	Occupation	Place of Birth	Cause of Death	Place of Burial
27-May	*Child of John T. Lind, Jr. (Livid)	M	W		S	315 W. Pine/ Pensacola, Fla	1 da		Orlando	Died in Uterus 6 Mos after Conception	Catholic
27-May	*Mrs Vivian M. Gould	F	W	49	M	626 Woodward Ave/ O.G.H.	7 mos	At Home	Fosterville, N.Y.	Intestional Obstruction	Buffalo, N.Y.
28-May	Caroline Peroy (Pery)	F	C	67	W	410 W. Jackson		House-work	Monticello	Acute Paren-chymous Nephritis	Greenwood
29-May	*Theada B. Walker	F	W	3	S	10 mi S of City/ O.G.H.	4 ds		Pollock, La	Acute ?__ Colitis	Pollock, La
30-May	Baby of John T. McDuffie	F	W	3 ds	S	O.G.H.	3 ds		Orlando	Inmature	Travares, Fla
1-Jun	Jire Boatwright	M	C	9m	S	612 W. Robinson	9 mos	None	Orlando	Gastritis	Greenwood
1-Jun	Allen Wilson	M	C	50 a	M	E Orlando		Labor		Died Sudden. No Attending Physician	Greenwood
1-Jun	David James McClining	M	C	13	S	612 W Long	1 yr	None	Groveland	Endo-carditis	Greenwood
2-Jun	Martha D. Stebbins	F	W	94	W	South & Bumby	47 yrs	Retired	Amherst, Mass	Old Age	Greenwood
2-Jun	*Jasper C. Seeley	M	W	82	M	Evans Ave	2 yr 6 mo	Carpenter Retired	Clarksville, N.Y.	Organic Heart Disease	Hornell, N.Y
3-Jun	Author Henson	M	C	26	M	1136 Federal	1 mo	Laborer	Mariana, Fla	Uremia	Greenwood
3-Jun	*Joseph Wint	M	W	79	W	Fowlersville, Mich/ 812 N. Summerlin	4 mos	Gardner	Rochester, N.Y.	Edema of Brain	Fowlersville, N.Y.
4-Jun	Alven Eliz-abeth Bartley	F	C		S	Orlando	1 da	None	Orlando	Asphyxia	Greenwood
5-Jun	W. T. Thomas	M	C		M	600 Jackson		Laborer	Fla	Cerebral Hemorrhage	Greenwood
19-May	Rosa Lee Scott	F	C	25	M	128 Gardner	8 mos	Domestic	Orangeburg, S.C.	Tuberculosis of Lungs	Greenwood
3-Jan	Lee Bryan	M	W	27 a	S	O.G.H.	1 mo	Day Labor		Parotid? Gland Abscess	County Home
4-Jun	*Mrs Lottie M. Briggs	F	W	44	M	O.G.H./ Cocoa, Fla	1 da	Registered Nurse	Charleston, S.C.	Shock Following Operation, Incarcerated Rectal Hernia	Charleston, S.C.
5-Jun	William H. Tunnicliffe	M	W	91	W	St. Cloud, Fla/ Fla Sanit	2 mo	Retired Soldier	Penn	Senility	St. Cloud
6-Jun	Frank Edwards	M	C	24 a	M	515 W. Jackson	5 mos	Laborer	Gainesville	Gun Shot Wound of Chest	Waldo, Fla
7-Jun	*Mrs. Minnie A. Diebold	F	W	55	M	Groveland, Fla/ O.G.H.	2 ds	At Home	On Atlantic Steamer near New York port	Strangulated Umbilical Hernia	Groveland, Fla
5-Jun	*William T. Entrican	M	W	49	M	1750 N. Mills/ Orlando Sanitarium	13 yrs	Painting?	Ind	Cirrhosis of Liver, Chronic	Greenwood

1925	Name of Deceased	Sex	Race	Age	Marital	Residence/Place of Death	Orlando Resident	Occupation	Place of Birth	Cause of Death	Place of Burial
7-Jun	*John R. Williams	M	W	71	M	Citra, Fla/ O.G.H.	1 m 24 d	Citrus Grower	S.C.	Pulmonary Tuberculosis	Ocala, Fla
7-Jun	*John (Joseph) Scocraft	M	W	80	M	Adair Circle	2 yrs	Clerical Work L & N., Cin.	England	Acute Broncho Penumonia	Greenwood
9-Jun	Francis N. Calvin	M	W	69	M	Fla Sanit/ Bartow, Fla	1 yr	Active Minister	Pike Co., Mo	Carcinoma of Stomach, Liver	Bartow (Wildwood)
10-Jun	*Osman Hutchs Mathews	M	W	79	M	Winter Park Road	43 yrs	Mechanic Stair Builder	New Hampshire	Organic Disease of Heart	Conway
10-Jun	*Hugh K. Ector	M	W	75	W	Miami, Fla/ Fla Sanitarium	1 mo	Retired	Marietta Co., Ga	Cancer of Coco_?	Miami, Fla
11-Jun	*Mrs Amanda E. Clark	F	W	59	M	Lockhart, Fla	4 yrs	At Home	Freeport, Pa	Organic Disease of Heart	Greenwood
12-Jun	*George W. Gray	M	W	56	M	Canton & Fern Creek Ave	8 yrs	Real Estate Agent	Waynes-ville, Ill	Uremic Poisoning	Greenwood
13-Jun	*Henry Webeking	M	W	82	M	411 W Concord Ave	7 yrs	Fruit Grower	Germany	Cerebral Hemorrhage	Greenwood
15-Jun	*Infant of Mr & Mrs Linton R. Briley	M	W		S	O.G.H.			Orlando	Stillbirth	Oakland
16-Jun	*Paul Oliver Mitchell	M	W	13	S	O.G.H.	8 mos	Student	Moore Sta, Seminole Co	Colitis	Sanford
19-Jun	James Thomas	M	C		S	910 Edner St			Orlando	Syphilitic, Active of Father	Greenwood
20-Jun	*Douglas Ev-erett Newman	M	W	2	S	642 Hughey St.	2 yrs		Orlando	Cholera, Infantum	Greenwood
21-Jun	John Smith	M	C	53	M	O.G.H.	1 da	Laborer	S.C.	Shot through Chest	Mascotte, Fla
22-Jun	*Homer Bethea	M	W	18	S	O.G.H./ 406 Gertrude St	14 ds	Day Labor	Stillmore, Ga	Peritonitis	Stillmore, Ga
20-Jun	*Stephen Chick	M	W	81	M	O.G.H./ Taft, Fla	20 ds	Day Labor	Lemerick, Maine	Broncho Pneumonia	County Home
22-Jun	*Mrs Minnie M. Patterson	F	W	49	W	Asbury Park, N.J./ 517 Highland Ave	8 mos	At Home	Farmingdale N.J.	Cancer of Pancreas	Asbury Park, N.J.
24-Jun	Amelia Reed	F	C	67 a	W	441 S. Division	10 yrs	Laundress	Madison, Fla	Hepatic Cor_osis?	Greenwood
25-Jun	*Bertha Reinertson	F	W	33	M	808 E. Washington	6 yrs	At Home	Springfield, Minn	Pernicious Anemia	Greenwood
24-Jun	*Caroline B. Ceman	F	W	77	W	Kingsley, Kans/ Bonnie Lock, Orlando	1 mo	At Home	Canodice?, N.Y.	Senility & Nephritis	Belding, Mich
25-Jun	*Mrs Lydia J. Bachelder	F	W	62	W	960 W. Central Ave	8 mos	At Home	Lynn, Mass	Organic Heart Disease	Lowell, Mass
29-Jun	David Zeigler	M	C	8	S	Globe St?	1 mo 8 ds	School Boy	Brownwood Ga	Remittent Malaria	Greenwood Cem
4-Jun	Zick Walker	M	C	18	S	O.G.H.	12 hrs		Leesburg, Fla	Peritonitis	Orange Bend, Fla

1925	Name of Deceased	Sex	Race	Age	Marital	Residence/Place of Death	Orlando Resident	Occupation	Place of Birth	Cause of Death	Place of Burial
26-Jun	*Mathew Bivins Hawkins	M	W	56	W	530 Conway Ave	3 mos	Day Labor	Plant City, Fla	Mitral Regurgitation	Plant City, Fla
28-Jun	*Geo Allen Dodd	M	W	73	M	Rock Lake	4 yrs	Retired U.S. Army	Penn	Chronic Myocarditis	Washington, D.C.
28-Jun	*Child of Mr & Mrs Blaine Edwards	M	W		S	Princeton Ave	about 8 mos		Orlando, Fla	Stillborn	Greenwood
28-Jun	*Martin Wm Crossley	M	W	48	M	O.G.H.	15 yrs	Contractor	Mich	Accidental Burn	Greenwood
1-Jul	Robt Washington	M	C	65	S	County Home	65 yrs	Day Labor	Orlando, Fla	Syphillis	County Home
2-Jul	*Wm Eugean Hobbs	M	W	1 d	S	O.G.H/ New Smyrna, Fla.	1 da		New Smyrna, Fla	Meningitis	New Smyrna, Fla
2-Jul	Jas Arthur Pearce	M	W	64	M	O.G.H./ St Cloud, Fla	2 ds	Mining Engineer	Tenn	Acute Dilitation of Heart	St. Cloud, Fla
2-Jul	Francis Salter	F	W	37	M	Church & Lee? St.	5 yrs	House-keeper	Ga	Apoplexy	Greenwood
4-Jul	*Cecil Robinson	M	W	4	S	O.G.H./ 414 America St.	1 mo		Odern, Ga	Cerebro-spinal Meningitis	Greenwood
5-Jul	*Mrs Sara Eliza Willcox	F	W	75	M	O.G.H./ 119 N. Hyer St	7 mos	At Home	Conn	Cerebral Hemorrhage	Bristol, Conn
6-Jul	*Miss May Carrol Darnell	F	W	18	S	O.G.H./ Anderson St.	1 yr	College Girl	Miss	Fracture Base of Skull	Medrian, Miss
7-Jul	*Gertrude Reynolds	F	W	22	M	Box 1786	4 yr 7 mo	At Home	Ky	Childbirth	Greenwood
8-Jul	Infant of Joe Livingston	M	B			Orlando			Orlando	Stillborn	Greenwood
7-Jul	Margaret Smith	F	C	26	M	508 S. Parramore	5 mos	HW	Orlando	Tuberculosis Pulmonary	Greenwood
9-Jul	James Tyson	M	C	80	S	County Home	Several yrs	Day Labor	Fla	Luetic Atrophy of Liver	County Home
13-Jul	*Emily Holley	F	W	11	S	O.G.H./ Ferndale, Fla	7 ds	In School	Palmetto, Fla	Streptococcus Infection / Lower Lip spreading over face	Ferndale Cem
12-Jul	*Mrs Elizabeth Richardson	F	W	47	W	117 E. Amelia Ave	1 yr 6 mo	At Home	London, England	Acute Dilation of Heart	Greenwood
13-Jul	*A. E. Wigglesworth	M	W	59	S	Fla Sanit/ Live Oak, Fla	4 mos	Merchant	Chicago, Ill	Chronic Nephritis	Live Oak, Fla
15-Jul	*Rebecca Napier	F	W	77	W	Fla Sanit/ 9 E. Washington	1 yr 9 mos	At Home	Ky	Senility	Jefferston, KY?
17-Jul	*Sara H. DeWitt	F	W	24	M	O.G.H/ Haines City, Fl	1 da	At Home	Ga	Eclampsia	Hohira, Ga
17-Jul	Infant Edw Dorsey	M	C	1	S	Holden St.	1 yr 12 ds	None	Orlando	Bone Deformation	Greenwood
18-Jul	*Alfred J. Casson	M	W	61	M	Chicago, Ill/ O.G.H.	10 mos	City Fireman	England	Myocardial Insufficiency	Chicago, Ill
18-Jul	Infant Fred J. Brown	M	C	1 y	S	Holden St.	1 mo	None	Orlando	Acute Diarrhea	Greenwood
20-Jul	Francis Williams	F	C	70	D	E South St.	35 mo	Domestic	Leon Co.	Apoplexy	Greenwood

1925	Name of Deceased	Sex	Race	Age	Marital	Residence/Place of Death	Orlando Resident	Occupation	Place of Birth	Cause of Death	Place of Burial
20-Jul	*James Fuller	M	W	24	M	O.G.H./ Cocoa, Fla	2 ds	Printer	Boston, Mass	Asphyxiation	Moultrie, Ga
21-Jul	*Edward Benn	M	W			O.G.H./ Jackson, Miss	8 mos			Cerebral Hemorrhage	Jackson, Mich
22-Jul	*Luther Baxter Long	M	W	70	M	502 S. Hughey	45 yrs	Merchant, Retired	Charlotte, N.C.	Uncompensated Heart	Greenwood
23-Jul	*James Palmer Taylor	M	W	64	M	E Central Ave	a 15 yrs	Retired	Monticello, Fla	Parkinson's Disease	Geneva, Fla
24-Jul	*Lou Henry	F	W	63	W	513 W. Washington	33 yrs	At Home	Davidson, N.C.	Apoplectic Paralysis	Greenwood
25-Jul	*Wm Harris Dolive	M	W	36	M	O.G.H./ Corner of Amelia and Mills	36 yrs	Truck Driver, Standard Oil Co.	Orlando	Uremia	Greenwood
26-Jul	Henry King	M	C	50	S	910 W. Holden	14 yrs	Laborer	Clinton, N.C.	Paralysis	Greenwood
27-Jul	*Samuel J. T. Lanier	M	W	39	M	O.G.H./ Eau Gallie, Fla	10 ds	Restaurant, Madison, Fla	Madison, Fla	Multiple Carbuncle	Madison, Fla
28-Jul	*Edward M. Pettes	M	W	77	W	O.G.H./ Canaan, N.H.	8 mos	Retired	Canada	Uremia	Greenwood
30-Jul	*Charlie Sloan	M	W	58	M	O.G.H./ Minneola, Fla	4 ds	Day Laborer	Fla	Streptococcus Infection	Groveland, Fla
31-Jul	Tina Burnam	F	C	35	W	914 South St.	1 mo 7 ds	Domestic	Americus, Ga	Mitral Regurgitation	DeLand, Fla
2-Aug	Ella Moore	F	C	60	W	Pepper Hill	12 mo	Domestic	Unknown	Acute Gastritis	Greenwood
2-Aug	*Harriet Susan Wilson	F	W	63	M	RFD #3 Orlando	6 yrs	At Home	Clay Co., Ala	Nephritis, Acute, Parenchymatous	Greenwood
4-Aug	*Wm Meade	M	W	65	D	O.G.H./ Grand Rapids, Mich	1 da	Amusement Co.	Orleans Co. N.Y.	Septicemia	Grand Rapids, Mich
4-Aug	*Lewis D. Gallagher	M	W	50	M	O.G.H./ 520 Amelia	3 yrs 6 mo	Stockman, Cadillac Auto Co.	Boston, Mass	Broncho Pneumonia	Green Cove Springs
4-Aug	Blaney Bennett	F	C		S	O.G.H.			Orlando	Stillborn	Greenwood
5-Aug	*Hubert L. Clark, Jr	M	W		S	O.G.H.			Orlando	Respiratory Failure in New Born	Catholic Cemetery
8-Aug	*Mrs Mary S. Nelson	F	W	38	M	Holden Hills	1 yr 2 mos	At Home	Chattanooga Tenn	Peritonitis	Catholic Cemetery
9-Aug	*Mamie Locklear	F	W	6 mo	S	Holden Ave	6 mos		Orlando	Acute Gastric Enteritis	Greenwood
11-Aug	*Geo Peffer	M	W	82	M	431 S. Hughey	6 yrs	Contractor & Builder Retired	Ohio	Pneumonia	Punxsutawney, Pa
9-Aug	*Joseph Fekany	M	W	21 or 24	S	212 S. Parramore	2 yrs		Orlando	Burn	Catholic Cemetery
9-Aug	Johnnie Johnson	M	C	50	M	O.G.H./ Eustis, Fla	8 ds	Labor	Fla	Acute Nephritis	Eustis, Fla

1925	Name of Deceased	Sex	Race	Age	Marital	Residence/Place of Death	Orlando Resident	Occupation	Place of Birth	Cause of Death	Place of Burial
10-Aug	Jim McLaine	M	C	a 65	S	County Home	a 7 ds	Day Labor	Ga?	Senility	County Home
11-Aug	Milton Butler	M	C	10 ds	Infant	912 W. Edner	10 ds		Orlando	Not Known	Greenwood
11-Aug	Peter O. Peterson	M	W	87	M	315 W. Concord	6 yrs	Retired	Sweden	Acute Nephritis	Algora, Iowa
11-Aug	*Mrs Linda Townsend	F	W	76	W	422 E. Pine	12 yrs	At Home	Hartford, Ohio	Angina Pectoris	Sharon, Pa
12-Aug	*Lillian M. Kemp	F	W	37	M	O.G.H./ Apopka, Fla	3 mos	At Home	Hamilton Co., Fla	Nephritis of Pregnancy	Jennings, Fla
12-Aug	Infant of Mr & Mrs Kenneth Henry	F	W		S	Orlando			Orlando	Stillborn	Greenwood
12-Aug	Isaac Robinson	M	C	73	W	822 S. Division	2 yrs	Day Labor	Decatur Co., Ga	Acute Indigestion	Greenwood
13-Aug	*Florence McCormack	F	W	69	M	34 Park Lake Ave	2 yrs	At Home	Ralls Co., Mo	Carcinoma of Liver	Apopka Cemetery
14-Aug	*Infant of Mr & Mrs Hugh R. Miller	M	W		S	N. Reel St.			Orlando	Stillborn	Greenwood
14-Aug	*Fannie A. Young	F	W	78	W	Lockhart, Fla/ Miami, Fla	14 ds	At Home	Greensboro, Ga	Cerebral Hemorrhage	Quitman, Ga
14-Aug	*Jefferson Davis Prescott	M	W	61	W	48 W. South St.	60 yrs	Stockman	S. Carolina	Cerebral Hemorrhage	Shingle Creek Cemetery
14-Aug	Eli L. Drew	M	C	43	M	318 W. South St.	14 ds	Blacksmith	Monticello Fla	Apoplexy	Tallahassee, Fla
17-Aug	*Anna M. Rattle	F	W	72	W	116 Lucerne Circle	20 yrs	At Home	S.C.	Pyelitis Left	Greenwood
18-Aug	Infant of Wm Bryant Wiley	M	W		S	Fla Sanitarium & Hosp			Orlando	Stillborn	Umatilla, Fla
19-Aug	*Jimmie Lee Ritter	F	W	4	S	O.G.H./ 1034 W. Jackson	4 yrs		Orlando	Post Operative Hemorrhage	Greenwood
19-Aug	*Mrs Carolyn T. Stapp	F	W	82	W	13 E. Pine St.	24 yrs	At Home	New York	Broncho Pneumonia	Greenwood
20-Aug	*Mrs Abbie Louise Johnson	F	W	55	M	509 E. Anderson	20 yrs	At Home	Batavia, Ill	Carcinoma of Breast	Greenwood
21-Aug	*Wm Fred Simmons	F	W	1	S	112 Hill St.	1 yr 6 mo		Orlando, Fla	IleoColitis	Greenwood
21-Aug	*Infant of Mr & Mrs E D Berdler	M	W		S	119 E. Concord Ave			Orlando, Fla	Stillborn	Greenwood
21-Aug	*Mrs Helen Keyes Kibbe	F	W	56	M	Fla San/ Melbourne, Fla	2 mos	At Home	Wisconsin	Embolis Lodged in Heart	Melbourne, Fla
21-Aug	*Elmer Smith Robinson	M	W	56	S	Fla Sanit/ Orlando	56 yrs	Painter	Orlando	Pernicious Anemia	Lake Hill Cemetery
22-Aug	*Infant of Mr & Mrs Chas B. Hunt		W		S	Orlando			Orlando	Stillborn	Greenwood
25-Aug	Dorothy Jane Archer	F	C	6 ds	S	Orlando/ 1029 Bentley St.	6 ds		Orlando	Unknown	Greenwood
27-Aug	*Mrs Donnell C, Sloan	F	W	72	W	303 S Liberty St.	30 yrs	At Home	Lake City, Fla	Chronic Nephritis	Greenwood

1925	Name of Deceased	Sex	Race	Age	Marital	Residence/Place of Death	Orlando Resident	Occupation	Place of Birth	Cause of Death	Place of Burial
26-Aug	Henry Davis	M	C	48	M	807 Carter	2 yrs	Laborer	Whigham, Ga	Ruptured Aneurysm? Of Middle Third of Femoral Artery	Greenwood
28-Aug	J. C. Harris	M	C	5 ds	Inf	1003 W. Livingston	5 ds		Orlando	Unknown	Greenwood, A. J. Smith Co
29-Aug	*Francis Roberts	M	C	55	M	County Home	60 mos	Day Labor	Fla	Pulmonary T B	Greenwood, Carey Hand
30-Aug	Polly Woodbury	F	C	62	W	South St	2 yrs	Laundress	Tallahassee	Acute Gastritis	Greenwood, A. J. Smith Co
1-Sep	Samuel Haines	M	C	24	M	541 W. Church	13 yrs	Merchant	Madison, Fla	Gun Shot Wound	Greenwood
1-Sep	*Anna Hellen Phepps	F	W	26	M	O.G.H./ Kissimmee, Fla	24 yrs	H.W.	Punta Gorda, Fla	Parturition over Term	Rose Hill Cemetery
1-Sep	Stillborn of Above	F	W	Inf	S	O.G.H.		None	Orlando	Stillborn	Rose Hill Cemetery
4-Sep	*Amanda Carver	F	W	63	W	RFD #4, Orlando	3 yrs	At Home	Gilmore Co., Ga`	Cerebral Thrombosis	Greenwood
4-Sep	*Patrick J. Kilcullen	M	W	58	M	803 Palmer St.	3 mos	Retired	St. Louis, Mo	Carcinoma of Stomach	St. Louis, Mo
4-Sep	*Infant of Mr & Mrs Lewis Kilgore	F	W		S	O.G.H.			Orlando, Fla	Stillbirth	Greenwood
4-Sep	Infant of Mr & Mrs Ira Odekirk	F	W		S	Fla San			Orlando, Fla	Stillbirth	Greenwood
4-Sep	*Infant of Mr & Mrs O.A. Dearing	M	W	4 ds	S	12 Glenn	4 ds		Orlando, Fla	Cerebral Traumatism	Palatka, Fla
5-Sep	Infant of Mr & Mrs J. G. Ray	M	W	10 hrs	S	O.G.H.	10 hrs		Orlando, Fla	Immature Featus (Fetus)	Forest Cemetery, Mt Dora
5-Sep	*J T. Young	M	C	45	M	Co. Home; Pine Hurst Turpentine Camp, 9 mi E. of Orlando	1 mo	Laborer	Don't Know	Cirrhosis of Liver	County Home
6-Sep	*Sybil Howington	F	W	7	S	966 W. Central	7 ds		Atlanta, Ga	Cerebral Tumor	Atlanta, Ga
6-Sep	*Harry Johnson	M	W	52	M	Melbourne, Fla/ Fla San	7 ds	Printer	Asborg, Denmark	Myocarditis	Melbourne, Fla
6-Sep	Henry Night	M	C	35	M	O.G.H.	1 da	Merchant	Fla	Gunshot Wound	Harthorn, Fla
8-Sep	*Charles D. Lee	M	W	58	D	Main & Church	4 yrs	Vocal Teacher	Oxford, N.Y.	Died During Night, Unknown	Oxford, N.Y.
8-Sep	Mrs Belle Foss	F	W	77	W	536 S Lake St	10 yrs	At Home	Vermont	Uremia	Greenwood
8-Sep	*Infant of Mr & Mrs J. B. Williams	F	W		S	Orlando, Fla			Orlando	Stillborn	Greenwood
9-Sep	*R. W. Rhodes	M	W	35	S	O.G.H./ Orlando	1 yr	Sawyer	S.C.	Ruptured Blood Vessel	Branchville, S.C.

1925	Name of Deceased	Sex	Race	Age	Marital	Residence/Place of Death	Orlando Resident	Occupation	Place of Birth	Cause of Death	Place of Burial
10-Sep	Walter Thomas	M	C	68	M	4 John St.	3 yrs	Laborer	Ga	Acute Gastric Indigestion	Greenwood
10-Sep	A. P. Sparrow	M	C	48	W	O.G.H.	1 da	Plasterer	Tallahassee, Fla	Stricture Urethra	Greenwood
10-Sep	*William Guy Jacobs	M	W	23	S	Winter Garden/ O.G.H.	1 yr	Farming	Ala	Tuberculosis	Winter Garden
10-Sep	William Harris Crooms	M	C	52	W	417 W. Washington	35 mo	Barber?	Monticello Fla	Acute Bronchial Asthma	Greenwood
12-Sep	Dave Brown, Jr	M	C	10 ds	S	908 S. Division	10 ds		Orlando	Icterus Neonatorum?	Greenwood
13-Sep	*Infant of Mr & Mrs H. Harris	W	M		S	127 W. Church			Orlando	Premature Infant	Greenwood
13-Sep	Smith Jackson	M	C	41	M	503 W. South St	15 yrs	Laborer	Fla	Cerebral Hemorrhage	Greenwood
14-Sep	*Wynn Edward Peterson	M	W	1 yr	S	Myrtle Heights	1yr 7 mo		Orlando	Acute Citis	Greenwood
14-Sep	Allen Sanders	M	C	16	S	S Ky Ave	12 yrs	Student	Ft. Meade	Malaria Fever	Apopka, Fla
15-Sep	*William D. Tucker	M	W	73	D	O.G.H./ Lockhart, Fla	15 yrs	Farming	Ga	Carcinoma of Bladder	Greenwood
16-Sep	*Frank E. Bosse	M	W	69	M	Orlando	40 yrs	Retired	Germany	Paralysis	Greenwood
17-Sep	Daphny Burnett	F	C	77	M	503 W Pine	35 yrs	Cook	Fla	Absorbing Toxins from Gangrene Greenwood	
18-Sep	*Anna M. Wintersdorf	F	W	47	M	O.G.H./ Yalaha, Fla	16 ds	At Home	G.D. Luxenburg	Shock Following Operation	Leesburg, Fla
18-Sep	George Tillman	M	C		S	215 N. Parramore	1 da	None	Orlando	Stillborn	Greenwood
17-Sep	*Wm L. Hughlett	M	W	63	M	O.G.H./ Cocoa, Fla	5 ds	Physician	Lancaster, Va	General Peritonitis	Cocoa, Fla
20-Sep	*Hannah Williamson	F	C	93	W	Orlando	3 yrs	At Home		Senility	County
21-Sep	*Murry S. King	M	W	55	M	748 N. Orange	20 yrs	Architect	Murryvile, Pa	Starvation	Greenwood
22-Sep	Gennie Patterson	F	C	62	S	30 N. Paramore	3 mos	Cook	Fla	Mitral Regurgitation	Greenwood
23-Sep	*Elmer Lewis Short	M	W	19	M	Orlando	4 ds	Electrician	Bloomington, Ill	Accidently Drowned	Bloomington, Ill
25-Sep	*Catherine Ellis	F	W	63	S	430 E. Jackson	2yrs	At Home	Oswego, N.Y.	Hemoplegia ? Following Starvation	Greenwood
26-Sep	Wesley Roberts	M	W	27	S	Sanford Ave	1 da	Carpenter	Ala	Fracture of the Parietal? Bone of Left Side	Jasper, Ala
29-Sep	John Newton	M	C	1 da	S	715 W. Carter	1 da	Infant	Orlando	Premature	
30-Sep	Carry Wilson	F	C	26	M	Haines City, Fla/ O.G.H.	3 ds	Housewife	Ga	Macerated Fetus	Haines City, Fla
1-Oct	Willie Moris	M	C	47	S	O.G.H.	12 ds	Laborer	S.C.	Abscess	Greenwood

1925	Name of Deceased	Sex	Race	Age	Marital	Residence/Place of Death	Orlando Resident	Occupation	Place of Birth	Cause of Death	Place of Burial
1-Oct	*Mrs Grace L. Parrott	F	W	55	M	Fla San	11 mos	At Home	Bridgeport, Conn	Myocarditis	Bridgeport, Conn
3-Oct	John Cunningham	M	C	81	W	9 Washington, City	6 mos	Laborer	Greenwood, S. C.	Don't Know	Apopka
3-Oct	*Margaret G. Lewis	F	W	45	M	219 Liberty St./ Orlando Sanit	2 yrs	At Home	Lowell, Mass	Broncho Pneumonia	Greenwood
3-Oct	*Hubert Woolf	M	W	5	S	O.G.H./ 1121 Catherine	3 yrs		Clay Co., Ala	Shock from Burns, Accidental	Blakely, Ga
5-Oct	*Meik Breikenbach	M	W	77 a	S	County Home		None	Germany	Pneumonia	County Home
6-Oct	Annie Thompson	F	W	52	W	511 Carter	4 mos	Domestic	Edysfield?, S.C.	Luro Tertiary	Lakeland, Fla
6-Oct	Grace Davis	F	C	78	W	601 W. Jackson	14 mo	Domestic	Orangeburg, S.C.	Accites	Jacksonville, Fla
6-Oct	Allie Ruth Belford	F	C		S	806 W. Robinson			Orlando	Stillbirth	Greenwood
7-Oct	Hyrum Nepo-lion Lester	M	C	11 mo	Inf	Orlando	11 mos	Infant	Orlando	Pneumonia	Greenwood
8-Oct	*Stanfield D. Hardaway	M	W	52	M	Michigan Ave	15 yrs	Retail Salesman	St Louis, Mo	Abscess of R. Lung	Greenwood
9-Oct	*Welcome Richard Greaton	M	W	18	S	Mims, Fla	4 ds	Day Laborer	Vancouver, B.C., Can	General Peritonitis	Mims, Fla
9-Oct	*Mrs Lizzie Long	F	W	39	M	RFD/ Orlando	8 mos	At Home	Quatman Co., Ga	Heart Dropsy	Mariana, Fla
11-Oct	*Infant of Mr & Mrs Morris Levenstein	M	W		S	629 E Cen.Ave/ O.G.H.	about 4 mo		Orlando	Stillborn	Tampa, Fla
12-Oct	*Edward Ringhausen	M	W	61	M	Conway, Fla/ O.G.H.	1 da	Farming	Mo	Cerebral Hemorrhage	Conway
14-Oct	*Joseph H. Lewis	M	W	36	M	21 N. Garland	1 yr	Day Labor	Baxter, Tenn	Typhoid, Pneumonia	Baxter, Tenn
14-Oct	Ollie Allen	M	C	26 a	?	Olando/ O.G.H.	2 da	Day Laborer	Cottontown, Ala	Gunshot Wound	Oakland
14-Oct	*Fred Badger	M	W	76	W	25 N. Hughey	6 yrs	Retired	Redding, Mass	Apoplexy	Oshkosh, Wis
14-Oct	*George A. Snook	M	W	68	S	507 Grove Park Drive	6 yrs	Carpenter Work	New Jersey	Apoplexy	Newton, N.J.
14-Oct	*Chas Gustave Medlin, 3rd	M	W	1 mo	S	820 Otey Place, Fla San	1 mo		Orlando	Surgical Shock	Greenwood
15-Oct	Alonzo Kirkland	M	C	78	S	828 S. Parramore	3 yrs	Watchman	Augusta, Ga	No Doctor in Attendance	Greenwood
18-Oct	*Ben P. Brown	M	W	66	M	Orlando/ O.G.H.	Several yrs	Day Laborer	N.C.	Cerebral Concussion	Greenwood
17-Oct	*Anna A. Robbins	F	W	56	S	500 Grove Park Drive	5 yrs	Trained Nurse	Edwards-ville, Ill	Carcinoma of Liver	Mt. Vernon, Ill
18-Oct	*Jacob Otto	M	W	74	M	Watseka, Ill/ O.G.H.	20 ds	Restaurant	Canal Dover, Ohio	Apoplexy	Watseka, Ill
19-Oct	*Mrs Amelia Ludwick	F	W	64	M	Belleview, Kas/ 730 W. Colonial Dr	2 ds	At Home	Chicago, Ill	Carcinoma of Rt Heart	Greenwood
19-Oct	*Mary Etta Scott	F	W	9 mo	S	RFD #1, Conway, Fla/ O.G.H.	1 da		Conway, Fla	Acidosis	Conway Cemetery

Date	Name of Deceased	Sex	Race	Age	Marital	Residence/Place of Death	Orlando Resident	Occupation	Place of Birth	Cause of Death	Place of Burial
20-Oct	*John William Jernigan	M	W	9	S	Clermont, Fla/ O.G.H.	2 ds		Clermont, Fla	Acidosis	Clermont, Fla
24-Oct	*Neils Clausen	M	W	74	M	1019 N. Mills	3 yrs	Ministery, Retired	Denmark	Angina Pectoris	Greenwood
24-Oct	Henry Williams	M	C	47	M	54 W. Holden/ O.G.H.	5 yrs	Laborer	Loyeds (Lloyds?), Fla	Lacerated Intestine	Loyeds (Lloyds?), Fla
25-Oct	*Mrs Lydia E. Edwards	F	W	34	M	Princeton Ave/ O.G.H.	1 yr	At Home	Bevis, Ohio	Diabetes Mellitus	Bevis, Ohio
25-Oct	*Henry Frerking	M	W	74	M	Lockhart, Fla	3 yrs	Retired	Germany	Cancer of throat	Greenwood
26-Oct	*Mrs Amelia S. Langdon	F	W	59	M	St. Johns Park, Fla/ Fla San	14 ds	At Home	Switzerland	Tuberculus Bowel	Greenwood
26-Oct	*Damie Steffy	F		73	a W	RFD#2, Orlando	1 yr	At Home	Michigan	Mitral Regurgitation	Greenwood
27-Oct	*Infant of Mr & Mrs Homer L. Quilling	F	W	10 hrs	S	105 W. Livingston Ave			Orlando	Premature Delivery	Patrick
31-Oct	*Edward J. Reilly	M	W	43	M	338 N. Orange	2 yrs	Real Estate	Pa	Acute Alcoholism	Pittsburgh, Pa
2-Nov	*Chas F. Lewis	M	W	65	M	Gore & Rio Grande Ave	3 yrs	Farming	Ga	Carcinoma of Prostate Gland	Hartsfield, Ga
4-Nov	Leonea Shine	F	C		S	614 W Jackson		None	Orlando	Stillborn	Greenwood
2-Nov	Infant of Willie Wilson	F	C		S	3018 Parramore		None	Orlando	Premature	Greenwood
3-Nov	*Mary Elizabeth Westover	F	W	96	W	143 E. Livingston	21 yrs	At Home	Conn	Acute Indigestion	Greenwood
4-Nov	*Lemuel Martin Streetman	M	W	80	W	Howard, Ga/ R #2, Box 143D	8 mo	Farming	Ga	Evidently Cerebral Hemorrhage	Butler, Ga
4-Nov	*Hugh A. Dollins	M	W	77	W	114 S, Garland	37 yrs	Retired	Tenn	Arterio-sclerosis	Lake Hill
5-Nov	Jessie Johnson	M	C		S	530 W. Pine St			Orlando	Stillborn	Greenwood
8-Nov	*Geo Washington Belk	M	W	66	M	132 E Church	3 mos	Minister	Union Co.	Cerebral Hemorrhage	Ft. Mill, S.C.
8-Nov	*Frederick J. Behm	M	W	68	M	Central & Bumby	4 yrs	Retired	Maeville, Wis	Myocarditis, etc.	Greenwood
8-Nov	*Frank Pearson Trammell	M	W	2	S	Melbourne, Fla/ O.G.H	7 ds		Dallas, Texas	Vincent's Angina of Throat	Tampa, Fla
8-Nov	*Mrs Olive Blanch Burn	F	W	35	M	512? N. Lake St/ O.G.H.	3 yrs	At Home	Canada	Post Operative Peritonitis	Greenwood
9-Nov	*Mrs Vivian Seeman	F	W	21	M	O.G.H.	4 yrs	At Home	Tampa, Fla	Lobar Pneumonia	Tampa, Fla
8-Nov	George Allen Hill	M	C	31	W	108 N. Bryant	25 yrs	Clergyman	Quincy, Fla	Pulmonary Tuberculosis	Greenwood
11-Nov	Emmer [Emma?] Bradley	F	C	37	S	710 Avondale	2 mo	Laundress	China, S.C.	Carcinoma of Stomach	DeLand, Fla
10-Nov	*Mrs Daisy Postom	F	W	42	W	OGH. / General Delivery, Orlando	5 yrs	At Home	Manuel Co., Ga	Cardiac Dilitation	Greenwood

1925	Name of Deceased	Sex	Race	Age	Marital	Residence/Place of Death	Orlando Resident	Occupation	Place of Birth	Cause of Death	Place of Burial
10-Nov	*Kenneth Evans Powers	M	W	10 ds	S	Evans Ave	10 ds		Orlando, Fla	Hemorrhage	Greenwood
10-Nov	*Infant of Mr & Mrs M. E. Brown	M	W	3 hrs	S	S. Munell? Ave			Orlando, Fla	Premature Birth	Conway
11-Nov	*Rev. B. DeValt	M	W	a 60	W	Winter Park/ County Home	14 ds	Minister of Gospel, Retired	S.C.	Splen-omogly?	Winter Park
13-Nov	*Mrs Cornelia B. Magruder	F	W	81	W	Rockledge, Fla/ 618 E Central	7 ds	At Home	Ga	Angina Pectoris	Cocoa, Fla
6-Nov	Son of Paul & Neta Drawdy	M	W	4 h	S	1112 E. Gore Ave	4 hrs		Orlando	Premature Birth	Greenwood
11-Nov	Clarence Brown	M	C	7 d	S	America St.	7 ds		Orlando	Not Known	Greenwood
13-Nov	Rose Flemming	F	C	21	S	608 W. Church	1 mo	Cook	Ga	Septicemia	Cuthburt, Ga
12-Nov	*John H. Lidell	M	W	a 86	W	327 E. Livingston/ Schuyler Lake, N.Y.	3 ds	Retired	N.Y.	Pulmonary Edema	Schuyler Lake, N.Y.
13-Nov	*Joseph Harris	M	W	a 57	M	O.G.H./ Brooklyn, N.Y.	1 mo	Merchant	Romania	Angina Pectoris	Brooklyn, N.Y.
16-Nov	*Seth W Parker	M	W	66	M	O.G.H./ Ohio	11 ds	Farming	Ohio	Carcinoma Prostate	Mayfield Village, Ohio
16-Nov	*Chas B. Roberson	M	W	56	W	551 W. Church/ O.G.H.		56 Labor	Winter Park, Fla	Fracture Base of Skull	Lake Hill Cemetery
16-Nov	*Richard Leon Holland	M	W	67	M	9 N. Hughey	41 yrs	Carriage Builder	Ky	Uremia	Greenwood
13-Nov	Mabel Jones	F	C	4 mo	S	811 Edner St.	4 mos		Orlando	Malnutrition	Greenwood
16-Nov	John McCloud	M	C	a 90	W	824 Avondale	1 yr	Farmer	Brooks Co., Ga	Capillary Bronchitis	Greenwood
14-Nov	*Infant of Mr & Mrs Samuel C. Bass	F	W		S	Fla San			Orlando, Fla	Stillbirth	Winter Park
15-Nov	*Andrew M. Carnes	M	W	a 60	W	Fla Sant/ Kenmore, N.Y.	1 yr 11 ds	Contractor		Acute Obstruction of Ileum Adjacent to Large Liver Tuberculum	Linesville, Pa
18-Nov	Porter Nettles	M	W	24	S	Rosalee, Fla	24 y 2 d	Laborer	Osceola Co., Fla	Extensive Burns	Pleasant Hill, Kissimmee
19-Nov	*Infant of Mr & Mrs Leon H. Smith	F	W		S	E. South St.			Orlando, Fla	Premature Still Birth	Greenwood
19-Nov	*Infant of Mr & Mrs Wayne Sanders	F	W		S	502 S. Hughey			Orlando, Fla	Premature Still Birth	Greenwood
21-Nov	*Infant of Mr & Mrs E. H. McCloud	F	W	3 mo	S	Grand Ave	3 mo 6 ds		Orlando	Acidosis	Mt. Pleasant, Ga
14-Nov	George M. Coar	M	C	64	M	O.G.H.	20 yrs	Clergy-man	Tallahassee Fla	Pulmonary Edema	Greenwood

	Name of Deceased	Sex	Race	Age	Marital	Residence/Place of Death	Orlando Resident	Occupation	Place of Birth	Cause of Death	Place of Burial
23-Nov	Geo. Williams	M	C	46	S	O.G.H.	2 mo	Common Labor	Lloyds, Fla	Tubercular Pluerisy & Meningitis	Lloyds, Fla
18-Nov	*Harry T. Kelsey	M	W	41	M	1309 E. Washington/ O.G.H.	8 yrs	Mechanic	Lynnville, Tenn	Shock Following Accident	Greenwood
19-Nov	*Chas Winslow Deane	M	W	68	M	Monroe, Conn/ O.G.H.	1 mo	Retired	Springfield Pa	Cardio Nephritis	Amsterdam, N.Y.
23-Nov	*Mrs Bessie Elizabeth Johnston	F	W	76	W	Coconut Grove, Fla/ Pinelock Ave	1 m 10 d	At Home	Caroline, N.Y.	Nephritis	Vault, St. James, Minn
23-Nov	*Edward James Holland	M	W	90	W	Kentucky Ave	45 yrs	Retired	Lexington, Ky	Broncho Pneumonia	Greenwood
23-Nov	John C. Leonard	M	C	33	S	945 South	20 yrs	Taylor	Fla	Hemorrhage	Greenwood
25-Nov	*Rebecca Anna Frazer	F	W	70	M	350 E. South st.	11 yrs	At Home	Indiana	Angina Pectoris	Greenwood Cem
19-Nov	Infant of Ed Moultrie	M	C		S	710 Parramore			Orlando	Not Known	Greenwood Cem
25-Nov	Mariah Johnson	F	C	50	M	E. Orlando	2 yrs	Domestic	Ga	Acute Gastric Indigestion	Greenwood Cem
22-Nov	Pauline Barbara Winn	F	W	3 min	S	Fla Sanit			Orlando	Still Birth	Maitland Cemetery
23-Nov	Mrs A. C. Hinton	F	W	55	M	Fla San/ Sanford, Fla	3 yrs	Housewife	Wis	Acute Dilitation of Heart	Sanford, Fla
24-Nov	Ruhton Davidson	M	C	40	M a	Wildwood, Fla/ O.G.H.	2 mo 7 ds	Laborer	D.K.	Fracture Neck, Etc.	Monroe, N.C.
25-Nov	Mrs Mary A. Leighty	F	W	44	M	RFD #3	1 yr	At Home	Pa	Leukemia	Lake Hill Cemetery
26-Nov	*John H. Derby	M	W	80	W	Hudson Falls, N.Y./ 15 W. Gore Ave	2 mo	Retired	N.Y.	Cerebral Hemorrhage	Hudson Falls, N.Y.
27-Nov	*Mrs Opal Sommerville	F	W	36	M	Apopka/ O.G.H.	4 yrs 1 da	At Home	W Va	Diabetic Coma	Clarksburg, W.Va
28-Nov	*Gus T. Thomas	M	W	60	M	Sharps, Fla/ O.G.H.	11 ds	Real Estate	Indiana	Chr Interstitial Nephritis	Cocoa, Fla
28-Nov	*Rasmus Christensen	M	W	76	M	Wilson Ave	24 yrs	Retired	Denmark	Heart Block	Greenwood
28-Nov	*Infant of Mr & Mrs Jessie F. Boyd	M	W		S	O.G.H.			Orlando, Fla	Stillborn 6 1/2 months	Lake Hill Cemetery
29-Nov	Elbert L. McGanah	M	W	19	S	Fla San/ Winter Park	12 ds	Labor	Ga	Vincent's Infection	Ashburn, Ga
30-Nov	William Herman Griffin	M	W	30	M	Louise St. City/ O.G.H.	3 mo 15 ds	Merchant Auto Accessories	Ala	Influenza	Gadsden, Ala
30-Nov	Edward Richardson	M	C	23	S	Washington, Ga/ O.G.H.	3 mo	Truck Driver	Ga	Concussion of Brain	Washington, Ga
1-Dec	Charlie Rosese (Rouse?)	M	C	50	S	1111 South St.	50 yrs	Labor	S.C.	Cerebral Hemorrhage	Greenwood

1925	Name of Deceased	Sex	Race	Age	Marital	Residence/Place of Death	Orlando Resident	Occupation	Place of Birth	Cause of Death	Place of Burial
1-Dec	*Mrs Norah Ann King	F	W	59	M	421 W, Amelia Ave/ Fla San	15 yrs	At Home	Ky	Fat Embolism in the Lungs	Greenwood
4-Dec	*Gertrude W. Riemann	F	W	36	M	Meadville, Pa/ 957 DeWitt Dr	2 mo	At Home	Pa	Tuberculosis	Meadville, Pa
4-Dec	*Helen Sheriff	F	W	84	S	437 S. Hughey	4 ds	At Home	Canada	Angina Pectoris	Huntingdon, Quebec, Canada
30-Nov	Louis Parker	M	C	29	S	403 McFall	3 yrs	Car Washer	Waynesboro Ga	Tuberculosis	Greenwood
26-Nov	Artha Henry	M	C	35	M	S.E. Orlando/ 526 Long St.	1 yr	Laborer	Fla	Gun Shot Wound	Lake City, Fla
28-Nov	William Strickland Graham	M	W	54	M	Kissimmee, Fla/ O.G.H.	6 ds	Ticket Agent RR Work	N.C.	Pneumonia	Rose Hill
3-Dec	*Sydney Chas Faulkner	M	W	65	M	6353 Conial Drive	a 7 yrs	Accountant Retired	Montreal, Canada	Precinious Anemia	Vault
5-Dec	*Louis Jefferson Davis	M	W	67	M	Wrightsville, Ga/ 421 W Gore Ave	14 ds	Farming	Wrightsville, Ga	Uncompensated Heart	Greenwood
5-Dec	*Benjamin Adams	M	W	79	M	433 W. Livingstont	15 yrs	Retired	Beverly, Mass	Carcinoma of Stomach	Greenwood
6-Dec	Henry Lipscomb	M	C	35	M	S. Melbourne, Fla/ O.G.H.	1 da	Laborer	Melbourne Fla	Ruptured Deuodenum	S. Melbourne, Fla
6-Dec	*Mrs Winnie Limerick	F	W	52	W	Galatia, Ill/ O.G.H.	7 ds	At Home	Raleigh, Ill	Cholery-thrin? With Acute Obstruction of bowels	Galatia, Ill
7-Dec	*Mrs Gussie McMillan	F	W	37	S	River Junction, Fla/ Fla San	21 ds	School Teacher	River Junction, Fla	Acute Nephritis	River Junction, Fla
7-Dec	Will Allen	M	C	62	W	46 1/2 Parramore St	2 yrs	Day Laborer, Retired	N.C.	Found Dead	Greenwood
7-Dec	*Troy Eldrige Wade	M	W	38	M	Sorrento, Fla/ O.G.H.	2 ds	Farmer	N.C.	Paralysis of Bowels	Sorrento
8-Dec	*Harford A. Davis	M	W	61	M	Orlando/ RRD #3	7 ds	Carpenter	N.Y.	Carcinoma of Stomach	Greenwood
9-Dec	Sarah Bellany	F	C	29	M	1112 E South St.	1 yr	Cook	Fla	Knife Wound (L) Chest to Heart	Greenwood
9-Dec	Charlie Bryant	M	C	30	M	520 John/ O.G.H.	1 yr	Labor	Ga	Shot through Left Shoulder, Etc.	Greenwood
13-Dec	James Spaulding	M	C	4 d	S	418 Long St	4 ds	None	Orlando	Acute Catanbal? Jaundice	Greenwood
10-Dec	*Isabelle T. Beard	F	W	76	M	709 Lucerne Terrace	5 yrs	At Home	Monroe Co., Tenn	Endocarditis	McLeansboro, Ill
10-Dec	*Oliver Lee Richardson	M	W	47	M	Charlotte, N.C./ Orlando	about 3 yrs	Traveling Salesman	Gerard, Ala	Chronic Nephritis	Charlotte, N.C.
10-Dec	Lewis M. Cleaver	M	W	88	M	512 W. Central Ave	24 yrs	Druggist, Retired	Pa	Bronchitis, Acute	Arlington Natl Cem, Washington, D.C.

1925	Name of Deceased	Sex	Race	Age	Marital	Residence/Place of Death	Orlando Resident	Occupation	Place of Birth	Cause of Death	Place of Burial
10-Dec	*John Ramke	M	W	75	D	S. Garland	40 yrs	Retired	Germany	Chronic Nephritis	Greenwood
11-Dec	*Felicue (Felicia?) Yoder	F	W	70 a	W	County Home	Several mos		Oklahoma	Pulmonary T B	Greenwood
13-Dec	*John Hamel-ton Polhill	M	W	29	M	O.G.H./ 339 W. Central	6 mos	Druggist	Ga	Gun Shot Wound	Thomasville, Ga
14-Dec	*Infant of Mr & Mrs Ellis Richardson		W		S	O.G.H.	1 da		Orlando, Fla	Still Birth	Lisbon, Fla
14-Dec	*R. L. Bunum (Burrum?)	M	W	60 a	M	O. Winter Garden Road	2 mo	Carpenter	Tenn	Fracture of Base of Skull	Nashville, Tenn
14-Dec	*Wm C. Holcomb	M	W	70	M	R F D #4	2 mo	Farming	Dresden, N.Y.	Apoplexy	Greenwood
15-Dec	*Billie J. Parker	M	W	6 ds	S	433 1/ 2 Hughey	6 ds		Orlando	Impact Bowel	Greenwood
15-Dec	Mrs Nancy K. Smith	F	W	83	W	816 Central	5 yrs	At Home	Ohio	Hypostatis Pneumonia	Crawford-ville, Ind
16-Dec	Rosa Worthey	F	C		S	723 S. Jernigan			Orlando	Stillborn	Greenwood
19-Dec	Amos Parrish	M	C	49	M	612 W Church	1 da	Merchant	Fla	Dilitation of Heart	Lloyd, Fla
29-Nov	Floyd E. Osborn	M	W	55 a	W	Youngstown, Ohio/ O.G.H.	2 ds	Real Estate	?	Probable Cause Acute Indigestion	Greenwood
1-Dec	Myrtle L. Parkerson	F	W	1y	S	829 S. Div	2 mo		Eastman, Ga	Intestional Toxemia	Eastman, Ga
14-Dec	Mattie R. Carter	F	W	75 a	W	Winter Haven, Fla/ Fla San	3 mo	Retired	Texas	Acute Pancreatitis	Winter Haven
15-Dec	*Cecil Bates Williams	M	W	23	M	315 Concord	1 m 14 ds	RR Rate Clerk	Ga	Pulmonary T B	Greenwood
15-Dec	*Infant of Mr & Mrs J F Steinmetz	F	W		S	O.G.H.	P 3 mo		Orlando	Due to Asphyxiation	Greenwood
15-Dec	*Mrs Hattie Atha	F	W	69	M	Laurel, Md/ 215 E. Livingston	1 mo	At Home	Va	Anemia & Pustation?	Greenwood
16-Dec	*Lillian Bradt	F	W	2	S	44 1/ 2 W Church	6 mos		London, Ontario, Canada	Acute Broncho Pneumonia	Greenwood
17-Dec	*Mrs Julia Richardson	F	W	22	M	Lisbon, Fla/ O.G.H.	3 ds	At Home	Ga	Eclampsia	Willocoochee
17-Dec	*Arthur Lindley Tracy	M	W	68	M	212 S Rosalind	15 ds	Mechanical Engineer	Conn	Cardio-nephritis	Bridgeport, Conn
19-Dec	*Chas Rudman	M	W	61	W	Gates, N.Y./ O.G.H.	about 2 mos	Farming	N.Y.	Hypostatic Pneumonia	Rochester, N.Y.
19-Dec	*Willie C. Dantzler	M	W	39	M	Orlando/ RFD #2	8 mo	Carpenter	S.C.	Double Lobar Pneumonia	Orangeberg, S.C.
20-Dec	*Thomas J. Lynch	M	W	38	M	354 E South/ Fla San	8 mo	Real Estate	Ga	Lobar Pneumonia	Atlanta, Ga
21-Dec	*Mrs Caroline McC. Smith	F	W	61	W	Cambridge, N.Y./ 17 E Gore Ave	26 ds	At Home	N.Y.	Cardio-nephritis	Cambridge, N.Y.
23-Dec	Isbell Williams	F	C	49	M	514 W Washington	20 yrs	House-wife	Fla	Influenza, Pneumonia	Waldo, Fla

1925	Name of Deceased	Sex	Race	Age	Marital	Residence/Place of Death	Orlando Resident	Occupation	Place of Birth	Cause of Death	Place of Burial
19-Dec	*Geo Lewis Lowery	M	W	81	S	RFD #3	14 yrs	Farming	Ga	Heart Disease	Lake Hill Cemetery
21-Dec	*Etha Henderson	F	W	3	S	Lockhart	3 yrs		Lockhart	Bronchopneumonia	Apopka
21-Dec	Loretta Julia Walentiny	F	W	1	S	O.G.H.	1 mo		Aberdeen, S.D.	Acute Ileo Colitis	Greenwood
26-Dec	*Mrs Annella Lochman	F	W	70	M	Summerlin Hotel/ Bellmont, Mass	2 mo	At Home	N.Y.	Cerebral Hemorrhage	Salem, Mass
28-Dec	*Chas R. Smith	M	W	48	M	O.G.H./ Morris St.	5 mo	Painter	Washington, D.C.	Aortic Aneurysm	Greenwood
28-Dec	*Mrs Nancy Headley	F	W	58	M	O.G.H./ Merritt, Fla	21 ds	At Home	Green Co., Pa	Carcinoma of Sigmoid	Cocoa, Fla
16-Dec	Baxter Reed	M	C	52	W	Mims, Fla/ O.G.H.	6 ds	Laborer	Sanford, N.C.	Peritonitis	Greenwood
23-Dec	*Emma Marsh	F	W	5	S	Winter Garden/ O.G.H.	3 ds		Windermere Fla	Acute Myocarditis	Winter Garden
25-Dec	*Henry B. Evans	M	W	69	M	Wauwatosa, Wis/ 715 Edgewater Dr	2 mos	Printer	Oshkosh, Wis	Angina Pectoris	Milwaukee, Wis
28-Dec	*Gertrude G. Hester	F	W	49	M	Miami, Fla/ Avalon Hotel	1 da	At Home	Conn	Hypertension Nephritis	Miami, Fla
28-Dec	*Lyle Wm Jourden	M	W	18	S	21 E Amelia Ave/ O.G.H.	2 mo	Real Estate	New York,.City	Right Lobar Pneumonia	Greenwood
29-Dec	*Joseph B. Cook	M	W	74	M	Vermillion Grove, Ill/ O.G.H.	26 ds	Farming, Retired	Ill	Uremic Coma	Vermillion Grove, Ill
30-Dec	*Mrs Mary Bevans	F	W	77	M	424 E Church	8 yrs	At Home	Rushville, Ind	Mitral Regurgitation	Chicago, Ill
16-Dec	Neal M. Alexander	M	W	64	S	Fla San/ Deland	2 mos +	Retired	N.C.	Nephritis	Beauford, Fla?
30-Dec	*Chas Allen Walsh	M	W	69	a W	Waukegan, Ill/ 304 E. Central	3 mos	Retired	McHenry, Ill	Angina Pectoris	Elgin, Ill
31-Dec	*Carrie Frances Putnam	F	W	82	W	646 N. Orange Ave	27 yrs	At Home	Chicago, Ill	Pneumonia, Lobar	Greenwood
31-Dec	*Jessie Marie Maxwell	F	W	41	W	Miami, Fla/ Fla San	12 ds	At Home	Memphis, Mo	Cancer Involving Pelvic Wall	Atlanta, Ga
29-Dec	*Mrs Leona P. Partin	F	W	47	M	Ft. Christmas, Fla/ Fla Sant	29 ds	At Home	Ft Christmas, Fla	Chronic Nephritis	Ft. Christmas

1926	Name of Deceased	Sex	Race	Age	Marital	Residence & Place of Death	Orlando Resident	Occupation	Place of Birth	Cause of Death	Place of Burial
1-Jan	*Mrs. Laura Stock	F	W	48	W	Walpole, Mass /801 W. Amelia	10 ds	At Home	Sherwin, Mass	Chronic Brights Disease	Boston, Mass
1-Jan	Gus Goldy	M	C	101	S	County Home	4 yrs	Laborer	Ga.	Senility	County Home
1-Jan	Ernestine Roberson	F	C	26	M	608 W. Jackson	1 yr	Domestic	Ga.	Stab Wound	Greenwood
2-Jan	*Charles X. Chism	M	W	23	M	N. Shine St./W. Church St.	5 yrs	Bread Salesman	Ga.	Auto Accident	Ray City, Ga.
2-Jan	*Edork Lee Crosset	M	W	50	M	128 E. Washington	8 mos	Book-keeper	Tenn.	Acute Cardiac Dililation	Jacksonville, Fla.
2-Jan	*Job Bratt	M	W	76	M	Washington & Mirimar	2 mos	Farming	Ind.	Pernicious Anemia	Riley, Ind.
3-Jan	*Mrs. Amelia C. Smith	F	W	81	M	721 Park Lake Ave.	1 mo	At Home	Wis.	Intestinal Obstruction	Waukesha, Wis.
3-Jan	Samuel Williams	M	C	1	Inf	203 Division	4 mos		Camilla, Ga.	Acute (Toxic) Gastritis	Camilla, Ga.
3-Jan	*Mrs. Elizabeth Scocroft	F	W	83	W	Pearl Hotel	3 yrs	At Home	England	Chronic Myocarditis	Greenwood
4-Jan	*Mrs. Marguerite Bellamy Meredith	F	W	28	M	419 Ruth	4 mos	At Home	Iowa	Nephritis	Knoxville, Iowa
4-Jan	Infant of Candace Scott	F	C		S	218 off Parramore			Orlando	Stillborn	Greenwood
5-Jan	Marcus Orine Williams	M	W	35	M	O.G.H./Mt. Dora	2 ds	Real Estate Broker	Adrian, Ga.	Secondary Infection	Mt. Dora, Fla.
5-Jan	Nelsey Cey	F	C	41	M	300 W. Robinson	2 yrs	H.W.	Ga.	Gunshot Wound	Dundee, Fla.
5-Jan	Martha E. Hull	F	W	64	M	St. Cloud, Fla.	4 yrs	H.W.	Ind.	Carcinoma of Pancreas	Mt. Peace Cemetery
6-Jan	Maxwell Green	M	C	10 m	S	843 Avondale	10 m		Orlando	Broncho Pneumonia	Greenwood
6-Jan	*Max R. Weiss	M	W	23	S	O.H.G.	1 mo	Mechanic	Germany	Spinal Meningitis	Detroit, Mich.
6-Jan	*Infant of Mr. & Mrs. Emmett Pengh	M	W		S	325 W. Long			Orlando	Premature Birth	Greenwood
7-Jan	Mary Norman Hazen	F	W	87	W	825 W. Church St.		House-keeper	N.Y.	Carcinoma of Liver	Deland
4-Jan	*Infant of Mr. & Mrs. Jas. R. Hudson	M	W		S	Zellwood, Fla/O.G.H.			Orlando	Stillborn	Apopka
5-Jan	Infant of Don & Isom Rollins	F	C		S	America St.			Orlando	Stillborn	Greenwood
6-Jan	*Mrs. Maggie Hudson	F	W	18	M	Zellwood/O.G.H.	2 ds	At Home	Ala.	Eclampsia Puerpal	Greenwood
6-Jan	*Ollis Allen Jillson	M	W	80	M	Providence R.I. /S. Orlando on Pine Castle Rd	1 mo	Cashier of bank	R.I.	Nephritis, acute	In vault - Providence, R.I.
6-Jan	*Thos. Clyde Hanna	M	W	14	S	540 Park Lake Ave.	1 mo		Mich.	Cardiac failure	Greenwood
8-Jan	*Winnie Elizabeth Savage	F	W	73	W	Ft. Christmas /O.G.H.	7 ds	At Home	Ga.	Abscess Gall Bladder	Ft. Christmas
9-Jan	Gertrude Parker	F	C	22	M	403 McFall /O.G.H.	4 mos	H.W.	Chattanooga,Tn	Pulmonary Tuberculosis	Chattanooga, Tenn.

1926	Name of Deceased	Sex	Race	Age	Marital	Residence & Place of Death	Orlando Resident	Occupation	Place of Birth	Cause of Death	Place of Burial
9-Jan	*Conrad Molter	M	W	86	S	Huntington, W. Va /217 E. Amelia Ave	3 mos	Retired	Germany	Pneumonia	Huntington, W. Va.
9-Jan	*John Presswood	M	W	35 a	W	Rockwood, Tenn./O.G.H.	1 mo	Farming	Rockwood, Tenn.	Pulmonary TB	Rockwood, Tenn.
9-Jan	*Ambrous Hanner	M	W	23	S	La Grange, Ga. /O.G.H.	12 ds	Day Labor	Ga.	Lobar Pneumonia	La Grange, Ga.
10-Jan	*Alva Sample	M	W	80	W	424 Ruth	3 yrs	Retired	Morgan-town, WV	Myocardial Degeneration	Morgantown, W. Va.
10-Jan	*John Henry Harvey	M	W	79	W	Lucerne Court	a 18 yrs	Retired	Ray Nau? N.Y.	Chronic Myocarditis	Greenwood
11-Jan	Charles Horace Hall	M	W	27	M	Fla. San/Umatilla	27 da	Labor	Fort Mc-Coy, Fla.	Nephritis	Umatilla, Fla.
11-Jan	*Margaret Smith	F	C	60 a	W	439 Holden St.	14 yrs	At Home	Don't Know	Carcinoma of uterus	Greenwood
12-Jan	*J. Freeman Short	M	W	38	M	510 E. Jackson /O.G.H.	6 mos	Salesman	Ky.	Septocemia	Greenwood
13-Jan	*Mrs. Etta C. Ruh	F	W	44	M	178 S. Osceola /Sandusky, Ohio	2 mo 12da	At Home	Ohio	Cancer	Sandusky, Ohio
16-Jan	Osema Hadrick	F	C	8	S	700 Paramore	1 yr		Ga.	Scarlet fever	Greenwood
4-Jan	Wm. C. Woodside	M	W	55 a	S	W. Church St./6 Columbia Ave.	Abt 1 yr	Day Work		Accident, fell from house	Greenwood
12-Jan	*John H. Shook	M	W	65	W	Goshen, N.Y./O.G.H.	1 mo 5 da	Horse-man	Versailles, Ind.	Chr. Myocarditis	Versailles, Ind.
13-Jan	*Miss Martha Haywood Kimball	F	W	57	S	Littleton, Mass./O.G.H.	1 mo 1 da	At Home	Littleton, Mass.	Emphysema	Littleton, Mass.
14-Jan	*John C. Anno	M	W	80	S	Pine Castle Road	50 yrs	Merchant retired	Orange-burg, Ky.	Senility	Greenwood
15-Jan	*William Emanuel Lilja	M	W	46	D	811 W. Church St./Rockford, Ill.	5 mos	Ornamen-tal Iron Worker	Sweden	Pulmonary TB	Greenwood
17-Jan	*Myron Dickson	M	W	80	W	Martinsville, Ind./Fla. San.	3 mos	Merchant retired	Fulton, Ill.	Cardiac Decom-pensation	Indianapolis, Ind.
18-Jan	Mixon McCloud	M	C	23	S	Garden St.	1 yr	Laborer	Ozark, Ala.	Broncho Pneumonia	Ozark, Ala.
19-Jan	Sarrahmay Chase	F	C	28	M	308 Terry St.	2 yrs	Cook	Mich.	Acidi-nephritis ?	Greenwood
19-Jan	Alice Berryhill	F	C	24	M	190 N. Division	3 yrs	H.W.	Americus, Ga.	Ulcerative Enteritis	Desoto, Ga.
20-Jan	*Infant of Mr. & Mrs. A. M. Wetherall	M	W		S	O.G.H.			Orlando, Fla.	Premature Birth	Tampa
21-Jan	Infant of Lois Nixon	M	C		S	423 Long St.			Orlando, Fla.	Stillborn	Greenwood
11-Jan	Bessie Aulstin	F	C	1m	Inf	1226 W. Jefferson	1 mo	Infant	Orlando	D.K.	Greenwood
23-Jan	Mathis Rivers	M	C	34	S	800 W. South	3 yrs	S	Ga.	Spine Paralysis	Greenwood
23-Jan	Isom Rolins	F	C	33	M	America	6 yrs	H.W.	Forest City, Fla.	Septicemia	Greenwood
6-Jan	Jack Wright Ross	M	W	2	S	1401 Division	6 mos		Ga.	Burned to death, sat in tub of boiling water	Greenwood
15-Jan	*Infant of Mr & Mrs L M Cochran	F	W		S	O.G.H./Bourne Place			Orlando	Stillborn	Greenwood

1926	Name of Deceased	Sex	Race	Age	Marital	Residence & Place of Death	Orlando Resident	Occupation	Place of Birth	Cause of Death	Place of Burial
17-Jan	*Infant of Mr & Mrs Wm Brown	F	W		S	O.G.H./Highland Ave			Orlando	Stillborn	Locoochee, Fla
17-Jan	*Edwin W Kennedy	M	W	78	M	Lake Placid, N.Y./316 W Amelia	3 mos	Merchant	Wellington N.Y.	Angina Pectoris	Lake Placid, N.Y.
20-Jan	*Carolyn Adelle Laycock	F	W	9m	S	613 Woodward	9 m		Orlando	Septicemia	Greenwood
21-Jan	*Jas B. Watson	M	W	66	M	R 3 Box 16/O.G.H.	4 yrs	Merchant Grocery	Alamance Co., N.C.	Alcoholism	Goldsboro, N.C.
22-Jan	*Evan Morris Frack	W	M	59	M	Niles, Ohio/Fla San	24 ds	R R Engineer	Gerard, Ohio	Uremia	Niles, Ohio
22-Jan	*Mrs Luella A. Mansfield	F	W	75	M	Westminister, Mass/S Cornell	2 mo	At Home	Linboro, N.H.	Chr Myocardiitis	Fitchburg, Mass
23-Jan	*Mrs Ruby Lee Slade	F	W	22	M	263 Ridgewood Ave/Fla San	8 yrs	At Home	Rochester, Pa	Parturition?	Greenwood
23-Jan	*Catherine Brandt	F	W	5	S	Camden, N.J. /E Central Tourist Camp	2 mo		Camden, N.J.	Diphtheria	Camden, N.J.
23-Jan	*Infant of Mr & Mrs J. A. Slade	F	W		S	Orlando/Fla San			Orlando, Fla	Stillbirth	Greenwood
24-Jan	*James Hunter	M	W	66 a	D	Maitland, Fla/O.G.H.	1 da	Citrus Fruit Grower	Volusia	Auto & RR Accident, etc	DeLand, Fla
24-Jan	Eva Gladden	F	W	5	S	534 ½ W Cen Ave	1 yr		Fitzgerald, Ga	Mastoiditis	Fitzgerald, Ga
24-Jan	*Thos Lee Lankford	M	W	39 a	M	Lavonia, Ga/O.G.H.	3 ds	Farming	Hart Co., Ga	Fractured Skull	Lavonia, Ga
24-Jan	*Mrs Sarah R. Falkenburgh	F	W	81	W	Jersey City, N.J./Duke Hall	16 ds	At Home	Barnegat	Cardiac Failure	Jersey City, N.J.
25-Jan	*Carl R. Rice	W	M	47	M	Grand Rapids, Mich/O.G.H.	1 mo 7 ds	Plaster/ Brick Mason	Sparta, Mich	Gen Peritonitis	Sparta, Mich
29-Jan	Manervia Walker	F	C	65	W	902 Long	2 mo	H W	Ga	Cancer of Uterus	Dawson, Ga
30-Jan	William Shackelford	M	C	38	M	838 W Jackson	1 mo	Barber	Ga	Valvular HeartDisease w/ Dropsy	Greenwood
26-Jan	*Fred Samuel Smith	M	W	73	M	Oak Lodge	4 mos	Tin Smith & Plumber	Skowhegan, Maine	Chronic Val-vular Heart Disease	Andover, Maine
27-Jan	*Melvin Wise Callender	M	W	69	M	Wilkinsburg, Pa/29 N. Brown	7 ds	Retired	Peckville,	Gangrene, Etc	Wilkinsburg, Pa
27-Jan	*Infant of Mr & Mrs Lyman Ange	F	W		S	O.G.H.			Orlando	Premature Birth	Greenwood
27-Jan	*Ida Floyd	F	W	71	M	Mich Ave	14 yrs	At Home	Ga	Pulmonary T B	Conway
28-Jan	*Capt Samuel T. Stevens	M	W	75	M	714 Elmer? St.	2 yrs 9 mo	Retired	Haven, Canada	Carcinoma of Stomach	Greenwood
29-Jan	*Infant of Mr & Mrs W E Crawford	M	W	1 d	S	Cor Dade & Evan			Orlando	Premature	Greenwood
28-Jan	*Peter Ross	M	W	83	W	Wayland, Mich /Dade St	4 yrs	Retired	Don't Know	Embolus	Wayland, Mich
29-Jan	*Infant of Mr & Mrs W L Hutto	M	W		S	42 W Church / Fla San	7 yrs		Orlando	Premature	Greenwood
30-Jan	*Martin M. Matting	M	W	85	W	Rockledge, Fla /O.G.H.	1 da	Mer-chant	Dearborn Co., Ind	Uremia	Ft. Thomas, Ky

84

Date	Name of Deceased	Sex	Race	Age	Marital	Residence & Place of Death	Orlando Resident	Occupation	Place of Birth	Cause of Death	Place of Burial
30-Jan	*Franklin Thos Burke	M	W	11	S	Melbourne, Fla /O.G.H	5 ds		Springfield, Oh	Gas Bacillus?	Melbourne, Fla
31-Jan	*Miss Stella E. Hill	F	W	76	S	Pine Castle Road	3 yrs	At Home	Clarksville, Pa	Morbis Cardiac? Valvular	Wattsburg, Pa
2-Feb	*Ouida Fay May	F	W	1	S	Holapaw, Fla /Near Clinic Bldg	1 hr		Miss	Influenza	St. Cloud, Fla
2-Feb	Mette? Calston	F	C	31	M	502 W Pine	23 yrs	Cook	Orlando	Acute Salpingitis	Greenwood
3-Feb	*Ruth Elnora Wilson	F	W	2	S	N Philadelphia St.	2 mo		Orlando	Marasmus	Greenwood
4-Feb	*Infant of Mr & Mrs Archie Lott	M	W		S	610 S. Division			Orlando	Stillborn	Greenwood
4-Feb	*Mrs Emma Jessie Dyrenforth	F	W	54	M	Clearwater, Fla /Fla San	7 ds	Trained Nurse	Buckingham, Quebec, Can	Myocarditis	Quebec, Canada
5-Feb	Paris William Singleton	M	C	2 ds	S	413 S Parramore	2 ds		Orlando	Icterus Monaton?	Greenwood
5-Feb	Malcom Gemloch?	M	C	26	M	516 W Long	26 yrs	Chauffeur	Orlando	Uremia	Greenwood
5-Feb	Geo Buggs, Jr	M	C	9 ds	S	1232 W Robinson	9 ds		Orlando	Don't Know	
5-Feb	*Henry D. Finnin	M	W	50	S	215 S Garland	20 yrs	Transfer Business	N Y City	Cerebral Apoplexy	Greenwood
6-Feb	Maria Fudge	F	C	6	S	525 W Robinson	3 yrs	School Girl	Silverton, Ga	Broncho Pneumonia	Greenwood
6-Feb	*Betty Joe Vining	F	W	1	S	Rosewood Ave	1 yr 2mos		Orlando	Lobar Pneumonia	Greenwood
6-Feb	*Infant of Mr & Mrs Joseph Peach	M	W	1 da	S	9 Grove Hill Court	1 mo		Orlando	Prematurity	Greenwood
6-Feb	*Frank Power Hassler	M	W	61	M	Chicago, Ill /O.G.H.	2 ds	Journalist	Cochranton, Pa	Myocarditis	Chicago, Ill
7-Feb	*Mrs Esther A. Haight	F	W	79	W	Hesperia, Mich /Orlando Ave	2 mo	At Home	Barry Co., Mich	Angina Pectoris	Hesperia, Mich
7-Feb	*Mrs Ella Adams	F	W	42	M	Grant Ave	5 yrs	At Home	Ga	Carcinoma of Sigmoid	Greenwood
7-Feb	*Marguerite Wait	F	W	16	S	Wilford Drive	5 yrs		Battle Creek, Mi	Embolism	Greenwood
7-Feb	*Leumas Thomas Bailey	M	W	46	M	Cocoa, Fla /O.G.H.	3 ds	Farming	Clinton, S.C.	Cerebral Laceration	Clinton, S.C.
7-Feb	*Andrew Branch	M	C	72	M	Federal St	6 yrs	Day Labor	Clay Co, Ga	Pistol Shot Wounds	Greenwood
8-Feb	*Ed Stoner, Jr	M	W	42	M	Cocoa, Fla /O.G.H.	3 ds	Cement Finisher	Neb	Gun Shot Wound	Plattsmouth, Neb
8-Feb	*Maurice Edward Collins	M	W	3 yr	S	Melbourne, Fla /O.G.H	1 da		Dayton, Ohio	Gun Shot Wound	Greenwood
8-Feb	*Alice Ruby Hall	F	W	23	M	Lakeland, Fla /O.G.H.	7 ds	At Home	Canon, Ga	General Peritonitis	Winter Park
9-Feb	Jessie Bradshaw	F	C		S	428 Holden			Orlando	Stillborn	Greenwood
10-Feb	*Thos O. Cox	M	W	52	M	Clay St	4 yrs	Real Estate Salesman	Lincoln Co., Mo	Emtro instrannial malaria	Greenwood
16-Feb	Palean Gadson	F	C	2m	Inf	1116 W Robinson	2 mo		Orlando	Broncho Pneumonia	Greenwood
10-Feb	*Wilfred K. Poellien	M	W	4 d	M	208 W Washington /O.G.H.	4 ds		Orlando, Fla	Arterio sclerosis?	Greenwood

1926	Name of Deceased	Sex	Race	Age	Marital	Residence & Place of Death	Orlando Resident	Occupation	Place of Birth	Cause of Death	Place of Burial
14-Feb	Jonia? Watson	M	C	1 m	Inf	1009? Randal	1 mo	Infant	Orlando, Fla	Not Attended by Physician	Greenwood
11-Feb	*Augustis Milton Nicholson	M	W	66	M	618 S. Div	45 yrs	Taxi-dermist	Fayette-ville, N.C.	Pulmonary TB	Greenwood
12-Feb	*William McCormack	M	W	76	W	34 Park Lake Ave	2 yrs 5 mo	Retired	Pike Co., Mis	Myocarditis	Apopka
12-Feb	*Mrs Ada S. Morrison	F	W	45	M	Fla San /E King St	4 mos	At Home	Chatham, Ontario, Can	Acute Nephritis	Sarnia, Ontario, Canada
13-Feb	Robert A. Fistoe	M	W	68	M	Haines City, Fla / O.G.H.	6 ds	Painter	Mo	Intestinal Obstruction	Haines City, Fla
13-Feb	*Joseph H. Treen	M	W	73	W	Wilford Drive	1 y 6 m	Farming	Nov [Nova Scotia?]	Multiple Arthritis	Vault
14-Feb	Leaford Lamps	M	B	27	S	Taxi Driver /502 W. Pine St	27 yrs	Taxi Driver	Orlando, Fla	Mitral Stenosis	Greenwood
14-Feb	*Infant of Mr & Mrs John Wadley Parker	M	W	18 hrs	S	O.G.H.			Orlando, Fla	Premature Birth	Greenwood
15-Feb	Wilber Berry	F	C	41	W	203 Chatham	a 6 yrs	Domes-tic	Ga	Apoplexy	Greenwood
17-Feb	David H. Cottnell	M	C	1	Inf	738 Avondale	1 yr 4 mo	Infant	Orlando	Broncho Pneumonia	Greenwood
18-Feb	Willie Cofield	M	C	29	M	1011 Randall	6 mos	Laborer	Ga	Bright's Disease	Greenwood
12-Feb	*Mrs Katie Mae Summerford	F	W	37	M	Winter Garden /O.G.H.	12 ds	At Home	Tenn	Shock From Operation	Culleka
15-Feb	*Henry Martin Webster	M	W	76	W	918 Greenwood Ave /Glenn Falls, N.Y.	1 yr 6 mo	Farming	Vermont	Cerebral Hemorrhage	Glenn Falls, N.Y.
16-Feb	*Mrs Miria Register	F	W	59	M	Conway Road	3 yrs	At Home	Ga	Apoplexy	Fitzgerald, Ga
17-Feb	*Thos M. Lay	M	W	74	W	Johnson City, Ill /Conway Road	4 mos	Carpen-ter	Livingston Co., Ky	Apoplexy	Marion, Ill
18-Feb	*Pat Auger	M	W	68	M	717 Grand /O.G.H.	5 yrs	Farmer	Toronto, Canada	Coma due to Intestinal Toxemia	Saxon, Wis
19-Feb	*Elsie Julia Johnson	F	W	1 yr	S	631 W Pine	8 mos		Winter Garden, Fla	Diphtheria	Manchester, Ga
20-Feb	*Mrs Addie Rose	F	W	68	M	417 E. Church	3 mos		N.Y.	Influenza, Pneumonia	Schuyler Lake, N.Y.
21-Feb	*Samuel A Robinson	M	W	76	W	128 E. Washington	49 yr 4 mo	Civil En-gineer	Mich	Senile Peritonitis	Greenwood
21-Feb	Emma Fenderson	F	C	60	W	Hilton Hospital /W. Church St	5 ds	School Teacher	N.C.	Lobar Pneumonia	Asheville
22-Feb	Jasper Brady	M	C	1 yr	S	Carter & Hogan	6 mos		Dublin, Ga	Acute Broncho Pneumonia	Greenwood
22-Feb	*Infant of Mr & Mrs Wm H. Taylor	M	W		S	E Cen.			Orlando	Stillborn	Greenwood
22-Feb	*Nora E. Hall	F	W	36	M	Lockhart	1 yr 5 mo	At Home	Triangle, N.Y.	Broncho Pneumonia	Triangle, NY
22-Feb	*Wm F. May	M	W	26	S	521 Macy St /about 7 mi W of Orlando	3 yrs 5 mo	Auto Mec-hanic	N.Y. City	Chest Crushed, Auto Accident	Greenwood

1926	Name of Deceased	Sex	Race	Age	Marital	Residence & Place of Death	Orlando Resident	Occupation	Place of Birth	Cause of Death	Place of Burial
17-Feb	*Samuel Lewis Versoy	M	W	83	W	O.G.H.	9 yrs	Retired	Brooklyn, N.Y.	Senility	Greenwood
19-Feb	*John Kratz	M	W	76	M	Titusville, Fla /Spier's San	6 ds	Retired	Germany	Cardio Nephritis	Vault - Akron, Ohio
20-Feb	Luke Williams	M	C	21	S	213 Chapman	3 yrs	Cement Finisher	Madison	Broncho Pneumonia	Greenwood
22-Feb	*Infant of Mr & Mrs L E Benefield	M	W	4 hrs	S	1206 Rosewood Ave	4 hrs		Orlando	Premature Birth	Lake Hill
22-Feb	*Joseph Heininger	M	W	77	M	21 N Hyer	abt 1 yr	Retired	Penn	Pulmonary Edema	Catholic Cemetery
22-Feb	*Viola Libby	F	W	18	S	West Pownal, Me /7 mi W of Orlando	2 mo		West Pownal, Me	Chest Crushed, AutoAccident	West Pownal, Me
23-Feb	*Infant of Mr & Mrs W. O. Powell	M	W	4 hr	S	Fla San	4 hrs		Orlando	Premature 6½ months	Greenwood
23-Feb	*Wm Roger Abernathy	M	W	15	S	Page Ave	3 yrs		McLean, Texas	Cardiac Failure	Greenwood
24-Feb	*Howard E. Bidwell	M	W	60	M	East Hartford, Conn /Fla San	2 mo 7 ds	Retired, Mfe	Chicago, Ill	Chronic Nephritis	Hartford, Conn
24-Feb	*John P. Spalding	M	W	50	M	1209 ½ Martin, S Nashville, Tenn /O.G.H.	1 mo 6 ds	Plasterer	Logan Co., Ky	Pneumonia	Nashville, Tenn
24-Feb	Henry Coleman	M	C	48	M	219 Lime St	4 yrs	Laborer	Macon Co., Ga	Pulmonary TB	Greenwood
24-Feb	*Randall E. Elmore	M	W	66	W	Ponce De Leon	7 ds	Farming	Ga	Pulmonary TB	Bainbridge, Ga
25-Feb	*Mrs Mary Rich Miller	F	W	67	M	Norristown, Pa / 401 E Hillcrest	5 mo	At Home	Middle-town, Pa	Apoplexy	Norristown, PA
26-Feb	*Geo D. Bridges	M	W	64	M	West Soumerville	1 mo	RR Em-ployee	N Spring-field, Vt	Angina Pectoris	Boston, Mass
26-Feb	*Valentine Bernhardt	M	W	69	M	Fla San /9 Alexander Place	2 mo	Retired	Germany	Miliary Tuberculosis	Jersey City, N.J.
26-Feb	*Florence E. Hamilton	F	W	83	W	Savannah, Ga / Kaley Ave	about 1 yr	At Home	Oliver, Ga	Angina Pectoris	Greenwood
26-Feb	Mollie Cleveland	F	C	85	W	Jackson		Domes-tic	Marianna Fla	Apoplexy	Greenwood
26-Feb	*Infant of Mr & Mrs Clay Benion	M	W		S	O.G.H.			Orlando, Fla	Prematurity	Near Orlando on Home Place
27-Feb	*Theo F. Martin	M	W	84	W	Eldoroda Hotel	2 yrs 6 mo	Retired	?	Myocarditis	Greenwood
27-Feb	Waren Bryant, Jr	M	C	7 ds	S	17 John St	7 ds		Orlando, Fla	Don't Know - No Doctor	Greenwood
28-Feb	Ostella Smith	F	C	30	S	20 Ossie		Laun-dress	Albany, Ga	Pulmonary T B	Greenwood
28-Feb	*Thomas Raymond Dandridge	M	W	1 yr	S	O.G.H. /901 1 /2 W Central Ave	4 mos		Valdosta, Ga	Cerebral Spinal Meningitis	Lakeland, Ga
1-Mar	*Mrs Martha Tyler	F	W	87	W	400 W Central	40 yr	At Home	Orange Co., Fla	Senility	Lake Hill Cemetery
4-Mar	*Mrs Sarah E. Clier	F	W	89	W	800 E. Robinson	5 mos	At Home	Marietta, Ohio	Probably Cerebral Hemorrhage	Clermont, Fla
4-Mar	Will Gilliams	M	C	48	S	717 Long	2 mos	Laborer	Quincy, Fla	Influenza	Quincy, Fla
4-Mar	Viola Webb	F	C	23	M	O.G.H. /Oakland, Fla	1 da	Cook	Fla	Peritonitis	Oakland, Fla

87

1926	Name of Deceased	Sex	Race	Age	Marital	Residence & Place of Death	Orlando Resident	Occupation	Place of Birth	Cause of Death	Place of Burial
4-Mar	Luther Williams	M	C	39	M	446 Jonikin	2 mos	Labor	N.C.	Chronic Int(erstitial) Nephritis	Greenwood
6-Mar	*Georgia Post	F	W	a 40	S	Clarksburg, Wva /122 Hillcrest	3 mos	Office Work		Apoplexy	Clerksburg, Wva
6-Mar	Philip Hunt	M	C	59	M	921 Randall	1 yr	Gardner	Ga	Pulmonary T B	Brooksville, Fla
7-Mar	*Mrs Ruth Collins	F	W	23	M	Haines City, Fla / O.G.H.	5 ds	At Home	Arkansas	Ptomaine Poison	Greenwood
7-Mar	Frank Ruthford	M	C	72	M	720 Parramore	40 y	Labor	Newburg, S.C.	Influenza	Greenwood
5-Mar	*Infant of Mr & Mrs H F Achenbach	F	W		S	Steel St			Orlando	Atelectasis	Cremated
6-Mar	*Patrick Cullen	M	W	52	S	Orlando Sanitarium	6 ds	Gen Work	Ireland	Influenza	Greenwood
8-Mar	*Frank M. Frederickson	M	W	47	M	O.G.H. /Winter Park	4 mos	Clerical Wk	Germany	Acute Dilation of Heart	Des Moines, Iowa
9-Mar	*Jimmie Diefendorf	M	W	5	S	Schenectady, NY /E Cen. Ave	a 5 mos	In School	Schenectady, N.Y.	Accidental Fall	Schenectady, N.Y
14-Mar	Handy Miller	M	C	19	S	213 1 /2 S. Division	3 yrs	Cleaning Cans	Woodbine, Ga	Meningitis	Woodbine, Ga
10-Mar	Tony Pierce	M	C	62	W	502 1 /2 Pine St	33 yr	Porter	Laudens Co, Ga	Apoplexy	Greenwood Cemetery
11-Mar	*Mrs Laura Provost	F	W	80	W	Michigan Ave /Newark, N.J.	3 mo	At Home	N.J.	Broncho Pneumonia	Morristown, N.J.
11-Mar	*Mrs Augusta Krause	F	W	70	W	801 E Washington	9 yrs	At Home	Germany	Pulmonary Edema	Greenwood
12-Mar	*Mrs Rachel Duncan	F	W	85	W	Oil City, Pa /San Juan Hotel	1 mo	At Home	Pittsburgh, Pa	Acute Dilation of Heart	Oil City, Pa
13-Mar	*Edward Christie	M	W	1 yr	S	Lockhart, Fla	5 mos		Orlando, Fla	Broncho Pneumonia	Greenwood
13-Mar	*Dr Wm Jas Maynard	M	W	81	M	Orlando, RFD #3, Box 86 B	15 yrs	Retired	Ann Arbor, Mich	Paralysis, Agitans / Senility	Winter Park
13-Mar	Mason Woodby	M	C	27	M	Lee St. near Carter	3 yrs	Truck Driver	Monro	Anasarca	Greenwood
14-Mar	*Martha Alice Barnes	F	W	53	W	Buffalo, N.Y. /O.G.H.	4 mos	At Home	Phillipsburg	Pulmonary Oedema, Cardiac Failure	Phillipsburg, Pa
15-Mar	*Mrs Sarah A. Clary Reinhard	F	W	55	W	624 N. Hughey	5 yrs	At Home	Taunton	Cardio Nephritis	Greenwood
15-Mar	*Peter Boller	M	W	63	M	Fern Creek Drive	5 mos	Mrg, Retired	Chicago, Ill	Cardiac Incompensation	Chicago, Ill
15-Mar	Jewell Burnadeau [Carey Hand records give surname Miller]	F	W	4	S	237 ½ Boone St	9 mos		Birmingham, Ala	Post Dyphtheria	Purvis, Miss
17-Mar	*William Virden Sipple	M	W	78	W	Milford, Delaware /27 W Conial Drive	18 ds	Monument Dealer, Retired	Milford, Del	Cardiac Failure	Milford, Del
17-Mar	Curtis Nelson	M	C	1yr	S	900 Carter St	1 y 5 d	None	Fla	Lobar Pneumonia	Greenwood

1926	Name of Deceased	Sex	Race	Age	Marital	Residence & Place of Death	Orlando Resident	Occupation	Place of Birth	Cause of Death	Place of Burial
18-Mar	Chas S. Hannah	M	W	53	M	Johnson City, Tenn /O.G.H.	4 ds	Whole-sale Dry Goods Notions	Green Co, Tenn	Chr Myocarditis	Umatilla
19-Mar	*John C. Tibbetts	M	W	70	M	Racine, Wis /Wyoming Hotel	4 mo 7 d	Retired	Covington, Ky	Broncho Pneumonia	Racine, Wis
19-Mar	Infant of Mr & Mrs Walter Riddle	F	W		S	W Church St			Orlando	Stillborn	Lake Hill Cemetery
20-Mar	*Mrs Dena Kestner	F	W	41	M	RFD -Box 671	3 mos	At Home	Ill	Tuberculosis of Hip Joint	Evansville, Ind
21-Mar	*Eugean Alonzo Wimbish	M	W	57	M	Macon, Ga /Fla San	1 mo 4 ds	Supt Const of Roads & Bridges	Macon, Ga	Cardiac Insufficiency	Macon, Ga
21-Mar	*Infant of Mr & Mrs E R Johnson	M	W		S	Fla San			Orlando, Fla	Asphyxia Neonatorum	Greenwood
21-Mar	*Carl T. Link	M	W	27 a	S	Fla San	20 yrs	Entomo-logist	Newport, Ky	Cardiac In-compensation	Greenwood
21-Mar	*Bignaute Batista	M	W	42 a	S	Cheney	1 yr 6 mo	Day Labor	Italy	Auto Accident	Greenwood
22-Mar	*Samuel N. Willner	M	W	56	M	Newark, N.J.	4 ds	Retired	Austria	Suicide by Hanging	Newark, N.J.
22-Mar	Nell Molphur	F	C			409 Holden	1 da		Orlando	Aborted	Greenwood
24-Mar	*Mrs Dora L Garner	F	W	50 a	M	Clear Lake Garden	2 yrs 6 mo	At Home	W. Va.	Organic Heart Disease	Kingwood, W. Va
21-Mar	*Chas W Fields	M	W	78	M	203 Harwood Ave	32 yrs	Retired	Providence R I	Senility	Greenwood
24-Mar	*Pauline May	F	W	11 m	S	S. Delaney St	11m 5 d		Orlando	Acute Pyelitis?	Greenwood
21-Mar	Marshial F. Griffin	M	C	80	W	320 W Patrick	30	Farming	S.C.	Paralysis	Greenwood
25-Mar	*Walter Lee Crews	M	W	36	M	938 E Palmer	9 mos	Manager of Citrus Exchange	Fla	Lobar Pneumonia	Greenwood
26-Mar	*Mrs Ellen J. Miner	F	W	67	M	1507 E Central Ave	3 mos	At Home	Ohio	Carcinoma of Rectum	Bambridge, Ohio
26-Mar	*Leonard E. Benefeld	M	W	1 yr	S	Garvin St	1 yr 26 ds		Orlando	Pneumonia	Lake Hill Cemetery
26-Mar	James E Handshaw	M	W	70	M	O.G.H. /Long Island, N.Y.	1 da	Retired	N.Y.	Senile Dementia due to Gen Auto Toxemia	St. Cloud, Fla
26-Mar	Susie Williams	F	C	66	W	523 W Jackson	16 yrs	Rooming House	Jax, Fla	Intestinal Nephritis	Greenwood
27-Mar	*Infant of Mr & Mrs Berkley Blackman	F	W		S	Fla San			Orlando, Fla	Stillborn	Winter Park
29-Mar	James Blount	M	W	11 ds	S	6 mi E of O.	12 ds		Orange Co	Icterus Neonatorum	6 mi E of O
30-Mar	*Mrs Mary E Devier	F	W	72	M	615 Broadway /Belmar, N.Y.	2 mos	At Home	Philadel-phia, PA	Organic Heart Disease	West Lawn Branch, N.Y.
26-Mar	*James Theodore Venable	M	W	43	M	O.G.H.	3 mo	RR Switch-man	Texas	Shock & Hemorrhage, Engine Turned Over on him in accident, McAllister, Okla	
29-Mar	*James Laverne McKenzie	M	W	5yr	S	O.G.H.	5 y +		Ark	Diabetic Coma	Greenwood
2-Apr	Roy Page	M	C	2m 19d	S	504 Jernigan	2 mo 19 ds		Orlando	Acute Gastritis	Greenwood Cemetery

1926	Name of Deceased	Sex	Race	Age	Marital	Residence & Place of Death	Orlando Resident	Occupation	Place of Birth	Cause of Death	Place of Burial
29-Mar	Dan Austin	M	C	24	M	O.G.H. / Savannah, Ga	1 da	Laborer	S.C.	Hemorrhage	Greenwood
1-Apr	*Mrs Sarah C. Cannon	F	W	62	M	RFD #1	9 mo	At Home	Ky	Cerebral Hemorrhage	Greenwood
2-Apr	*Fred J. Simmons	M	W	80	M	Detroit, Mich /O.G.H.	1 mo	Retired	N.Y.	Bronchopneumonia	Detroit, Mich
2-Apr	*John T. Thorne	M	W	76	W	Forrest, Ill /O.G.H.	2 ds	Retired	England	Broncho pneumonia	Forrest, Ill
2-Apr	*John A. Barclay	M	W	67	M	4128 DeLaney	15 yrs	Real Estate	N.Y.	Cerebral Hemorrhage	Sioux City, Iowa
3-Apr	*John Edward Frye	M	W	64	M	RFD#3 /Star Garage, W Church St	2 yrs	Farming	N.C.	Fell Dead, Probably Apoplexy	Lake Hill
3-Apr	*Larney Pitcher Carr	M	W	77	M	Farimont, W. Va.	4 mos	Retired	W. Va.	Double Lobar Pneumonia	Fairmont, W. Va.
3-Apr	*Mary C. Stearns	F	W	71	S	Hudson, N.H. /E Concord Ave	2 mos	At Home	N.Y.	Colitis	Hudson, N.H.
4-Apr	*Annetta B. McConnell	F	W	52	M	RFD /Fla San	12 yrs	At Home	Ohio	Cancer	Greenwood
4-Apr	*Mrs Alice Yeakel Bannard	F	W	69	M	Chicago, Ill /Wyoming Hotel	7 ds	At Home	Ind	Angina Pectoris	Chicago, Ill
4-Apr	*Columbus Richard Gilbert	M	W	23	S	Marianna,	6 ds	Engineer	Marriana, Fla	Embolus in Coronary Artery	Marriana, Fla
5-Apr	Mary L. Reese	F	C	34	M	Hilton Hospital	2 yrs	House-wife	Ga	Collapse of Heart	Harris, Ga
5-Apr	Richard Cobs	M	C	16	S	815 W Jefferson	6 mos	Laborer	Ga	Pneumonia	Greenwood
7-Apr	Infant of Anderson & Gertrude Hendricks	M	C		S	932 W Bentley			Orlando	Stillborn	Greenwood
3-Apr	*John P Glasgow	M	W	60	M	133 Earnestine /O.G.H.	5 mo	Teacher	Newberry, S.C.	Nephritis	Newberry, S.Car
3-Apr	*Infant of Mr & Mrs E J Weimer	M	W		S	1012 E Jackson			Orlando, Fla	Stillborn	Greenwood
3-Apr	*Infant of Mr & Mrs M O Gordon	M	W		S	Fla San			Orlando, Fla	Stillborn	Greenwood
6-Apr	*Lewis Reiss	M	W	a 65	unk	Fla San	5 yrs	Day Labor	Germany	Senility	Winter Park
6-Apr	*Herman Hudson	M	W	5	S	Orange Heights	1 yr 6 mo		Columbus, Ga	Rapidly Growing Neuro Blastoma	Greenwood
6-Apr	*Mrs Ella M Drew	F	W	a 65	W	Chevy Chase, Md /Fremont Hotel	3 mo	At Home	D.C.	Myocarditis	Washington, D.C.
7-Apr	*W A Edwards	M	W	4 mo	S	Altoma St	4 mo 5 ds		Orlando	Marasmus & Wasting from Birth	Greenwood
8-Apr	*Infant of Mr & Mrs Walter S. Scott	F	W		S	Fla San			Orlando	Premature Birth	Greenwood
8-Apr	*George H. Green	M	W	50	M	100 N. Main	5 yrs	Potter	Pa	Broncho pneumonia	Greenwood
9-Apr	Roma Smith	M	C	12	S	Spring Lake	1 yr	None	Ga	Drowned	Tifton, Ga
10-Apr	Isiah Hall	M	W	23	M	922 S Division	4 mos	Labor	Ga	Acute Nephritis	Cuthbert, Ga

90

1926	Name of Deceased	Sex	Race	Age	Marital	Residence & Place of Death	Orlando Resident	Occupation	Place of Birth	Cause of Death	Place of Burial
10-Apr	*Mrs Fannie Bridges Davis	F	W	61	W	Orlando	9 yrs	At Home	Ky	Angina Pectoris	Carrollton, Ky
12-Apr	*Mrs Mary R Dean	F	W	72	M	310 Long	42 yrs	At Home	Germany	Nephritis & Hypertension	Greenwood
12-Apr	*Chas A Finzel	M	W	55	M	Miami, Fla /Fla San	2 mos	Real Estate	Ohio	Unresolved Broncho Pneumonia	Miami, Fla
12-Apr	James Braswell	M	C	10 hrs	S	850 Otis St	1 da		Orlando	Stillborn	Greenwood
13-Apr	*Alvin Jefferson Nye	M	W	57	M	305 E Church St	20 yrs	Fruit Grower	Romeo, Mich	Anaphylaxis	Greenwood
15-Apr	*Mrs Martha Elizabeth Johnson	F	W	76	W	19 Princeton	40 yrs	At Home	Ga	Chr Myocarditis	Greenwood
15-Apr	*Ernest C Evans	M	W	5 mo	S	Conway Road /O.G.H.	5 mo 19 ds		Conway, Fla	Acute Gastric Con	Conway
16-Apr	*John T Bohen	M	W	a 63	M	Live Oak, Fla /Fla San	14 ds	Mechanic	S.C.	Myocarditis	Live Oak, Fla
16-Apr	*Joseph L. Laube	M	W		S	Fla San			Orlando	Stillborn	Bloomington, Ind
16-Apr	Stillborn of Homer Pryer	M	C		S	McFall St			Orlando	Stillborn	Greenwood
17-Apr	*Lydia J. Thompson	F	W	65	W	Clermont, Fla /O.G.H.	14 yrs	House keeper	Ohio	Chronic Nephritis	Clermont, Fla
18-Apr	*Maggie Bushbee	F	W	14	S	Fuller Crossing, Fla /O.G.H.	3 ds		Ala	Mesenteric Abscess	Ocoee, Fla
18-Apr	Diniah Neason	F	C	24	M	513 Gore Ave	6 yrs	Cook	Ga	Broncho Pneumonia	Greenwood
19-Apr	*Clara Louis Johnson	F	W	26	M	Kaley Ave / Fla San	3 yrs	At Home	Ohio	Eclampsia	Zanesville, Ohio
19-Apr	*Infant of Mr & Mrs C Johnson	F	W		S	Fla San /Ka			Orlando, Fla	Stillborn	Zanesville, Ohio
21-Apr	*Soven Gutar Holmquist	M	W	66	M	710 N Summerlin	4 yrs	Mason, Contractor	Sweden	Myocarditis	Greenwood
21-Apr	Frederick W Rice Jr	M	W	4	S	Amherst Apt /O.G.H.	3 mos		Brooklyn, N.Y.	Acute Broncho Pneumonia	Brooklyn, N.Y.
22-Apr	*Jackson Byrd	M	W	77	M	RFD, Orlando	40 yrs	Farming	Ga	Pulmonary Edema	Lake Hill Cemetery
23-Apr	Johnny Taylor	M	C	19	S	Carter /Armory Bldg	19 yrs	Laborer	Orlando	Acute Cardiac Dilatation	Greenwood
15-Apr	Mrs. Martha Elizabeth Johnson [duplicate]	F	W	76	W	19 Princeton Ave	40 yrs	At Home	Eaton, Ga	Uremia	Greenwood
23-Apr	*Josephine Adams	F	W	75	M	Citrus Ave	14 yrs	At Home	Mo	Cardiac Failure	Greenwood
23-Apr	*Harriet E Underhill	F	W	74	M	Fern Creek & Harding	6 mos	At Home	Mass	Cancer of Uterus	Vault
27-Apr	*Infant of Mr & Mrs Roy W Sylvester		W		S	S Fern Creek Drive			Orlando, Fla	Stillborn	Conway Cemetery
27-Apr	*Robert English	M	W	48	M	Tampa Ave	2 mos	Moulder in Foundry	Fort Valley, Ga	Pernicious Anemia	Winter Garden
9-Mar	Damon C Parker, Jr	M	W		S	Fla San Hosp			Orlando	Stillborn	D K
24-Apr	Infant of Mr & Mrs John H. Caldwell	M	W		S	O.G.H.			Orlando	Asphyxia	Leesburg, Fla

1926	Name of Deceased	Sex	Race	Age	Marital	Residence & Place of Death	Orlando Resident	Occupation	Place of Birth	Cause of Death	Place of Burial
24-Apr	Elvira Mae Caldwell	F	W	33	M	Astor Park, Fla /O.G.H.	few days	House-work	Mo	Rupture of Uterus	Leesburg, Fla
25-Apr	Unknown (Found Apr. 25)	M	W	a 65	?	Conway Road	?	?	?	?	County Home
25-Apr	Wanan Alan Bass	M	C	49	M	512 S Division	5 yrs	Carpenter	S.C.	Pericarditis	Greenwood
26-Apr	*Fred Johnson	M	W	49	M	Daytona Beach, Fla /Fla San	1 mo 2 ds	Cafeteria	Penn	Cardiac De-compensation	Kane, Penn
26-Apr	Taylor J. Gilbert	M	C	36	M	Titusville, Fla /O.G.H.	abt a mo	Common Labor	Ga	Fracture of First Lumbar Vertebra	Titusville, Fla
27-Apr	Wesley Grimes	M	C	4 h	Inf	Newman & Williams Sts	4 hrs		Orlando	Premature Birth	Greenwood
28-Apr	*Helen Lee Redditt	F	W	53	M	Maitland, Fla /O.G.H.	a 1mo	At Home	Tenn	Lobar Pneumonia	Lake Howell
29-Apr	Infant of Hillard Johnson	F	C			1115 Randall			Orlando	Injury to Cord	Greenwood
29-Apr	*Samuel A. Sage	M	W	a 65	M	Marked Tree, Ark /O.G.H.	a 3 mos	Surveyor	Ark	Toxemia	Marked Tree, Ark
29-Apr	*Dedrick Joseph Harper, Jr	M	W	3 yr	S	Weldona Dr /O.G.H.	3 yrs		Orle?, Mass	Acute IleoColitis	Catholic
1-May	*Wm Arthur Libby	M	W	51	M	221 S Garland	6 yrs	Real Estate	Maine	Angina Pectoris	Greenwood
3-May	*Geo W. Cannada	M	W	a 56	M	Gen Del	2 mos	Farming	Fla	Apoplexy	Drowdy Cemetery
5-May	Agnes Ellis	F	C	6 m	S	215 S Division	6 mos		Orlando	Broncho Pneumonia	Greenwood
3-May	Rosa L. Taylor	F	C	a 15	S	415 S. Parramore	3 yrs	School GIrl	Fla	Endocarditis	Greenwood
5-May	*Ada Rachel Kelly	F	W	36	M	St Cloud /Fla San.	16 ds	At Home	Ala	Streptococcic Laryngitis	Perdido, Ala
5-May	*Mrs Mary Whitaker	F	W	63	M	834 Highland /Chicago, Ill	a 9 mos	At Home	Tenn	Carcinoma of Liver	Cremated
7-May	Alena Williams	F	C	40	M	905 Carter	4 mos	Cafe	Barnsville, Ga	Chronic Nephritis	Greenwood
8-May	Joseph F. Williams	M	C	54	M	907 Long St	10 ds	Minister	Fla	Mitral Stenosis	Lake City, Fla
9-May	Alice Woodley	F	C	51	M	427 Chapman	3 yrs	Laun-dress	Ga	Uterine Cancer	Greenwood Cem
11-May	Isac Alfonce Peepler	M	C	19 d	S	728 W South St	19 ds		Orlando	Measles	Greenwood
2-May	Adrian Mc Nerve	M	C	28	M	O.G.H. /Barbados, BWI	2 yrs 1 da	Tailor	Granada, BWI	Bullet Wound of Head	Greenwood
9-May	Mose Calloway	M	C	52	M	700 S Parramore	4 yrs	Labor	Ga	Senility	Greenwood
7-May	*Hassie Ricks	F	W	82	S	1008 E Concord Ave /Spiers San	2 yrs	At Home	Ala	Bronchial Pneumonia	Greenwood
8-May	*Jessie Hardy Caldwell	M	W	64	M	24 West	21 yrs	Retired	Americus, Ga	Bronchial Pneumonia	Greenwood
9-May	*Mrs Clara D Barrows	F	W	68	W	501 Grand Ave	30 yrs	At Home	Ill	Myocarditis	Greenwood
9-May	*Mrs Harriet Halley	F	W	44	M	Forest City Road	13 yrs	At Home	Wis	Pellagra	Greenwood
12-May	*John Martin Sheehy	M	W	32	M	Schroon River, N.Y. /O.G.H.	6 mos	Hotel Business	N.Y.	Acute Cardiac Dilitation	Riverside, N.Y.

92

1926	Name of Deceased	Sex	Race	Age	Marital	Residence & Place of Death	Orlando Resident	Occupation	Place of Birth	Cause of Death	Place of Burial
13-May	*Mrs Eva A Paul	F	W	70	W	O.G.H. /21 Palmer Ave, Buffalo, N.Y.	1 da	At Home	N.Y.	Adema Carcinoma of Stomach	Brodine, N.Y.
16-May	Queen Ester Harkans	F	C	3m	S	900 E South St	3 mo		Orlando	Don't Know	Greenwood
16-May	Ella Dow	F	W	68	M	O.G.H.	14 ds	House-wife	Ill	General Toxemia	White Heath, Ill
16-May	Johnnie Johnson	M	C	22	S	O.G.H. /Groveland	1 da	Laborer	Ga	Gun Shot Wounds	Greenwood
17-May	*Albert Geo Foster	M	W	22	M	O.G.H. / 115 America St	a 2 yrs	Clerk in P.O.	N.J.	Gun Shot Wound in Head	Dover, N.J.
18-May	*Caroline Hazel Decker Foster	F	W	17	M	115 America St	a 3 yrs	At Home	N.Y.	Gun Shot Wound of Head & Chest	Greenwood
18-May	Mrs Effie Demastus	F	W	28	M	O.G.H. /Winter Garden, Fla	12 ds	At Home	Tenn	Septicemia	Culleoka, Tenn
18-May	*Luciell McBride	F	C	22	D	O.G.H. /529 S Division	3 yrs	Domestic Wk at O.G.H.	Ga	Pneumonia	Louisville, Ga
18-May	*Samuel Lenard Parker	M	W	51	M	206 E Livingston	2 yrs 6 mo	Sales Mgr O. Posteners	N.Y	Angina Pectoris	Felmington, N.J.
9-May	Charles N. Lindner	M	W	11	S	Maitland Fla /Lake Lillian	1 yr 6 mo		S.D	Accidentally Drowned	Winter Park
18-May	Infant of Mr & Mrs Ed D. Gallops	F	W		S	N.W. Part of City /O.G.H.			Orlando, Fla	Premature Birth	Greenwood
20-May	Harry Farrer	M	C	52	M	1100 W South St	10 yrs	Labor	Va	Chronic Atrophy of Liver	Burksville, Va
21-May	Chas A. Waldron	M	W	59	M	E Orange Ave /Ft Meyers, Fla	1 yr 6 mo	Carpenter, Retired	Washington, D.C.	Organic Heart Disease	Greenwood
21-May	Frank A. Parker	M	W	58	M	Daytona Beach	11 ds	City Clerk	Ill	Embolus	Daytona Beach, Fla
22-May	*Infant of J. H. & Elnora Coleman	M	C		S	417 S Paramore			Orlando, Fla	Stillborn	Greenwood
26-May	J. C. Mumford	M	C	10 mo	S	1204 E South St	10 mos	Chronic Colitis	Orlando, Fla	Chronic Colitis	Greenwood
23-May	Stepney Adams	M	C	43	M	910 Edna	1 yr 1 mo	Common Labor	Ga	Paralysis	Apalachicola
23-May	*Mrs Emelie Moeckel	F	W	71	W	O.G.H. /Atlanta, Ga	4 mos	At Home	Ind	Acute Dilitation of Heart	Atlanta, Ga
23-May	*William Thomas Wilson	M	W	13	S	Fern Creek & Gatlin	1 yr 7 mo	At Home	Pa	Organic Heart Disease	Greenwood
23-May	*Mary Louise Murray	F	W	1 yr	S	Clermont, Fla /O.G.H.	20 ds		Clermont, Fla	Vincents Angina	Clermont, Fla
24-May	*Mrs Amelia Thom	F	W	a 63	M	101 Key Ave, Eustis /Fla San & Hosp	1 da 6 wks	House-wife	Penn	Cardiac Asthma	Eustis, Fla
24-May	*Hattie A. Wood	F	W	72	M	417 E Anderson / Battle Creek	8 yrs	At Home	Mich	Carcinoma of Uterus	Greenwood
26-May	*Infant of Mrs Evert Rowland	F	W		S	E Washington St			Orlando, Fla	Stillborn	Davenport, Fla

1926	Name of Deceased	Sex	Race	Age	Marital	Residence & Place of Death	Orlando Resident	Occupation	Place of Birth	Cause of Death	Place of Burial
25-May	Corneluis Stoothoff	M	W	58	M	Sanford, Fla /Fla San & Hosp	3 mos	Farmer	L.I., N.Y.	Cerebral Hemorrhage	Sanford, Fla
27-May	Addie Williams	F	C	24	M	547 W Holden	3 mos	House-wife	N.C.	Acute Nephritis, Dilitation of Heart	Greenwood
27-May	Lizzie Thomas	F	C	51	W	601 W Jackson	28 yrs	House-keeper	Monti-cello	Carcinoma of Stomach	Greenwood
27-May	*Ballie C. Crisp	M	W	72	M	O.G.H. /Davenport, Fla	3 ds	Holly Hill Grove & Fruit Co	Laurens Co., S.C.	Acute Dilitation of Heart	Davenport, Fla
27-May	Viola Demps	F	C	50	S	9 Routherford	10 yr	Cook	Fla	Broncho-pneumonia	Greenwood
27-May	*Ruth Mary Wilson	F	W	8	S	Keyston Drive	8 mo		Orlando, Fla	Congenital Hydro-cephalic	Greenwood
28-May	*Russel M. Sparks	M	W	17	S	O.G.H. /1724 Portland	7 yrs	Student	Akron, Ohio	Fracture of 5 & 6 Cervices, Spinal Cord	Vault
29-May	*Valton H. Sphaler	M	W	28	M	O.G.H. /400 Tampa Ave	20 yrs	Labor	McRae, Ala	Acute Gastritis	Greenwood
29-May	*Mrs Allie Joslin	F	W	67	M	610 W Concord	abt 4 yrs	At Home	Alpena, Mich	Organic Heart Disease	Carey Hand
30-May	*Albert E Schue	M	W	42	M	O.G..H. /S Fern Creek	a 7 yrs	Farming & Grove Wk	Fulda	Acute Cardiac Dilitation	Greenwood
30-May	*Infant of Mr & Mrs Frank D Bloodworth	M	W		S	114 N. Garland			Orlando, Fla	Stillborn	Greenwood
30-May	*Harrold Lee Wilson	M	W	13	S	O.G.H. /Umatilla	18 ds	School	Va	Acute Pericarditis, Acute Endocarditis	Umatilla, Fla
31-May	Quinton Clarence Davis	M	W	63	M	O.G.H. /Eustis, Fla	10 mos	Minister	N.C.	Shock-Operation for Diverticula?	Portsmouth, Va
1-Jun	*Max L. Mathews	M	W	1 yr	S	O.G.H. /Holopaw, Fla	1 da		Holopaw, Fla	Acute Broncho Pneumonia	St Cloud, Fla
30-May	*Louis Kellog	M	W	79	W	O.G.H. /Ferris Drive	4 yrs	Retired	Troy, N.Y	Chr Nephritis	Greenwood
27-May	*Infant of Mr & Mrs W R Smythe	F	W		S	O.G.H.			Orlando, Fla	Anaphylaxis	Greenwood
27-May	Gineatha O'Neal	F	C	6 m	S	Federal St	6 mos	Infant	Orlando, Fla	Broncho Pneumonia	Greenwood
30-May	Elvine Sweet	F	C	71	W	507 W Long	32 yrs	House-keeper	Quincy, Fla	Mitral Re-gurgitation	Greenwood
3-Jun	Curtis Sceley	M	C	16	S	319 Short	11 mos	None	Fla	Acute Lobar Pneumonia	Greenwood
4-Jun	Rufis Williams	M	C	46	M	447 Lincoln Court	10 ds	Farmer	Center Hill, Fla	Acute Uremia	Center Hill, Fla
2-Jun	*Othey Lee Duke, Jr	M	W	1 m	S	O.G.H. / Haines City, Fla	1 da		Haines City, Fla	Acute IleoColitis	Haines City, Fla
2-Jun	Othey Lee Duke, Jr [duplicate record?]	M	W	2 m	S	O.G.H. / Haines City, Fla	1 da	Infant	Haines City, Fla	Acute IleoColitis	Haines City, Fla
4-Jun	*Geo W Cameron	M	W	59	M	1247 Minnesota Ave	10 mo	Retired	Fairbanks Iowa	Acute Indigestion	Independence, Iowa

1926	Name of Deceased	Sex	Race	Age	Marital	Residence & Place of Death	Orlando Resident	Occupation	Place of Birth	Cause of Death	Place of Burial
4-Jun	*Adolphus J. Paulnot	M	W	65	W	415 W Central	9 mo	Carpenter	Ogle-thorpe, Ga	Shock Following Operation for Ruptured Appendix	Oglethorpe, Ga
5-Jun	*Burton Clarence Datson	M	W	52	M	Conway Road /Winter Garden Road	11 yrs	Dairy Business	Cleveland Ohio	Cerebral Hemorrhage	Greenwood
5-Jun	*Mrs Marie De Porter	F	W	43	M	RFD 19 /O.G.H.	20 yrs	At Home	Belgium	Fracture of Spine	Greenwood
6-Jun	*Perry R. Holland	M	W	46	M	448 Cherokee Drive	7 yrs	Builder	Lawrence Mich	Acute Dilation of Heart	Greenwood
7-Jun	*Russell Pope Johnson	M	W	48	M	817 E. Livingston	17 yrs	Salesman	Griffin, Ga	Chronic Myocarditis	Greenwood
7-Jun	*Loyd Lee Pace	M	W	6	S	2116 N. Orange / O.G.H.	2 mo 15 ds		Phoenix City	Shock Following Operation	Gastonia, N.C.
8-Jun	Lillian Sims	F	C	4	S	611 McFall St.	4 mo 7 ds		Orlando	Malaria Fever	Greenwood
8-Jun	*James L. Lineberger	M	W	14	S	W Kaley Ave	3 yrs	School	Tift Co., Ga	Accidental Drowning	Greenwood
8-Jun	*Infant of Mr & Mrs R. H. Tedder, Jr [twin]	M	W		S	Atlanta, Ga /Fla San			Orlando, Fla	Stillborn	Greenwood
8-Jun	*Infant of Mr & Mrs R. H. Tedder, Jr [twin]	M	W		S	Atlanta, Ga /Fla San			Orlando, Fla	Stillborn	Greenwood
10-Jun	*Elwood Hammond	M	W	7	S	Tangerine, Fla /Fla San	3 ds		Brewster, Fla	Acidosis	Apopka
9-Jun	Riley Whitfield Jennings	M	W	57	M	Kissimmee, Fla /O.G.H.	4 ds	Hotel Proprietor	Dawson, Ga	Auto? Uremia	Dawson, Ga
7-Jun	Robert Leslie	M	C	a 35	S	Chatanooga /O.G.H.	2 mos	Day Labor	?	TB Pneumonia	County Home
8-Jun	Leathen Brown	F	C	a 47	S	16 Ossie	1 yr	Laundress	Quincy, Fla	Pulmonary Hemorrhage	Greenwood
9-Jun	James Bell	M	C	9 mo	S	800 S. Parramore	9 mos		Orlando	Lobar Pneumonia	Greenwood
11-Jun	Doris May McNeal	F	C	7 mo	S	826 W Livingston	7 mos			Gastro Enteritis	Greenwood
11-Jun	Sopha Holland	F	C	a 42	M	E Jackson	3 yrs	House-wife	White Co., Ga	Acute Gastritis, Indigestion	Greenwood
13-Jun	Fred Edwards Jones	M	C	a 10 mo	S	1415 E South St	10 mos		Orlando, Fla	Acute Colitis	Greenwood
13-Jun	*Infant of Mr & Mrs J M Williams	M	W			Forest & E Robinson			Orlando, Fla	Bad Conditon of Mother	Greenwood
14-Jun	Willie Sarey	F	C	38	S	612 W Church St	14 ds	Cook	Ga	Parenchyma-tous Nephritis	Highsprings, Fla
14-Jun	Timmatha Luckus	M	C		S	O.G.H.			Orlando	Stillborn	Greenwood
15-Jun	Susie Pears	F	C	52	S	6 Ossie St	8 yrs	None	S.C.	Malaria Fever	Greenwood
15-Jun	Jane May Cutts	F	C	1 y	S	714 Woods	1 yr	Infant	Orlando	Whooping Cough	Greenwood
16-Jun	*Infant of Mr & Mrs A. J. Webb	F	W		S	McBro Court		Infant	Orlando	Stillborn	Greenwood
16-Jun	*Kassie K. Powell	M	W	48	M	122 E South St /O.G.H.	4 yrs	Real Estate	Hamilton Co, Fla	Carcinoma of Colon	Greenwood

1926	Name of Deceased	Sex	Race	Age	Marital	Residence & Place of Death	Orlando Resident	Occupation	Place of Birth	Cause of Death	Place of Burial
17-Jun	*Sarah J. Farmer	F	W	4	S	O.G.H. /Ocoee	2 ds		Ocoee, Fla	Acute Broncho Pneumonia	Lathonia, Ga
17-Jun	*Grace Quin	F	W	1 m	S	O.G.H. /McComb, Miss	1 mo	At Home	Miss	Accidental Poisoning	McComb, Miss
17-Jun	*Arial Porter Case	M	W	63	M	Plant City, Fla / Fla San	7 ds	Mechan-ical Foreman	Kans	Apoplexy	Plant City, Fla
21-Jun	Bert Smith	M	W	a 55	DK	Lake Eola / 28 Garland St	6 or 7 mo	Labor	D K	Drowning, Suicidal	Greenwood
16-Jun	Fannie E. Holliday	F	W	63	M	1910 N. Mills	abt 7 y	At Home	Clyde, N.Y.	Apoplexy	Greenwood
16-Jun	Charles Hankerson	M	C	2m	S	431 S Parramore	2m +	None	Orlando	EnteroColitis	Greenwood
20-Jun	*Marshall Lee Dudley	M	W	9hr	S	Fla San	9 hrs 5 min	None	Orlando	Premature	Oxford, Fla
21-Jun	*Albert Lee Bass	M	W	3	S	O.G.H. / Kissimmee, Fla	11 ds		Rome, Ga	Empyema	Kissimmee, Fla
22-Jun	*Ruby Mae Hall	F	W	27	M	O.G.H. / Conway Road	4 mo	At Home	Sampson City, Fla	Shock & Toxemia	Palatka, Fla
22-Jun	*Mrs. Clara N. Patterson	F	W	54	M	540 Princeton Ave / St. Catherine, Ont Canada	9 mo	At Home	Philadel-phia	Myocardial Degeneration	St Catherine, Ont., Canada
23-Jun	G. I. Dyer	M	W	52	M	Heights Sani-tarium /Sanford, Fla	6 ds	Painter	Tenn	Broncho-pneumonia with Effusion	John City, Tenn
23-Jun	Amos Smith	M	C	74	M	O.G.H. /Zellwood, Fla	3 ds	Farmer	Wilming-ton, N.C.	Uremia	Zellwood, Fla
23-Jun	*Chas V. Tanner	M	W	68	M	RFD Orlando	65 yrs	Retired	Ga	Aneurysm of Aorta Ruptured	Oak Ridge
23-Jun	James Smith	M	C	20 min	Inf				Orlando	Premature	Greenwood
24-Jun	*Virginia Agness Myers	F	W	4 m	S	S. Mill St	4 mo 8 ds		Orlando	Acute Gastritis, Intest. Intox	Greenwood
24-Jun	*William Carey Lanter, Jr	M	W	3	S	O.G.H.	9 mos		Middle-town, Ohio	Fracture of Skull	Middletown, Ohio
24-Jun	Janie May Smith	F	C		Inf	315 S Byron	1 hr		Orlando	Premature	Greenwood
25-Jun	*Infant of Mr & Mrs Wm McFarland	F	W		Inf	928 S. Mill			Orlando	Stillborn	Greenwood
25-Jun	*Harry B. Cover, Jr	M	W	33	M	O.G.H. /Vienna, Ga	1 mo 7 ds	Cabinet Maker	Peoria, Ill	Bullet Wound Perforating Bladder	Vienna, Ga
24-Jun	Garfield Wellington Johnson	M	C		Inf	706 W Long			Orlando	Stillborn	Greenwood
27-Jun	Jam_ Donell	F	C	39	M	828 S Parramore	9 mo	Cook	Ga	Pellagra	Greenwood
27-Jun	*Infant of Mr & Mrs Louis Kilgore	F	W		Inf	O.G.H. /Pine Castle, Fla			Orlando	Premature	Greenwood
27-Jun	*Elizabeth Gorvett	F	W	58	M	O.G.H. /Ocoee	4 ds	At Home	Canada	Diabetes Mellitus	St. Thomas, Ont
28-Jun	*Linnie Evans	F	W	1 y	S	Atlanta Ave	2 mo		Tenn	IleoColitis	Greenwood
29-Jun	Fla Sant? [probably *Ruth Ward Eckels]	F	W	4 d	S	Fla San /Ocoee	4 ds		Orlando	Intracranial Hemorrhage	Ocoee, Fla

96

1926	Name of Deceased	Sex	Race	Age	Marital	Residence & Place of Death	Orlando Resident	Occupation	Place of Birth	Cause of Death	Place of Burial
29-Jun	Oliver Lewis	M	C	7m	S	611 McFall St.	12 ds		Ga	Measles	Valdosta, Ga
30-Jun	Helen May Goodrum	F	C	11 m	S	Forest City	11 mos		Fla	Whooping Cough	Forest City
1-Jul	Stella Leaman	F	W	20	M	O.G.H. /Holopaw, Fla	1 da	H W	Miss	Shock Following Operation for Mylitis	St Cloud, Fla
3-Jul	Cannealia Williams	F	C	67 a	M	552 W Long St	40 yrs	House-wife	Talla-hassee	Heart Failure	Greenwood
4-Jul	*Louis V Cook	F	W	1	S	925 W Jackson	a 6 mos		Ga	Acute Nephritis	Nashville, Ga
6-Jul	W M Virgin	M	C	45 a	M	O.G.H. /Jax, Fla	3 mos	Waiter	Jackson-ville, Fla.	Fall from window	Jacksonville
30-Jun	*Mrs Mary Elizabeth Kerce	F	W	35	M	O.G.H. /Ocoee	2 hrs	At Home	Douglas, Ga	Acute Nephritis	Ocoee, Fla
1-Jul	*Infant of Mr & Mrs Willie Kerce?	F	W	1 da	S	O.G.H.	1 da		Orlando, Fla	Alytulosa?	Ocoee, Fla
3-Jul	*Mrs Alice S. Willis	F	W	47 a	D	O.G.H. /Miami, Fla	4 mos	Sales lady, Real Estate	?	Partial Obstruction of Intestine	Reading, Pa
3-Jul	*Mrs Christanna McAllister	F	W	64	W	123 W Church St	10 mos	At Home	England	Chronic Myocarditis	Greenwood
3-Jul	*Harriett Randolf Parkhill	F	W	85	S	615 Woodward Ave	21 yrs	Deacon-ess	Fla	Senility	Jacksonville, Fla.
4-Jul	*Infant of Mr & Mrs Shug Crane	M	W		S	O.G.H. /817 W Central			Orlando, Fla	Failure to Deliver after Coming?	Greenwood
4-Jul	*Mrs Amanda Tyson	F	W	67	W	39 Princeton Avenue /Nashville, Ga	12 mos	At Home	Marion Co., Ga	Cardiac Insufficiency	Adel, Ga
5-Jul	Gertrude Hendricks	F	C	30	M	932 Bentley St	4 yrs	Domestic Work	Camilla, Ga	Acute Gastric Indigestion	Camilla, Ga
3-Jul	*Stephen Jone Bullman	M	W	65	unk	Fla San & Hosp /Bunker Hill, Ill	1 mo	Laborer	Bunker Hill, Ill	Myocarditis	Bunker Hill, Ill
6-Jul	*Frederick A. Sherman	M	W	78	M	203 Annie St	12 yrs	Jewelry Business, Retired	Lonsdale, R.I.	Senile Dementia	Providence, R.I.
7-Jul	Ruth Madison	F	C	30 a	M	612 W Church	abt 2 mos	Don't Know	Dk	Acute Cirrhosis of the Liver	Greenwood
10-Jul	Willie Stoker	M	C	22	S	1664 Kaley Ave	22 ds	None	Orlando	Gastro-enteritis	Greenwood
7-Jul	*Edwin Beeman	M	W	34	M	O.G.H. /Gore Ave	34 yrs	Real Estate	Orlando	Acute Dilation of Heart	Greenwood
13-Jul	*John Bernard Doerr	M	W	61	M	O.G.H. /1107 E Concord	15 yrs	Mechanic, S & L RR	Germany	Pulmonary Edema	Greenwood
14-Jul	Wilbert Springs	M	C	19	S	O.G.H / McMinnville, Tenn	1 da	Labor	McMinn-ville, Tenn	Gun Shot Wound	McMinn-ville, Tenn
8-Jul	*Milledge J. Holley	M	W	44	M	O.G.H. /1710 Long St	1 yr 8 ds	Lineman, Utilities	Akin, S.C.	Came in Contact with Live Wire	Lakeland, Fla
9-Jul	*Albert Harlon Pomeroy	M	W	70 a	M	West Central Ave) /Hartford, Conn	7 ds	Real Estate	Hartford, Conn	Crushed Chest, Auto Accident	Hartford, Conn
14-Jul	*Virginia Doris Smith	F	W	9 mo	S	619 N Parramore	9 mos		Medford, Mass	Status Laryngitis	Greenwood

1926	Name of Deceased	Sex	Race	Age	Marital	Residence & Place of Death	Orlando Resident	Occupation	Place of Birth	Cause of Death	Place of Burial
16-Jul	Lula Chambliss	F	C	46	M	Roberson Alley	3 yrs	Cook	Houston Co., Ga	Carbunculosis	Greenwood
16-Jul	G. W. Washington	M	C	a 70	W	612 W Church St.	4 yrs	Common Labor	Va	Prostatitis	Greenwood
16-Jul	Cealer Moltte	M	C	34	M	229 Westmoreland	1 mo 7 ds	Housewife	McClendonville, S.C.	Acute Dilitation of Heart	Charleston, S.C.
16-Jul	*Infant of Mr & Mrs Perry J. Williams	F	W	4 hrs	S	428 S Rosalind Ave	4 hrs		Orlando, Fla	Premature Birth	Greenwood
17-Jul	*Patrick Henry Thomson	M	W	a 58	M	O.G.H. /Ft. Launderdale	1 da	Real Estate	Lexington Ky	Fracture of Cerebral Vertebra	Lexington, Ky
18-Jul	*Hallie Self Crane	F	W	19	M	O.G.H.	1 yr	At Home	Cherokee, Ala	Pueperal Septicemia	Stevenson, Ala
18-Jul	*Joseph H. Hull	M	W	a 53	M	Sunset Park	53 yrs	Day Labor	Orange Co., Fla	Cardiac Valvular, Diabetic	Greenwood
20-Jul	Infant of Rosa Lap Porter	F	C		S	414 Parramore Alley			Orlando	Stillborn	Greenwood
11-Jul	Maggie J. Lupfer	F	W	a 60	M	O.G.H. /Kissimmee, Fla	15 d /39 y	Home	Penn	General Septicemia	Rose Hill - Kissimmee
18-Jul	Zoby Hartzog	M	W		S	O.G.H.			Orlando	Stillborn	Rose Hill - Kissimmee
21-Jul	*Mrs Catherine E. Wincher?	F	W	75	M	315 Copeland Drive	5 yrs	At Home	Monroe Co., Ohio	Diabetes Mellitus	Greenwood
22-Jul	John Adams	M	C	60	M	O.G.H. /Melbourne, Fla	6 ds	Laborer	Savannah, Ga	Carcinoma of Stomach	S Melbourne, Fla
23-Jul	*Wm C. McElroy	M	W	21	S	O.G.H. /Philips Apts	1 yr 1 mo	Filling Sta	Columbus, Ohio	Starvation - Acidosis	Greenwood
23-Jul	*John Walter Rehse	M	W	59	M	Fairbanks Ave	11 yrs	Retired	Minn	Myocarditis w/ Acute Dilitation of Heart	Minneapolis, Minn
24-Jul	*John A. Assheir	M	W	69	M	O.G.H. /Clermont, Fla	4 ds	Citrus Grower	Norway, Europe	Fish Bone	Bode, Iowa
24-Jul	John Davis	M	C	64	W	217 Chatham	7 mos	Laborer	Ala	Perineal Abscess	Greenwood
26-Jul	*Julia Klosterman	F	W	37	M	O.G.H. /Umatilla, Fla	2 ds	At Home	Ky	Peritonitis from Pelvic Abscess	Greenwood
26-Jul	*Edith Davis Boland	F	W	43	M	O.G.H. /Plymouth, Fla	3 ds	At Home	Ind	Retrocecal Appendix Abscess	Greenwood
25-Jul	Katie Bell Williams	F	C	5 mo	Inf	938 W Washington	5 mos		Orlando, Fla	Gastroenteritis	Greenwood
25-Jul	Hattie Perrin	F	C	46	M	1202 Jefferson	17 yrs	Domestic	Ga	Rheumatic Arthritis	Greenwood
22-Jul	*Infant of Mr & Mrs M K Van Duzor	M	W		S	1019 Noble St		None	Orlando, Fla	Premature Birth	Greenwood
25-Jul	*Bobby S. Hamilton	M	W	1	S	Fla San / 431 E Concord Ave	1 yr +		Orlando, Fla	Acute Enteritis	Greenwood
25-Jul	*Wm D. Nydegger	M	W	66	M	861 N Orange	2 yrs	Real	Alleghany	Carcinomato	Oakland, Md
26-Jul	*Infant of Mr & Mrs H. Jas Gut	M	W		S	15 W Livingston /Sanford, Fla			Orlando, Fla	Stillborn Twin, Full Term	Greenwood

1926	Name of Deceased	Sex	Race	Age	Marital	Residence & Place of Death	Orlando Resident	Occupation	Place of Birth	Cause of Death	Place of Burial
26-Jul	Albert Smith	M	C	49	M	805 Carter	15 ds	Laborer S A L RR	N.C.	Septicemia	Bradenton, Fla
27-Jul	*Mrs Vida R. Pemberton	F	W	43	W	701 W. Central	4 yrs	At Home	Sturgis? Ky	Exhaustion following Septic f___? operation	Greenwood
28-Jul	*Alfred Lilja	M	W	55	M	Highland Ave /Sanford, Fla	abt 1h	Engineer ACL	Cambron, Sweden	Scalded to Death	Sanford, Fla
28-Jul	Indiana Crofford	M	C	25	M	O.G.H. /Holopaw, Fla	4 ds	Cook	Ala	Shock	York, Ala
22-Jul	James Willis Hickey	M	W	51	M	728 Alemeda Ave	3 yrs	Merchant, Retired	Miss	Myocarditis	Greenwood
24-Jul	John William	M	C	54 a	S	6 mi S E of O.	3 yrs	Labor	Ga	Apoplexy	Gabrella, Fla
22-Jul	Lorethia Burns	F	C	1	S	436 Parramore Alley	1 y 1 m	Infant	Orlando	Broncho Pneumonia	Greenwood
26-Jul	*Edith Davis Boland (duplicate)	F	W	43	M	O.G.H.	4 ds	At Home	Ind	Retrocecal Appendical Abscess	Vault
30-Jul	*Infant of Mr & Mrs D. D. Green	M	W		S	O.G.H. /Courtney, Fla			Orlando, Fla	Anaphylaxis	Titusville, Fla
31-Jul	*Winfield S. Loe	M	W	69 a	W	Orlando	7 yrs	Carpenter	Ohio	Angina Pectoris	Toledo, Ohio
31-Jul	*Jay Campbell	M	W	88	W	606 W Cen	25 yrs	Retired	Indiana	Organic Heart Disease	Milton, Ind
31-Jul	No name - 199 N Division	F	C	9 ds	S	199 N. Division	9 ds	Infant	Orlando	Don't Know	Greenwood
2-Aug	*Mrs Lillian A. Tripp	F	W	36	M	201 Liberty	5 yrs	At Home	Ohio	Empyema, Chest	Greendoow
2-Aug	*Earl Lewis Paddock	M	W	33	M	400 W Gore Ave	9 yrs	Mgr Barber Shop	Mich	Hodgkin's Disease	Greenwood
3-Aug	Clara Sharpe	F	C	62	M	O.G.H. / Eustis, Fla	6 ds	Housewife	Ga	Gangrene of Rt Foot	Eustis, Fla
3-Aug	*Florence S Smith	F	W	65	M	McElroy Apts /Nashville, Tenn	10 mos	At Home	Tenn	Acute Dilation of Heart	Nashville, Tenn
4-Aug	*Infant of Mr & Mrs G. Frank Milam	M	W		S	O.G.H. /Holopaw, Fla			Orlando	Stillborn	Greenwood
5-Aug	Elnora Williams	F	C	12	S	O.G.H. / Panasoffkee, Fl	12 ds	School Girl	Fla	Genl Peritonitis	Panasoffkee, Fla
5-Aug	*Champion Jefferson	M	W	17	S	O.G.H. /Taft, Fla	15 ds		S.C.	Frontal Brain Tumor Eroded through Skull	Kissimmee, Fla
5-Aug	*Infant of Mr & Mrs H. C. Harrison	M	W		S	O.G.H. / Winter Park	1 da		Orlando	Anaphylaxis	Greenwood
6-Aug	Infant of A. L. Simmons	F	C		S	820 W. Livingston		None	Orlando	Stillborn	Greenwood
6-Aug	Clara Mack	F	C	47 a	M	442 S. Division	3 yrs	Housewife	Dublin, Ga	Carcinoma of Left Breast	Dublin, Ga
6-Aug	*Edwin Foster	M	W	45 a	M	Orlando /Cincinnati	7 yrs	Citrus Fruit Grower	Ohio	IleoColitis	Greenwood
7-Aug	*Rosetta W. Giles	F	W	53	M	O.G.H. /Winter Park	9 ds	At Home	Va	Stenosis of Pylorus, Pyelitis, & Nephritis	Winter Park
7-Aug	*Virginia Clark Podmore	F	W	31	M	O.G.H. /Winter Park	4 yrs	At Home	Va	Septicemia	Winter Park

1926	Name of Deceased	Sex	Race	Age	Marital	Residence & Place of Death	Orlando Resident	Occupation	Place of Birth	Cause of Death	Place of Burial
7-Aug	*Rosa Chiusano	F	W	27	M	915 S Division /Brooklyn, N.Y.	3 mos	At Home	N.Y.	Pulmonary Tuberculosis	Greenwood
9-Aug	Alonzo Roberts, Jr	M	C	6 hr	S	418 McFall			Orlando	Atelectasis of Lung	Greenwood
10-Aug	Julus C Stephen	M	C	1 yr		925 Raynold	3 yrs		Orlando	IleoColitis	Greenwood
11-Aug	*Elva H. Linder	F	W	50	M	Fla San /Deland	7 ds	At Home	Md	Chronic Inter-stitial Nephritis	Deland
11-Aug	Ruth Leach	F	C	3 ds	S	Hilton Street	3 ds	None	Orlando	Atelectasis	Greenwood
11-Aug	Middie Ola Milam	F	W	34	M	O.G.H. /Holopaw, Fla	2 yrs	House-wife	La	Post Eclamptic Nephritis	Mt Peace Cemetery
11-Aug	*Levi H Crisler	M	W	74	M	119 Golf View Ave	40 yrs	Retired	Ohio	Paralysis Agitans	Greenwood
12-Aug	J. B. Fedrick	M	C	6 mo	Infant	908 S Division	6 mos		Orlando	Not Determined	Greenwood
13-Aug	*Warren Chas Lockwood	M	W	13	S	Fla San /2613 N Orange	18 mos		Conn	W___? To Lungs, Ribs and Chest	Greenwood
13-Aug	*Robert Lee Fox	M	W	54	M	O.G.H. /Leesburg	3 ds	Garage	Ga	Genl Peritonitis	St Marys, Ga
14-Aug	J. C. Crane	M	W	72 a	W	County Home	4 yrs	Day Labor	England	Chronic Nephritis	County Home
16-Aug	*Mrs Roberta Beacham	F	W	57	W	O.G.H. /N Orange Ave	40 yrs	At Home	Ky	General Peritonitis	Greenwood
16-Aug	*Mrs Tryphenia Harris	F	W	64	W	Tampa St	3 yrs	At Home	Ga	Uremia	Port Orange, Fla
17-Aug	Naden Owens	F	C	3 ds	S	27 N. Bryant	3 ds	None	Orlando	Status Lymplotism?	Greenwood
17-Aug	Henry Bunn	M	C	2 m	Inf	436 Parramore Alley	2 mo	None	Orlando	Gastro-enteritis	Greenwood
17-Aug	Lizzie Benett	F	C	58 a	W	613 W Carter	2 yrs	Cook	S.C.	Bronchial Pneumonia, Asthma	Bartow, Fla
17-Aug	Willie Mack Smith	F	C	23	M	O.G.H. /711 Jackson	20 yrs	H W	Orlando	Pneumonia, Lobar	Greenwood
19-Aug	*Daniel Mann	M	W	50	M	1400 Avondale	4 yrs	Builder & Con-tractor	Scotland	Myocardial Degeneration	Greenwood
22-Aug	Infant D. G. Green	F	C		S	709 Quail	6 yrs		Orlando	Miscarriage	Greenwood
22-Aug	Eller Smith	F	C	65	S	345 Beach	7 mos	House-wife	Ga	Acute Heart Failure	Washington
23-Aug	*Geo. S. Deming	M	W	82	W	Fla San /Winter Park	5 ds	Retired	Conn	Myocarditis	Winter Park
23-Aug	*G. Irving Tillotson	M	W	71	W	Chaney Hgh [Hwy]	2 yrs	Retired	N.Y.	General Debility	Mt Kisco, N.Y.
24-Aug	*Chas C. Hall	M	W	52	M	Fla San /1200 S W	10 yrs	Gardner	Fla	Embolus Lodged in Brain	Greenwood
24-Aug	Annie Fulton Maston	F	C	33	M	702 W Robinson	5 yrs	House-wife	Eufala, Ala	Accidentally Drowned	Greenwood
24-Aug	Mrs Mary E. Sweetapple	F	W	90	W	259 E Robinson	43 yrs	At Home	Canada	Hemorrhage of Chronic Gastric Ulcer	Toronto, Canada

Date	Name of Deceased	Sex	Race	Age	Marital	Residence & Place of Death	Orlando Resident	Occupation	Place of Birth	Cause of Death	Place of Burial
25-Aug	*Mrs Bevora B. Clark	F	W	44	M	Holden Ave	6 yrs	At Home	N.Y.	Organic Heart Disease	Binghanton [sic]
26-Aug	*Fannie E. McCloud	F	W	33	M (a)	O.G.H. /Ocoee	24 ds	At Home	Ocoee, Fla	Septicemia	Ocoee, Fla
26-Aug	*Preston Huston	M	W	88	W	Orlando Sanitarium /Blandinsville, Ill	1 yr 6 mos	Retired	Don't Know	Senility	Blandinsville
26-Aug	*Robert L. Odom	M	W	56	M	O.G.H. /Travares, Fla	6 ds	Boarding House Business	Ga	Diabetes Mellitus	Rockledge, Ga
27-Aug	Joseph Gonzalez	M	W	1 mo	S	619 Myrtle Ave, Sanford, Fla	1 mo 7 ds		Sanford, Fla	Acute Broncho Pneumonia	Sanford, Fla
27-Aug	*Infant of Mr & Mrs L. M. Studdard	W	M		S	315 N. Rosalind Ave			Orlando, Fla	Asphyxia, intrauterine	Greenwood
27-Aug	*Catherine F. Murphy	F	W	58	W	O.G.H. /423 E Pine St	12 yrs	At Home	Ireland	Acute Uremia	New York, N.Y.
29-Aug	*Earl Hannah	M	W	36 (a)	S	Fla San / Lake Monroe, Fla	1 da	Labor	King Tree, S.C.	Fracture of Base of Skull From Auto Accident	King Tree, S.C.
29-Aug	*Ruth Edna Buchan	F	W	20	S	726 Shady Lane	2 yrs	At Home	Buffalo, N.Y.	Uremia	Greenwood
29-Aug	*Wm Heberger, Jr	M	W	51	M	Winter Garden Road	1 yr	Grocery	Rochester N.Y.	Carbuncle	Greenwood
30-Aug	Euthie May Walter	F	C	1y +	Inf	809 McFall St	1y 8m	Infant	Orlando	Lobar Pneumonia	Greenwood
3-Sep	*Benjamin Franklin Hudson	M	W	1 yr	S	O.G.H. /Lake Alfred	about 10 hrs		Grady Co., Ga	Foreign Body in both fr___?	Lake Alfred
31-Aug	Mack Makinzie	M	C	3	S	740 S. Division	3 yrs 11mo	Child	Winter Haven, Fla	Acute Gastritis	Greenwood
31-Aug	*Mrs Minnie Hall	F	W	51	M	1505 Canton Ave	20 y (a)	At Home	Ill	Uremia	Greenwood
31-Aug	*Grace Marsh	F	W	23	S	O.G.H. /Winter Park	3 yrs	?	Penn	Pyelo-nephritis	West Chester, Pa
1-Sep	*Ralph D. Jackson	M	W	27	S	O.G.H. /Winter Garden R R	30 min	Farming	Troy, Ala	Crushed by Tractor	Ocoee
1-Sep	*Alma Catherine Karr	F	W	7	S	O.G.H. /Kissimmee	1 da		Ala	General Peritonitis	Albertville, Ala
2-Sep	*Catherine L. Lingold	F	W	1	S	742 W Church St	1 yr 6mos		Orlando	Broncho Pneumonia	Lake Underhill
3-Sep	*Robert H. Millington	M	W	6	S	O.G.H. /Route #3	1 da		Ga	Septicemia	Lake Hill
4-Sep	Infant of Sam Jones	M	C		Inf	Terry			Orlando	Stillborn	Greenwood
4-Sep	Mahala Huston	F	C	46	M	424 W Robinson	20 yr	Cook	Fla	Gastric Ulcer	Greenwood
5-Sep	*Mark Judson Smith	M	W	57	W	207 E. Livingston	5 yrs	Contractor & Builder	Iowa	Chr. Nephritis	Elmwood, Ill
5-Sep	*Francis Demitha? (Perilla)	F	W	83	W	R F D #2	2 yrs	At Home	Miss	Chronic Interstitial Nephritis	Biloxi, Miss
6-Sep	*Delilah R. Shell	F	W	23	M	O.G.H. /R R #4	10 ds	At Home	Mich	Toxemia of Pregnancy	Greenwood

1926	Name of Deceased	Sex	Race	Age	Marital	Residence & Place of Death	Orlando Resident	Occupation	Place of Birth	Cause of Death	Place of Burial
6-Sep	*Mrs Anne Kirkland	F	W	53	M	O.G.H. /517 N. Hughey	2 mo	At Home	Ont.	Pernicious Anemia	Grafton, N.D.
6-Sep	*Helen Elizabeth Gilmartin	F	W	19	M	O.G.H. /Orlando	2 mo	At Home	Iowa	Pueperal Sepsis	Greenwood
6-Sep	*Michael M. Schultz	M	W	62	M	33 E Washington / Charlotte, N.C.	7 mo	Contrac-tor	Iowa	Apoplexy	Charlotte, N.C.
7-Sep	*Mrs Caroline G. Mitchell	F	W	75	W	Howell Sanit / N.Y. City	1 yr 5 mo	At Home	Ky	Cancer of Right Leg	Greenwood
7-Sep	*Will E. Lee	M	W	38	M	O.G.H. /Clermont, Fla	4 ds	Truck Driver	Ga	Compound Fractuare of Left Leg	Jonesboro, Ga
7-Sep	Ida Wright	F	C	50 a	W	34 Parramore Alley	9 yrs	Laun-dress	Fla	Mitral Incompetence	Greenwood
7-Sep	James Adolphus Cyer	M	C	80 a	W	318 S. Terry St.	30 yr	Tailor	Mariland?	Cystitis	Greenwood
7-Sep	*Wm Thos Moore	M	W	94	M	Fla San /Clearwater	2 mo	Minister of Gospel	Ky	Pneumonia	Cincinnati, Ohio
9-Sep	Jessie Means, Jr.	M	C	8 da	Inf	740 S. Division	8 ds		Orlando	Bronchitis	Greenwood
7-Sep	*Infant of Sam Watson	M	W		S	Lockhart			Lockhart	Stillbirth	Greenwood
9-Sep	*Infant of Mr & Mrs. Chas. Vogt	M	W		S	1729 Bellevue			Orlando		Greenwood
9-Sep	*Mrs. Ida Campbell	F	W	54	M	26 N. Hughey	5 mo	At Home	Mass	Peritonitis	Leesburg, Fla
9-Sep	*Robert Briss	M	W	46	M	338 E. South St.	2 yrs	Assistant Salesman	Scotland	Heart Disease	Greenwood
7-Sep	Edith Exion	F	C		Inf	914 Reynold	2 yrs		Orlando	Stillborn	Greenwood
9-Sep	*Lillian Griggs	F	W	39	M	O.G.H. /Winter Park	12 da	At Home	Fla	Shock Following Operation	Winter Park
11-Sep	Moses Jessup McGough	M	W	6	S	O.G.H. /Eustis, Fla	2 d	At Home	Eustis, Fla	Meningitis & Hemiplegia	Eustis, Fla
12-Sep	*Phillip R. Dann	M	W	3	S	Fla San /Clarcona	1 da		Clarcona, Fla	Tetanus	Patrick Cemetery
12-Sep	*James Robt. Brown	M	W	42	S	Fla San /Orlando	2 yrs	Carpenter	Lynchburg, Va	Carcinoma of Bowels	Greenwood
13-Sep	Mamie L. King	F	C	4 ds	S	817 Wood St.	8 mos		Orlando	Icterus Neonatorum	Greenwood
13-Sep	*Thos Lorenzo Langley	M	W	59	M	Fla Sant /1308 Long St	a 2 mos	Farming	Dawson, Ga	Nephritis Acute	Calvary, Ga
14-Sep	Cathrene Lyanch	F	C	1 yr	S	539 Holden	1 yr 5 mo	None	Fla	Acute Nephritis & Congenital Liver?	Greenwood
12-Sep	*Infant of Mr & Mrs J. E. Thompson	F	W	1 da	S	Clear Lake	14 ds		Orlando	Prematurity	Tifton, Ga
14-Sep	*Sam Gentile	M	W	52 a	M	1053 W Church	5 yrs	Merchant	Italy	Angina Pectoris	Greenwood
15-Sep	*Harriett Ann Browne	F	W	3 ds	S	401 E. Rollins Ave	3 ds		Orlando, Fla	Status Lymphemia	Greenwood
15-Sep	Derris (Dorria) Harris	F	W	24	S	143 W. Pine St.	2 yrs	At Home	N.C.	Pulmonary & Intestinal TB	Greenwood
17-Sep	Ruth Anne Spires	F	C	4 mo	S	233 Chatham	17 yrs	Infant	Orlando	Don't Know	Greenwood
18-Sep	*Mrs Maggie Weaver	F	W	40 a	M	O.G.H. /Leesburg, Fla	9 ds	At Home		Acute Acidosis	Leesburg, Fla

102

1926	Name of Deceased	Sex	Race	Age	Marital	Residence & Place of Death	Orlando Resident	Occupation	Place of Birth	Cause of Death	Place of Burial
17-Sep	Jennie G. Lane	F	W	61	M	Fla San /Winter Haven	1 mo	HW	Canton, Ohio	Cancer of Uterus	Winter Haven
22-Jul	Infant of Mr & Mrs S. J. Parrott	F	W		S	O.G.H.			Orlando	Stillborn	Specimen
18-Sep	*Infant of Mr & Mrs Artie Simkowitz	F	W		S	Fla San Hosp			Orlando	Asphyxia Neonatorum	Ohev Shalom Cemetery
21-Sep	*Stella L. Cruse	F	W	8 mo s	S	O.G.H. /Plymouth, Fla	1 da		Plymouth, Fla	Acute Broncho Pneumonia	Bay Ridge
21-Sep	*Orvile Wood	M	W	46	M	Bonnie Lock Drive	1 yr	Accountant	Kan	Chronic Myocarditis	Hiawatha, Kan
22-Sep	*Chas. M. Sullivan	M	W	a 42	W	O.G.H. /Greenville, S.C.	a 6 mos	Clerk in Grocery Store	Ga	Convulsions	McCormick, S.C.
24-Sep	*Sally Avera	F	W	7 ds	S	946 W Jackson	8 ds		Orlando, Fla	Tetanus neonatorum	Lake Hill Cem
26-Sep	*George M. Murdock	M	W	29	S	O.G.H. /St. Cloud, Fla	3 hrs	Electrician	Mass	Shock	Worcester, Mass
26-Sep	*Ruben Adams Cort	M	W	59	M	Fla San / Charleston, S.C.	1 yr	Clerk	Ind	Incompentency of all Valves of Heart	Charleston, S.C.
26-Sep	*Edward Lewis	M	C	72	S	County Home	2 mos	DK		Valvular Heart Disease	County Home
27-Sep	*Milford A. Corey	M	W	58	D	Lockhart, Fla	1 yr 6 mos	Farming	Oskosh, Wis	Cerebral Hemorrhage	Greenwood
29-Sep	*Josiah S. Henderson	M	W	a 75	W	O.G.H. /Apopka, Fla	1 da	Retired	W Va	Obstruction Common Gall Duct	Oklaloosa, Iowa
28-Sep	*Adam G. Stevens	M	C	79	M	1038 Washington	7 ds	Carpenter	Clinton, N.C.	Senility	Greenwood
29-Sep	Ruffus Boysdon	M	C	64	M	404 W Moreland Dr	15 yrs	Labor	Ga	Panophthalmitis	Greenwood
30-Sep	Mrs Esther M. Cogswell	F	W	88	W	61 E Amelia	3 yrs	At Home	Maine	Mitral Regurgitation	Portland, Maine
30-Sep	*Jackson H. Hoffman	M	W	72	S	Eola Park /632 S. Hughey	1 yr	Watchman	Ind	Suicide	County Home
30-Sep	Janie Roberts	F	C	15	M	O.G.H. /219 W Moreland Dr	3 yrs	HW	Monticello, Fla	Eclampsia	Monticello
30-Sep	Infant of Harison Robinson & Jane Alexander	F	C		S	O.G.H.	30 min		Orlando	Stillborn	Greenwood
1-Oct	*Infant of Mr & Mrs Wm R. Roose		W		S	O.G.H.			Orlando	Stillborn	Greenwood
29-Sep	Fredrick Oscar Daniels	M	C	39	M	37 Bryan	25 yrs	Tailor	Winter Park	Influenza	Greenwood
1-Oct	Dave Sirmon	M	C	50	M	817 Wood		Laborer	Ga	Mitral Stenosis	Greenwood
5-Oct	Fannie Smith	F	C	55	M	647 Bentley St	2 yrs	Cook	Ga	La Grippe	Americus, Ga
1-Oct	West Long	M	C	63	W	1020 Federal St	2 yrs	Laborer	Fla	Broncho Pneumonia	Swort?, Jackson Co.
5-Oct	Stewart R. Greiner	M	W	43	M	O.G.H. /Kissimmee	12 hrs	Realtor	Fla	Gastric Hemorrhage	Kissimmee
5-Oct	Emanuel Scott	M	C	49	S	O.G.H. /320 N. Parramore	5 yrs	Labor	Fla	Acute Nephritis	High Springs, Fla

1926	Name of Deceased	Sex	Race	Age	Marital	Residence & Place of Death	Orlando Resident	Occupation	Place of Birth	Cause of Death	Place of Burial
24-Sep	Evelyn Smith	F	C		S	617 S. Parramore			Orlando	Stillborn	Greenwood
5-Oct	*Sallie C. Ellis	F	W	43	M	O.G.H. /108 S. Tampa	4 yrs	At Home	Ala	Placenta Previa & Hemorrhage	Lake Hill, Fla
5-Oct	*Infant of Mr & Mrs Allen M. Ellis	M	W		S	O.G.H. /Tampa, Fla.			Orlando	Premature Birth	Lake Hill
6-Oct	Willie James	M	C	3 ds	S	237 S. Division	3 ds		Orlando	Edema of Lungs	Greenwood
6-Oct	*Infant of Mr & Mrs Fred A. Falkner	F	W	9 ds	S	910 Maxwell Ave	9 ds		Orlando	Convulsions, etc.	Greenwood
6-Oct	*Mrs Effie Barbere	F	W	38	M	Fla San /Kissimmee	8 ds	At Home	Mich	Pneumonia	Kissimmee, Fla
8-Oct	*Luther C. Townsend	M	W	48	M	312 N. Magnolia	13 yrs	Contractor & Builder	S.C.	Acute Uremia	Iva, S.C.
8-Oct	*Wm Tyler Carroll	M	W	19	S	Fla San / Mt. Verde, Fla	1 da		Ala	Myocarditis	Mt. Verde
9-Oct	Louis Davis	M	C	2 hrs	S	532 John Street	2 hrs		Orlando	Status Lymphatism	Greenwood
9-Oct	Cecil Cornell Hazel	M	C	18	S	764 Avondale	13 yrs	Laborer	Webster, Fla	Broncho Pneumonia	Greenwood
10-Oct	Manther Bradley	F	C	85 a	W	632 W Washington	1 yr	Invalid	Tallahas-see, Fla	Mitral Regurgitation	Jacksonville, Fla
10-Oct	Dennis Webster	M	C	21	S	Tampa Ave / 805 Edna St	15 yr	Laborer	Fla	Homicidal	Greenwood
9-Oct	*Allie Elizabeth Banner	F	W	46	M	Fla San / Apopka R F D #1	6 ds	At Home	Wis	Cancer of Liver	Greenwood
10-Oct	*Donald Elmer Barclay	M	W	30	S	OGH /304 DeSota Circle	10 mos	Auto Mechanic	Neb	Veroval? Poisoning	Greenwood
11-Oct	*Chas. Henry Carter	M	W	46	M	535 N. Summerlin	8 mos	Prof. Of English	Pa	Mitral Regurgitation	Greenwood
11-Oct	*Infant of Mr & Mrs Millard McMillan	M	W		S	Wahsateh St.			Orlando	Stillborn	Greenwood
12-Oct	*Infant of Mr & Mrs Chas Rutledge	F	W		S	O.G.H. / 206 Coast St., Tampa, Fla			Orlando	Intracranial Injury	Greenwood
15-Oct	Corene Johnson	M	C		S	1028 W Jefferson			Orlando	Don't Know	Greenwood
15-Oct	*Joseph Komada	M	W	65	M	OGH /1020 S. Parramore	1 mo 14 ds	Wire Factory	Europe	Acute Asthma	Blue Island, Ill
15-Oct	*Infant of Mr & Mrs Wm Bennett	M	W	1 da	S	526 Piedmont			Orlando	Atelectasis	Greenwood
15-Oct	*Francis M. Kenney	M	W	80	M	845 N. Mill	14 yrs	Wholesale Merchant	Ga	Angina Pectoris	Greenwood
16-Oct	*Mrs Martha Jane Waters	F	W	24	M	O.G.H. / Haines City, Fla	2 ds	At Home	Ark	Chronic Paren-chymalores	Davenport, Fla
16-Oct	*Harriett S. Keys	F	W	60 a	M	Lake View Drive	6 yrs	At Home	Ohio	Carcinoma of Uterine	Leesville, Ohio
16-Oct	*Mrs Minnie Watson	F	W	56 a	M	Fla San /Grove Hill Court	6 ds	At Home	Canada	Cardiac Asthma	Boston, Mass
17-Oct	Emma Virginia Woodall	M?	W	13	S	O.G.H. /Kissimmee, Fla	5 ds	At Home	Kissimmee Fla	Septicemia	Rose Hill
17-Oct	Jake Crumly	M	C	29	M	723 R. R. Ave	10 yrs	Common Labor	Ga	Nephritis	Greenwood

1926	Name of Deceased	Sex	Race	Age	Marital	Residence & Place of Death	Orlando Resident	Occupation	Place of Birth	Cause of Death	Place of Burial
17-Oct	*John Worthy	M	C	45	M	Hilton Sant	28 ds	Day Labor	Ga	Apoplexy	Winter Park
19-Oct	*Tom J. Voss	M	W	50	M	O.G.H. /Winter Garden	2 hrs	Day Labor	Ala	Pulmonary Edema	Ocoee
16-Aug	Ruth Leach	F	C	5 ds	S	612 W. Church	3 ds	None	Orlando	D__hold?	Greenwood
19-Oct	Jim Armstead	M	C	47	M	809 McFarland St.	4 yrs	Carpenter	Fla	Acute Gastritis	Greenwood
19-Oct	*Minnie Lehman	F	W	54	W	Howell San /Iowa	14 yrs	At Home	Wis	Cancer of Liver	Greenwood
22-Oct	*Everett E. Hansen	M	W	1	S	Fla San /Clear Lake	1yr +		Orlando	Acute Gastroenteritis	Greenwood
22-Oct	*Frances Wm Topliff	M	W	67	W	1304 N. Mills	12 yrs	Retored	N.H.	Ruptured Abdominal Aneurysm	Greenwood
24-Oct	*Infant of Mr & Mrs John C. Lynch	M	W		S	618 W. Pine			Orlando	Congenital Defect	Crosland, Ga
24-Oct	*Christiana Carolina Farmer	F	W	72	W	707 W Pine	1 yr	At Home	Spring Hill, Ga	Apoplexy	Lumber City, Ga
25-Oct	*Lucy Louise Rodney	F	W	1	S	O.G.H.	1 da		Sanford, Fla	Acute Broncho Pneumonia	Quitman, Ga
25-Oct	*Isadore A. Stein	M	W	66	M	Lockhart, Fla	4 yrs	Insurance	Russia	Pulmonary Tuberculosis	Greenwood
26-Oct	*Mrs Gertrude Ruskin	F	W	35	M	O.G.H. /Oviedo, Fla	1 da	At Home	Orlando, Fla	Shock Following Operation for Gallbladder	Greenwood
26-Oct	*Mrs Jennie Amelia Schole (Scholey)	F	W	60	M	Dubstred Circle	5 yrs	At Home	Conn	Lobar Pneumonia	Guilford, Conn
26-Oct	*Frederick H. Medley	M	W	54	M	O.G.H. / Huntington, WV	9 ds	Real Estate Agt	Ark	Endartiritis?	Huntington, W Va
27-Oct	*Richard Honeycutt	M	W	35 a	M	O.G.H. /Altamonte Sps	1 da	Laborer	N.C.	Gunshot Wound	Cooper, N.C.
30-Sep	Eddie Kitchen	M	W	35	M	DK	3 ds	Day Labor		Gunshot Wound	County Home
22-Oct	Cary Mack	F	C	31	M	623 Carter	5 yrs	HW	Jacksonville	Child Birth	Greenwood
22-Oct	Girl of Cary Mack	F	C						Orlando	Toxemia from Mother	Greenwood
25-Oct	Johnie McNight	M	C	34	M	W Jefferson	3 yrs	Clothes Presser	Charleston, S.C.	Acute Pneumonia; Phthisis	Greenwood
??-Oct	Dola Bivins	F	C	19	S	1202 W Carter	4 mo	Laborer	Harrison, Ga	Puerperal Eclampsia	Greenwood
29-Oct	*Infant of Mr & Mrs John R. Graham	M	W		S	O.G.H. /1606 E Central Ave			Orlando	Premature Birth	Greenwood
30-Oct	Elvin (Elvis) W. Watson	M	W	79	W	Amhurst Apts	3 mo	Retired	Ky	Uremia	Cartersville, Ill
30-Oct	Willie Mack	M	C	45	M	508 S. Division	4 yrs	Laborer	Resipe?, Ga	Accidental Death	Dublin, Ga
30-Oct	Johnnie Mack	M	C		S	619 S. Lee			Orlando	Stillborn	Greenwood
31-Oct	*Ruth Caroline Segers	F	W	4	S	O.G.H. / Plymouth, Fla	1 da		Cornelia, Ga	Acute Nephritis	Cornelia, Ga

1926	Name of Deceased	Sex	Race	Age	Marital	Residence & Place of Death	Orlando Resident	Occupation	Place of Birth	Cause of Death	Place of Burial
31-Oct	*Mary Eula Jones	F	W	56	M	Fla San /Miami, Fla	15 ds	At Home	Va	Pneumonia	Jacksonville, Fla
1-Nov	*John Douglas Rowland	M	W	65	M	762 Westmoreland	3 yrs	Jeweler	Minn	Angina Pectoris	Cremation
1-Nov	*Infant of Mr & Mrs Wm W. Morrow	M	W		S	Woodhaven			Orlando	Stillborn	Greenwood
2-Nov	Infant of Edward Golden & Julia Oxford	M	C		S	214 N Hughey			Orlando	Stillborn	Greenwood
2-Nov	Wedlow West	M	C	a 50	M	533 S Parramore	4 yrs	Laborer	Ward, S.C.	Carcinoma of Liver	Ridge Spring, S.C.
2-Nov	*John Franklin Price	M	W	a 61	M	Perdue St.	a 5 yrs	Carpenter	N.C.	Cerebral Hemorrhage	Greenwood
3-Nov	*Carl Wray Diehl	M	W	3 m	S	Miami, Fla	1 da		Miami, Fla	Broncho Pneumonia	Greenwood
3-Nov	*Frank A. Wallace	M	W	60	M	229 S. Garland	15 yrs	Real Estate	Athens, Ga	Pulmonary TB	Greenwood
4-Nov	*Lenora Cogswell	F	W	a 5	S	Fla San	a 3 yr		Methuen, Mass	Burns	Greenwood
4-Nov	Clara M. Lindsey	F	W	58	M	O.G.H. / Eustis, Fla	6 ds	At Home	Popa,	Appendicitis & Peritonitis	Eustis
6-Nov	*Anna Louise Herring	F	W	61	S	1110 S. Division	5 mo	At Home	Ohio	Chronic Nephritis	Greenwood
7-Nov	*David Britt Wingo	M	W	21	M	O.G.H. /1508 E Gore	1 mo	Carpenter	Atlanta, Ga	Contusion of Chest	Atlanta, Ga
8-Nov	*Luther Cephas McCarley	M	W	49	M	O.G.H. / 624 W Gore Ave	1 yr	Farming	Seneca, S.C.	Chronic Nephritis	Senica, S.C.
9-Nov	D. Stokes	M	C	41	M	Quincy Ave	2 yrs	Laborer	Ga	Mitral Regurgitation	Greenwood
9-Nov	*Infant of Mr & Mrs Thomas E. May	F	W	1 hr	S	530 Lakeview			Orlando	Premature Birth	Greenwood
9-Nov	*Jerome Palmer	M	W	83	M	1622 Kuhl Ave	10 yrs	Retired	Vt	Uremia	Greenwood
10-Nov	*James H. Wilkins	M	W	81	M	619 E. Concord Ave	16 yrs	Retired	Mass	Senility	Greenwood
11-Nov	*Andrew Guernsey	M	W	a 69	W	County Home / Taft, Fla	1 mo	Retired	Australia	Pulmonary TB	County
11-Nov	*Catherine Brown	F	W	1 yr	S	O.G.H. /Ocoee	1 da		Ocoee, Fla	Strangulation	Ocoee
11-Nov	Will Denis	M	C	35	M	419 S. Division	5 yrs		Atlanta, Ga	Otitis	Greenwood
13-Nov	*Mary Louise Venerable	F	W	9	S	2116 N. Orange Ave	8 mo			Broncho Pneumonia	Greenwood
14-Nov	Wesley Bradly	M	C	45	M	305 S Fern Creek	6 mo	Shoe-maker	Ga	Broncho Pneumonia	Greenwood
15-Nov	*Mrs Allie Waelde	F	W	58	W	O.G.H. /1918 Hilcrest Ave.	1 mo	At Home	Cleveland, Ohio	General Carcinomatsis?	Cleveland, Ohio
15-Nov	*Mrs Mary Elsie Boyer	F	W	59	W	525 E Central	9 yrs	At Home	Salem, N.J.	Acute Endocarditis	Greenwood
15-Nov	*Infant of Mr & Mrs Henry H. Guerin	M	W		S	O.G.H. /Melbourne, Fla			Orlando	Asphyxia, Foot Prolapse	Greenwood
16-Nov	Orange Bailey	M	C	23	S	O.G.H. /429 W Robinson	2 yrs	Laborer	Blakely, Ga	Pistol Shot Wound	Blakely, Ga

1926	Name of Deceased	Sex	Race	Age	Marital	Residence & Place of Death	Orlando Resident	Occupation	Place of Birth	Cause of Death	Place of Burial
17-Nov	Infant of Wheeler Gary & Catherine Gary	M	C		S	737 W Long			Orlando	Born Dead	Greenwood
13-Nov	*Mrs Augusta F. Payne	F	W	63	M	E Winter Park Road	30 yrs	At Home	Sweden	Influenza	Greenwood
17-Nov	*Mrs Rose Warren	F	W	58	M	O.G.H. / 1 Gore Ave	8 yrs	At Home	Kan	Gertian?	Greenwood
18-Nov	*Catherine McGraw	F	M	72	M	O.G.H. / Indiana Ave	12 ds	At Home	Miss	Malarial Fever	Ft. Smith, Ark
18-Nov	*Infant of Mr & Mrs Athansios Demopulos	F	W		S	O.G.H. /23 W Church			Orlando	Congenital Malformation	Greenwood
19-Nov	*Edmund Swabey	M	W	a 67	W	O.G.H. /Narcoossee, Fla	14 ds	Retired	England	Broncho Pneumonia	Greenwood
19-Nov	*Luthella V. Aldrich	F	W	59	M	West Central Ave	a 3 yrs	At Home	Penn	Cerebral Hemorrhage	Greenwood
20-Nov	*Infant of Jessie F. Boyd	M	W		S	1410 Osceola St			Orlando, Fla	Stillborn	Lake Hill Cemetery
21-Nov	George Williams	M	C	a 80	S	County Home	27 yrs	Retired	Don't Know	Valvular Heart Disease	County Home
21-Nov	*Mrs Alsina Myers	F	W	76	W	Crystal Lake	6 yrs	At Home	Ohio	Arterio-sclerosis	Caledonia, Mich
2-Nov	*Infant of Mr & Mrs Carl G. Ahik	F	W	2 hr	S	Fla San / Winter Park			Orlando	Premature Birth	Winter Park
20-Nov	Thomas Dewing	M	C	a 38	W	810 W. Livingston	9 yrs	Laborer	Tallahassee Fla	Acute Dilation of Heart	A. J. Smith Co.
22-Nov	Jery Sales	M	C	77	W	423 S. Parramore	34 mo	Laborer	Fla	Prostatitis	Greenwood
24-Nov	E. Bigsbee	M	C	88	S	510 S Parramore	7 mos	Minister	Ga	Chronic Bronchitis	Greenwood
25-Nov	Odesa Robinson	F	C	21	M	514 W Pine	4 mo	House-wife	Ga	Lobar Pneumonia	Moultrie, Ga
25-Nov	Susan Zanders?	F	C	a 90	W	435 S Terry	10 mo	Invalid	Atlanta, Ga	Gangrene of Leg	Greenwood
26-Nov	J. C. Cromer	M	C	9 m		1026 W. Bentley	9 mo		Orlando	Lumbricoids	Greenwood
23-Nov	*Emma Johnson	F	C	57	M	O.G.H. / Plymouth, Fla	1 da	At Home	N.C.	Auto Accident	Apopka
23-Nov	*Mrs Ann A. Hull	F	W	a 78	W	College Hill / Lynne, Fla	1 mo	At Home	N.C.	Apoplexy	Ocala, Fla
24-Nov	*Frank Johnson	M	W	a 68	W	Howell Sant / 646 Ridgewood	7 yrs	Painter & Decorator	Mass	Chronic Nephritis	Greenwood
24-Nov	*Infant of Mr & Mrs Frank P. Burch	M	W		S	427 N Shine			Orlando	Stillborn	Greenwood
25-Nov	*Alice Miller	F	W	57	W	O.G.H. / Aurora, Ill	a1 mo	At Home	Big Rock, Ill	Chonic Nephritis	Aurora, Ill
25-Nov	*Samuel Andress	M	W	69	W	529 N Magnolia	20 yrs	Real Estate	N.J.	Angina Pectoris	Greenwood
26-Nov	*William Geo. Thompson	M	W	68	M	508 N Mills	5 yrs	Retired	S.C.	Pellagra	Summerville, S.C.
26-Nov	*Daniel M. McGraw	M	W	76	W	O.G.H, /812 E Livingston	1 mo 7 ds	Retired	Miss	Malaria Fever	Ft. Smith, Ark
27-Nov	*David M. Luttrell	M	W	70	M	4 Kaley Ave	1 yr	Retired	Ohio	Myocarditis	Greenwood

1926	Name of Deceased	Sex	Race	Age	Marital	Residence & Place of Death	Orlando Resident	Occupation	Place of Birth	Cause of Death	Place of Burial
28-Nov	*Earnest O. Britt	M	W	20	S	O.G.H. /Ocoee, Fla	10 ds	Day Labor	Ala	Acute Mye-logenous Leukemia	Jackson Gap, Ala
30-Nov	*Sarah S. Holcomb	F	W	73	W	Fla San	1 mo 7 ds	At Home	Mo	Cholelithiasis with Pyemia of GB	Greenwood
29-Nov	*Jasper Thomas Rooks	M	W	3 m	S	Fairvilla	3 mo 9 ds		Orlando	Broncho Pneumonia	Greenwood
1-Dec	*Horace T. A. Carmichael	M	W	2	S	1906 Park Lake Ave	1 yr		Maxton, N.C.	Acute Broncho Pneumonia	Maxton, N.C.
3-Dec	*Mrs Bessie Mae Richards	F	W	58	M	R F D #4	2 yrs	At Home	N.Y.	Chronic Nephritis	Vault
3-Dec	*Georgia A. Axtell	F	W	67	M	1640 DeLaney	5 mo	At Home	N.Y.	Carcinoma of Breast	Greenwood
4-Dec	George Henry Hollie	M	C		S	502 Parramore		None	Orlando	Hydro-cephalus	Greenwood
4-Dec	*Johnie M. Crozier	M	W	5	S	Conway Ave	a 4 yrs		Ashburn, Ga	Lobar Pneumonia	Lake Hill
4-Dec	*Emmet J. Parker	M	W	57	M	N. Mills /Keene, N.Y.	11 ds	Retired	N.Y.	Fractured Skull; Auto Accident	Keene, N.Y.
5-Dec	*Charles E. Vinson	M	W	60	M	107 W Princeton	2 yrs	Auto Repairs	Milledge-ville, Ga	Cerebral Hemorrhage	Savannah, Ga
5-Dec	Maude Grace Pray	F	W	38	M	117 E. Livingston	1 yr 1 mo	At Home	Maine	Endocarditis	Augusta, Maine
6-Dec	*Adelbert J. Reed	M	W	82	M	239 W Orlando Ave	2 mos	Retired	N.Y.	Chronic Bright's Disease	GAR Greenwood
6-Dec	*John Gardner	M	W	65	M	119 E Concord /Toronto	16 ds	Retired	Ireland	Acute Cardiac Dilitation	Toronto, Canada
6-Dec	*Geo W. Hanlon	M	W	67	M	Fla San /Winter Garden	7 ds	Real Estate	N.Y.	Gen Peritonitis	Tampa
6-Dec	*James H. Eller	M	W	89	W	112 S. Lake /Canton, Ohio	24 ds	Retired	Ohio	Uremia	Canton, Ohio
7-Dec	James M. Riddle	M	W	80	M	O.G.H. /Grand Island, Fla	10 ds	Farmer	Ga	Chronic Endocarditis	Grand Island, Fla
7-Dec	Henry Arthur Wheeler, Jr.	M	W	18	S	O.G.H. /St. Cloud, Fla	2 ds	At School	Ga	Infected Limb	Mt. Peace Cemetery
7-Dec	*Chas A. Gutke	M	W	68	M	O.G.H. /Plymouth, Fla	1 da	Salesman, Retired	Berlin, Germany	High Blood Pressure	St. Louis, Mo
7-Dec	*Melinda Stowell	F	W	86	W	Gatlin Ave /Oswego, N.Y.	a 20 ds	At Home	N.Y.	Pulmonary Edema	Oswego, N.Y.
8-Dec	*Frances M. Lane	F	W	41	M	405 S. Osceola /Whitehall, NY	6 ds	At Home	N.Y.	Cerebral Hemorrhage	Ausable Forks, N.Y.
8-Dec	*Infant of Mr & Mrs Chas T. Simerly	M	W		S	Lucerne Park			Orlando, Fla	Large Child & Contracted Pelvis	Greenwood
8-Dec	*Leon Bas	M	W	77	W	O.G.H. /1724 S Kuhl Ave	39 yrs	Retired	Paris, France	Concussion of Brain	Greenwood
8-Dec	*George H. Horn	M	W	73	W	O.G.H. / S Fern Creek Av	5 yrs	Retired	London, England	Operation for Urinary Retention	Greenwood
9-Dec	*James W. O'Brien	M	W	28	S	O.G.H. / Ellicottville, N.Y.	9 mos	Book-keeper	N.Y.	Pneumonia, Broncho	Ellicottville, N.Y.

1926	Name of Deceased	Sex	Race	Age	Marital	Residence & Place of Death	Orlando Resident	Occupation	Place of Birth	Cause of Death	Place of Burial
9-Dec	*Florida H. Bermenter	F	W	73	W	St. Regis Apts /Jacksonville, Fla	8 mos	At Home	Tallahassee, Fla	Uremia	Tallahassee, Fla
9-Dec	*Mrs Annie J. Rowland	F	W	65	M	Dixie Apt	42 yrs	At Home	Tallahassee, Fla	Chronic Interstitial Nephritis	Greenwood
11-Dec	*Mrs Euphemia Ryerson	F	W	85	W	612 N. Hughey	1 yr	At Home	N.J.	Myocarditis	Newark, N.J.
9-Dec	James H. Hunter	M	C	53	M	737 W Long	5 yrs	Laundry-man	Maryana	Acute Gastritis	Jacksonville, Fla
14-Dec	*Jacob G Moorman	M	W	65	M a	W King St / Tampa, Fla	2 yrs	Day Labor	DK	Angina Pectoris	Greenwood
26-Nov	Infant of Ray & Bessie Quarterman	F	C	St		603 Lee St			Orlando	Stillborn	Greenwood
16-Nov	Infant of Isaac & Lucender Shuler	M	C	Inf		Newman			Orlando	Stillborn	Greenwood
15-Dec	Infant of James & Susie _?_	F	C	St		415 S Chatham			Orlando	Stillborn	Greenwood
13-Dec	*Infant of Mr & Mrs Thos Hage	F	W	4	S	500 W Gore			Orlando, Fla	Atelectasis	Greenwood
13-Dec	*Malivina M. Blanchard	F	W	69	W	S. Dixie Road	1 mo	At Home	Canada	Acute Dilation of Heart	Bangor, Maine
13-Dec	*Frank [Francis] Fish	F	W	69	W	W Orlando / Heart Lake, Penn	2 mos	At Home	Penn	Myocarditis	Greenwood
15-Dec	*John S. Bryan	M	W	59	M	828 N. Mills	2 yrs	Retired	Jasper, Fla	Paralysis	Greenwood
15-Dec	*Donia Seferian	M	W	46	M	711 W Central Ave	2 mo	Hotel Keeper	Armenia	Pulmonary TB	Greenwood
15-Dec	*Mrs Josie E. Howard	F	W	76	M	436 Anderson Ct.	1 yr 2mos	At Home	Irondequoit, NY	Purecutor?	Rochester, N.Y.
16-Dec	*Edward H. Reynolds	M	W	57	S	Apopka Road	a 1yr	Retired	Ky	Cardiac Insufficiency	Paris, Mo
16-Dec	*George Segroves	M	W	29	M	O.G.H.	2 ds	Day Laborer	Tenn	Active Tuberculosis	Greenwood
16-Dec	*Marie G. Rooch [Roach]	F	W	31	S	Fla Sant / Minnesota St	2 yrs	Steno-grapher	Canada	Cellulitis	Sussex-New Brunswick, Can
16-Dec	Will Rice	M	C	35	S a	O.G.H.	1 da	Labor	Ga	Stab Wound	County Home
17-Dec	Infant of A. B. & Alice Wells	F	C		S	318 N Parramore			Orlando	Stillborn	Greenwood
18-Dec	*Houston Gillyin Tubb	M	W	45	M	O.G.H. / Winter Garden	5 ds	Farming	Amory, Miss	Gas Gangrene	Winter Garden
19-Dec	*Harry Edward Brenenstuhl	M	W	42	M	Fla Sant / Lockhart, Fla.	2 mo	Lineman Fla Public Serv.	New York	Embolus	Lake George, N.Y.
9-Dec	Eveline Alexander	F	C	74	M	200 N. Division	34 yrs	Laun-dress	Va	Cerebral Hemorrhage	Greenwood
19-Dec	George Simmons	M	C	55	M	517 Holden	3 yrs	Laborer	Ga	Acute Gastritis	Greenwood
20-Dec	*Mrs Sarah G. Coker	F	W	63	M	502 N Mills St / Rome, Ga	1 yr	At Home	Cherokee Co., Ala	Chronic Myocarditis	Rome, Ga
21-Dec	*Hannah A. Farmer	F	W	67	S	O.G.H. / Concord, N.H.	1 mo 6 ds	At Home	Hooksett, N.H.	Broncho Pneumonia	Vault - Hooksett, NH
21-Dec	*Henry W. Stiles	M	W	27	S a	O.G.H. /Canada	1 mo	Laborer	Canada	Shock Following Auto Accident	Petitcodiac, Canada

109

	Name of Deceased	Sex	Race	Age	Marital	Residence & Place of Death	Orlando Resident	Occupation	Place of Birth	Cause of Death	Place of Burial
22-Dec	*Clarence R. Knox	M	W	34	S	O.G.H. /Tavares	1 da	Labor	Neb	Gunshot Wound	Shenandoah, Iowa
22-Dec	*Geo T Williams	M	W	47	M	616 Park Lake Ave	12 yrs	Real Estate	Iowa	Chr Myocarditis	Greenwood
23-Dec	*Charlotte C. Meistermann	F	W	92	W	311 S Rosalind A	27 yrs	At Home	Germany	Valvular Heart Disease	Greenwood
24-Dec	*Wilfred Horton	M	W	58	M	1211 Greenwood Ave / Lynbrook, L.I., N.Y.	2 mo	Salesman	Valley Strain	Cerebral Hemorrhage	Lynbrook, L.I., N.Y.
24-Dec	Will Bennett	M	C	a 38	S	O.G.H. /S E of City	2 ds	Day Labor	D K	Tetanus	County Home
24-Dec	Ed Gibbs	M	C	a 40	M	O.G.H. / S of Orlando	2 ds	Day Labor	S.C.	Stabbed in Abdomen	County Home
26-Dec	*Alfred Warren Frost	M	W	57	M	O.G.H. /N. Y.	1 mo 14 ds	Fruit & Produce	Red Creek, NY	Meningitis	Newark, N.J.
26-Dec	Aider Davis	F	C	a 43	M	616 W Church St. /Kissimmee	5 yrs	House-wife	Thomasville, Ga	Chronic Interstitial Nephritis	Kissimmee
27-Dec	Richard B. Williams	M	C	76	M	730 South	4 mo	Minister	Fla	Uremia Toxemia	Greenwood
27-Dec	*Sarah Inda [Ida] Shafer	F	W	73	M	330 Clay St	2 mo	At Home	Michigan	Cardiac Insufficiency	Cassopolis, Mich
27-Dec	Robert Lee Lucas	M	C	44	M	242 N. Bryan	17 yrs	Laborer	Macon, Ga	Acute Gastric Indigestion	Macon, Ga
27-Dec	*Mrs A. Maude Wallace	F	W	60	M	60 S Bamboo	10 yrs	At Home	Canada	Uremia	Greenwood
27-Dec	*James A. Bass	M	W	16	S	O.G.H.	10 yrs	In School	Orange Co., Fla	Auto Accident	Greenwood
28-Dec	*John Wesley Smith	M	W	83	M	505 Eola Drive	18 ds	Fruit Grower	Canada	Angina Pectoris	Fruitland, Ont, Can.
28-Dec	Frank C. Hart	M	W	62	M	O.G.H. /Kissimmee, Fla	6 yrs	Grocier	Tenn	Septicemia	St. Cloud, Fla
29-Dec	*Bart Henard	M	W	28	M	1006 W. Church St	9 mo	Carpenter	Huntsville, Ala	Pulmonary T B	Murfreesboro, Tenn
29-Dec	*Robert Adair McTyer	M	W	68	M	627 E. Robinson	9 yrs	Retired	Barber Co., Ala	Locomotive Ataxia	Bainbridge, Ga
29-Dec	Elizabeth Turner	F	C	18	S	412 Division Alley	6 yrs	Housework	Live Oak, Fla	Pulmonary Tuberculosis	Live Oak, Fla
26-Dec	Louis Anderson	M	W	75	?	127 W Pine	a 6 mo	?	?	Evidently Heart Disease	County Home
27-Dec	*Mrs Alice E. Cook	F	W	69	W	817 Atlanta Ave	13 yrs	At Home	Tenn	Senility	Greenwood
28-Dec	*Eleanor G. Wilmott	F	W	38	M	O.G.H. /521 E Jackson	9 yrs	At Home	Crescent City, Fla	Toxemia	Greenwood
29-Dec	*Ernest Ternest	M	W	18	S	O.G.H. /Route #4	3 hrs	Day Laborer	Waycross, Ga	Gunshot Wound	Ocoee, Fla
29-Dec	*Ranson B. Collier	M	W	70	M	Masonic Temple / 625 E Cen Ave	1 yr 3 mo	Retired	Blanchester, Ohio	Presumably Angina Pectoris	Vault
31-Dec	*Mrs Lillian Smith	F	W	50	W	1424 Mt Vernon Ave	8 yrs	At Home	Montgomery, Ala	Pneumonia	Greenwood
9-Nov	Infant of Brice & Annie Mobley	M	B		S				Orlando	Stillborn	Greenwood

1927	Name of Deceased	Sex	Race	Age	Marital	Residence & Place of Death	Orlando Resident	Occupation	Place of Birth	Cause of Death	Place of Burial
1-Jan	Naoma Young	F	C	1 yr	Inf	721 S. Westmoreland	1 yr		Orlando	Not Known	Greenwood
1-Jan	*Mrs Anna Jenks	F	W	a 80	W	219 S. Liberty	1 da	At Home	Mass	Carbon Monoxide Poisoning	Nantucket, Mass
2-Jan	Jennie H. Colton	F	W	57	M	Fla Sanitarium /St. Cloud	7 yrs	H.W.	N.Y.	Uremia, Chronic Nephritis	St. Cloud, Fla
2-Jan	*Harry Flash	M	W	70	W	O.G.H. / 315 S. Garland	5 yrs	Day Labor	D.K (Don't Know)	Heart Block	Greenwood
3-Jan	Nathaniel Parks	M	C	5 m	Inf	1044 Randel	4 yrs		Orlando	Don't know	Greenwood
3-Jan	*Hope Starbuck	F	W	51	S	615 E. Livingston	Abt 37 y	At Home	Arkansas	Uremic Poison	Greenwood
4-Jan	*Mr Chas. Howard	M	W	75	W	436 Anderson Court	1 yr 5 mo	Retired	England	Lobar Pneumonia	Rochelle, N.Y.
4-Jan	Janie Floid	F	C	a 90	W	113 N. Terry	1 yr	Invalid	Virginia	Uremic Toxemia	Eastman, Ga
4-Jan	*Mrs Ollie Weiss	F	W	52	M	O.G.H. / RFD#3	2 yrs	At Home	Tenn	Skull Fracture	Oakdale, Tenn
4-Jan	*Bert Harding	M	W	a 40	S	Fla Sanit / Pittsburgh, Pa	1 mo	Real Estate	N. J.	Angina Pectoris	Philadelphia, Pa
4-Jan	*Christopher C. Wilmeth	M	W	64	M	42 E Church St/ Galveston, Texas	10 mo	Real Estate Agent	Tenn	Myocarditis, Degeneration	Florence, Ala
4-Jan	John T. Reddicks [Raddicks]	M	C	52	W	917 W. South	4 yrs	Carpenter	Ga	Uremia, Toxemia	Greenwood
5-Jan	*George Wm. Roberson	M	W	10	S	O.G.H. / 39 N. Terry St.	2 yrs	School	Ark	Septicemia	Malvern, Ark
6-Jan	*Buford Dean	M	W	80	W	310 Long	42y	Retired	Ga	Chronic Myocarditis	Greenwood
7-Jan	*Mrs. Clara Morse	F	W	a 78	W	511 N. Parramore	4 yrs	At Home	Mass	Mitral Regurgitation	East Walpole, Mass
7-Jan	*William Lidsay Nightingale	M	W	14	S	O.G.H. / 1508 E. Concord	1 yr 4 m	School	Va	Streptococcal Endocarditis	Greenwood
9-Jan	Almira Washburn	F	W	77	W	Barlow St.	2 yrs	House wife	N.Y.	Carcinoma Gall Bladder & liver	St. Cloud, Fla
9-Jan	William Shine	M	C			555 W. Church			Orlando	Stillborn	Greenwood
9-Jan	*Hillary N. Neal	M	W	58	M	O.G.H. / Sanford, Fla	5 ds	Market	Ala	Carcinoma of Stomach	Crescent City, Fla
9-Jan	*Albert Sarver	M	W	58	M	Oak Lodge / Milton, Ind	1 mo	Farming	Hamilton, Ohio	Chronic Nephritis	Pershing, Ind
10-Jan	*Eunice C. Ives	F	W	58	S	O.G.H. / 7 W. Gore Ave	45 yr	At Home	Xenia, Ill	Cerebral Hemorrhage	Greenwood
11-Jan	Henry Lawson	M	C	60	W	Americus	3 mo	Laborer	Ga	Anasarca	Greenwood
11-Jan	Leroy Bouyer	M	C	2 m	S	1008 Long	2 mo		Orlando	Pneumonia	Greenwood
12-Jan	Wilbert Robbenson	M	C	4 m	S	514 W. Pine	2 mo	None	Orlando	Cholongitis? Obstruction	Greenwood
12-Jan	*Berry M. Stephens	M	W	60	M	Marks & Mill	5 yrs	Grove Work	Ga	Hypertrophy of Heart	Greenwood
23-Jan	*James Lane Allen	M	W	79	M	Fla Sanit / Montclair, N.J.	8 days	Retired Lawyer	Ky	Interstitial Nephritis	Waukegan, Ill.
13-Jan	*Mrs. Jessie A. Fletcher	F	W	64	W	O.G.H. / Clarcona, Fla	2 ds	At Home	N.Y.	Carcinoma of Stomach	Brooklyn, N.Y.

1927	Name of Deceased	Sex	Race	Age	Marital	Residence & Place of Death	Orlando Resident	Occupation	Place of Birth	Cause of Death	Place of Burial
19-Jan	*Florence Madora Jackson	F	W	6	S	701 W. Central	9 mo		Atlanta, Ga	Acute Dilation of Heart	Atlanta, Ga
7-Jan	Nora Ross	F	C	Abt 51	W	515 W. Washington	4 mos	Laundress	Macon, Ga	Lobar Pneumonia	Greenwood
13-Jan	*Clarence Isabel	W	M	a 9 yrs	S	Peele Ave	8 mo	School	N.Y.	Burns of Back	Vault
15-Jan	*Mrs. Elizabeth Cunningham	F	W	62	W	O.G.H. / N. Rosalind Ave	8 yrs	Dickson Ives Dept. Store	Hannibal, Mo	Pneumonia	Sedalia, Mo
15-Jan	*Mrs. Elizabeth Josephine Colbert	F	W	54	M	O.G.H. / Providence, R.I.	7 ds	At Home	Mass	Uremia	Providence R.I.
19-Jan	*Florence Cornwright	F	W	a 38	M	3205 Clay St /Lewis, N.Y.	2 mo	At Home	Lewis,N.Y	Organic Heart Disease	Lewis, N.Y.
17-Jan	*Willa Davis	F	W	38	M	223 W. Irwin	16 yr	At Home	Brunson, S.C.	Acute Uremia	Greenwood
17-Jan	*Ella S. Kendry	F	W	63	M	8182 Anderson	1 yr	At Home	Conn	Acute Dilitation of Heart	Vault
17-Jan	*Edwin Clayton McDowell	M	W	54	M	W Central Ave	41 yrs	Deputy Sheriff	Ashville, N.C.	Arterio-sclerosis	Greenwood
19-Jan	*Mary Louise Scott	F	W	58	M	982 Marks	1 yr	At Home	Penn	Broncho Pneumonia	Danville, Penn
19-Jan	Thomas H. Sanders	M	C	52	M	921 Edna	4 yrs	Laborer	Ga	Acute Dilitation of Heart	Greenwood
19-Jan	John McFerson	M	C	31	S	O.G.H. / Taft, Fla	2 ds	Laborer	Ga	Fracture of Spine	Conway, Fla
20-Jan	*William D. Wethington	M	W	35	M	Washington & Main Sts /717 W Church	2 yrs	Brick Mason	Ala	Prob. Acute Dilatation of Heart	Greenwood
21-Jan	James Thomas	M	C		S	332 N. Parramore			Orlando	Stillborn	Greenwood
14-Jan	Allen L. Simmons	M	C	51	M	820 W. Livingston	3 yrs	Soda Water Mfg	Ga	Diabetic Gangrene of Legs	Greenwood
22-Jan	Ollie Houts	F	C	44	W	632 W. Washington	5 mo	House-work	Ga	Gunshot	Cairo, Ga
21-Jan	William Kernon	M	W	87	M	435 Broadway	14 yrs	Retired	Ireland	Senility	Sanford, Maine
22-Jan	*Thomas J. Wood	M	W	71	M	Country Club	3ds	Com. Merchant	Ireland	Prob. Chronic Heart Condition	Staten Island, N.Y.
24-Jan	*Martha W. Stowell	F	W	80	S	Gatlin Ave	2 mo+	Retired Teacher	Oswego Co, N.Y.	Organic Heart Disease	Oswego, N.Y.
30-Jan	Stillborn of Elsie Buchanan	M	W		Inf				Orlando	Stillborn	
31-Jan	William Betterson	M	C	1	Inf	1032 W. Livingston	1 yr		Orlando	Unknown	Greenwood
13-Jan	James Gavin	M	C		Inf	209 N. Lee	1 yr	Infant	Fla		Greenwood
23-Jan	John Williams	M	C	11m	Inf	606 Albany Ave	6 mo	Infant	Fla		Greenwood
24-Jan	*Lillian Neppner	F	W	39	S	1605 Asher	11 mos	At Home	Chicago, Ill	Carcinoma of Uterus	Cremation

1927	Name of Deceased	Sex	Race	Age	Marital	Residence & Place of Death	Orlando Resident	Occupation	Place of Birth	Cause of Death	Place of Burial
24-Jan	*Reuben Pratt Foley	M	W	63	M	O.G.H. / Winter Park, Fla	7 ds	Wellsboro, Ga	Seminole Hotel	Chr. Nephritis	Winter Park
24-Jan	*Jas. Barto Christian	M	W	1	S	O.G.H. / Ocoee, Fla	2 ds		Porterdale, Ga	Acute Broncho Pneumonia	Covington, Ga
24-Jan	John Vance	M	C	abt 25	M	Kentucky & Amelia	1 yr	Laborer	Hilhouse, Ga	Septicemia	Greenwood
25-Jan	A. L. Smiley	M	C	abt 43	S	1230 W. Carter	6 mos	Store Keeper	Ruffin, S.C.	Acute Nephritis	Greenwood
26-Jan	*Belton O'Neal Stansell	M	W	82	W	623 N. Broadway /Tampa, Fla	abt 3 yrs	Retired Farmer	Barnwell, S.C.	Myocarditis, Degeneration	Elko, S.C.
26-Jan	*Mrs. Sarah F. Boone	F	W	71	W	112 Grace	65 yrs	At Home	Reideville, Ga	Pneumonia, Lobar	Greenwood
26-Jan	*J. Franklin Wilkins	M	W	62	D	306 S. Thornton St.	6 wks	Salesman, Grocery	Girard, Ga?	Cardiac Failure	Waynesboro, Ga
27-Jan	*Louise W. Achstetter	F	W	63	W	County Home	1 yr	At Home	New York	Carcinoma of Uterus	Greenwood
27-Jan	*Arimida A. Thomas	F	W	76	W	436 Revere	12 yrs	At Home	Canton, Ill	Chr. Myocarditis	Greene, Iowa
28-Jan	*Lester Powell Schilling	M	W	18	S	2022 Nebraska Ave	4 yrs		Meadsgrove, Neb	Heart Failure	Greenwood
28-Jan	*Chester Milton Hanks	M	W	9	S	O.G.H. / St. Johns Berry, Vt	3 mo		N.H.	General Septicemia	Rumney, NH
28-Jan	*Irene Daizie Jones	F	W	40	M	Fla San	4 wk	HW	Nova Scotia	Suicide from drowning	Sarasota, Fla
29-Jan	O. B. Harrison	M	C		S	523 W. Church		None	Orlando	Stillborn	Greenwood
30-Jan	*Frederick Mass	F	W	79	W	1213 Eastin	8 mo	At Home	Germany	Pneumonia, Lobar	Greenwood
30-Jan	Ulee Anderson	F	C	25	W	1035 W. Jefferson	7 yrs	Domestic Duties	Winfield, Fla	Pulmonary Tuberculosis	Greenwood
31-Jan	*Rodney Hansel Prescott	M	W	1 da	S	O.G.H. / RFD Box 100	1 da		Orlando	Amafblepys?	Greenwood
31-Jan	*Howard R. Meacham	M	W	60	M	OG.H. / Cortland, N.Y.	1 mo 9 ds	Dealer in Live Stock	Cortland, N.Y.	Cardio-nephritis	Cortland, N.Y.
31-Jan	*Myrtle B. Batey	F	W	50	M	11316 E. Robinson	4 yrs	At Home	Nashville, Tenn	Acute Cardiac Dilitation	Greenwood
31-Jan	Charlie Minor	M	C	23	S	592 W. Church	1 mo	Laborer	N.C.	Gunshot Wound	Greenwood
1-Feb	*Emma O. Brewer	F	W	82	W	101 E. Colonial	9 yrs	At Home	Demoplis, Fla	Angina Pectoris	Greenwood
2-Feb	*Maurice Murray	M	W	54	M	OG.H.	14 ds	Day Labor	Manuel Co., Ga	Pneumonia, Lobar	Stillmore, Ga
3-Feb	*Raymond J. Woodbery	M	W	39	D	O.G.H.	14 ds	Laborer	Quincy, Fla	Strangulated Bowel	Quincy, Fla
3-Feb	*Marjorie C. Clark	F	W	15	S	O.G.H. / 1003 E. Jackson	18 mos	In School	Lakewood, Ohio	Peritonitis Following Appendicitis	Cremated
4-Feb	*Mrs. Anna Randall	F	W	72	W	335 W. Carter	8 yrs	At Home	Black Rock, Ark	Cardiac Asthma	Greenwood
4-Feb	*Mrs. Edith Victoria Carter	F	W	69	W	1311 N. Mill	6 yrs	At Home	Boxley, Ga	Acute Broncho Pneumonia	Boxley, Ga
5-Feb	J. H. Younge	M	C	54	M	O.G.H. / Eustis, Fla	2 ds	Farmer	Stokes, Fla	Gangrene of Intestine	Eustis, Fla

1927	Name of Deceased	Sex	Race	Age	Marital	Residence & Place of Death	Orlando Resident	Occupation	Place of Birth	Cause of Death	Place of Burial
5-Feb	*Infant of Mr & Mrs Walter Griffin	M	W		S	O.G.H.			Orlando	Immature Fetus	Greenwood
7-Feb	Laura Brantly	F	C	35	W	501 W. Robinson	4 ds	Evangelist	Fla	Tubercular	Greenwood
8-Feb	Johnie Stuart	M	C	2 m	Inf	721 West-moreland	2 mos		Orlando	Colitis	Greenwood
9-Feb	Infant of L. & Allie Daniels	M	C			412 W. Pine			Orlando	Stillbirth	Greenwood
4-Feb	*M. L. Gage	M	W	68	W	O.G.H. / Detroit, Mich	1 da	Real Estate	Lockport, N.Y.	Arterio-sclerosis	Lockport, N.Y.
8-Feb	*Preston Sowell	M	C	46	M	O.G.H.	1 da	Laborer	N.C.	Perforated Duodenal Ulcer	Charlotte, N.C.
9-Feb	*Chas. W. Mason	M	W	66	M	1420 N.Y. Ave /Chicago, Ill	1 yr	Carpenter	Belleview, Fla	Myocarditis	Greenwood
10-Feb	*Edward Hobbs Walker	M	W	65	M	O.G.H. / 211 America	45 yrs	Fruit Grower	Jefferson Co,. N.Y.	Chronic Nephritis	Greenwood
10-Feb	*Anna M. Donahue	F	W	56	W	Route #1	6 yrs	At Home	Iowa	Tuberculosis	Greenwood
11-Feb	*Alick A. Marshall	M	W	69	W	920 Beaver? Ave	7 yrs	Retired	Ga	Lobar Pneumonia	Greenwood
12-Feb	*Laney Leon Gannon	M	W		S	O.G.H. / Sanford, Fla	1 da		Sanford, Fla	Encephalitis	Sanford, Fla
12-Feb	Nancy Smith	F	C	57	M	219 S. Division St.	14 ds	H.W.	Ga	Gangrene of Intestine	Zellwood
13-Feb	James Jackson	M	C	1	S	810 S. Parramore	9 mos	None	Orlando	Bronco Pneumonia	Greenwood
13-Feb	*John T. Moore	M	W	65	M	Lockhart /Orlando	1 da	Minister of Gospel	Blaine, Ky	Organic Heart Disease	Ashland, Ky
13-Feb	*Iver R. Carlson	M	W	36	M	O.B.H. / Keokuk, Iowa	6 mos	Traffic Mgr	Keokuk, Iowa	Pachy meningitis	Keokuk, Iowa
14-Feb	*Mrs. Elizabeth Ewing	F	W	67	W	O.G.H. / Ewington, Ohio	1 da	At Home	Ohio	Pneumonia	Vinton, Ohio
14-Feb	*Mrs. Jessie S. Phelps	F	W	51	M	Fla Sant /Batavia, N.Y.	21 ds	At Home	Hermitage N.Y.	Surgical Shock	Boston, N.Y.
15-Feb	*Loui Leopold Boyle	M	W	48	M	Orlando Ave	2 yrs	Clerk	Agusta, Ga	Apoplexy	Greenwood
16-Feb	Mrs. Bessie Macreadie	F	W	50	M	Fla San	12 ds	HW	Portland, Me	Cerebral Hemorrhage	Daytona Beach, Fla
16-Feb	*Frank Robt. Roe	M	W	41	M	Howell Sant / Orlando	1 yr	Manager of Transfer Co.	Tenn	Tuberculosis	Daytona, Fla
17-Feb	Catherine Carter	F	W	9 mo	Inf	428 W. Roberson	1 yr	Infant	Orlando	Broncho Pneumonia	Greenwood
17-Feb	*Mrs Alice McCorkle Dunlop	F	W	abt 67	W	51 E Concord	2 mo 14ds	At Home	Va	Angina Pectoris	Lexington, Va
18-Feb	*Mrs Ellen Francis Burnett	F	W	87	W	212 N. Rosalind Ave	16 yrs	At Home	Mass	Nephritis	Greenwood
19-Feb	Mammie William Harley	F	C	33	M	502 Parramore	15 yrs	Seam-stress	Fla	Cardiac Drop-sy, Acute Nephritis	Store Butler - Greenwood
19-Feb	Hattie May Nebbick	F	C	3 mos	S	511 Lee	3 mo		Orlando	Broncho Pneumonia	Greenwood

1927	Name of Deceased	Sex	Race	Age	Marital	Residence & Place of Death	Orlando Resident	Occupation	Place of Birth	Cause of Death	Place of Burial
21-Feb	Osbourne T. Eales	M	W	54	M	O.G.H. / Umatilla, Fla	6	U.S. Soldier	England	Acute Abdominal Peritonitis	Umatilla, Fla
21-Feb	*William Walace Rutherford	M	W	57	M	328 N. Main /Canton, N.Y.	3 mo	Supt State School Farm Canton	Madrid, N.Y.	Carbon Monoxide Affixation	Rochester, N.Y.
21-Feb	Edward David Culver	M	W	5	S	Orlando /38 D	5 mo		Orlando	Acute Dysentery	Lake Hill Cemetery
22-Feb	*Infant of Mr & Mrs John Stone	F	W		S	22 Hanks Auto Camp			Orlando	Stillborn	Cremation
22-Feb	*Paul Patterson Mohler	M	W	6 ds	S	O.G.H. / 15 W Moreland Dr.	6 ds		Orlando	Immature?	Cremation
22-Feb	Verneta Berkins	F	C	27	S	532 Holden Ave	22 yrs	Seamstress	Fla	Pulmonary Hemorrhage	Greenwood
22-Feb	Essie Mae Johnson	F	C			419 Quincy Ave			Fla	Stillborn	Greenwood
23-Feb	Essie Neblish	F	C	3 m	S	511 Lee	3 mo		Orlando	Broncho Pneumonia	Greenwood
23-Feb	*Nina Rachel Hollis	F	W	64	W	113 N. Hyer St	3 yrs	At Home	Tenn	Pulmonary Tuberculosis	Ruppertown, Tenn
23-Feb	*Infant of Mr & Mrs B J Hutchins	M	W		S	O.G.H.			Orlando	Stillborn	Greenwood
24-Feb	*Tina King	F	W	18	M	Orlando /Sanitarium	8 yrs	At Home	Iowa	Acute Heart Dilitation	Cremation
25-Feb	*David V. Doyle	M	W	32	M	County Home	32 yrs	Glazier	Orlando, Fla	Pulmonary Tuberculosis	Greenwood
25-Feb	*Margaret Edith Dickens	F	W	7	S	635 W. Pine	8 mo		Fitzgerald, Ga	Broncho Pneumonia	Locus Grove, Ga
26-Feb	*Mrs Anna B. Nyblom	F	W	74	W	510 E. Concord	2 yrs	At Home	Sweden	Carcinoma of Liver	Jacksonville, Fla
26-Feb	*Robt Allen Jenkins	M	W	69	W	Fla San / Longwood, Fla	7 ds	Retired	Americus, Ga	Pneumonia, Bronchial, Double	Longwood, Fla
27-Feb	A. Felton Purcell	M	W	34	M	Fla Sant /500 Crystal Place	10 yrs	Merchant	Mize, Ga.	Tubercular Peritonitis	Greenwood
28-Feb	*Etta Matthews	F	W	45	M	O.G.H. / 415 Gunty Ave	2 yrs	At Home	Racine, Wis	Ch. Myocarditis	Racine, Wis
28-Feb	Mattie Brown	F	C	26	M	48 N. Parramore	3 yrs	HW	Fla	Acute Gastritis	Greenwood
13-Feb	Louise Peasley	F	W	82	W	Seminole Hotel Winter Park / Chicago, Ill	2 mo	At Home	?	Broncho Pneumonia	Chicago, Ill
19-Feb	Elsie Mae Piner	F	C	5 m	Inf	1015 Bentley	5 mo		Orlando	Pulmonary Tuberculosis	Greenwood
24-Feb	Bernis Daniels	F	C	10 ds	Inf	1203 Conley	10 ds		Orlando	Marasmus	Greenwood
24-Feb	E. D. Boone	M	C	25	M	O.G.H. / Sand Hill, Fla		Laborer	Don't Know	Perforation of Ileum and Bladder	Greenwood
1-Mar	*Infant of Mr & Mrs John R. Stewart	M	W		S	1216 Wilson Ave			Orlando	Premature not viable	Cremated
1-Mar	*Infant of Mr & Mrs Chas. O. Patrick	M	W		S	Angebilt Add			Orlando	Infancy	Lake Hill Cemetery

1927	Name of Deceased	Sex	Race	Age	Marital	Residence & Place of Death	Orlando Resident	Occupation	Place of Birth	Cause of Death	Place of Burial
2-Mar	*J. E. Little	M	W	68	M	O.G.H. / Winter Garden	2 mo	Day Labor	Miss	Chr. Myocarditis	Oakland
2-Mar	Infant of Robert & Julia Calhoun	F	C		S	Newmart /William Ave			Orlando	Stillborn	Greenwood
4-Mar	*Infant of Mr & Mrs Wm. V. Deming	M	W		S	1012 E. Jackson			Orlando	Stillborn	Cremated
4-Mar	*James Scott	M	W	71	M	O.G.H./ Hamilton, Ont	4 mo	Merchant	Hamilton, Ont	Cardiac Asthma	Hamilton, Ont
5-Mar	917 Long [Richard Brown]	M	C	43	M	917 Long	4 yrs	Cook	Ga	Chr. Myocarditis	Greenwood
5-Mar	Joseph B. Midgett	M	W	2 mo	S	1219 W. Church	2 mo		Orlando	Colitis	Lake Hill Cemetery
5-Mar	*Samuel Robt. Pooser	M	W	41	M	Fla. San /5508 S. Seminole, Tampa	17 ds	Book-keeper	Ocala, Fla	Myocarditis	Tampa, Fla
5-Mar	*James Pierce	M	W	12	S	OGH / Lake Gem	1 da	School	Ga	Gunshot Wound, Right Chest	Ocoee
5-Mar	*Mrs Minnie Henderson	F	W	55	M	617 Lexington	4 yrs	At Home	Ind	Carcinoma of Liver	Brazil, Ind
6-Mar	*Bryant Turneage	M	W	29	S	O.G.H. / Webster, Fla	2 ds	Day Labor	Webster, Fla	Fractured Pelvis	Webster, Fla
6-Mar	*Andrew Bisset	M	W	50	M	405 S. America	10 yrs	Laborer	Scotland	Pulmonary Tuberculosis	Greenwood
6-Mar	*Mrs. Minnie McDaniels	F	W	41	M	O.G.H.	1	HW	Asheville, N.C.	Broncho Pneumonia	Anderson, S.C.
7-Mar	Mary Demps	F	C	13	S	735 Erin?	3	None	Orlando	Acute Endocarditis	Greenwood
7-Mar	*Mrs Mary S. Cobb	F	W	58	M	54 Revere /Marion, Mass	3 mos	At Home	Newton, Mass	Angina Pectoris	Marion, Mass
7-Mar	*Patrick Henry Swann	M	W	68	M	O.G.H. / Hunt-ington, Wva	1 da	Retired	Cabell, WVa	Cerebral Hemorrhage	Huntington Wva
8-Mar	*Amos Lawton Woodworth	M	W	71	M	E. Rob	3 yrs		Sterling, N.Y.	Cerebral Hemorrhage	Fulton, N.Y.
8-Mar	*Infant of Mr & Mrs M E Brown	F	W	1 da	S	O.G.H. / RFD#1	few min-utes		Orlando, Fla	Prematurity	Conway, Fla
8-Mar	*Ethel Duplantis	F	W	10	S	O.G.H.	6 mo	School	Covington La	Acute Intestinal Obstruction	Covington, La
9-Mar	*Mrs Florence E. Fennelle	F	W	41	M	O.G.H. / Rochester, N.Y.	14 ds	At Home	Grenadier Island, Canada	Chronic Par-enchymatous Nephritis	Rochester, N.Y.
9-Mar	Infant of Robert & Charlie Mae Smith	M	C		S	John St across Parramore			Orlando	Stillborn	Don't know
3-Mar	May Pearl Randall	F	C	3 mo	S	1210 Carter St.	7 ds		Fla	Don't know	Greenwood
5-Mar	*Mrs Francis Hoskins Harrod	F	W	35	W	Col & R /Sioux City, Iowa	2 mo	At Home	Sioux City, Iowa	RR Crossing Accident	Cremation
6-Mar	*Mrs Alice May Lord	F	W	70	M	600 Lucere Circle	42 yr	At Home	Pontiac, Mich	Acute Dili-tation of Heart	Greenwood
7-Mar	Infant of Ossie Johnson	F	C			812 W. Long			Fla	Stillborn	Greenwood

1927	Name of Deceased	Sex	Race	Age	Marital	Residence & Place of Death	Orlando Resident	Occupation	Place of Birth	Cause of Death	Place of Burial
7-Mar	*Edward J. Patterson	M	W	50	M	1410 Canton Ave	5 mo	Baggage Master	Dorchester, N.H.	Influenza	Rumley, N.H.
8-Mar	*John A. Watson	M	W	70	M	Fla Sant /1821 Garland	4 mo	Retired	Canada	Lobar Pneumonia	Greenwood
9-Mar	Infant of Hezekiah Baker	M	C	1	Inf	745 Avondale	1 da		Fla	Don't know	Greenwood
28-Mar	Dr. Oliver Cone	M	C	50	W	606 W. South	1 mo	Doctor	Ga	Abscess of the Lung	Apalacha-cola, Fla
9-Mar	*Legone States, Jr.	M	W	8 mo	S	Orlando, Fla	8 mo 19 d		Orlando	Acute Ileocolitis	Greenwood
10-Mar	Calvin G. Jackson	M	C	3 mo	Inf	807 W South	9 mo		Orlando	Gastro-enteritis	Greenwood
10-Mar	Abram Herrin	M	C	86	W	427 S. Terry	10 yrs	Laborer	Ga	Acute Dilita-tions of Heart	Greenwood
10-Mar	*Thos. Jefferson Wolford	M	W	76	M	Lockhart	6 ys	Retired	Ga	Broncho Pneumonia	Lake Hill
11-Mar	*Cleveland A. Savell	M	W	37	M	O.G.H. / Eustis, Fla	3 ds	Real Estate Broker	Ala	Uremia	Hartford, Ala
15-Mar	William Jordon	M	C	22	M	O.G.H. / 545 Link Ave	1 yr	Laborer	S.C.	Cerebral Hemorrhage	Charleston, S.C.
12-Mar	*Tom Seacy	M	C	abt 40	M	O.G.H. / Maitland, Fla	30 min	Day Labor	Ga	Pistol Shot	County Home
12-Mar	*Samuel Enos Prather	M	W	76	M	8 W. Woodlawn Blvd	a 3 mos	Farming	Ohio	Lobar Pneumonia	Springfield, Ill
12-Mar	Lena Norwood	F	W	8 m	S	Fla Sant / Titusville, Fla	few hrs		S.C.	Influenza	Titusville, Fla
13-Mar	Carrie B. Davis	F	C	29	M	437 W. Moreland	1 wk	Domestic Duties	Ala	Acute Gastritis	Enterprise, Ala
13-Mar	*Dominick Poncia	M	W	27	S	O.G.H. / Boston, Mass	1 mo 15 d	Prof. Boxer	Italy	Fractured Spine - Auto Wreck	Greenwood
14-Mar	*Geo. Williams, Jr.	M	W	3 mo	S	1044 Citrus & Parramore	3 mo 1 da		Orlando	Colitis	Greenwood
16-Mar	Wern Harding Brown	M	C	1	S	Fla /730 Long	1/8 /25		Fla	Acute Broncho Pneumonia	Satsuma, Fla
16-Mar	*Mrs Elizabeth P. Brookshire	F	W	90	W	N. Orange Ave	12 yrs	At Home	N.C.	Senility	Raleigh, N.C.
16-Mar	A. J. Swain	M	W	60	M	Fla San /Lakeland, Fla	3 mo	Retired	Mich	Carcinoma of the Pros-tate Gland	Boise, Idaho
16-Mar	*Wm Clinton Jurnigan	M	W	74	M	Ky Ave	6 yrs	Retired	Clint Co., Ga	Chronic Myocarditis	Greenwood
17-Mar	*Mrs Mamie S. Gray	F	W	61	W	1606 E. Robinson	7 mo		Columbia Co., Ga	Primary Pernicious Anemia	Greenwood
18-Mar	Julia Murray	F	C	63	S	604 Delaney	7 yrs		S.C.	Uremia	Greenwood
19-Mar	*Haywood Tell Chastain	M	W	1	S	O.G.H. / Ocoee,Fla	4 ds		Ocoee, Fla	Acute Gas-tric Intestinal Intoxication	Ocoee, Fla
19-Mar	*Jas H. Nixon	M	W	46	M	103 Hillards	1/5 /14		Ireland	Leukemia	Brestwood, N.H.
20-Mar	*Bettie Jo Botsford	F	W	2 m	S	1406 S. Westmoreland	2 mo		Orlando	Acute Meningitis	Greenwood
20-Mar	*Mrs Ada H. Garrett	F	W	86	W	628 N. Orange	6 yrs	At Home	Miss	Senility	Nashville, Tenn

1927	Name of Deceased	Sex	Race	Age	Marital	Residence & Place of Death	Orlando Resident	Occupation	Place of Birth	Cause of Death	Place of Burial
20-Mar	*Infant of Mr & Mrs W. D. Williams	F	W		S	101 W Moreland			Orlando	Premature Not Viable	Greenwood
20-Mar	*Mary Hurst	F	W	a 30	W	333 W Pine	7 yrs	At Home	Va	Broncho Pneumonia	Greenwood
21-Mar	V. Marie Creamer	F	W	2 m	S	1034 W. Jackson	2 mo 7 ds		Orlando	Congenital Heart Disease	Greenwood
22-Mar	*Mrs Blanche L. Smith	F	W	55	M	Fla Sant /Mt Dora, Fla	2 ds	At Home	N.J.	Apoplexy	Mt Dora, Fla
22-Mar	*Ruff Whitson	M	W	54	M	Howell Sant / Grand Ave	7 mo	Deputy Sheriff	Tenn	Interstitial Nephritis	Herrion, Ill
22-Mar	*Wm J. Smith	M	W	81?	M	Fla Sant /Ohio	18 mos	Retired	Canada	Septicemia	Cleveland, Ohio
22-Mar	Lillie Withams	F	C	34	M	714 Conley	4 yrs	Laundress	Ga	Asthma	Greenwood
23-Mar	*Harry Miller Fitzgerald	M	W	57	M	O.G.H. / Crofton, Penn	3 mo 1 da	Special Agt Tariff Bureau	W.Va	Pernicious Anemia	Cameron, Wva.
23-Mar	*Mrs. Amanda E. White	F	W	68	M	O.G.H. / 502 Raehn Ave	43 yrs	At Home	Ga	Angina Pectoris	Greenwood
24-Mar	*Floyd E. Darling	M	W	50	M	O.G.H. / RFD	1 yr 7 mo	Mechanist	Mass	Carcinoma of Stomach	Greenwood
24-Mar	Infant of Mr & Mrs W. F. Smith	F	W		S	Michigan Ave			Orlando	Stillborn	Conway
24-Mar	Earnest Davis	M	C	4 m	S	1013 Long St	9 mo		Orlando	Ascaris? Lumbricoids?	Greenwood
24-Mar	Inez Demps	F	C	6 m	S	311 S. Bryan	6 mo		Orlando	Ascaris? Lumbricoids?	Greenwood
25-Mar	*Jas. P. Luby	M	W	a 76	S	O.G.H. / 208 Bryant	6 yrs	Retired	Canada	Cerebral Embollus?	Greenwood
25-Mar	M. S. Hill	M	C	57	M	618 W. Jackson	30 yrs	Merchant	Fla	Toxemia	Greenwood
26-Mar	Gladys Hayes Jackson	F	W	25	M	O.G.H. / Altoona, Fla	9 ds	House wife	Altoona, Fla	Pneumonia, Lobar	Umatilla, Fla
26-Mar	*Joseph Allie Wells	M	W	68	M	O.G.H. / 1136 Lexington	3 yrs	Hotel Business	Maine	Acute Appendicitis	Kissimmee
26-Mar	*Mrs. Adelaide L. Kintner	F	W	32	M	2311 E Cen. Ave / Pains-ville, Ohio	1 yr	At Home	Mich	Organic Heart Disease	Painsville, O
27-Mar	*Robt. Mitchell Buckmaster	M	W	81	M	106 N. Hill	13 yrs	Retired	Ohio	Pneumonia	St. Cloud, Fla
27-Mar	Louis Williams	M	C	3 mo	S	O.G.H. / City Point, Fla	1 da		Fla	Strangulated Bowel	City Point, Fla
28-Mar	*Mary A. Clark	F	W	80	W	316 E. Pine	16 yrs	At Home	Tenn	Acute Uremia	Greenwood
28-Mar	Charles Edwin Wills	M	W	42	M	O.G.H. / St. Cloud, Fla	2 hrs	Mechanic	N.Y.	Gun Shot	St. Cloud, Fla
29-Mar	*Annie Ethel Cobb	F	W	55	M	130 America? /Stoughton, Mass	1 mo	At Home	Mass	Cerebral Hemorrhage	Stoughton, Mass
29-Mar	*Infant of Mr & Mrs John A Gray	F	W		S	O.G.H. / Mt Dora, Fla			Orlando	Stillborn	Cremation
29-Mar	Mildred Simms?	F	C	8 mo		550 John	8 mo		Fla	Amebic Dysentery	Greenwood

1927	Name of Deceased	Sex	Race	Age	Marital	Residence & Place of Death	Orlando Resident	Occupation	Place of Birth	Cause of Death	Place of Burial
30-Mar	Miriam R. Wright	F	W	25	S	O.G.H. / Howey, Fla	1 da	Principal Howey School	Washington D.C.	Accidental Burn ?	Vault
31-Mar	*Robt. Craig	M	W	25	M	O.G.H. / Pine Castle	4 ds	Laborer	Ohio	Streptoies? Meningitis	Greenwood
31-Mar	*George W. Peck	F	W	47	M	O.G.H. / 31 N. Mill	4 yrs	Accountant & Auditor	Morley, Mich	Uremia	Greenwood
1-Apr	Infant of Mr & Mrs Homer Quilling	M	W		S	837 Talloka			Orlando	Premature Labor	Lake Hill Cemetery
1-Apr	*Marilyn Buell	F	W	7 ds	S	E. Auto Camp	2 ds		Orlando	Hemophiliac Hemorrhage	Greenwood
3-Apr	*LeRoy Vern Pratt	M	W	21	S	O.G.H. / Holden Ave	14 yrs	Fireman	Albany, Ill	Acute Cardiac Dilitation	Greewood
3-Apr	*Leola Evlyn Fenn	F	W	4	S	O.G.H. / Winter Garden	1 da	Teacher	Rochelle, Ga	Pelvic Peritonitis	Rochelle, Ga
3-Apr	*Mrs Annie Stanners	F	W	76	W	1502 E. Hillvert?	20 yrs		Fairfield, S.C.	Stroke of Paralysis	Ft. Christmas
5-Apr	*Grace Earl Willis	F	W	1	S	335 Long St	13 mos		Orlando	Lobar Pneumonia	Greenwood
6-Apr	Charles Henderson	M	C	21	S	O.G.H. / Groveland, Fla	1 yr	Laborer	Fla	Post Operative Shock	Greenwood
3-Apr	Nancy Clinton	F	C	64	M	732 America	13 yrs	H W	Ga	Acute Dilatation of Heart	Greenwood
4-Apr	Doris Turner	F	C	3 mo	Inf	412 Division Cty	3 mo		Orlando	Septic Pyemia	Greenwood
8-Apr	*David B. Foster	M	W	63	M	Fla Sant /Dravoburg, Pa	Since Aprl	Watch-man	Penn	Cardiac Decompensation	Homestead, Pa
9-Apr	*Mattie Leona Woodward	F	W	28	M	O.G.H. / Winter Garden	6 wk	At Home	Aiken, S.C.	Septic Endocarditis	Aiken, S.C.
2-Apr	*Wilks Spivey	M	W	4	S	O.G.H. / Winter Garden	4 yrs		Winter Garden, Fla	Typhoid Fever	Beulah Cemetery
3-Apr	Infant of Walter Stephens	M - F	C		Inf	908 John Court	4 yrs parents		Orlando, Fla	No physician	Greenwood
4-Apr	Mae Bell Murry	F	C	18	S	423 Chathorn St.	6 yrs	School Girl	S.C.	Appendicitis	Greenwood
8-Apr	*Sarah Cole Skillman	F	W	87	W	614 E. Concord	sev. yrs	At Home	Ohio	Acute Dilitation of Heart	Greenwood
11-Apr	*Mrs Clara Hayes Caryell	F	W	a 80	M	S. Fern Creek Dr.	10 yrs	At Home	N.Y.	Hypostatic Pneumonia	Chicago, Ill
12-Apr	*Rev. Father John M. Barry	M	W	76	S	Fla San	22 ds	Priest	Maryland	Multiple Sclerosis Of Liver	Baltimore, Md
12-Apr	*Mrs Cora A. Vreeland	F	W	67	W	521 Carter	4 yrs	At Home	New Jersey	Pulmonary Edema & Uremia	Greenwood
13-Apr	A. L. Mongomery	M	C	55	S	O.G.H / Groveland Fl.	8 ds	Laborer	N.C.	Acute Enteritis	Groveland, Fla
13-Apr	Louise Charlott Gersendorfer	F	W	34	M	Fla San / Tavares	30 hrs	At Home	Cleveland, Ohio	Uremia	Cleveland, Ohio
13-Apr	Albert Wise Dowdell	M	C	55	W	501 S Parramore	30 yrs	Brick Mason	Ala	Hemorrhage of Lungs	Greenwood

1927	Name of Deceased	Sex	Race	Age	Marital	Residence & Place of Death	Orlando Resident	Occupation	Place of Birth	Cause of Death	Place of Burial
14-Apr	Josephine Bullard	F	C	5ds	Inf	19 Hicks	5 yrs		Ga	Don't know	Greenwood
17-Apr	Cornelius Branham	M	C	35	M	312 W. Jackson	7 yrs	Orange Cutter	Hamburg, Fla	Peritonitis	Greenwood
13-Apr	Eli Lott	M	C	26	S	800 Avondale	2 yrs	Presser	Ga	Tuberculosis	Greenwood
14-Apr	*Winiford Burkhalter	F	W	8 mos	S	O.G.H. / 334 Carter	8 mo		Orlando	Surgical Shock	Greenwood
15-Apr	Unknown	M	C	a 50	unk	612 Carter	1 da	Day Labor	DK	Probably Alcoholism	Greenwood
17-Apr	*William Stych	M	W	71	W	2612 Sanitarium Ave	8 yrs	Retired	Bradda, Isle of Mann	Epilepsy	Greenwood
17-Apr	*Mrs. Annie Parnell	F	W	64	W	O.G.H. / R 1 Box 51-0	2 yrs	At Home	Columbia Co., Fla	Apoplexy	Largo, Fla
17-Apr	*Wendall Cox	M	W	4 mos	S	O.G.H. / Melbourne, Fla	3 ds		Atlanta, Ga	Acute Broncho Pneumonia	Greenwood
18-Apr	*Henry Gero	M	W	53	M	410 E Amelia	4 yrs	Book-keeper	Budapest, Hungary	Apoplipea?	Cremation
9-Apr	Lottie Cain	F	C	45	W	14 N.Bryan	39 yrs	Midwife	Fla	Vascular Tumor of Liver	Greenwood
26-Apr	*Hughey Goolsby	M	W	42	M	O.GH. / E Central Ave	6 mo	Grove Work	Orange Co., Fla	Amebic Dysentery	Greenwood
20-Apr	*Joseph Dawson	M	W	66	W	420 S. DeLaney	32 yrs	Salesman	S.C.	Arterio-sclerosis	Greenwood
20-Apr	*Mrs Phoebe Nelson Bingham	F	W	72	M	224 Lucerne Circle	12 yrs	At Home	N.Y.	Chronic Intestinal Nephritis	Brooklyn, N.Y.
22-Apr	*Mary Bell Brooks	F	W	55	M	O.G.H. / Apopka	22 ds	At Home	Grady Co., Ga	Cardiac Dilitation	Greenwood
23-Apr	*Thomas P. Grant	M	W	72	M	430 S. Maine	24 yrs	Retired	Butler Co, Penn	Cerebral Hemorrhage	Beaver, Penn
24-Apr	*Lewis Simmons, Jr.	M	W	62	M	Fla San /Claricona, Fla	5 da	Retired	N.J.	Carcinoma of Pyloria	Greenwood
25-Apr	*William Barnette McClure	M	W	79	W	Fla Sanitarium / Chattanooga, Tenn	3 mo	Retired	Pittsburgh, Pa	Cancer of Bladder	Chatta-nooga, Tenn
24-Apr	*Thos. J. Dresen	M	W	64	M	530 S. Eola Drive	7 yrs	Retired	Wis	Pulmonary Edema	Greenwood
24-Apr	*Geo. T. Lovell	M	W	67	M		4 yrs	Retired	Mich	Suicide by Drowning	Cremation
25-Apr	*Mrs. Celestia J. Jones	F	W	91	W	720 Hilcrest Ave	3 yrs	At Home	La Porte, Ind	Myocarditis	Evanston, Ill
27-Apr	*Addison M. Scott	M	W	84	M	Fla San /Charles-ton, WVa	2 yrs 3 mo	Retired	Aetna, N.Y.	Broncho Pneumonia	Dryden, N.Y.
27-Apr	*Richard Caldwell	M	C	25	S	115 N. Terry	2 yrs	Laborer	Quincy, S.C.	Myocarditis	Greenwood
28-Apr	Emma Tilman	F	C	19	S	44 W. Jefferson	3 yrs	HW	Thomas-ville, Ga	Aortic Re-gurgitation	Greenwood
30-Apr	*Infant of Fred & Mary DeFord	F	W		S	Lockhart			Lockhart	Premature	Cremated
1-May	Noah Green	M	C	63	M	139 Beggs	32 yrs	Laborer	Quincy	Acute Nephritis	Greenwood

1927	Name of Deceased	Sex	Race	Age	Marital	Residence & Place of Death	Orlando Resident	Occupation	Place of Birth	Cause of Death	Place of Burial
2-May	*Parker Enwright	M	W	23	M	E Robinson Ave	4 yrs	Judge Municipal Court	West Va.	Chronic Glomerular Nephritis	Greenwood
3-May	*Myrtle Law	F	W	1 ½ ds?	S	531 Carter	1 2 /4 da		Orlando	Right Lobar Pneumonia	Greenwood
4-May	*Louis Watson Toles	M	W	60	M	O.G.H. / Lansing, Mich	1 yr 6 mo	Retired	Mich	Uremia	Lancing, Mich
4-May	*Audrey Wren	F	W	4 mos	S	1019 W Amelia	4 mo 2 ds		Orlando	Acute Broncho Pneumonia	Mt Verde, Fla
5-May	Perry Oliver, Jr.	M	C	19	S	1059 W. Washington	11 yrs	Labor	Ga	Arthritis & Osteo Stetitis? Acute	Greenwood
5-May	*Jimmie Holliday	M	W	3 ds	S	1037 Wilfred Dr.	3 ds		Orlando	Atelectasis; Premature & Underdeveloped	Greenwood
4-May	*Louraine C. Boylen	F	W	46	M	425 Kuhl Ave	16 yrs	At Home	West Va.	Lymphatic Leukemia	Greenwood
6-May	*Anna L. Buchan	F	W	73	M	Orlando	4yrs	At Home	Canada	Apoplexy	Greenwood
6-May	*Mrs Gertrude Mink	F	W	46	M	O.G.H / Winter Garden, Fla	1 mo	At Home	Volney, Va	Pernicious Anemia	Oakland Cemetery
7-May	*Stark H. Dennis	F	W	87	W	2 mi E of city	6 mo	At Home	Eatonton, Ga	Myocarditis	Eatonton, Ga
2-May	Ella Williams	F	C	56	W	40 Ossie?	40 yrs	Laundress	Jordan, Ala	Toxemia	Greenwood
4-May	Henry Williams	M	W	54	M	RFD #3 /Raleigh St	6 yrs	Gardner	London, Eng	Carcinoma	Greenwood
5-May	Sylvia Barnett	F	C	62	W	1028 W. Washington	16 yrs	Laundress	Ga	Uterine Carcinoma	Greenwood
8-May	*Infant of Mr & Mrs Robert [Lindsay]	M	W	1 da	S	1217 Illa Ave	1 da		Orlando	Failure of Foramen Vavla	Greenwood
9-May	Samuel Harris	M	W	64	M	O.G.H. / RFD	2 yrs	Carpenter /Contractor	California, Pa	Coronary Embolism	California, Pa
7-May	*Ida K. Ammam	F	W	53	M	S. Fern Creek Dr.	20 yrs	At Home	N.J.	Chr. Interstitial Nephritis	Greenwood
10-May	*James D. Webb	M	W	82	W	628 E. Washington	33 yrs	Retired	Appomatox Va	Organic Heart Disease	Greenwood
11-May	*Nettie E. Morison	F	W	35	S	O.G.H. / 20 N. Eola Dr.	1 yr 6 mo	Book-keeper	Sussex Co, Canada	Post Operation	Sussex, New Brunswick, Canada
11-May	*Ralph H Biggs	M	W	31	M	O.G.H. / 4 E. Kaley	1 yr 6 mo	Carpenter	Jackson Co., Ill	Ileus Paraylitic	Murphysboro, Ill
6-May	*Chas. Wesley Baker	M	W	75	M	710 E. Colonial Dr	4 yrs	Farming	Ohio	Heart Trouble	Greenwood
10-May	Verdell Morgan	F	C	16	S	205 N. Division	2 m	School Girl	Quincy, Fla	Tuberculosis	Greenwood
10-May	Littie Bryant	F	C	29	M	762 John St. City	4 yrs	HW	Putnam Hall, Fla	Acute Gastric Indigestion	Putnam Hall, Fla
12-May	*Charles Archie Lott	M	W	4 m	S	606 S. Division	4 m		Orlando	Broncho Pneumonia	Greenwood
12-May	*Infant of Mr & Mrs Marvin Dickson	M	W		S	503 Perdue Ave			Orlando	Stillborn	Greenwood

121

1927	Name of Deceased	Sex	Race	Age	Marital	Residence & Place of Death	Orlando Resident	Occupation	Place of Birth	Cause of Death	Place of Burial
13-May	*Infant of Mr & Mrs S.T. Simpson	F	W	10 hrs	S	635 Brookhaven Dr.	10 hrs		Orlando	Atelecatasis	Cremation
15-May	*Lottie E. Cobb	F	W	74	M	120 E. Concord / Sinclairsville, N.Y.	5 mos	At Home	Sinclairsville, N.Y.	Uremia	Jamestown, N.Y.
15-May	*Vernon E. Shealey	M	W	22	M	O.G.H. / Cocoa	2 ds	Day Labor	Lexington Co., S.C.	Shock & Hemorrhage	Leeville, S.C.
15-May	Sam Hall	M	C	37	M	612 W. Long	4 yrs	Laborer	Ind	Cerebral Hemorrhage	Greenwood
13-May	W.A. Thomas	M	C	1 da	S	1008 Newman	2 yrs		Fla	Don't know	Greenwood
18-May	*Mable Sentell	F	W	38	M	O.G.H. / 3068 S. Thornton	2 yrs	At Home	Girard, Ga	Mitral Stenosis	Waynsboro Ga
19-May	*Mrs Lola S. Kingsland	F	W	67	W	1402 E. Robinson	4 yrs 6 mo	At Home	Albanie, Ohio	Encephalitis, Lethargica	Albany, Ohio
20-May	*Charlotte Grubbs	F	W	11 mos	S	O.G.H. / Okeechobee, FL	5 ds		Fla	Acute Pyelo Nephritis	Okeechobee, Fla
20-May	Fannie Washington	F	C	17	M	O.G.H.	2 yrs	HW	Mariannah, Fla	Pelvic Patria Onitis? Acute	Greenwood
22-May	*Robt. Julia Gillman	M	W	2mo	S	O.G.H. / Titusville, Fla	3 ds		Titusville, Fla	Acute Malnutrition	Titusville, Fla
21-May	*Frederick T. Lawton	M	W	1	S	Lake Jennie Jewell	1 yr		Orlando	Drowning	Vault
22-May	*Hazel Agness Carpenter	F	W	2 mo	S	466 Macay St.	21 da		Ala	Cardiac Incompetency	Greenwood
22-May	*M. Kerkorian	M	W	60	S	Oregon Ave	4 yrs	Laborer	Armenia	Apparent Cause Myo-carditis with Valvular Disease	Lynn, Mass
23-May	Millard B. Smith, Jr.	M	W	1	S	O.G.H. / Titusville, Fla	5 ds	Infant	Titusville, Fla	Primary Acute Broncho Pneumonia	Titusville, Fla
24-May	*Minnie [Winnie] Vaughn Williams	F	W	76	W	Alton, Va	5 yrs	HW	Va	Broncho Pneumonia	Alton, Va
24-May	Emma Lee Woodard	F	C	16	S	OG.H. / 508 S. Westmoreland	7 yrs	School Girl	Waynesboro, S.C.	Peritonitis Following Abortion	Greenwood
26-May	*Carl Bembry	M	W	10 m	S	Lockhart	9 mo		Williston, Fla	Broncho Pneumonia	McAlpin, Fla
28-May	*Elizabeth Langley	F	W	72	W	1309 Long St.	2 yrs	At Home	N.C.	Chronic Myocarditis	Calvary, Ga
29-May	Dan Boles	M	C	53	M	720 Woods	2 yrs	Laborer	Thrift, Ga	Mitral Stenosis	Greenwood
28-May	*William Pattigrew [Pettigrew]	M	W	24	M	2013 W. South	3 mo	Construction Work	N.C.	Pulmonary T.B.	Greenwood
28-May	Elizabeth Sloan	F	W	39	W	O.G.H. / Groveland, Fla	24 yrs	Housekeeper	Leesburg	Pellagra	Groveland, Fla
30-May	*Lelia M. Whitehead	F	W	52	W	Spiers Sant. / 30 Grove Park Dr	12 yrs	At Home	Commerce, Ga	Diabetes	Winder, Ga
31-May	*Chas Adelbert Mariner	M	W	49	M	Heights San /Oviedo, Fla	2 mo	Blacksmith	Ills	Mitral Regurgitation	Oviedo
30-May	Richard Floid	M	C	a 23	S	737 W. South	5 yrs	Laborer	Ga	Appendicitis, Acute	Quincy, Fla

1927	Name of Deceased	Sex	Race	Age	Marital	Residence & Place of Death	Orlando Resident	Occupation	Place of Birth	Cause of Death	Place of Burial
22-May	Infant of Lula Scrivins?	F	C		S	430 Parramore Alley			Orlando	Stillborn	Greenwood
28-May	Vera May Childs	F	C	5	S	1003 Jefferson	2	School Girl	Ga	Acute Toxic Gastritis	Greenwood
4-Jun	*Albert Letcher Nottingham	M	W	66	M	Cottage Hill Ave	7 yrs	Retired	WVa	Cardiac Asthma	Greenwood
5-Jun	*Jane Holt	F	W	65	M	O.G.H. / 1312 E. Gore Ave	7 yrs	At Home	England	Cardio Renal	Cleveland, Ohio
6-Jun	*Margaret J. Scott	F	W	79	W	Fla Sant / Cordeal, Ga	4 ds	At Home	Ga	Cerebral Hemorrhage	Cordeal, Ga
6-Jun	*Mrs Anna L. Guernsey	F	W	70	M	427 E. Central	41 yrs	At Home	Ky	Chronic Arterio-sclerotic Nephritis	Greenwood
7-Jun	*Joseph S. Schrock	M	W	73	M	Fla Sant /Ft. Meade, Fla	22 ds	Minister of Gospel	Ind	Mitral incompetency w/ Myocarditis	St. Petersburg, Fla
4-Jun	Elijah L. Sweet	M	C	47	M	406 W. South	30 yrs	Stone Cuper?	Qunicy, Fla	Esophageal? Stenosis	Greenwood
6-Jun	E. D. Taylor	M	C	42	M	1038 W Randal	30 yrs	Laborer	Maitland, Fla	Heptic? Carbosis?	Greenwood
1-Jun	Edna Hankerson	F	C	9 da	S	503 S. Parramore	9 ds		Orlando	Cholycystitis	Greenwood
4-Jun	Lullie Stockton	F	C	37	M	306 W. Moreland	6 yrs	Cook	Fla	Pulmonary Phthisis	Greenwood
4-Jun	Henry T. Simmons, Jr	M	W	3+	S	Heitz San / 21 Drury Ave	6 ds	None	Fla	Broncho Pneumonia	Narcoosie
4-Jun	Napolion Thomas	M	C	25	S	414 W. Moreland	25	Cook	Fla	Bilateral Lobar Pneumonia	Greenwood
10-Jun	*Jacob Meschler, Jr	M	W	60	M	O.G.H. Howey, Fla	3 ds	Retired	Germany	Acute Appendicitis	Stickney, Ill
11-Jun	*Joe Migone	M	W	53	M	O.G.H. / Lake Fairview	5 yrs	Retired	Italy	Chronic Myocarditis	Bethel, Conn
11-Jun	*Ulyses Seward Anderson	M	W	62	M	Fla San /Lakeland, Fla	8 ds	Minister of Gospel	Ind	Cholelithiasis	Muncie, Ind
12-Jun	Jerry Brown	M	C	35	M	O.G.H. / Groveland, Fla	5 yrs	Laborer	Fla	Appendiceal Abscess	Groveland, Fla
12-Jun	*Mrs. Bernice Summitt	F	W	a 26	M	O.G.H. / Sorento, Fla	1 da	At Home	Iowa	Septicemia	Ottumwa, Iowa
12-Jun	*Francis Edwin Burke	M	W	75	M	435 Anderson Ct.	2 yrs	Retired	Wis	Uremic Coma	Greenwood
14-Jun	*James Banter Ervin	M	W	57	M	538 Columbia Ave	15 yrs	Carpenter	Fla	Mitral Stenosis	Higley Cemetery
14-Jun	*Owen Duane Culver	M	W	2	S	O.G.H. / 747 Arlington	2 y+		Orlando	Acute Gastric intestional Intoxication	Greenwood
9-Jun	*Josie D. O'Neal	F	W	57	S	Fla Sant /Belpre, Ohio	9 mos	At Home	Belpre, Ohio	Shock following Operation	Parkersburg, Wva
20-Jun	Isom Hill	M	C	65	W	430 Ocie St.	2 mo	Laborer	Ala	Pulmonary Hemorrhage	Sanford, Fla
20-Jun	*Quincy R. Tyner	M	W	52	M	RFD #3	52	Foreman Orange Grove	Orange Co, Fla	Lightning	Ocoee, Fla
21-Jun	*Lois Marie McMillan	F	W	3	S	O.G.H. / 21 Rosevear St.	3 mos		Orlando	Colitis	Greenwood

123

1927	Name of Deceased	Sex	Race	Age	Marital	Residence & Place of Death	Orlando Resident	Occupation	Place of Birth	Cause of Death	Place of Burial
22-Jun	Mary Jane Arnert	F	W	79	W	308 S. Tampa Ave	7 mo	At Home	Birmingham, Ohio	Cancer of the Stomach	Birmingham, Ohio
14-Jun	*Marshall Erwin Nicholson	M	W	10	S	O.G.H.	1 da		Detroit, Mich	Gunshot Wound	Clermont, Fla
24-Jun	*Mrs Kate Covington Dolive	F	W	69	M	19 W. Washington	40 yrs	At Home	Mobile, Ala	Uremia	Greenwood
24-Jun	Olivia Washington	F	C	1	S	913 Bentley	1 yr +	None	Orlando	Broncho Pneumonia	Greenwood
26-Jun	Eliza J. Dixon	F	C	81	W	8 W. Randall	1 yr	Housework	Ga	Apoplexy	Greenwood
26-Jun	Henry D. Osteen, Jr	M	W	22	S	O.G.H. / Ft. Christmas	1 da	Labor	Fla	Fracture base of Skull	Ft. Christmas
27-Jun	Mrs Arousyag T. Polovlian	F	W	a 46	M	Grand Ave	6 yrs	At Home	Armenia	Apoplexia	Greenwood
30-Jun	Classie Riley	F	C	51	M	12 Wood	3 yrs	HW	Ga	Nephritis	Dawson, Ga
30-Jun	*Mrs Emma A. Rogers	F	W	57	M	Gen Del	17 yrs	At Home	N.Y.	Embolus, Cerebral	Lake Hill Cemetery
20-Jun	Edward Otis Moore	M	C	1 m 6 ds	S	320 Beech St	1 mo 6 ds		Orlando	Broncho Pneumonia	Greenwood
20-Jun	Infant of G. W. Thomas	M	C	10 ds	S	217 Lime St	1 yr 5 mo		Orlando	Malnutrition	Greenwood
29-Jun	*Mrs Addie Tracy	F	W	72	W	513 Hillcrest	17 yrs	At Home	Howells, N.Y.	Organic Disease of Heart	Greenwood
1-Jul	Edward Love	M	C	54	M	547 W. Jefferson		Labor	Tallahassee, Fla	Cerebral Thrombosis	Greenwood
2-Jul	Girl of Charly & Nora Francis	F	C	7	S	9 Hicks	7 ds		Orlando	Jaundice	Greenwood
2-Jul	Sindy Harden	F	C	48	W	410 W. Jackson	5 mo	HW	Ga	Carcinoma of Uterus	Waynesboro, Ga
2-Jul	*Catherine McConnell	F	W	a 30	S	O.G.H. / Holopaw, Fla	1 da		Keenansville, Fla	Acute Broncho Pneumonia	Homerville, Ga
3-Jul	*James A. McAnally	M	W	36	M	O.G.H. / Tavares, Fla	13 ds	Day Labor	Wilcox Co., Ga	Acute Myocarditis	Travares, Fla
4-Jul	Mary Johnson	F	C	21	S	O.G.H. / Eustis, Fla	4 ds	Laundress	W Fla	Shock Post Operation	Eustis, Fla
4-Jul	*Infant of Mr & Mrs E O Cooper	M	W		S	730 W. Central			Orlando	Asphyxiation	Greenwood
5-Jul	*Patrick Cleveland Kittrell	M	W	62	W	O.G.H. / Mt Pleasant, Tenn	4 ds	Retired	Tenn	Pneumonia	Mt. Pleasant, Tenn
19-Mar	Infant of Walter Cleo? & Sallie Williams	F	W		S	101 S. Westmoreland			Orlando	Stillborn	
21-May	Helen Wilphrd?	F	C		S	430 McFall			Orlando	Stillborn	
6-Jul	*Aboud Fekany	M	W	105	M	600 W. Gore	7 yrs	Retired	Syria	Senility	Greenwood
12-Jul	*Willie Beasley	M	C	35	S	O.G.H. / S.W. part of City	1 yr	Day Labor	Ga	Syphilis	Greenwood
5-Jul	*Infant of Mr & Mrs Robt M. Howard	F	W		S	O.G.H. / 318 Hughey Court			Orlando	Stillborn	Cremated
6-Jul	*Frank Hays	M	W	55	W	County Home	10 yrs	Retired	Hillsboro Co., Fla	Bronchitis	Greenwood
8-Jul	Ella Chapel	F	C	26	M	728 Avondale	3 mo	Housewife	Ga		Ocala

124

1927	Name of Deceased	Sex	Race	Age	Marital	Residence & Place of Death	Orlando Resident	Occupation	Place of Birth	Cause of Death	Place of Burial
10-Jul	*Cecelia Hall Moseley	F	W	73	M	634 E. Concord Ave	15 yrs	At Home	Miss		Greenwood
7-Jul	*Infant of Mr & Mrs August Kasper	M	W		S	Columbia Ave			Orlando	Premature	Greenwood
14-Jul	*Margaret Jarvis	F	W	a 50	S	O.G.H. / E Rob. Ave	5 yrs	Steno-grapher	Wis	Toxemia	Cremation
15-Jul	*William T. Cheesebrough	M	W	54	M	O.G.H. / 914 Lake View Ave	7 yrs	Contractor	Chicago, Ill	Carcinoma of Omenta	Vault
18-Jul	*Mrs Emma Tucker	F	W	46	W	Lake Mann	2 yrs	At Home	Bibb Co., Ga	Acute Dila-tion of Heart	Bryon, Ga
19-Jul	*Infant of Mr & Mrs Erle Spear	M	W	1 hr	S	O.G.H. / Pine Castle, Fla			Orlando	Paralysis	Greenwood
17-Jul	Mrs Ada B. Spahr	F	W	76	W	Fla Sant /St. Cloud, Fla	6 mos	House-wife	Not Known	Senility	St. Cloud, Fla
19-Jul	*William B. Childers	M	W	81	M	1612 Ill Ave	5 yrs	Retired	Ky	Intersticial Nephritis	St. Cloud, Fla
22-Jul	*Wm H. McGrory	M	W	77	M	1137 Dixie Ave	7 yrs	Retired	New York City	Acute Colitis	New York, N.Y.
21-Jul	*Wm J. Masters	M	W	54	M	Merritt Park	9 mos	Furniture	Mandarin Co., Fla	Angina Pectoris	Middle-burg, Fla
1-Jun	Ella Beal	F	W	57	M	Fla Sant /Cocoa, Fla		House-wife	Marion Co., Fla	Myocarditis	Cocoa, Fla
17-Jul	Mattie Sampson	F	C	43	W	1026 Bently	6 yrs	Laundress	Quinton, Ga	Acute Hep-atic Cirrhosis	Greenwood
22-Jul	Anna Moye	F	C	47	M	745 W South St	1 yr 7 mo	Domestic	Ga	Acute Cardiac Dilitation	Smithville, Ga
21-Jul	*William E. Bishop	M	W	81	W	323 E Amelia Avenue	16 yrs	Retired	Conn	Organic Heart Disease	Greenwood
22-Jul	*Sarah Young Hamlin	F	W	63	W	520 E Anderson	3 yrs	At Home	Mich	Cerebral Hemorrhage	Carey Hand
24-Jul	*Mrs Pauline Behm	F	W	70	W	Central & Bumby	5 yrs	At Home	Germany	Carcinoma of Uterus	Greenwood
25-Jul	*Joseph Reahn	M	W	64	M	Fla Sant /1525 S Delaney	27 yrs	Well Drilling	Germany	Apoplexy	Greenwood
28-Jul	Silas Cooke	M	W	84	W	O. G. H. / Michigan & 8th	11 ds	Retired Minister	Penn	Hemorrhage	Carnegie, Pa
28-Jul	Rose Lee Barran	F	C	34	M	547 W Jefferson	34 yrs	Seam-stress	Orlando	Pulmonary Phthisis	Greenwood
18-Jul	Robbert Watson	M	C	23	S	O.G.H. / Groveland	1 yr	Laborer	S.C.	Septicemia	Greenwood
26-Jun	Infant of B T & Lillie Washington	?	C		S	646 W Long			Orlando, Fla	Don't know	Backyard at Home
27-Jul	*Mrs Clara Emma McCandless	F	W	55	S	O.G.H. / 125 E Copeland Dr	3 yrs	Prof. Trained Nurse	Penn	Stricture of Pylorus	Butler, Penn
28-Jul	*Jefferson Lamar McGehee, Jr.	M	W	47	M	612 W Concord	1 yr 6 mo	Contractor	Tenn	Acute Gastric	Cremation
29-Jul	Jerome Moore	M	W	52	M	Lockhart	2 yrs	Dairy	Mo	Apoplexy	Apopka
30-Jul	*Daniel W. Prescott	M	W	72	M	Pine Castle Road	50	Farming	Green Coral Springs, Fla	Acute Dilitation of Heart	Greenwood

125

1927	Name of Deceased	Sex	Race	Age	Marital	Residence & Place of Death	Orlando Resident	Occupation	Place of Birth	Cause of Death	Place of Burial
30-Jul	*Infant of Catherine B. Burns	M	W		S	Fla Sant			Orlando	Stillborn	Cremated
30-Jul	*Infant of Mr & Mrs E E Harris	F	W		S	O.G.H.			Orlando	Stillborn	Cremated
31-Jul	*Clarence Bunnell	M	W	61	M	600 W Lake View Avenue	1 yr	Real Estate	Wis	Acute Nephritis	Greenwood
31-Jul	*Thad Oliver Blackman	M	W	22	M	O.G.H. / 605 E Pine	2 yrs 6 mo	Employee of Western Union	Ala	Hemorrahage	Pensacola, Fla
1-Aug	*Frances Jasinskie	F	W	69	M	714 E Washington	6 yrs	At Home	Germany	Organic Heart Disease	Cleveland, Ohio
2-Aug	*John S. Lang	M	W	80	W	1018 Lake	2 yrs	Retired	Penn	Apoplexy	Coffeyville, Kan
25-Jul	Shank Williams	M	C	50	S	O.G.H. / Parramore & S A L	2 yrs	Day Labor		Uremia	Greenwood
30-Jul	Limeul B. Board	M	C	50	M	O.G.H. / Apopka	15ds /16y	Farming	Bowling Green	Hypertrophy of Prostate	Apopka, Fla
1-Aug	Millie Powell	F	C	52	S	207 Garden	4 yrs	H W	Fla	Acute Nephritis	Greenwood
2-Aug	Jerldene Dunley	F	C	3 ds	S	100 N. Bryan	3 ds		Orlando	Anapholyxis?	Greenwood
3-Aug	Virgil Blount	M	C	40	M	O.G.H. / Taft, Fla Don't Know	30 min	Day Labor	Don't Know	Gunshot	County Home
6-Aug	*Andrew P. Thayer	M	W	89	W	O.G.H. / 430 Anderson Ct	4 yrs	Retired	Conn	Bronchopneumonia	Hammond, Wis
4-Aug	*Infant of Mr & Mrs David A Williams	F	W	18 hrs	S	416 Esther St	1 da		Orlando	Prematurity	Greenwood
6-Aug	*Carl Hunt	M	W	47	M	37 Howard	2 yrs	Advertising	Coatsville, Ind	Hodgkins Disease	Cremation
10-Aug	*Augusta A. Lockewood	F	W	70	S	120 E Washington	1 yr 3 mo	At Home	Troy, N.Y.	Cerebral Hemorrhage	Saratoga Springs, NY
10-Aug	*Mrs Drew Russell Stafford	F	W	51	W	228 S Hughey	51 yrs	At Home	Orlando	Fever Typhoidmalarial	Mizell Cemetery
11-Aug	*Irvin B. Kenner	M	W	22 ds	S	O.G.H. / 627 W. Pine	22 ds		Orlando	Ictersis Veutroum?	Jewish Cemetery
11-Aug	*Gladys B. Christenson	F	W	5 yrs	S	O.G.H. / Grant, Fla	10 ds		Grant, Fla	Acute Nephritis	Grant, Fla
9-Aug	Robert Dozier	M	C	30	S	O.G.H. / Groveland	1 yr	Laborer	Fla	Cerebral Hemorrhage	Greenwood
12-Aug	*Wilson Oscar Royal	M	W	66	M	10 Esther	2 yrs	Retired Farming	Ga	Bronchopneumonia	Tifton, Ga
15-Aug	*Mrs Flora Martha Parker	F	W	86	W	243 S. Garland	10 yrs	At Home	Maine	Uremia; Coma	Cremation
15-Aug	*Katie V. Hodges	F	W	71	M	9 Kaley Ave	1 yr 6 mo	At Home	Ga	Cerebral Hemorrhage	Greenwood
3-Apr	Infant of Walter & Caroline Stephens	F	?	C	S	908 Johns Court			Orlando	Stillborn	Greenwood
13-Aug	*Mynus D. Bailey	M	W	12	S	Lake N E Of Orlando /2012 W. Jackson	2 yrs		Okla	Drowning	Greenwood

1927	Name of Deceased	Sex	Race	Age	Marital	Residence & Place of Death	Orlando Resident	Occupation	Place of Birth	Cause of Death	Place of Burial
2-Jul	Geo Smith	M	W	72	W	O.G.H. / Travares, Fla	2 ds	Labor	D K	Senility & Chronic Nephritis	Greenwood
11-Aug	Emarell Harris	F	C	13 ds	Inf	808 S. McFall	4 yrs		Orlando	Acute Toxic Gastritis	Greenwood
12-Aug	James Conway	M	W	a 81	W	In Howells Hosp	18 mo	Minister	Scotland	Pneumonia	Orange City, Fla
17-Aug	Maggie Willis	F	C	31	M	642 W. South	5 yrs	Cook	Macon, Ga	Acute Cardiac Dilitation	Greenwood
19-Aug	Clary Johnson	F	C	31	M	800 Avondale	7 mo	H W	Ga	Peritonitis	Americus, Ga
19-Aug	*Infant of Mr & Mrs James T. Murphy	M	W		S	O.G.H. / Lancaster Pk			Orlando, Fla	Stillborn	Greenwood
20-Aug	Eddie Williams	M	C	50	M	704 Easy	4 yrs	Day Labor	Ga	D K	Greenwood
20-Aug	Infant of G. Barber	F	W		S	E Rob Ave			Orlando	Stillborn	E of Orlando
24-Aug	Edie Mae Frank	F	C	17	S	O.G.H. / Winter Garden	5 mo	Cook	Ga	Following Operation	Montgom- ery, Ga
19-Aug	Gus Owens	M	C	50	DK	O.G.H.		Labor		Don't Know	Greenwood
22-Aug	*Elmer B. Fitzpatrick	M	W	43	M	239 W Orlando Ave	2 yrs	Merchant	N. H.	Angina Pectoris	Vault
23-Aug	A. M. Zinzer	M	W	11 ds	S	O.G.H. / Sanford, Fla	1 da		Sanford, Fla	Congenital Malformition of Circulation System	Sanford
24-Aug	*Infant of Mr & Mrs Jessie Ramsdell	M	W		S	Fla Sant			Orlando	Stillborn	Greenwood
24-Aug	Mrs Lida H. MacDougall	F	W	51	W	Howell Sanit / Philadelphia, Pa	9 mo	At Home	Philadel- phia, Pa	Pulmonary Tuberculosis	Philadelphia, Pa
24-Aug	*Mrs Louise J. Barlow	F	W	57	W	Apopka Road	35 yrs	At Home	Lake Howell, Fla	Cerebral Hemorrhage	Greenwood
24-Aug	*Jeramiah O. Beck	M	W	71	M	819 Park Lake Ave	9 mo	School Principal	Clermont, Ohio	Nervous Protration	Bethel, Ohio
25-Aug	*Mrs Annie Catherine Bohlen	F	W	75	W	229 S. Garland	42 yrs	At Home	Germany	Pneumonia	Greenwood
25-Aug	*Infant of Mr. & Mrs Wm H. Sanders	M	W	1	S	Fla Sant			Orlando	Transmatic? Meningitis	Cremation
27-Aug	Infant of U W & Minna Cunningham	M	W		S	O.G.H.			Orlando	Stillborn	Eustis, Fla
17-Aug	Eddie James	M	C	2 ds	S	207 N. Division	2 ds		Orlando	Broncho- pneumonia	Greenwood
28-Aug	*Geo W. Wainwright	M	W	7 mo	S	O.G.H. / Winter Garden	1 da		Miami	Acute Gas- tric Enteritis	Folkston, Ga
29-Aug	*Mrs Nellie G. Frame	F	W	37	M	420 W Concord	7 mo	At Home	Broadrun, WVa	Pulmonary TB	Weston, Wva
29-Aug	Essie May Willis	F	C	18	S	801 W Long	4 yrs	House Servant	Washington Ga	Eclampsia	Greenwood
29-Aug	Geo Agness	M	C	a 50	DK	804 W Robinson	1 mo	Labor	D K	Pulmonary Hemorrhage	County Home
30-Aug	Irene Powell	F	C	a 36	M	406 Lee St	7 yrs	H W	Sanford, Fla	Asthe__?	Greenwood

1927	Name of Deceased	Sex	Race	Age	Marital	Residence & Place of Death	Orlando Resident	Occupation	Place of Birth	Cause of Death	Place of Burial
30-Aug	*Mrs Margaret J. Condit	F	W	82	W	138 E Amelia	11 yrs	At Home	Pa	Myocarditis	Lone Pine, Pa
10-Aug	Martha Dossey	F	C		S	619 S. Lee St.			Orlando, Fla	Stillborn	Don't know
2-Sep	Jackson H. Hawkins	M	C	84	S	733 W. Jackson	3 yrs	Laborer	Mass	Uremia	Greenwood
2-Sep	*Timothy B. Stephenson	M	W	65	W	123 Hill St.	6 yrs	Retired	Ky	Chronic Brights	Cremation
2-Sep	*Pauline K. Le Mon	F	W	71	M	214 Dollins	2 yrs	At Home	Ind	Carcinoma of Pancreas	Evansville, Ind
3-Sep	*Jeff T. White	M	W	76	W	Orla Vista	5 yrs	Retired	Vermont	Hypostatic Pneumonia	Cremated
4-Sep	*Earnest Dease	M	W	23	M	O.G.H.	1 da	Labor	Orange Co., Fla	Pneumonia, Traumatic	Conway
4-Sep	*Sherman E. Limpus	M	W	62	M	312 E. Scouth St.	16 yrs	Retired	Ind	Suicide by Gas	Greenwood
5-Sep	*Elijah McDaniel Littlefield	M	W	76	S	712 W Central	8 yrs	Farming	S.C.	Diabetic Coma	Greenwood
5-Sep	Infant of Mr & Mrs M K Van Duzor	M	W		S	1217 Noble Ave			Orlando	Premature	Cremated
5-Sep	Nick McClendon	M	C	14	S	741 Bentley	4 yrs	Delivery Boy	Ga	Drowned	Greenwood
15-Aug	Lucy Grizzle	F	C	42	M	1000 W Long	7 yrs	House-wife	Lillie, Ga	Chronic Myocarditis	Greenwood
29-Aug	Infant of Essie M. Willis	M	C		S	801 W Long			Orlando	Stillborn	Greenwood
20-Aug	Essie W. Martin	F	W	73	W	Springfield, Mass /Orlando	1 yr	At Home	Canada	Endarteritis, Obliterans	Oakwood, Troy, N.Y.
8-Sep	*Russell Hague	M	W	a 32	M	Fla Sant /Canton, Ohio	2 yrs	Real Estate	Ohio	Multiple Abscess of Liver	Canton, Ohio
9-Sep	*Clarence W. Rose	M	W	70	M	48 W Robinson Ave	16 yrs	Retired	Ind	Myocarditis	Greenwood
10-Sep	*Colesita Isobel Hill	F	W	56	M	511 S. Hughey	1 yr 8 mo	At Home	Dawson Co., Ga	Asthma	Greenwood
9-Sep	Lizzie Timmons	F	C	45	M	104 N. Parramore	17 yrs	Cook	Fla	Cerebral Hemorrhage	Greenwood
10-Sep	Susen P. Suker	F	C	66	W	243 Chatham	40 yrs	Sexton for Church	S.C.	Apoplexy	Greenwood
14-Sep	Infant of Bessie Wright	F	C		Inf	418 S Lee	8 ds		Orlando	Stillborn	Greenwood
10-Sep	*Mrs Lois Stephens	F	W	17	M	O.G.H./ Winter Garden, Fla	3 ds	At Home	Ga	Eclampsia	Moultrie, Ga
11-Sep	*Infant of Mr & Mrs M. B. Hill	M	W		S	O.G.H. / 1230 Golden Lane			Orlando	Stillborn	Cremation
15-Sep	*Mrs Bell Holes Scott	F	W	75	W	504 E Central	1 yr 3 mo	At Home	S.C.	Cerebral Hemorrhage	Montecello, S.C.
16-Sep	*Tyne Cheney Whitman	F	W	86	W	516 E. Jackson	26 yrs	At Home	Mass	Chr Bronchitis	Greenwood
18-Sep	*Walter Earnest Williams	M	W	40	M	O.G.H. / 317 N. Main	1 yr 6 mo	Pres Orlando Memorial Assoc	Nova Scotia	Peritonitis	Vault
19-Sep	Ruby M Crokan	F	W	27	M	Fla Sant /1222 Ridgewood	2 yrs	At Home	Mass	Puerperal Septicemia	Springfield Mass

1927	Name of Deceased	Sex	Race	Age	Marital	Residence & Place of Death	Orlando Resident	Occupation	Place of Birth	Cause of Death	Place of Burial
20-Sep	*Mrs Anna Gore	F	W	55	M	O.G.H. / Taft, Fla	4 ds	At Home	Ga	Shock Following Op	Greenwood
20-Sep	*Infant of Mr & Mrs A. B. Chapman	M	W		S	Peel Ave			Orlando	Premature Birth	Cremation
22-Sep	*Conttina Turrisi	F	W	21	M	911 W Church	3 yrs	At Home	Italy	Puerperal Eclampsia	Greenwood
23-Sep	*Mrs Daisy B. Smith	F	W	40	M	O.G.H. / Winter Park	1 da	At Home	S.C.	Eclampsia	Rambert, S.C.
24-Sep	*Mrs Mary Clayton McGehee	F	W	58	M	423 Palmer	6 mo	At Home	Tenn	Organic Heart Disease	Greenwood
25-Sep	Louis Forst	M	W	57	D	630 Park Lake Ave	4 yrs	Shoe Merchant	N.Y.	Cerebral Apoplexy	Bessemer, Ala
27-Sep	*Infant of Mr & Mrs Harley C Brown	F	W	2 ds	S	Midiran Dr, Dubsdread	3 ds		Orlando	Hemorrhage	Vault
27-Sep	*Helen Lee Daniels	F	W	6 mos	S	509 Grove Park Drive	6 mo		Orlando	Primary Acute Broncho Pneumonia	Greenwood
26-Sep	Helen Heath	F	C	23	S	920 Edner St.	23 yrs	House Service	Orlando	Pulmonary TB	Greenwood
28-Sep	Hattie Allens	F	C	32	W	400 Lee St.	2 yrs	Laundress	Tallahassee	Puerperal Septicemia	Tallahassee
29-Sep	Bula Bronson	F	C	34	M	O.G.H. / Winter Garden		Domestic	Eufala Ala	Septic Peritonitis	Oakland
28-Sep	Idella Sheffield	F	C	26	M	523 W South	2 mos	Chamber Maid	Wade, Fla	Acute Pulmonary Tuberculosis	Greenwood
28-Sep	*Thos E. Hampton	M	W	66	M	O.G.H. / 444 S Lake	10 yrs	Traveling Salesman	La Grange, Ga	Perforation of Ileum	Greenwood
29-Sep	*Marion R. Fillmore	M	W	51	S	1106 S. Parramore	8 yrs	Painter	Mich	Organic Heart Disease	Cremated
1-Oct	Clarence Williams	M	C	24	S	749 W South St.	24 ds		Orlando	Status Lymphatism	Greenwood
2-Oct	Mary E. Layton	F	W		M	O.G.H. / Tangerine, Fla	30 ds	H W	Jonesville, Ga	Cerebral Embolism	Tangarine, Fla
12-Sep	Marie Hentz	F	W	44	M	O.G.H. / Groveland, Fla	6 ds	H W	Berne, Switzerland	Peritonitis, General	Groveland, Fla
26-Sep	Infant of Sophia Wallace	M	C	1½ hrs	S	704 Easy St.	4 yrs		Orlando	Don't Know	Greenwood
27-Sep	Infant of Elizabeth Taylor	F	C		S	805 Reynold St	1 yr		Orlando	Don't Know	Greenwood
5-Oct	Susie Nelson	F	C	18	M	23 Ossie St.	2 yrs	House-work	Ga	Broncho Pneumonia	Greenwood
2-Oct	*Infant of Mr & Mrs O. J. Scroggins	F	W		S	612 Raleigh Ave			Orlando	Premature Still birth	Greenwood
2-Oct	*Joseph Griffith	M	W	63	M	713 Seminole Ave/Sanford, Fla	31 ds	Retired	Ohio	Pulmonary TB	Greenwood
4-Oct	*Mrs Ella D. Brown	F	W	70	M	634 N. Shine	5 yrs	At Home	Canada	Organic Heart Lesion	Vault
4-Oct	*Mrs Beatrice Lahman	F	W	46	M	O.G.H. / Route #4	2 yrs	At Home	Mich	Accidental Burns	Greenwood
4-Oct	Janie Jordan	F	C	48	M	812 W Carter	8 yrs	House-wife	Quincy, Fla	Cerebral Apoplexy	Greenwood

1927	Name of Deceased	Sex	Race	Age	Marital	Residence & Place of Death	Orlando Resident	Occupation	Place of Birth	Cause of Death	Place of Burial
5-Oct	Ezell Jackson Tyson	M	W	6	S	O.G.H. / Kissimmee	2 hrs	School	Fla	Appendicitis	Boggy Creek
5-Oct	*Elizabeth B. Whittaker	F	W	47	M	212 Ridgewood	8 yrs	At Home	Pa	Gastro-enterocolitis	Greenwood
5-Oct	*John B. Loyd	M	W	24	M `	526 Revere St	2 yrs	Labor	Tenn	Tuberculosis	New Market, Tenn
8-Oct	*Infant of Mr & Mrs Evert Rolland	M	W		S	22 East St			Orlando	Atelectasis, Premature Birth	Davenport, Fla
8-Oct	*Tom T. Spiers	M	W	a 25	S	O.G.H. / Augusta, Ga	5 mo	Mechanic	Ga	Fall From Window	Augusta, Ga
9-Oct	*Christian Wincher	M	W	80	W	O.G.H. / 315 Copeland Dr	6 yrs	Retired	West Va.	Shock from Fracture of Femur	Greenwood
10-Oct	E. Ola Davenport	F	W	57	W	19 N. Eola Dr / Elberton, Ga	1 yr 3 mo	At Home	Ga	Hodgkins Disease	Elberton, Ga
27-Sep	Ruby Irene Shuford	F	W	25	M	O.G.H. / Kenansville, Fla	6 ds	HW	Fla	General Septicemia, Post Mastoid Operation	Kenansville, Fla
10-Oct	Fannie Harvy	F	C	39	M	O.G.H. / 419 S. Division	1 yr	HW	Cuthbert, Ga	Syphilis	Cuthbert, Ga
10-Oct	*Sidney E. Ives, Sr.	M	W	73	M	12 W Gore Ave	45 yrs	Merchant	Macon, Ga	Broncho-pneumonia	Greenwood
12-Oct	*Frank J. Hartenstein	M	W	54	D	O.G.H. / Conway Drive	4 yrs	Salesman	Nashville, Ga	Stricture of Urethra	Nashville, Tenn
13-Oct	*Infant of Mr & Mrs Jas R Beach	F	W		S	Church & Glenn			Orlando, Fla	Premature Birth	Greenwood
13-Oct	*Infant of Mr & Mrs Jas R Beach	F	W		S	Church & Glenn			Orlando, Fla	Premature Birth	Greenwood
14-Oct	Catherine Pough	F	C		S	825 McFall			Orlando, Fla	Stillborn	Greenwood
28-Sep	Infant of Mr & Mrs Alvie Whitington	M	C		S	40 N. Bryan			Orlando	Stillborn	Greenwood
14-Oct	Thornton Snyder Keaton	M	W	32	M	O.G.H. / 802 13th? St	3 ds	Lineman	Ky	Fracture of Base of Skull	St. Petersburg
15-Oct	*Elizabeth Moseley	F	W	72	D	Lucerne Park	7 yrs	At Home	Fla	Acute Cardiac Dilitation	Greenwood
4-Oct	*Stephen Brosche	M	W	46	S	Orlando, RFD#4 / Lake Barton	21 ds	Mechanic	Germany	Pulmonary Edema	Greenwood
16-Oct	*Mrs Willie Augusta Stedman	F	W	45	W	O.G.H. / Forest City, Fla	3 ds	At Home	Isabelle, Ga	Septic Peritonitis	Greenwood
17-Oct	Lizzie Merriweather?	F	C	4 [40]	M	Wilton Infirmary	4 yrs	Laundress	Ga	Mitral Leak	Sparta, Ga
17-Oct	*Vernon Andrew Rice	M	W	37	D	308 Evans St / Holopaw, Fla	4 mo	Lumber Inspector	Ga	Cirrhosis of Liver with Ascites	Lakeland, Fla
12-Oct	*Infant of M A & Salomia Holly	M	W		S	O.G.H.	1 da		Orlando	Premature	Cremated

1927	Name of Deceased	Sex	Race	Age	Marital	Residence & Place of Death	Orlando Resident	Occupation	Place of Birth	Cause of Death	Place of Burial
16-Oct	Infant of Mr & Mrs W A Wottler?	F	W		S	Fla San			Orlando	Stillborn	
17-Oct	*Rena Lois Schrann	F	W	18	S	Fla San	3 yrs		Dayton, Ohio	Shock	Cremated
18-Oct	*John P Johnson	M	W	79	M	RFD #4 Box 187	3 yrs	Farming	Sweden	Myocarditis	Greenwood
21-Oct	Laura Anna McIntyre	F	W	57	M	Spears Hosp / Lakeland, Fla	1 mo	House wife	Washington, Ga	Hypostatic Pneumonia	Sanford, Fla
18-Oct	Edna Jackson	F	C	27	S	Lee St	DK	Domestic	Ga	Bronchial Asthma	County Home
20-Oct	*Infant of Mr & Mrs Joseph Pheifer	F	W		S	472 Macey			Orlando	Stillbirth	Greenwood
20-Oct	Will Maddox Matthews	M	C	14	S	O.G.H. / Colonial, Fla??	3 yrs	Laborer	Ga	Intestinal Obstruction	Oakland, Fla
21-Oct	*William C. Davis	M	W	47	M	435 N. Orange	2 yrs +	Candy Maker	Ga	Cerebral Hemorrhage	Greenwood
21-Oct	*Grechin [Gretchen] M. Dayton	F	W	37	M	102 Summerlin Place	1 mo	At Home	Brooklyn, N.Y.	Asphyxiation	Apopka, Fla
23-Oct	*Jas M Raleigh	M	W	69	M	O.G.H. / Lucerne Circle	40 yrs	Retired	Cleveland, Ohio	Uremia	St Augustine, Fla
24-Oct	James W. Brazwell	M	C	8 m	S	906 W Livingston	8 mo	None	Fla	Broncho Pneumonia	Greenwood
27-Oct	*Mrs Elizabeth Royal [Royall]	F	W	58	M	O.G.H. / 407 Raleigh	2 yrs	At Home	Vienna, Ga	Lobar Pneumonia	Tifton, Ga
27-Oct	*Mrs Mary M. Eales	F	W	77	W	618 N. Hughey	3 yrs	At Home	Canada	Cerebral Hemorrhage	Buffalo, N.Y.
24-Oct	Infant of Allie Daniels	F	W		S	729 Oakwood	15 yrs		Fla	Stillborn	Greenwood
25-Oct	*Mary A. Safford	F	W	75	S	811 S Main	20 yrs	Unitarian Minister	Quincy, Ill	Cerebral Hemorrhage	Hampton, Ill
29-Oct	*Mrs Mary Elizabeth Cleland	F	W	67	W	303 W Colonial Drive	1 yr	At Home	Ohio	Carcinoma of Uterus	Cremation
30-Oct	Irviss Bess	M	C	56	M	608 Albany	3 yrs	Laborer	S.C.	Tuberculosis	Greenwood
30-Oct	*Wilson F. Prescott	M	W	73	D	Clay Co., Fla	1 yr	Retired		Arteriosclerosis	Greenwood
1-Nov	*Arthur Towne	M	W	44	M	512 Revere St	3 yrs	Architect	Mass	Organic Heart Disease	Cremation
1-Nov	Ed Rucker	M	C	70	W	O.G.H.	2 ds	Laborer	Ga	Chr Nephritis	Greenwood
2-Nov	*Infant of Mr & Mrs B O Ryals	M	W	1 da	S	409 America	1 da		Orlando	Broncho Pneumonia	Greenwood
3-Nov	Infant of Allen Thomas	F	C		S	604 McFall	2 yrs		Orlando	Macerated Condition	Greenwood
30-Oct	*Wm Henry Johnston	M	W	79	M	Maitland	18 yrs	Retired	N.Y.	Cancer of Prostate Gland	Appleton, Wis
3-Nov	Mattie Brown	F	C	38	W	906 W Livingston	3 yrs	W	Ga	Acute Cardiac Dilatation	Greenwood
28-Oct	*Jim Smith	M	W	65	DK	O.G.H. / DK	1 da	DK	DK	Chronic Myocarditis	Greenwood
3-Nov	*Wm Schnarr	M	W	79	S	LaSalle	25 y	Germany	Retired	Exhaustion	Greenwood
4-Nov	*Mary Esther McQuarters	F	W	81	M	O.G.H. / 430 S Osceola	25 yrs	At Home	N.Y.	Lobar Pneumonia	Greenwood

1927	Name of Deceased	Sex	Race	Age	Marital	Residence & Place of Death	Orlando Resident	Occupation	Place of Birth	Cause of Death	Place of Burial
4-Nov	*Infant of Mr & Mrs H. L. Spear	M	W		S	2009 Joseph			Orlando	Stillborn	Webster Co., Fla
6-Nov	*John Fred Houser	M	W	60	M	Fla San /Winter Garden	21 ds	Retired	Columbia, Tenn	Cancer of Bladder	Winter Garden
7-Nov	Franklin Grant	M	B	39	W	Eatonville	5 ds	Day Work	Fla	Lightning	Maitland
21-Oct	*Edna Lee	F	W	5 m	S	3 mi E of Orlando			Orlando	Lobar Pneumonia	Winter Park
6-Nov	*Harry D. Hogan	M	W	57	M	Heights Sani /239 Palmetto	7 yrs	Claims Adjustor	N.J.	Cerebro Apoplexy	Millville, N.J.
6-Nov	Infant of Ed Steward	M	C		S	819 Reynold			Orlando	Stillborn	Greenwood
7-Nov	*Infant of Mr & Mrs Edward G. Pierce	M	W		S	O.G.H.			Orlando	Asphyxia Neonatorum	Greenwood
8-Nov	*Delbert Aldrich	M	W	31	M	O.G.H. / RFD #3 Box 44	4 yrs	Fireworks	Pa	Accidental Explosion	Greenwood
8-Nov	*Owen M Davis	M	W	31	S	O.G.H. / W Amelia Ave	6 yrs	Labor	Maine	Accidental Explosion	Wellsbeach, Maine
9-Nov	*Florence Shaffer Mills	F	W	26	M	O.G.H. / E Pine St.	1 yr	At Home	Mo	Puerperal Sepsis	Ocoee, Fla
10-Nov	*Mrs Ann Eliza Edwards	F	W	90	W	369 Cherokee Drive	2 yrs	At Home	Conn	Angina Pectoris	Granby, Conn
12-Nov	*Fred A. Lawrence	M	W	35	M	O.G.H. / Oakland, Fla	7 ds	Clerk	Ga	Chronic Active Tuberculosis	Chattanooga Tenn
12-Nov	*Thos I. Gregory	M	W	69	M	Angibelt Add /Denver, Colo	1 yr	Retired	Canton, Mo	Carcinoma of Prostate	Cremation
12-Nov	*Victor S. Bennett	M	W	38	S	O.G.H. / 706 E. Central Ave	38 yrs	Cigar Maker	Orlando	Dental Abscess	Greenwood
13-Nov	*James M. Ricketson, Jr.	M	W	19	M	O.G.H. / 1006 E Jackson	7 yrs	Laborer	Boston, Ga	Fracture of Base of Skull	Greenwood
15-Nov	John Lucwick Miller	M	W	57	M	Fla San /Sanford	15 ds	Baker	Houston, Texas	Myocarditis	Sanford, Fla
16-Nov	Hadley Robert Morris	M	W	58	M	120 America / Glenmora, La	2 mo	Book-keeper	Glenmora, La	Chronic Arteriosclerotic Nephritis	Glenmora, La
7-Nov	Infant of Arthur Davis	M	C			692 W Robinson Ave	4 yrs		Orlando	Stillborn	Greenwood
11-Nov	Bernice Stanly	F	C			740 W Carter	4 mo 13 d		Orlando	Intestinal Interruption	Greenwood
14-Nov	Emma E. Dallas	F	C	17	S	416 S Parramore	4 yrs	H W	Orlando	Acute Pulmonary Tuberculosis	Greenwood
17-Nov	*Daniel B. Summers	M	W	74	M	O.G.H. / 1111 S Division	25	Retired	Ill	Chr Myocarditis	Powell Cemetery
17-Nov	*Jas M. Williams, Jr	M	W	2 mo	S	Route 23	2 mo +		Orlando	Primary Acute Broncho Pneumonia	Greenwood
18-Nov	Chas Harris	M	C	a 53	M	903 W Livingston	35 yrs	Yardman	Ga	Cerebral Hemorrhage	Greenwood
19-Nov	James Stokes	M	C	36	M	104 N. Parramore	15 yrs	Machinist	Fla	Chronic Glanular Nephritis	Greenwood
19-Nov	Mrs Helen Wallen	F	W	a 52	D	Orlando	3 yrs	Sales Lady	Indiana	Heart Failure	Greenwood

1927	Name of Deceased	Sex	Race	Age	Marital	Residence & Place of Death	Orlando Resident	Occupation	Place of Birth	Cause of Death	Place of Burial
21-Nov	Infant of Cabot Wilson	M	C	Still		535 John St.	2 yrs		Orlando	Premature Birth	Greenwood
21-Nov	*Samuel B Estes	M	W	82	M	411 S Delaney	13 yr	Retired	Gibson Co., Ind	Myocardial Insufficiency	Madelia, Minn
22-Nov	*James C. Doty	M	W	67	M	O.G.H. / EauGallie, Fla	1 da	Shoe Repair	New York	Ruptured Gastric Ulcer with Peritonitis	Greenwood
18-Nov	*Mrs Mary Lyon Arrington	F	W	29	M	O.G.H. / 115 Liberty	3 yr+	At Home	Augusta, Ga	Myocardial Failure	Greenwood
16-Nov	*John Lee Bryant	M	W	21	S	Highland & RR /408 W Amelia	3 yrs	Lineman	Ind	Electric Shock	Terre Haute, Ind
22-Nov	*Mrs Thelma Yarborough Jones	F	W	25	M	O.G.H. / RFD #4	1 da	At Home	Ga	Right Lobar Pneumonia	Greenwood
29-Nov	*Martin Brown, Jr	M	W	1	S	O.G.H. / 1042 N Highland	1 yr		Orlando	Acute Gastric Intestinal	Durant, Fla
1-Dec	*Mrs Minnie C Kenyon	F	W	74?	W	Fla San	2 yrs	SDA Conference Worker	Mich	Cancer of Liver	Greenwood
1-Dec	*Samuel M. Dunmire	M	W	58	M	Apopka Road	3 yrs	Retired	Pa	Angina Pectoris	Pittsburgh, Pa
1-Dec	*Mrs Mary Ellen Sullivan	F	W	67	M	O.G.H. / Richmond, Va	1 mo	At Home	Conn	Exhaustion Psychosis	Richmond, Va
2-Dec	A B Le Vatt	M	C	58	S	O.G.H. / Okahumpka. Fla	6 ds	Day Labor	Ga	Broncho Pneumonia	Greenwood
1-Dec	Doris E. Bouton	F	W	2	S	Winter Garden Road	1 yr		Orlando	Fracture of Base of Skull	Greenwood
1-Dec	*Edgar Dawson	M	W	a 50	M	OGH / Williamsburg, Ohio	1 da	Carnival Show		Ruptured Duodenal Ulcer	Greenwood
2-Dec	*Adaline Williams	F	W	56	M	Forest City	3 mo	At Home	France	Acute Cardiac Dilitation	Akron, Ohio
2-Dec	Johnnie Lee McCullough	M	C	7 mo	S	602 S Parramore	7 mo	None	N.C.	Gastroenteritis	Greenwood
5-Dec	*Henry V. Bryan	M	W	63	S	O.G.H. / 829 N Thornton	15 yrs	Labor	Hamilton Co., Fla	Burns, 1st & 2nd Degree	Greenwood
6-Dec	*Mrs Julia D. Ewing	F	W	49	M	O.G.H. / RFD #3	2 mo	At Home	N.H.	Post Operation Shock	Clairmont, N.H.
6-Dec	James Standard Langmaid?	M	C	19	M	O.G.H. / Winter Park, Fla	9 yrs	Laborer	Fla	Appendicits	Winter Park, Fla
5-Dec	*Mrs Nancy H. Kingsley	F	W	70	M	1017 Park Lake Ave	14 yrs	At Home	Girard, Ohio	Ileus	Warren, Ohio
6-Dec	*Wm F. Noble	M	W	68	M	O.G.H. / 417 S Rosalind	4 yrs	Retired	Noble, Iowa	Chr Myocarditis	Cedar Falls, Iowa
7-Dec	*Carl P. Higginbotham	M	W	33	M	Fla San	28 ds	Machinist	Elbert Co., Ga	Acute Nephritis	Elberton, Ga
7-Dec	*Ward C. Rish	M	W	19 ds	S	1215 E Gore Ave	19 ds		Orlando	Malnutrition	Greenwood
8-Dec	*Mrs Margaret Campbell	F	W	53	M	Fla San / 721 Putman	1 mo / 14 ds	At Home	Mich	Myocarditis	Winter Park
9-Dec	*Abraham L. Stevens	M	W	63	M	715 Irma St	7 yrs	Retired	Mich	Angina Pectoris	Cremation
9-Dec	May Bell Hayer [Hayes?]	F	C	24	M	O.G.H.	1 da	H W	Fla	Bronchial Pneumonia	Winter Park

133

1927	Name of Deceased	Sex	Race	Age	Marital	Residence & Place of Death	Orlando Resident	Occupation	Place of Birth	Cause of Death	Place of Burial
11-Dec	Maude Anna Lake	F	W	55	M	Fla San / Sanford, Fla	1 mo	H W	Jacksonville, Fla	General Carcinomatosis	Sanford, Fla
8-Dec	John W. Knox	M	C	50	M	1003 W Jefferson	13 yrs	Minister	Fla	Acute Cardiac Dilatation	Greenwood
10-Dec	Anne Mae Fall	F	C	6	Inf	O.G.H. / 745 W Carter	3 yrs	School Girl		Shock	Greenwood
11-Dec	Frank Walker	M	C	36	M	805 W Carter	7 yrs	Common Laborer	Thomasville, Ga	Septicemia	Greenwood
13-Dec	*Infant of Mr & Mrs Topek Fekany	M	W		S	737 W Church			Orlando	Stillborn	Greenwood
14-Dec	*Lucy Ainsworth	F	W	73	S	Fla San	14 ds	At Home	Rock Island, Ill	Myocarditis	Geneseo, Ill
14-Dec	*William A. Ward	M	W	71	M	606 Hillcrest Ave	8 yrs	Retired	West Va.	Pernicious Anemia	Greenwood
15-Dec	*Catherine G. Edgar	F	W	83	W	Winter Park	14 yrs	At Home	Lewisburg, Pa	Hypertension	Lewisburg, Pa
16-Dec	Lawrence Edward Newman	M	C	1 da	S	523 W Jackson	1 da		Fla	Tor__? Of Cord	Greenwood
7-Dec	*Infant of Mr & Mrs Joseph Owens	M	W		S	O.G.H. / Merritt, Fla			Orlando	Stillborn	Indianold?, Fla
9-Dec	Infant of W M Wilson	F	C		S	719 Grove	10 yrs		Orlando	Stillborn	Greenwood
12-Dec	*Mrs Sarah E. Pierce	F	W	80	W	811 W Concord	11 yrs	At Home	Truxton, N.Y.	Cerebral Hemorrhage	Middleville, Mich
16-Dec	*Theodore Steir	M	W	76	M	Fla San	18 y	Retired	Germany	Chronic Nephritis	Greenwood
16-Dec	*Albert Maywood Davis	M	W	52	S	O.G.H. / Altamonte Sps	3 mo	Real Estate	Ohio	Cerebrial Embolism	Marietta, Ohio
17-Dec	*S. Marshall Sightler, Jr.	M	W	55	M	O.G.H. / 540 Grand Ave	16 yrs	Laborer	S.C.	Fracture 3 Lumbar Vertebra	Greenwood Cemetery
17-Dec	*Augustus Johnrowe	M	W	81	W	Fla San / Taft, Fla	2 ds	Retired	Farmer	Broncho Pneumonia	Alpina, Mich
17-Dec	*Mrs Mary Zoellner	F	W	77	W	230 Copeland	4 mo	At Home	Germany	Morbus Cardis Valvalarm	Springfield, Ill
18-Dec	*Mrs Mary Helen Goss	F	W	61	M	Weise Ave / Cuyahoga Falls, Ohio	2 mo	At Home	N.Y.	Chronic Myocarditis	Cremation
19-Dec	*David E. Gearheart	M	W	64	M	O.G.H. / Burbank, Ohio	6 ds	Farming	Burbank, Ohio	Fracture of Skull	Burbank, Ohio
20-Dec	*Mrs Lydia S. Chamberlin	F	W	82	W	O.G.H. / 722 E Concord Ave	6 yrs	At Home	Syracuse, N.Y.	Hypertension	Perry, Pike Co., Ill
20-Dec	Cyrus Ravannah	M	C	44	M	525 S Jackson	12 yrs	Woodman	S.C.	Bronchopneumonia	Tampa, Fla
20-Dec	*Wm F. Rosborough	M	W	55	M	O.G.H. / Micanopy, Fla	1 mo 14 d	Doctor of Medicine	Windsor, Fla	Encephalitis	Windsor, Fla
21-Dec	Hannah Wilson	F	C	50	W	513 S Westmoreland	5 yrs	Maid at Hotel	Leesburg, Fla	Acute Gastritis	Warwick, Ga
22-Dec	*Infant of Mr & Mrs Joseph Register	M	W	2 ds	S	411 Piedmont	2 ds		Orlando	Statuis Thymucios?	Greenwood
23-Dec	*Lawrence Garrett	M	W	79	M	O.G.H. / Conway, Fla	7 ds	Farming	Stan Tavern, Va	Chronic Myocarditis	Conway Cemetery

134

1927	Name of Deceased	Sex	Race	Age	Marital	Residence & Place of Death	Orlando Resident	Occupation	Place of Birth	Cause of Death	Place of Burial
24-Dec	*Otto Wettstein, Sr.	M	W	89	M	Heights Sant	3 mos	Retired	Germany	Apoplexy of Heart	Greenwood
25-Dec	*Mrs Sophonia McClelland	F	W	62	M	520 Clayton	7 ds	At Home	Covington Co., Ala	Acute Dilation of Heart	Andolusia, Ala
25-Dec	*Mrs Anna E. McCrary	F	W	66	W	RFD #3 Box 110	8 mo	At Home	Va	Organic Heart Disease	Henderson-ville, N.C.
26-Dec	*Ernest Ellsworth Elkins	M	W	66	M	208 W Pine	8 yrs	Retired	Camden, Ohio	Apoplexy	Arcadia, Fla
26-Dec	Charlie Johnson	M	C	45	S	O.G.H.	18 ds	Labor	Ga	Carcinoma of Liver	County Home
27-Dec	*Alvin G Becker, Jr	M	W	1	S	Conway & Kaley Aves	8 mo		Sanford, Fla	Broncho Pneumonia	Greenwood
21-Dec	Linnie Zee Jordan	F	C	27	M	314 Beech	6 yrs	House wife	Lake City, Fla	Pulmonary Tuberculosis	Greenwood
23-Dec	*Edward O Marshall	M	W	80	S	Fla San /New Ipswich, N.H.	8 ds	Retired	N.H.	Failure of Kidneys to Function	Naugatuch, Conn
25-Dec	*John Joseph Griffin	M	W	36	M	Fla San /New Berry, Fla	3 ds	Farming	Jonesville, Fla	Chr Acute Cellulitis	Jonesville, Fla
23-Dec	*W C Chandler	M	W	82	DK	O.G.H. / Orlando	2 mo	Retired		Chr Myocarditis	Greenwood
24-Dec	Louis Ridly	M	C	17	S	426 S Parramore	13 yrs	Chauffeur	Ga	Acute Pulmonary Phthisis	Greenwood
25-Dec	John Comodore	M	C	17	S	1606 E Jackson	3 yrs	Laborer	Ga	Broncho Pneumonia	Greenwood
28-Dec	Infant of Mr & Mrs Tilman Jones	F	W		S	O.G.H. / Kentucky Ave			Orlando	Premature Birth	Greenwood
29-Dec	Julia Schelley	F	C	48	W	426 McFall	3 yrs	Laundress	Ga	Cerebral Hemorrhage	Greenwood
29-Dec	*John Frank Sachse	M	W	37	M	Fla Sant /Winter Park	11 ds	Auto Sup Co	Germany	Bronchial Pneumonia	Winter Park
30-Dec	*Infant of Mr & Mrs J E A Padgett	M	W	1	S	O.G.H. / Kenansville, Fla	1 da		Orlando	Toxemia from Maternal Eclampsia	Kenansville, Fla
28-Dec	Nettie Sampson	F	C	39	M	521 E Jackson	2 yrs	Cook	Arlington, Ga	Acute Dilation of Heart	Greenwood
8-Dec	Emma Hightower	F	C	27	M	O.G.H. / Winter Park	3 mos	Maid	Davisboro, Ga	Shot	Eatonville
24-Dec	Margie Christina Hoskins	F	C	11 ds	S	1203 Conley	3 mos		Orlando	Don't Know	Greenwood

1928	Name of Deceased	Sex	Race	Age	Marital	Residence & Place of Death	Orlando Resident	Occupation	Place of Birth	Cause of Death	Place of Burial
2-Jan	A C Cotey	M	C	28	M	440 Parramore	2 mos	Labor	Fla	Pulmonary Tuberculosis	Greenwood
2-Jan	*J F Ludwick	M	W	62	D	O.G.H./ Astabula, Fla	1 mo 7 ds	Farming	Ky	Pulmonary Edema	Groveland
3-Jan	*Geo A. Wood	M	W	67	M	Fla Sant/N.H.	2 mos	Carpenter	N.H.	Cholecystitis with Periodic Septicemia	West Lebanon, N.H.
3-Jan	*John I. Hursh	M	W	71	W	O.G.H./ Canton, Ohio	3 wks	Retired	Ohio	Right Lower Lumbar Pneumonia	Canton, Ohio
3-Jan	*Christian H. Wright	M	W	84	W	617 E Harwood	3 yrs	Retired	Ind	Cardiorenal Disease	Winchester, Ind
4-Jan	Infant of Wheeler & Catherine Gary	F	C		S	725 W Robinson			Orlando	Stillborn	Greenwood
4-Jan	Tytus Scott	M	W	16	S	O.G.H./Ocoee	1 da	School	Millville, Fla	Tetanus	Ocoee, Fla
4-Jan	*Samuel Dallas Works	M	W	65	M	Merritt Park	4 yrs	Real Estate	N.Y.	Cerebral Hemorrhage	Cremation
4-Jan	Mary Elizabeth Johnson	F	W	7 ds	S	O.G.H./ Clermont	1 da		Clermont	Congenital mal-formation of Intestines	Clermont, Fla
7-Jan	*Mrs Mattie B. Frint	F	W	64	M	222 Weber Ave	1 yr 3 mos	At Home	Ohio	Broncho Pneumonia	Ironton, Ohio
11-Jan	*Leona Padgett	F	W	18	M	Kenansville, Fla	10 ds	At Home	Frost Proof, Fla	Puerperal Eclampsia	Kenansville, Fla
8-Jan	Henry Musser White	M	W	9	S	O.G.H./ Clermont, Fla	8 ds		W Va	Double Otitis Media Septicemia	Clermont, Fla
8-Jan	Charlie Hagan	M	C	81	M	O.G.H. / Clermont	42 yrs	Labor	Fla	Uremia, Cardeo?	Apopka, Fla
9-Jan	*Victor J. Borges	M	W	77	W	200 W Jackson / Taft, Fla	7 ds	Retired	Portugal	Apoplexy	Greenwood
9-Jan	*Myrtie May Maxey	F	W	33	D	N Eola Dr / 710 Ky Ave	2 yrs	At Home	Ohio	Broncho-pneumonia	Huntington, Wva
10-Jan	Leeroy Green	M	C	21		OGH/ Cocoa, Fla	2 yrs	Labor	S.C.	Auto Accident	Cocoa, Fla
11-Jan	*Infant of Mr & Mrs T. E. May	F	W		S	530 Lakeview Ave			Orlando, Fla	Premature Birth	Greenwood
11-Jan	*John McQuarters, Sr	M	W	91	W	430 Osceola	26 yrs	Retired	N Y CIty	Senility	Greenwood
11-Jan	Archie L. Anderson	M	C	40	S	O.G.H. / 121 N Div St	6 mos	Day Labor	?	Gunshot	County Home
12-Jan	*Mrs Antonie Hartemann	F	W	64	M	O.G.H. / Gotha, Fla	3 ds	At Home	Germany	Carcinoma of Stomach	Gotha
12-Jan	Donnie Archer	F	C	50	M	O.G.H. / Winter Garden	1 da	H W	Ga	Denvatitis? Colonica?	Oakland, Fla
13-Jan	Margaret May Armentrant	F	W	41	M	O.G.H.	2 ds	H W	Oklahoma	Carcinoma	St. Cloud, Fla
11-Jan	Susie Parramore	F	C	21	S	734 W Livingston	3 yrs	Laun-dress	Cuthbert, Ga	Pellagra	Cuthbert, Ga
14-Jan	Rosa Lee McPherson	F	C	15	S	1010 W South	3 mos	School	Fla	Pulmonary Tuberculosis	Greenwood
16-Jan	Annie Laster	F	C	30	M	O.G.H. / Winter Park	3 yrs	Cook	Ala	Pellagra	Winter Park
12-Jan	*Elisa C Bargar	F	W	91	M	714 Putnam St	3 mos	Retired	N.Y.	Valvular Heart Disease	Sinclairville, N.J.
13-Jan	*Mrs Anna Drew	F	W	36 a	M	O.G.H. / Ocoee	5 ds	At Home	Newton, Ala	Pellagra	Ocoee, Fla

136

1928	Name of Deceased	Sex	Race	Age	Marital	Residence & Place of Death	Orlando Resident	Occupation	Place of Birth	Cause of Death	Place of Burial
15-Jan	*Ulyses Grant Boak	M	W	60	M	Fla San / McDonald, Pa	21 ds	Retired	Pa	Myocarditis	McDonald, Pa
15-Jan	*Wm Thos Bland [sic]	F W	W	66	M	716 S. Orange	8 yrs	Banker	Weston, Va	Cerebral Hemorrhage	Greenwood
17-Jan	James Irving	M	C	40	M	321 Terry St	30 yrs	Laborer	Fla	Acute Gastric Indigestion	Greenwood
16-Jan	Le Roy Filmore	M	W	73 a	S	County Home		Farmer	Auburn, N.Y.	Senility	County Home
19-Jan	*Forest Sultzbach	M	W	48	M	436 N Parramore	7 yrs	Retired	Ohio	Organic Heart Disease	Springfield, Ohio
20-Jan	*Geo Hitchcok	M	W	55	M	O.G.H. / 368 E 194th St, N.Y.	1 mo	Retired	N.Y.	Chronic Nephritis	New Lawn Cemetery, N.Y.
22-Jan	*Lester A Lewis	M	W	82	W	O.G.H. / Highland Ave	10 yrs	Retired	N.Y.	Acute Gangrenous Appendicitis	Schuyler Lake, N.Y.
22-Jan	*Mrs Maggie J. Wicoff	F	W	50	W	30 E Copeland Dr	14 yrs	At Home	Ga	Diabetic Coma	Greenwood
23-Jan	*Infant of Mr & Mrs Wm E Argo	F	W		S	Clear Lake View/Orlando			Orlando	Not Determined	Greenwood
13-Jan	Albert Lee	M	C	34	M	O.G.H. / 524 W Jackson	2 yrs	Day Labor	Tallahas-see, Fla	Accidental Fall From Motor Car	Greenwood
21-Jan	Bessie Finley	F	C	27	M	922 Edna	6 yrs	Cook	Ga	Broncho Pneumonia	Greenwood
22-Jan	*John Richards	M	W	80	W	County Home	1 mo	Retired		Senility	County Home
24-Jan	Shadch Brimson	M	C	56	M	546 John	8 yrs	Laborer	Tallahas-see, Fla	Acute Bronchial Pneumonia	Greenwood
25-Jan	*Mrs Louise Williams	F	W	60	M	1121 N Mills	3 mos	At Home	N.Y.	Recurrent Carcinoma	Greenwood
26-Jan	Infant of Emma Garvin	F	C			Apopka Road	17 yrs		Fla	Syphilitic	Greenwood
27-Jan	Johnny Mae Phillips	F	C	12	S	Apopka	5 yrs	School Girl	Ga	Acute Broncho Pneumonia	Apopka, Fla
27-Jan	*Infant of Mr & Mrs Joseph Honour	F	W	3 ds	S	Lake Holden	3 ds		Orlando	Prematurity	Cremation
28-Jan	*Emma Bertha Williams	F	W	63	M	O.G.H. / Winter Park	2 mos	At Home	Oswego, N.Y.	Hypertension	Rochester, N.Y.
28-Jan	*Infant of Mr & Mrs W. G. Hawkins	F	W		S	216 E Evans			Orlando	Stillborn	Cremation
30-Jan	*Mrs Effie Claire Lavaron	F	W	37	M	14 La Salle	4 yrs	At Home	Quincy, Fla	Acute Myocarditis	Greenwood
30-Jan	Mary Elizabeth Clark	F	W	84	W	O.G.H.	28 ds	At Home	Ky	Chr Myocarditis	Eustis, Fla
30-Jan	*Harry A. Corbett	M	W	56	M	Heights Sant / Lovalletto, N.J.	5 ds	Electrical Engineer, Retired	Nova Scotia	Cerebral Apoplexy	Cremation
31-Jan	*Mrs Mary Jane Passmore	F	W	69	W	Duke Hall / Penn	1 mo	At Home	Pa	Cerebral Hemorrhage	Philadelphia, Pa
31-Jan	*Theodore A Long	M	W	9	S	S Rio Grande / New Hope, Pa	3 mos	School	Pa	Valvular Heart Disease	Mill Hall, Pa
2-Feb	Ugene Baty	M	C	17	S	O.G.H. / 320 Bentley	5 yrs	Labor	Fla	Burns	Greenwood
28-Jan	Joe Small	M	C	5 ds	S	528 John	5 yrs		Fla	Don't Know	Greenwood
29-Jan	*Mrs Hannah A. Hunt	F	W	37	M	O.G.H. / 812 N Thornton	9 yrs	At Home	Mass	Broncho Pneumonia	Marion, Mass
4-Feb	Obie Mincy	M	C	53	M	809 W South	4 yrs	Labor	Valdosta, Ga	Chronic Myocarditis	Greenwood

1928	Name of Deceased	Sex	Race	Age	Marital	Residence & Place of Death	Orlando Resident	Occupation	Place of Birth	Cause of Death	Place of Burial
5-Feb	*Claude U. Detwiler	M	W	41	M	Fla Sant / Winter Park St.	7 ds	Labor	Winter Park, Fla	Peritonitis, Abdominal	Winter Park
5-Feb	Robert Ridgeway	M	B	55	M	O.G.H. / St. Cloud, Fla	1 da	Day Laborer	Carolina	Acute Dilitation of Heart	St. Cloud, Fla
6-Feb	*Mary H. Bunson	F	W	73	M	237 Irvin St	17 yrs	At Home	N.C.	General Carcinomatosis of Eutae?	Brunson, S.C.
6-Feb	*Mrs Minie M. Paul	F	W	58	W	O.G.H. / Columbus, Ohio	3 mos	At Home	Ohio	Lobar Pneumonia	Columbus, Ohio
7-Feb	*Frank Huff Barker	M	W	11	S	RFD #3	5 yrs	In School	Ala	Organic Heart Disease	Greenwood
7-Feb	Infant of Dan Richardson	F	C		S	801 Carter			Orlando	Stillborn	Greenwood
8-Feb	Doris Mims	F	C	3 m	S	737 W South	2 mos		Fla	Don't Know	Greenwood
8-Feb	Ida Folsom	F	C	52	W	763 Powell Ave	4 yrs	Laun-dress	Flint, Ga	Carcinoma	Camilla, Ga
9-Feb	*Dan C. Swanner	M	W	27	S	Fla Sant	5 yrs	Sales-man	Geneva, Ala	Acute Nephritis	Geneva, Ala
6-Feb	*Jeff Davis	M	W	66	M	Lockhart	40 yrs	Farming	Ga	Acute Cardiac Dilitation	Greenwood
6-Feb	*James Burton Killian	M	W	9 m	S	223 E Spruce	9 mos		Orlando	Broncho Pneumonia	Greenwood
9-Feb	*Francis Harvey Packer	M	W	53	M	Orange Court Hotel	3 mos	Gift Shop	Hudson Falls, NY	Acute Myocarditis	Hudson Falls, N.Y.
9-Feb	*Norman Earl Dukes, Jr	M	W		S	O.G.H. / 140 E Livingston			Orlando	Injury at Birth	Cremated
10-Feb	Edwin C. Thawley	M	W	38	M	O.G.H. / Titusville, Fla	8 hrs	Auto Mech	Ind	Septicemia	Summitville, Ind
12-Feb	*Alice Roberts	F	W	1	S	O.G.H. / Winter Garden	1 da		Winter Garden, Fla	Acure Gastro Intestional Intoxication	Winter Garden
12-Feb	*Newton Rupert Bailey	M	W	28	D	251 Palmetto	10 ds	Mgr of Market at Palatka	S.C.	Abscess of Lung	Greenwood
12-Feb	*Rouyman P. Hurd	M	W	81	M	105 N Eola Drive	1 yr 6 mos	Retired	Carthage, N.Y.	Broncho-pneumonia	Watertown, N.Y.
13-Feb	*Willie S. Silas	F	W		M	O.G.H. / RFD #3	1 yr	At Home	Suwannee Co., Fla	Broncho-pneumonia	Greenwood
13-Feb	*Mrs Viola E. Voorhees	F	W	64	M	Gatlin Ave	8 yrs	At Home	Trenton, N.J.	Pulmonary & Spinal Tuberculosis	Trenton, N.J.
13-Feb	*Catherine Viola Hook	F	W	2	S	O.G.H. / Orlo Vista	4 ds		Orlando, Fla	Acute Ileocolitis	Greenwood
12-Feb	Infant of Ike Schuler	M	C	2		1608 E Jackdon	2 ds	Father Common Laborer	Orlando	Don't Know	Greenwood
12-Feb	Annie M Merrit	F	C	71 a	W	406 W. South	20 yrs	Domestic	Maryana, Fla	Mitral Insufficiency	Greenwood
13-Feb	John Edward Hampton	M	W	18	S	103 S Long	3 yrs	Common Labor	Ga	Broncho-pneumonia	Greenwood
15-Feb	Infant of Victor Sampson	M	C			539 S Parramore	13 yrs		Orlando	Torsion of Cord	Greenwood
15-Feb	Willie Daniels	M	C	18	S	409 Chapman	4 yrs	Common Labor	Ga	Mania	Dublin, Ga
16-Feb	Reed Murphy	M	C	64	M	515 John / 515 Murphy St	10 yrs	Janitor	Ga	Lobar Pneumonia	Greenwood

1928	Name of Deceased	Sex	Race	Age	Marital	Residence & Place of Death	Orlando Resident	Occupation	Place of Birth	Cause of Death	Place of Burial
17-Feb	Infant of Chas Woodly	M	C			507 Jernigan			Orlando	Eclampsia of Mother	Greenwood
8-Feb	Willie Walker	M	C	25	S	O.G.H. / Howey, Fla	1 da	Worked at Hotel	D K	Acute Dilitation of Heart	County Home
13-Feb	*John Herman Marsh	M	W	78	M	O.G.H.	2 mos	Retired	Arlington, Vt	Lobar Pneumonia	Cambridge, N.Y.
15-Feb	Elizabeth Williams	F	C	38	M		1 yr 4 mos	H W	Fla	Broncho-pneumonia	Greenwood
15-Feb	*Thos Preston Roney	M	W	70	M	412 E South	16 yrs	Retired	Pa	Cerebral Hemorrhage	Greenwood
16-Feb	*Mrs Eliza J Denning	F	W	88	W	232 N Magnolia	10 yrs	At Home	Scotland	Cardiac Insufficiency	Greenwood
16-Feb	*Jas F Watkins	M	W	68	M	32 Lucerne Circle	46 yrs	Real Estate	Ga	Arteriosclerosis	Greenwood
18-Feb	*Eddie Lancaster	M	W	37	D	1611 E Concord	20 yrs	Auto Me-chanic	Brunswick Ga	Carcinoma of Rectum	Greenwood
18-Feb	*Chas Joyce	M	W	64	D	1418 Beaver Ave	16 yrs	Retired	England	Pulmonary Tuberculosis	Greenwood
19-Feb	Pearlie Patrick	F	C	36	M	425 S. Lee	2 yrs	Cook	Ga	Lobar Pneumonia	Montezuma, Ga
20-Feb	*George W. Steele	M	W	66	M	510 E Jackson	1mos	Retired	Ind	Pernicious Anemia	Crawfordsville, Ind
24-Feb	*Luella Eubank	F	W	72	W	740 N. Mills / Port Orange, Fla	2 yrs	At Home	Richmond Va	Pneumonia, Lobar	Port Orange
5-Oct-27	Luscius Tomlinson	M	W	37	M	Groveland		Laborer	Mascotte Fla	Gunshot	Empire Cemetery
10-Jan	Infant of Purious Dow	M	W		S	O.G.H.		None	Orlando	Stillborn	Ocoee
16-Feb	Fennie Bell Jones	F	B	28	S	O.G.H. / Clermont, Fla	2 ds	House-keeper	Archer, Fla	Streptococcus	Clermont, Fla
18-Feb	John Putnam Bates	M	W	64	M	O.G.H. / Clermont, Fla	10 ds	Retired	Wiscon-sin	Carcinoma of Cecum	Clermont, Fla
26-Feb	Amanda Furnish	F	W	75	M	O.G.H. / St. Cloud, Fla	14 ds	House-wife	Ky	Diabetes Mellitus	St. Cloud, Fla
9-Feb	Infant of Abraham R. James	M	C		S	42 Ossie St.			Orlando	Stillborn	Greenwood
25-Feb	*Infant of Mr & Mrs John H Roberts	F	W		S	O.G.H./Win-ter Garden, Fla			Orlando	Stillborn	Winter Garden, Fla
26-Feb	*Leslie Denning	M	W	69	S	Howell Sanit / 232 S Main	14 ds	Retired Farmer	Iowa	Apoplexy	Waterloo, Iowa
26-Feb	*Margaret Ethel Carmicheal	F	W	2	S	2007 E Cen Ave	2+ yrs		Orlando	Ileocolitis	Greenwood
28-Feb	*Lindley M. Brackin	M	W	86	W	O.G.H. / Colerine, Ohio	10 ds	Retired Farming	Mt. Pleas-ant, Ohio	Chronic Interstitial Nephritis	Colerine, Ohio
24-Feb	John Reid Tyler	M	C			602 S. Parramore			Fla	Stillborn	Greenwood
24-Feb	Ivory Gibson	F	C	29	M	612 W Jackson	2 mos +	House-wife	Fla	Acute Pul-monary Phthisis	Greenwood
26-Feb	*Mrs Ellen Hall Luce	F	W	77	M	126 Orlando Ave	7 mos	At Home	Mich	Myocarditis	Grand Rapids, Mich
28-Feb	*Infant of Mr & Mrs L. Quilling	M	W		S	1837 Fellokas			Orlando	Premature Infant	Lake Highland Cemetery
29-Feb	*Hugh R. Barrentine	M	W	28	D	O.G.H. / Orlando	1 yr	Laborer	Bartow, Fla	Fracture Skull	Cremation
29-Feb	*Ira W. Leach	M	W	67	M	508 N. Garland	17 yrs	Confec-tionery Salesman	Niles, Mich	Carcinoma of Pancreas	Petakey, Mich

1928	Name of Deceased	Sex	Race	Age	Marital	Residence & Place of Death	Orlando Resident	Occupation	Place of Birth	Cause of Death	Place of Burial
1-Mar	*Mrs Sarah Ann Russell	F	W	70	W	20 W Moreland Dr	70 yrs	At Home	Mickopaney, Fla	Carcinoma of Rectum	Mizell Cemetery
2-Mar	*Elgin Wood	M	W	79	W	Jefferson Ct	2 mos 8 ds	Retired	Canada	Bronchopneumonia	Sarnia, Ontario, Canada
2-Mar	Marie Agnes Meinhardt	F	W	85	M	John J. Heirtz Hosp	1 mo	H W	Bohemia	Pulmonary Tuberculosis	Palm Bay, Fla
3-Mar	Infant of Rosa Lee Large	M	C		S	817 Avondale	3 yrs	Mother a Laundress	Fla	Stillborn	Woodlawn
3-Mar	Essie Geter	F	C	19	S	O.G.H. / S W part of City	1 yr	Domestic	Ga	Gunshot Wound of Abdomen	County Home
4-Mar	Geo H. Davis	M	C	61	M	1019 W Jefferson	35 yrs	Barber	Athens, Ga	Mitral Regurgitation	Greenwood
5-Mar	*J Frank Sallade	M	W	55	D	Heitz Sant	2 yrs 5 mos	Stone Cutter	Pa	Bronchial Pneumonia	Pottsville, Pa
5-Mar	*Infant of Mr & Mrs Loney Mele	F	W		S	RFD # 3			Orlando	Stillborn	Lake Hill Cemetery
5-Mar	*R T Hunt, Jr	M	W	3	S	Fla Sant / Sanford, Fla	6 ds		Sanford, Fla	Nephritis with Dropsy	Sanford, Fla
5-Mar	*Sarah Elizabeth Atha	F	W	83	W	415 W Pine Ave	5 yrs	At Home	Va	Cerebral Hemorrhage	Mannington, WVa
6-Mar	*Methias Kline	M	W	75	M	O.G.H. / Gotha, Fla	6 ds	Merchant	Ohio	Acute Appendicitis	Greenwood
6-Mar	John Dawson Hood	M	W	53	M	O.G.H.	3 ds	Retired	Sandersville, Ga	Acute Dilitation of Heart	Sanford, Fla
9-Mar	*Mrs Daisy Lawrence	F	W	56	D	ACL Crossing / W Church St	18 yrs	Rooming House	Bradford Co., Fla	R R Accident	DeLand, Fla
9-Mar	Infant of Mr & Mrs E D Holton	M	W	6 hr	S	O.G.H.			Orlando	Atelectasis	Titusville, Fla
12-Mar	Sarah H. Allen	F	W	85	W	806 Anderson	1 yr +	At Home	N.J.	Chronic Pyelonephritis	Vault
10-Mar	*Infant of Mr & Mrs Arthur Lee Wilson	M	W		S	14 Norton Ave			Orlando	Atelectasis	Cremation
10-Mar	*Mrs Dora Bell Mills	F	W	64	W	Greenwood Ave	5 mos	At Home	N.C.	Chr Myocarditis	Reidsville, N.C.
11-Mar	*Infant of Mr & Mrs Arthur Lee Wilson	M	W		S	14 Norton Ave	1 da		Orlando	Atelectasis	Cremation
11-Mar	*Mrs Lois M. Cady	F	W	57	M	O.G.H.	6 ds	At Home	Cincinnati	Intestinal Obstruction	Cremation
12-Mar	*Jeanette Turner	F	W	13 d	S	1404 Westmoreland	13 ds		Orlando	Premature Birth	Greenwood
13-Mar	*Mrs Mary L. Wallace	F	W	81	W	O.G.H. / Berwyn, Ill	4 mos	At Home	Dover, Ill	Arteriosclerosis	Berwyn, Ill
13-Mar	*Mrs Catherine Eaton	F	W	71	M	RFD #4	3 yrs	At Home	Belfast, Ireland	Uremia	Greenwood
15-Mar	*Mrs Anna M. Brewster	F	W	74	W	O.G.H. / Dover, N.H.	4 mos	At Home	D K	Hypertension	Dover, N.H.
15-Mar	*Violet M. Redman	F	W	58	M	635 Terrace Blvd, N.Y. City	2 mos	At Home	N.Y.	Pleurisy with Effusion	N Y City
15-Mar	*Infant of Mr & Mrs Hugh Ferriss	M	W		S	Fla Sant / 101 Park Ave, N.Y.			Orlando	Premature Birth	Cremation
16-Mar	*Ellen Millsap	F	W	17	S	O.G.H. / Ocoee, Fla	5 ds		Moultrie, Ga	Septicemia	Moultrie, Ga
16-Mar	*Mrs Mattie Hyer	F	W	74	M	O.G.H. / 612 W Concord	54 yrs	At Home	Merriwether, Ga	Uremia	Greenwood

140

1928	Name of Deceased	Sex	Race	Age	Marital	Residence & Place of Death	Orlando Resident	Occupation	Place of Birth	Cause of Death	Place of Burial
6-Mar	Susie Batson	F	C	26	M	531 Thomas	5 yrs	Domestic	Oscella, Fla	Peritonitis	Greenwood
10-Mar	Lucy Elizabeth Hobbs	F	C	85	W	1620 E South	37 yrs	Laundress	Fla	General Paralysis	Greenwood
13-Mar	James Corbitt	M	C	55	M	445 Quincy	9 yrs	Common Labor	N.C.	Chronic Intestinal Nephritis	Greenwood
14-Mar	John Solomon Hall	M	C	11		729 W Carter	11 yrs	School Boy	Fla	Hematoma of Throat	Greenwood
19-Mar	Gilbert Ellis	M	C	23	S	O.G.H.	4 ds	Laborer	Ga	Typhoid Fever	Savannah, Ga
19-Mar	*Daniel B Kurtz	M	W	73	M	1214 Westmoreland Dr	10 yrs	Retired	Ky	Pellagra	Greenwood
17-Mar	Robert Clark	M	C	64	M	537 W Robinson	1 mo	Laborer	S.C.	Endocarditis	Greenwood
20-Mar	*Infant of Mr & Mrs T J Johnson	M	W		S	O.G.H. / Holopaw, Fla			Orlando	Stillborn	Cremation
21-Mar	*William H. Search	M	W	84	W	O.G.H.	1 mo 14 ds	Retired	N.Y. City	Chr Myocarditis	New Rochelle, N.Y.
21-Mar	*Infant of Mr & Mrs Robert G Summers	F	W		S	O.G.H. / 417 S Eola Dr			Orlando	Stillborn	Greenwood
21-Mar	Elijah Johnson	F	C	51	M	641 Ossie St	9 mos	Domestic	Fla	Abscess of Lungs	Reddick, Fla
22-Mar	*Mrs Cora Simmons	F	W	37	M	O.G.H. / Orlando	3 mos	At Home	Ozark, Ala	Lobar Pneumonia	Greenwood
23-Mar	*Ida Ricketson	F	W	60	M	1006 W Jackson	6 yrs	At Home	Ware Co., Ga	Acute Dilitation of Heart	Greenwood
24-Mar	*John T Brierly	M	W	73	W	O.G.H.	5 mos	Retired	Milbubry? Mass	Cerebral Hemorrhage	Holden, Mass
24-Mar	*Mrs Mattie B Davis	F	W	60	a W	Amherst Apts	30 yrs	At Home	Lexington, Ky	Myocarditis	Arlington Cemetery, Ft Myers, Md
24-Mar	*Wm L. Myers	M	W	50	M	339 W Carter / Indianapolis, Ind	4 mos	Carpenter	Ind	Tubercular Peritonitis	Seymour, Ind
24-Mar	*Mrs Eva Lee Kelley	F	W	53	CW	O.G.H. / RFD #4	1 da	At Home	Petersburg Va	Angina Pectoris	Atlanta, Ga
26-Mar	*Frederick Hagens	M	W	64	M	2010 Nebraska Ave	6 mos	Retired	Germany	Acute Dilitation of Heart	Hoboken, N.J.
27-Mar	William Nelson	M	C			O.G.H.			Fla	Stillborn	Greenwood
27-Mar	Henry King	F	C		S	660 W Robinson		None	Orlando	Stillborn	Greenwood
28-Mar	*Mrs Emily E. Kingsley	F	W	59	M	407 E South	30 yrs	At Home	Portsmouth, N.H.	Chronic Ulcerative Colitis	Greenwood
30-Mar	*James Eugean Johnson	M	W	43	M	1913 Marks St.	2 yrs	Plasterer	N.C.	Pulmonary Tuberculosis	Greenwood
30-Mar	*Sarah Elizabeth Longenecker	F	W	17	S	Fla Sant / Winter Park	21 ds	At Home	Easton, Maryland	Acute Nephritis	Winter Park
6-Mar	Henderson Brown	M	C	27	M	729 Americus Alley	4 ds	Day Laborer	Ga	Left Lobe Pneumonia	Greenwood
23-Mar	Infant of Mr & Mrs J. B. Overton	F	W		S	Fla Sant			Orlando	Premature	Taken Care of By Family
27-Mar	Infant of Chas King & Carrie Murphy	M	C		Inf	660 W Robinson			Orlando	Stillborn	Greenwood
1-Apr	*William Edwin Boydston	M	W	17	S	O.G.H. / Mt Dora, Fla	1 da	Clerk	Water Valley, Miss	Fractured Skull	Mt Dora, Fla

141

1928	Name of Deceased	Sex	Race	Age	Marital	Residence & Place of Death	Orlando Resident	Occupation	Place of Birth	Cause of Death	Place of Burial
2-Apr	*Infant of Mr & Mrs Dallas Keenan	M	W		S	O.G.H. / 1007 Harwell St			Orlando, Fla	Asphyxia from Dystocia	Greenwood
3-Apr	Wm Felk	M	C	23	M	745 Carter St	3 ds	Day Work	Valdosta, Ga	Don't Know	Greenwood
5-Apr	Mamie Julia Anderson	F	W	49	M	Fla Sant	21 ds	House-wife	Kiran, Iowa	Ulcerative Colitis	Groveland, Fla
46707	Infant of Mr & Mrs A L Carmichael	M	W	8 hrs	S	2009 E Central Ave	8 hrs	None	Orlando	Infancy	Colonial Cemetery 3 mi NE Orlando
1-Apr	*Infant of Mr & Mrs L. S. Chubb	F	W		S	Fla San			Orlando	Stillborn	Cremation
4-Apr	*Alford [Alfred] A Riddle	M	W	a 68	M	Conroy Ave	6 yrs	Day Labor	Ga	Appendical Abscess	Lake Hill
6-Apr	*Mrs Isabella M S Thomson	F	W	a 71	W	O.G.H./Toronto, Canada	few hours	At Home	Scotland	Probable Skull Fracture	Montreal, Canada
8-Apr	*Miller D Galloway	M	W	61	S	RFD #4	5? yrs	Farming	Warren Co., Ky	Cardiac Dilatation, Acute	Bowling Green, Ky
9-Apr	*Theo W Arms	M	W	73	W	520 E Anderson	3 yrs	Retired	Norwich, Conn	Cerebral Hemorrhage	Brooklyn, N.Y.
10-Apr	Haywood Rigsbee	M	C	41	M	323 Westmoreland	8 yrs	Plasterer	Lake City, Fla	Gun Shot Wound	Greenwood
11-Apr	*Elmore William Way	M	W	78	M	419 E South	16 yrs	Retired	Ill	Arteriosclerosis	Glenn Ellyn, Ill
12-Apr	*Infant of Mr & Mrs A J Ruff	F	W		S	608 Amelia			Orlando	Stillborn	Greenwood
13-Apr	*Mrs Elizabeth L Martin	F	W	68	M	525 E Church	2 yrs	At Home	Pa	Cerebral Softening	Philadelphia, Pa
13-Apr	*Saumella Grace Pannell	F	W	75	W	O.G.H. / Apopka	1 da	At Home	Memphis, Tenn	Chronic Tuberculosis	Apopka, Fla
13-Apr	Cornelious D. Akerson [Ekerson]	M	W	82	W	612 N. Hughey	5 yrs	Retired	Ithacia, N.Y.	Angina Pectoris	Newark, N.J.
14-Apr	Lewis H. Bullis	M	W	91	M	818 Adair Blvd	6 yrs	Retired	N.Y.	Senility	West Concord, Minn
15-Apr	*James J. Vining	M	W	69	M	O.G.H. / Winter Garden	18 ds	Market	Ga	Cancer of Lip	Winter Garden
16-Apr	*Kate Lark Clement	F	W	68	W	316 N Main	8 yrs	At Home	Lawrence Co., S.C.	Myocarditis & Endocarditis	Greenwood
14-Apr	*Mrs Bessie N. Beerye	F	W	46	M	241 Ridgewood	5 yrs	At Home	Baltimore, Md	Angina Pectoris	Vault
1-Mar	Erbert Henry Johnson	M	W	4	S	Laughman, Fla	5 ds	None	Fla	Acute Lymphatic Leukemia	Rose Hill Cemetery
11-Apr	Olie May Jackson	F	C	5 m	S	846 Short	5 mos		Orlando	Status Lymphatium	Greenwood
14-Apr	*Infant of Mr & Mrs Tomas DeFoe	M	W		S	O.G.H.			Orlando	Prematurity	Greenwood
13-Apr	Jem McPherson	M	C	49	S	533 W South	2 mos	Labor	Fla	Cirrhosis of Liver	Greenwood
19-Apr	*Allen F. Sheffler	M	W	63	M	O.G.H. / 622 Anderson	4 yrs?	Retired	Bath, Penn	Acute Bacillaty?	Greenwood
19-Apr	*Rachel A. Dardonville	F	W	69	M	436 S. Osceola	7 yrs	At Home	New York City	Streptococcus	New York
20-Apr	*Frank M. Osborn	M	W	71	M	402 America	34 yrs	Carpenter Work	Conn	Apoplexy	Cremation
20-Apr	*Infant of Mr & Mrs Arthur Layton	F	W		S	O.G.H. / Tangerine, Fla			Orlando	Prematurity	Cremated

1928	Name of Deceased	Sex	Race	Age	Marital	Residence & Place of Death	Orlando Resident	Occupation	Place of Birth	Cause of Death	Place of Burial
21-Apr	*James A. Burney	M	W	38	M	511 E Jackson	1 yr	Travel-ing Salesman	Colquit Co., Ga	Angina Pectoris	In Vault
22-Apr	*Ruby C. Stinson	F	W	23	M	Orla Vista	2 yrs	At Home	Ala	Endocarditis	Brundridge, Ala
22-Apr	*Ivva [Ivo] J. Billingsley	F	W	31	M	O.G.H.	3 yrs	At Home	Chicago, Ill	Septicemia from Infection of Nose	Greenwood
23-Apr	*Margaret H. Smith	F	W	58	M	94 Marks St / Hudson, Fla	3 mos	At Home	Tenn	Apoplexy	Johnson City, Tenn
22-Apr	Walter Denson	M	C	22	S	Lake Mann/ 716 W Livingston	1 mo	Tailor	Ga	Accidental Drowning	Greenwood
23-Apr	*Margarette Clouser	F	W	63	M	Fla Sant / 1400 Clouser Ave	11 yrs	At Home	Pa	Shock Following Amputation of Leg	Greenwood
24-Apr	*Teresa Jannet Schlinkert	F	W	1	S	648 W Concord	1 yr		Orlando	Acute Gastrointestinal Intoxication	Detroit, Mich
25-Apr	*Infant of Maggie Mae Powell	F	C		S	737 W South			Orlando	Prematurity	Greenwood
28-Apr	*John Thomas Stephenson	M	W	45	M	O.G.H. / Groveland, Fla	9 yrs	Yard Foreman	Bruton, Ala	Fracture Base of Skull	Carey Hand
2-May	Lena Dysen	F	C	35	M	O.G.H. / Winter Garden	15 ds	House-wife	Fla	Carcinoma of Uterus	Oakland, Fla
4-May	Anna Banks	F	C		Inf	206 Quincy Ave			Orlando	Stillborn	Greenwood
11-Apr	Minie E. Lester	F	C	1 mo	Inf	Tampa Ave			Orlando	Status Lymphaticus?	Greenwood
25-Apr	Infant of Mr & Mrs Willie Pane	F	C			419 McFall			Orlando	Stillborn	Greenwood
26-Apr	Will Reed	M	C	48	M	Beech	20 yrs	Laborer	Caro, Ga	Acute Nephritis with Oedema	Greenwood
4-May	Mary Margaret Mincarelli	F	W	16 m	S	O.G.H.	7 days		Kissim-mee, Fla	Acute Bright's	Kissimmee, Fla
31-Mar	Calvin Nelson, Jr.	M	C	SB		O.G.H.			Orlando	Asphyxiation from Breech Delivery	Greenwood
28-Apr	*Charles A. Averill	M	W	78	M	830 N. Hyer	5 yrs	Retired	Stillwater, Maine	Cerebral Hemorrhage	Greenwood
30-Apr	*Ralph E. Smith	M	W	21	S	O.G.H. / 1506 Kuhl Ave	2 yrs	Auto Mecha-nic	Ohio	Fracture Lumbar	Ironton, Ohio
30-Apr	*Frederick Herman Worch	M	W	71	M	R 19 Box 79	5 yrs	Retired	Germany	Broncho-pneumonia	Brooklyn, N.Y.
2-May	*Austin Chas Starbird	M	W	66	M	O.G.H. / Apopka, Fla	3 ds	Retired	Maine	Acute Nephritis	Apopka
3-May	*Fred M. Preston	M	W	54	M	O.G.H. / R 3 Box 102	12 yrs	Real Estate	Mass	Carcinoma of Pancreas	Greenwood
4-May	*Benjamin L. Griffin	M	W	79	M	Hertz San / Ocoee, Fla	21 ds	Grove & Truck Farming	Ga	Carcinoma	Beulah Cemetery
4-May	*Alvin Miller Forsythe	M	W	72	M	OGH/ Canons-burg, Penn	1 mo 19 ds	Retired	Hickory, Penn	Chr Myocarditis	Canonsburg, Pa
6-May	*Wm D. Gleason	M	W	81	W	O.G.H. / 624 Lexington Ave	19 yrs	Retired	Oswego, N.Y.	Cerebral Hemorrhage	Greenwood
8-May	*Infant of Mr & Mrs L. Oscar Sangster	F	W		S	OG.H / Cheney Highway			Orlando	Stillborn	Greenwood

1928	Name of Deceased	Sex	Race	Age	Marital	Residence & Place of Death	Orlando Resident	Occupation	Place of Birth	Cause of Death	Place of Burial
9-May	*Mary Smith Harris	F	W	46	M	201 Oglethorp Ave	2 yrs	At Home	Deatsville, Ala	Apoplexy; Uremia	Coffee Springs, Ala
9-May	*Sarah H. Todd	F	W	82	W	508 E Washington/Liberty St	12 yrs	At Home	N.J.	Chronic Nephritis	Clermont, N.J.
8-May	Clara Edith Bradford	F	W	56	S	Fla Sant / 30 Gatlin Ave	2 ½ yrs	Trained Nurse	Indiana	Acute Obstruction of Bowel	Bloomington, Ind
10-May	*Anna Eliza Jones	F	W	87	W	2310 Amherst Ave	12 yrs	At Home	N.Y.	Uremia	Poundridge, N.Y.
12-May	*Oliver R. Cooke	M	W	78	M	RFD 3	3 yrs	Retired	Pa	Angina Pectoris	Carneig, Pa
13-May	*Helen Marie Chafin	F	W	9 m	S	O.G.H. / Ocoee, Fla	1 da		Gainesville, Fla	Septicemia	Washington, Ga
14-May	*James Francis Shultz	M	W	2	S	Fla Sant / Winer Park	1 da		Winter Park	Food Toxin Poisoning	Fountain City, Ind
21-May	*Louise C Felter	F	W	74	M	Route 19	16 yrs	At Home	Brooklyn, N.Y.	Chronic Myocarditis	Woodmere, Long Island, NY
21-May	*Lucina Bullis	F	W	87	W	819 Adair Blvd	4 yrs	At Home	East Auto, N.Y.	Mitral Regurgitation	West Concord, Minn
20-May	*Clara Roseman	F	W	46	M	O.G.H. / 539 N. Hughey	10 yrs	At Home	Romania	Broncho-pneumonia	New York City
19-May	*Edward Reid [Reed]	M	W	10 mo s	S	O.G.H. / 517 Yale Ave			Orlando	Acidosis	Greenwood
16-May	*Infant of Mr & Mrs Bertie Prescott	M	W		S	O.G.H. / Rt 19			Orlando	Stillborn	Greenwood
11-May	*William J. Payne	M	W	73	W	Fla Sant	10 ds	Retired	Clay Co, Ind	Auto Accident	Danville, Ill
18-May	Edward Griffith Dyer	M	W	71	M	704 S Summerlin	8 yrs	Builder	New York	Chronic Myocarditis	Greenwood
20-May	Frank Sidney Palmer	M	W	65	M	Fla San	21 ds	Oil Merchant	Conn	Uremia	DeLand, Fla
21-May	Eddie Walker	M	C	36	M	O.G.H/12 Jefferson St Court	2 yrs	Janitor	Ga	Gastric Ulcer	Greenwood
22-May	*Charles Patrick Fitzgerald	M	W	1	S	Fairvilla	4 mos		Orlando	Uremia	Greenwood
22-May	*Ada Reely Hickok	F	W	25	M	Fla San / Madison, Fla	12 ds	Graduate Nurse	Montana	Acute Nephritis	Greenwood
23-May	*Lena L. Johnson	F	W	41	M	O.G.H. / Conway Drive	3 yrs	At Home	Hart Co, Ky	Pyelonephritis	Mannforville, Ky
23-May	Melnotte H. Priest	M	W	77	W	Fla San	4 mos	Retired	N.Y.	Hemorrhage of Stomach	Little Falls, N.Y.
24-May	Infant of James & Carrie Preston	M	C			O.G.H.			Fla	Stillborn	Greenwood
24-May	Stella Dessesaw?	F	C	48	M	208 N. Bryant	12 yrs	Housework	Ga	Carcinoma of Uterus	Greenwood
24-May	*Glenn Henry Miller	M	W	1	S	O.G.H. / Lockhart, Fla	3 ds		Lockhart, Fla	Acute Ileocolitis	Cairo, Ga
24-May	*Lola R Balch	F	W	30	M	O.G.H. / Samsula, Fla	4 mos		Ind	Intestinal Obstruction	Cremation
25-May	*Thos Herbert Cook	M	W	42	M	O.G.H. / 918 Lakeview Ave	5 yrs	Salesman	Newberry, S.C.	Uremia	Jasper, Fla
15-May	Agnes Bradley	F	C	1	S	1107 W Holden	1 yr		Camphill, Fla	Acute Ileocolitis	Rochell, Fla
19-May	Will Hicks	M	C	52	M	49 Ossie St	5 yrs	Common Labor	Ga	Acute Dilation of Heart	Greenwood
21-May	Infant of Mollie Evelyn Rigsby	F	C	2 m	S	912 Bentley			Orlando	Broncho-pneumonia	Greenwood

144

1928	Name of Deceased	Sex	Race	Age	Marital	Residence & Place of Death	Orlando Resident	Occupation	Place of Birth	Cause of Death	Place of Burial
25-May	*Mrs Christina N Hofer	F	W	53	D	O.G.H. / 1003 E Jackson	2 mos	Southern Rep Calif Perfume Co	N.Y.	Pernicious Anemia	Cremation
26-May	James Danforth	M	C	36	M	713 Carter	5 yrs	Carpenter	Ga	Stab Wound of Back	Greenwood
29-May	Willie J. McCloud	M	C	2	S	818 Avondale	5 yrs		Orlando	Burn to Death	Greenwood
29-May	Samuel Law Kyles	M	W	76	W	O.G.H. / 1016 Elmwood	8 yrs	Retired Contrac- tor	Canada	Carcinoma of Stomach	Greenwood
1-Jun	Vernie Kathern Hall	F	W	1	S	O.G.H. / Umatilla, Fla	6 ds		Umatilla, Fla	Acute Ileocolitis	Umatilla, Fla
18-May	Ossie Lee Hunter	F	C	1 da	S	1203 Conly	1 da	Infant	Orlando	Stillborn	Greenwood
28-May	Bula Reese	F	C	42	M	225 S Butts	12 yrs	House- work	Ga	Valvular Heart Disease	Greenwood
17-May	Chas A. Baldwin	M	W	60	M	Park Lake Ave	4 yrs	Carpenter	D K	Apoplexy	Greenwood
26-May	*Edward A Ewers	M	W	62	M	1303 Catherine	7 mos	Painter	N.Y.	Acute Dilitation of Heart	Greenwood
30-May	*Infant of Mr & Mrs Michael J Smith	M	W		S	O.G.H. / RR 2			Orlando	Stillborn	Cremated
30-May	Henry Murphy	M	C	47 a	W	807 W Robinson	21 ds	Laborer	S.C.	Malaria Fever	Greenwood
31-May	*Minnie Elizabeth Peaden	F	W	1 da	S	1104 E Rob Ave	1 da		Orlando	Atelectasis	Greenwood
31-May	*Mary Olive Mitchell	F	W	45	M	1600 E Cen Av/Oviedo, Fl	9 mos	At Home	Chuluota, Fla	Parcomatosis? Gen Abdominal Cavity	Chuluota, Fla
2-Jun	*P. Bradley Martin	M	W	83	M	Fla San / Fair Shores	40 yrs	Retired	Blairs- town, N.J.	Senility	Blairstown, N.J.
3-Jun	*Oveda Gravitt	F	W	4	S	310 W Church	1 yr		Maitland, Fla	Laryycal? Diphtheria	McDonald Cemetery
1-Jun	*Chas F Edwards	M	W	50 a	W	710 W Central Ave	4 mos	Laundry	D K	Ruptured Aneurysm	Greenwood
3-Jun	Lewis Tyson	M	C	39	M	OGH/814 Lee	1 yr	Labor	Fla	Chr Myocarditis	Greenwood
3-Jun	*Mrs Elizabeth Jane Donhue [Donahue]	F	W	81	W	Conway Drive	8 yrs	Home	Ireland	Senile Dementia	Greenwood
4-Jun	*Edgar B. Whipple	M	W	77	W	RFD 3-72B / Plymouth, Fla	2 mos 7 ds	Retired	N.H.	Apoplexy	Crayden, N.H.
4-Jun	Willie Babb	M	C		S	1040 Holden St			Orlando	Premature Delivery	Greenwood
6-Jun	*Leon Barks	M	W	21	M	O.G.H. / Winter Garden	19 hrs	Labor	Ga	Burns	Bulah Cemetery
6-Jun	*Lorenzo Barks	M	W	48	M	O.G.H.	6 hrs	Labor	N.C.	Burns	Bulah Cemetery
5-Jun	*Infant of Mr & Mrs Fred B. Rawl	F	W		S	Fla Sant			Orlando	Asphyxia Neonatorum	Cremated
8-Jun	*Mrs Emily A. Welch	F	W	62 a	M	O.G.H.	5 yrs	At Home	N.Y.	Acute Dilatation of Heart	Greenwood
9-Jun	*Dale Frederick Richards	M	W	1	S	O.G.H.	3 ds		Winter Park	Acute Nephritis	Winter Park
11-Jun	*John Colin Murchison	M	W	60	M	O.G.H. / 6 Columbia	5 yrs	Exec Supt ACL	N.C.	Shock Following Operation	Charleston, S.C.

Date	Name of Deceased	Sex	Race	Age	Marital	Residence & Place of Death	Orlando Resident	Occupation	Place of Birth	Cause of Death	Place of Burial
11-Jun	Joe Eursepro Limini [Linzini]	M	W	22	S	O.G.H. / Mascotte, Fla	1 yr	Laborer	Italy	Burned to Death	Groveland, Fla
12-Jun	Annie Rains Patterson	F	W	61	W	Winter Garden Road	4 wks	None	Chairs, Fla	Cancer of Stomach	DeLand, Fla
13-Jun	Charles A. Reeve	M	W	51	S	Fla Sant & Hosp / DeLand	8 ds	Photographer	Ontario	Edema	DeLand, Fla
12-Jun	Carrie Preston	F	C	28	M	539 W Church St	4 yrs	Housewife	Tenn	La Grippe	South Pittsburg, Tenn
13-Jun	Lee Ora Demps	M	C	1	S	511 W Gore Ave	1 da	None	Orlando	Stillborn	Greenwood
7-Jun	Lois Wanda Padgett	F	W	3	S	O.G.H. / Kissimmee	1 da	None	Fla	Ileocolitis	Rose Hill
11-Jun	Viola Lemoure	F	W	35	M	O.G.H. / Kissimmee	8 ds	Housewife	Texas	Shock Following Rupture of Op	Rose Hill
8-Jun	*Thomas J. Noore	M	W	62	M	O.G.H. / 1001 E Cen Ave	11 yrs	Real Estate	Detroit, Mich	Intestional Obstruction	Vault
14-Jun	Thomas J. Dallas	M	C	40	M	416 S Parramore	15 yrs	Laborer	Fla	Acute Pulmonary Phthisis	Greenwood
14-Jun	*Mrs Sarah Ely Hodson	F	W	65	W	316 Winter Park Ave	2 yrs	At Home	Canada	Apoplexy	Grafton, N.D.
19-Jun	Newl Leon Whaley	M	W	12	S	O.G.H. / Kissimmee Park, Fla	1 da	Child	Kissimmee, Fla	Fracture of Base of Skull	Rose Hill Cemetery
19-Jun	*Cecil Harris Rodenbaugh	M	W	22	M	O.G.H. / Winter Park	2 ds	Auto Mechanic	Lockhart, Fla	Septicemia	Greenwood
19-Jun	*Infant of Mr & Mrs Dewey Hage	M	W		S	500 W Gore Ave			Orlando	Congenital Heart Defect	Greenwood
19-Jun	*Mrs Elizabeth S Styles	F	W	76	W	107 Liberty	3 yrs	At Home	Canada	Uremic Poison	Belvedere, Ill
21-Jun	*Lindberg Stewart	M	W	11 m	S	O.G.H. / Okeechobee City, Fla	1 da		Okeechobee City, Fla	Acute Ileocolitis	Okeechobee City, Fla
12-Jun	Wm T. Green	M	C	29	M	619 W Roberson	6 yrs	Bill Poster	West Va.	Drowned	Greenwood
14-Jun	Henry Gainey	M	C	38	S	O.G.H. / Winter Garden	15 yrs	Common Labor	N.C.	Pellagra	Winter Garden
21-Jun	Sarah Jane Pinckney	F	C	50	S	525 W Jackson	3 mos	Housekeeper	S.C.	Cerebral Hemorrhage	Savannah, Ga
21-Jun	*Grace L Vance	F	W	33	M	110 Park Lake Ave	4 yrs	Trained Nurse	Ohio	Chronic Interstitial Nephritis	Greenwood
22-Jun	*Sallie Thurman Barnard	F	W	71	W	519 Daniels	6 ds	At Home	Tenn	Hemiplegia, Left	Greenwood
19-Jun	*Anna L Carr	F	W	56	M	O.G.H. / 2721 N. Orange	4 yrs	At Home	Canada	General Debility	Cremated
25-Jun	*Florence Jobe	F	W	69	W	2611 E Wash	2 yrs	At Home	Ind	Chronic Myocarditis	Connersville, Ind
25-Jun	Michael Washington	M	C	31	S	701 W Robinson	15 ds	Ship Builder	S.C.	Mitral Stenosis	Taft, Fla
26-Jun	John Frank Reed	M	W	72	W	Bumby St / Conway Drive	3 yrs	Retired	Maine	Cerebral Hemorrhage	Rochester, N.H.
26-Jun	*Mrs Ollie B Segroves [Seagraves]	F	W	20	M	O.G.H. / Ocoee, Fla	5 ds	At Home	Ga	Ruptured Sepsis	Beulah Cemetery
26-Jun	William Alexander	M	W	47	S	114 Chatham	1 yr	Cement Finisher	Va	Brain Tumor	Greenwood
27-Jun	*Walter Newell	M	W	76 a	M	O.G.H. / Apopka	14 ds	Retired	N.H.	Uremia	Apopka

1928	Name of Deceased	Sex	Race	Age	Marital	Residence & Place of Death	Orlando Resident	Occupation	Place of Birth	Cause of Death	Place of Burial
28-Jun	*Stephen Parker Morrey	M	W	7 mo	S	S Fern Creek Drive	3 mos		Apopka	Tremnotine?	Apopka
28-Jun	Infant of Mr & Mrs Roy P Douberley	F	W		S	24 Glenn			Orlando	Stillborn	Cremated
29-Jun	Geo Holmes	M	C	45 a	M	OGH/Carter St	3 ds	Labor	D K	Acute Nephritis	Greenwood
29-Jun	*Mrs Emely Hewitt	F	W	78	W	Lockhart		At Home	England	Diabetes	Greenwood
30-Jun	Infant of Mr & Mrs L L Latham	M	W	0	S	Fla San	0	None	Orlando	Stillborn	Greenwood
30-Jun	*Bessie Luke	F	C	40 a		O.G.H. / Div St	D K	House-work	Ga	Pellagra	Greenwood
30-Jun	*Louis Cyrus Demain	M	W	67	S	732 Concord	7 yrs	Retired	Vt	Cardiac Insufficiency	Fairfax, Vt
30-Jun	*William Henry Drake	M	W	11	S	Fla San / Grand Ave	8 yrs		Mich	Primary Acute Lobar Pneumonia	Greenwood
1-Jul	*Mrs Hilda Kratzer	F	W	41	M	Fla San / Apopka	21 ds	At Home	Apopka	Pyonephritis	Apopka
1-Jul	*Geo E Macy	M	W	77	M	421 S Rosalind	52 yrs	Retired	Tenn	Hypostatic Pneumonia	Greenwood
2-Jul	Claude Bridges	M	C	37	M	811 S Division St	9 yrs	Laborer	Va	Pulmonary Edema	Greenwood
20-Jul	*James B F Thomas	M	W	37	M	Las Animas?	8 yrs	Labor	Fla	Pulmonary Tuberculosis	Greenwood
12-Jul	*Mrs Emelia R Kimball	F	W	70	W	Angebilt Hotel /Birmingham, Al		At Home	N. Y. City	Food Poisoning	Long Island, N.Y.
2-Jul	*Ben Wesley Johnson	M	W	39	M	O.G.H. / Ocoee, Fla	3 ds	Fruit Grower	Ala	Acute Appendicitis	Pell City, Ala
2-Jul	Tom Council	M	C	24 a	S	O.G.H. / Holopaw, Fla	2 ds	Day Laborer	Ala	Homicide	St Cloud, Fla
3-Jul	Bill Williams	M	C	46	M	O.G.H.		Laborer	Ga	Acute Dysentery	Greenwood
3-Jul	Maria Whitaker	F	C	87 a	W	713 W South	36 yrs	Domes-tic	Ga	Acute Nephritis	Greenwood
3-Jul	*Mrs Theresa Sirlin	F	W	65	M	O.G.H. / 1419 Pine Crest	3 yrs	At Home	Germany	Intestinal Obstruction	Millville, Pa
5-Jul	*Eugene Booth	M	W	4	S	O.G.H. / Titusville, Fla	1 da		Fla	Auto Accident	Titusville, Fla
5-Jul	*Harry Botto	M	W	3 ds	S	O.G.H. / Kissimmee, Fla	3 ds		Orlando	Infancy	Kissimmee
6-Jul	*Mrs Eldora Allice Hill	F	W	52 a	M	Carlton Road	4 yrs	At Home	Howard, Ga	Nephritis	Manke, Ga
6-Jul	*Infant of Mr & Mrs David E Wheeler	M	W		S	O.G.H. / 715 Bamboo			Orlando	Stillborn	Cremated
7-Jul	Eddie Wilson	M	C	40	M	432 S Parramore	3 yrs	Common Labor	N.C.	Post Typhoid	Greenwood
7-Jul	Almeda Freeberg	F	W	42	W	O.G.H.	5 ds	House work	Sweden	Myocarditis	Chicago, Ill
7-Jul	Dorothy B Cooley	F	C	6 mo	S	14 Hicks	3 mos		Fla	Stomach Trouble	Greenwood
7-Jul	George J. Spoctsy	M	C	56	M	313 W Pine St	2 yrs	Labor	Va	Acute Pulmonaty Phthisis	Greenwood
7-Jul	Calvin Hightower	M	C	36	W	O.G.H. / Winter Park	1 da	Labor	S.C.	Intestinal Obstruction	County
8-Jul	Martha Reims	F	C	44	M	1410 W Washington	11 yrs	H W	S. C.	Mitral Regurgitation	Greenwood
12-Jul	*Rudolph Menzel	M	W	68	M	O.G.H. / 12 Copeland Dr	5 yrs	Retired	Ohio	Acute Dilation of Heart	Greenwood

Date	Name of Deceased	Sex	Race	Age	Marital	Residence & Place of Death	Orlando Resident	Occupation	Place of Birth	Cause of Death	Place of Burial
12-Jul	*Infant of Mr & Mrs T E Whaley	F	W	14 hrs	S	O.G.H. / 906 E Cen Ave			Orlando	Atelectasis	Greenwood
13-Jul	Sarah Wheeler	F	C		M	1849 S Division St	30 yrs	H W	Ga	Lobar Pneumonia	Greenwood
13-Jul	*Infant of Mr & Mrs Laurence Wade	M	W	6 hrs	S	O.G.H.			Orlando	Enlarged Thymus	Greenwood
13-Jul	Robert E Lee	M	W	14	S	Fla San	9 ds		Groveland, Fla	Fractured Vertebra	Groveland, Fla
14-Jul	*Emily B McMullin	F	W	60	M	520 Lakeview	1 mo	At Home	Ga	Apoplexy	Moultrie, Ga
14-Jul	Waldense Nixon	M	C	34	M	621 S Kentucky	2 yrs	Dentist	Fla	Acute Gastritis	Sanford, Fla
14-Jul	Infant of Robt Williams	F	C		S	909 Bently			Orlando	Stillbirth	Greenwood
14-Jul	Cassie Mae Mitchell	F	C	12	S	735 S Parramore	6 yrs	School Girl	Ga	Acute Pulmonary Phthisis	Greenwood
14-Jul	*Mrs Mary L. Frank	F	W	78	W	O.G.H. / Orlando	10 mos	At Home	Pa	Accident	DeLand, Fla
15-Jul	*Evan Eugene Davis	M	W	1	S	Lake Lorna/ 1630 S Delaney	1 yr		Orlando	Drowning	Greenwood
16-Jul	*Mrs Mary M Mathews	F	W	77	W	801 W Jackson	15 yrs	At Home	N.C.	Acute Uremia	Greenwood
17-Jul	*Ira Pratt Humphrey	M	W	76	M	O.G.H. / 804 Smith Ave	6 yrs	Retired	N.Y.	Septicemia	Greenwood
18-Jul	Amos Bryant	M	C	65	M	835 S Parramore/ 210 Garden	2 yrs	Common Labor	Fla	Broncho-pneumonia	Greenwood
18-Jul	*Thomas Jefferson Herndon	M	W	71	W	Grand / Rio Grand Ave	2 yrs	Retired	Fla	Myocarditis	Arcadia, Fla
21-Jul	Rogers Weary	M	C	11	S	735 S Parramore	2 yrs	School Boy	Ga	Influenza	Greenwood
23-Jul	*Infant of Mr & Mrs Harold V Semling	F	W	1	S	O.G.H. /1702 N Shore Terrace			Orlando	Asphyxia Pallida	Cremation
24-Jul	*Henry V Bucks	M	W	48 a	S	100 S Hughey	8 yrs	Raidator	Montana	Myocarditis	Cannibol, Mo
24-Jul	Eula Carter	F	C	43	W	O.G.H.	5 yrs	Cook	Ga	Syphilis	Smithville, Ga
24-Jul	Levi Mandol	M	C	40	D K	O.G.H. / Lockhart	1 da	Day Labor		Septicemia	County Home
25-Jul	*Victor Berion Newton	M	W	37	D	O.G.H. / Amherst Apts	12 yrs	Fruit Broker	Ga	Secondary Hemorrhage	Oliver, Ga
25-Jul	Charity Smith	F	C	40 a		Lockhart	7 mos	H W	S.C.	Mitral Regurgitation	County Home
26-Jul	Stephen Andrew White	M	W	11 mo	S	624 Citrus Ave	11 mos	None	Orlando	Acute Intestinal Intoxication	Greenwood
24-Jul	*Clarence G. Guerny, Jr.	M	W	2 ds	S	515 Trenton St	2 ds		Orlando	Hemorrhage	Greenwood
29-Jul	*Wade Hampton McRainey	M	W	59	M	Fla Sant / 322 E Central Ave	8 yrs	Retired	N.C.	Atropic Hepatic Cirrhosis	Gainesville, Fla
4-Aug	Arthur Jones	M	C	42	M	O.G.H. / Oviedo	1 mo	Celery Farm	N.C.	Tertiary Syphilis	Abbeville, Ga
2-Jul	Mildred Chappel	F	C		S	3 Harmily Quarters			Orlando	Stillborn	Greenwood
29-Jul	Eddie Anderson	M	C		S	819 Edna			Orlando	Stillborn	Greenwood
1-Aug	Edner Mims	F	C	24	M	44½ N Parramore	5 ds	H W	Fla	Pellagra	Memorial Park

1928	Name of Deceased	Sex	Race	Age	Marital	Residence & Place of Death	Orlando Resident	Occupation	Place of Birth	Cause of Death	Place of Burial
2-Aug	*Infant of Mr & Mrs H S Robertson	M	W		S	O.G.H. / 416 E Concord Ave			Orlando	Asphyxia	Greenwood
5-Aug	*Mrs Barbara Becker	F	W	57	M	1219 Park Lake Ave	18 yrs	At Home	Germany	Carcinoma Colon	Greenwood
5-Aug	*Iva Lee Hicks	F	W	15	S	Orlando/ Macy St	9 mos		Tenn	Endocarditis	Athens, Tenn
6-Aug	*Satrach Kazarian	M	W	36	W	Orlando	5 yrs	Grocer	Turkey	Double Bronchopneumonia	Greenwood
6-Aug	*Infant of Mr & Mrs Granville Eaton		W		S	Fla San			Orlando	Asphyxia, Premature	Greenwood
6-Aug	*Jane Eaton	F	W	42	M	Fla San	1 da	At Home	Scotland	Hemorrhage	Greenwood
8-Aug	*Josia W Chase	M	W	43	M	RFD #4	8 yrs	None	Boston, Mass	Alcoholism	Greenwood
10-Aug	Mary Louise Knight	F	W	62	W	120 E Washington	8 mos	None	Conn	Cardiac Decompensation	Hartford, Conn
11-Aug	*Infant of James & Nannie Snipes	M	W		S	O.G.H.			Orlando	Stillborn	Cremation
8-Aug	Grant Nelson	M	C	53	W	739 Bentley	7 yrs	Common Labor	Jax, Miss	Heart Trouble	Greenwood
12-Aug	Rosa Moore Williams	F	C	40	M	722 America	3 yrs	Laundress	Ga	Acute Pneumonia Phthisis	Greenwood
19-Aug	____ Robinson	M	C	40 a	DK	DK	Several Days	Day Labor	Don't Know	Accidentally Drowned	County Home
29-May	*Ruth C Bell	F	W	72	W			At Home	Gainesville, Fla	Myocarditis, Chronic	Liberty Hill, S.C.
7-Aug	*Frank G Hall	M	W	61	M	511 Virginia Dr	3 yrs	Retired	Detroit, Mich	Apoplexy	Greenwood
8-Aug	Estella Patterson	F	C	40	S	706 W Jackson	15 yrs	Cook	S.C.	Cerebral Hemorrhage	Greenwood
11-Aug	*Annie B Flint	F	W	57	M	O.G.H. / 1600 S Osceola	5 yrs	At Home	Maine	Peritonitis	Bangor, Maine
13-Aug	*Julia Hughes	F	W	58	M	O.G.H. / Bithlo	1 da	At Home	Ala	Myocarditis	Chuluota, Fla
13-Aug	*J J Davis	M	W	53	M	2315 Dade	6 yrs	Brick Mason	Ga	Acute Dilation of Heart	Royston, Ga
13-Aug	*John A Sikes	M	W	52	M	606 Columbia	7 yrs	City Employee	Jacksonville, Fla	Angina Pectoris	Greenwood
13-Aug	*Carl Rummell	M	W	73	W	RFD #3	2 yrs	Retired	Germany	Ulceration of Stomach	Cremation
17-Aug	Infant of James & Inez Canther [Cauthen]	M	C		S	25 S Jernigan			Orlando	Status Lymphatism?	Greenwood
17-Aug	*Madison Monroe Storrs	M	W	85	M	Lockhart	6 yrs	Retired	Connecticut	Cardiovascular Renal Disease	Greenwood
17-Aug	*Phebe E Tower	F	W	55	D	O.G.H. / Apopka	8 ds	At Home	Kan	Chronic Arteriosclerotic Nephritis	Perry, Kan
17-Aug	Janes Lane	M	C	24	S	720 W South	10 yrs	School Boy	Brooksville, Fla	Tubercular Infection	Greenwood
18-Aug	Infant of Thomas Mays	M	C		S	1040 Carter			Orlando	Prematurity	Memorial Park
19-Aug	Infant of Carrie Stephens	F	C		S	914 Randall			Orlando	Stillborn	Memorial Park
20-Aug	*Elizabeth Biggerstaff	F	W	1	S	O.G.H. / Winter Park	1 da		Winter Park	Acute Pyolitis	Winter Park
23-Aug	*James Edward Priest	M	W		S	Fla San / 1908 S Oregon Ave			Orlando	Stillborn	Lake Hill Cemetery
24-Aug	*Infant of Ruth Johns	M	W		S	O.G.H. / 315 Spruce			Orlando	5 mos Fetus	Cremation

1928	Name of Deceased	Sex	Race	Age	Marital	Residence & Place of Death	Orlando Resident	Occupation	Place of Birth	Cause of Death	Place of Burial
25-Aug	Lucinda Argrett	F	C	65	W	804 Frederick	10 ds	House work	Fla	Cerebral Hemorrhage	Tallahassee, Fla
26-Aug	*Wm Shephard	W	M	79	M	431 Summerlin	5 yrs	Retired	England	Hypostatic Pneumonia	Greenwood
28-Aug	*Infant of Mr & Mrs K F Seymour	F	W		S	Fla San / Pine Castle			Orlando	Asphyxia	Cremated
28-Aug	*Bernard S Litherland	M	W	21	S	Ocoee	3 yrs	Labor	Ill	Typhoid Fever	Ocoee Cemetery
29-Aug	*Grover C Schmitt	M	W	43	M	O.G.H. / Winter Garden	9 ds	Carpenter	Ga	Acute Nephritis	Chattanooga, Tenn
2-Sep	Joe Richardson	M	C	6 m	S	6 Hicks St	6 mos	None	Orlando	Broncho Pneumonia	Memorial Park
31-Aug	Wm Horton Gafford	M	W	60	M	O.G.H. / Plant City	1 mo	Farmer	Stewart Co., Ga	Acute Cardiac Dilitation	Thomasville, Ga
1-Sep	*James W Boring	M	W	43	M	1322 S Bryant / Jefferson Court	10 yrs	Collector	Decatur, Ga	Bullet Wound	Decatur
4-Sep	*Mrs Margaret E Hall	F	W	62	W	511 Virginia Dr	3 yrs	At Home	New Castle, Thyne, Eng	Encephalitis Lethargica	Greenwood
5-Sep	*Jessie H Hurlburt	F	W	67	M	723 Lucerne Terrace	16 yrs	At Home	N.Y.	Uremia	Greenwood
9-Sep	Dale N Boydston	M	W	21	S	O.G.H. / Mt Dora, Fla	10 hrs	Clerk	Miss	Fractured Skull	Mt Dora, Fla
7-Sep	*J Lewis Kilgore	M	W	32	M	O.G.H. / Pine Castle	1 hr	Real Estate	S.C.	Crushed Chest	Greenwood
7-Sep	*Marcus James Buchanan	M	W	2	S	RFD #4	2 hrs 7 ds?		RFD #4	Accidental Drowning	Greenwood
7-Sep	*William Rogers	M	W	72	S	O.G.H. / Bithlo, Fla	10 ds	Cattle Business	S.C.	Chronic Nephritis	Cremation
10-Sep	*Infant of Mr & Mrs Eugean M Boone	M	W		S	Fla San / 9 W Kaley			Orlando	Stillborn	Greenwood
10-Sep	*Horace O Greer	M	W	17	S	173 W Jackson	1 yr		Miss	Acute Dilitation of Heart	Brook Haven, Miss
10-Sep	Infant of Cabot Wilson	F	C	11 ½ h	S	535 Johns St	½ da		Orlando	Don't Know	Greenwood
12-Sep	Elling King	F	C	32	S	OGH/ Mt Dora, Fla	6 ds	House-work	Ga	Gen Peritonitis	Zellwood, Fla
13-Sep	*Robt Lee Head	M	W	5	S	O.G.H. / RFD #3	7 ds		Atlanta, Ga	Acute Broncho-pneumonia	Drake Town, Ga
27-Aug	Ermanda Taylor	F	C	43	M	639 W Jefferson / O.G.H.	4 yrs	House-work	Fla	Lobar Pneumonia	Greenwood
11-Sep	John Piner	M	C	26	M	740 Jernigan	8 yrs	Day Laborer	Fla	Cerebral Hemorrhage	Greenwood
14-Sep	Nick Holmes	M	C	44	M	21 N Bryant	3 yrs	Laborer	Ala	Concussion of Brain	Dothan, Ala
14-Sep	*Wm P Sherman	M	W	92	W	County Home	50 yrs	Retired	Maine	Chronic Intestinal Nephritis	Greenwood
14-Sep	*Nannie E Barlow	F	W	56	M	1529 Hollenbeck Dr	56 yrs	At Home	Orlando, Fla	Chronic Intestinal Nephritis	Greenwood
16-Sep	Walker Fedge	M	C	27	M	113 N Terry	6 yrs	Common Labor	Ga	Acute Pulmonary Phthisis	Greenwood
16-Sep	*Thomas Walter Walsh	M	W	72	M	1322 Muriel Ave	7 yrs	Contrac-tor	Nova Scotia	Morbus Cardis Valvalarm	Griffin, Ga
16-Sep	*Infant of Mr & Mrs Sam Dean	M	W		S	Fla San			Orlando	Stillborn	Apopka, Fla

1928	Name of Deceased	Sex	Race	Age	Marital	Residence & Place of Death	Orlando Resident	Occupation	Place of Birth	Cause of Death	Place of Burial
16-Sep	*James Columbus Lemerand	M	W	71	M	Gatlin Ave	5 yrs	Retired	Mich	Sarcoma	Greenwood
17-Sep	Infant of Wright Drane	M	C		S	920 Edna			Orlando	Stillborn	Woodlawn Memo
17-Sep	*Mrs Dollie B Stamps	F	W	71	W	421 S Lake	7 yrs	At Home	Ky	Carcinoma of Pancreas	Tampa, Fla
18-Sep	*James Harry Reed	M	W	58	M	125 E Copeland	7 yrs	Retired	Penn	Electrocution	Tarentown, Penn
19-Sep	*Sallie C Hayes	F	W	82	S	O.G.H. / 628 N Orange	15 yrs	At Home	Miss	Fracture of Hip	Nashville, Tenn
20-Sep	*John Joseph Shea, 3rd	M	W		S	O.G.H. / Melbourne, Fl	2 ds		Melbourne Fla	Acute Broncho-pneumonia	Melbourne, Fla
13-Sep	F. W. White	M	C	60	M	Orlando, Fla	15 yrs	Laborer	Fla	Stroke, Paralysis	Greenwood
18-Sep	Alfred Weaver	M	C			Orlando, Fla			Fla	Stillborn	Memorial Park
21-Sep	Baby Francis	F	C			9 Hicks St			Orlando	Stillborn	Memorial Park
22-Sep	*Mrs Ida D Calhoun	F	W	49	W	215 Yale Ave	10 yrs	House-wife	Blount? Co., Ala	Cancer	Ocoee
23-Sep	*Dereta Gardiner	F	W	5		Grand Ave			Kissim-mee	Broncho-pneumonia	Kissimmee, Fla
23-Sep	*John A Paulk	M	W	27	M	O.G.H.	11 yrs	Laborer	Covington Co., Ala	Gunshot Wound	Ocoee
24-Sep	Florence Gillstroy	F	C	26	M	O.G.H.	1 yr	Domestic	Lake City, Fla	Shock After Operation	Lake City, Fla
24-Sep	*Mrs Minie Campbell	F	W	58	M	Fla Sant	7 yrs	House-keeper	Iron City, Iowa	Chronic Myocarditis	Winter Park, Fla
25-Sep	*John A Warren	M	W	2	S	1024 W Church St	1 yr		Ft Laud-erdale, Fla	Acute Sipelic?	Greenwood
25-Sep	*William Conger	M	W		S	Rt 3 / Orlando	6 mos		Orlando, Fla	Broncho-pneumonia	Fruitland, Fla
25-Sep	*Moses D Fuller	M	W		M	430 S Rosalind	10 yrs	Minister	Sussex Co., N.J.	N? Endocarditis	Greenwood
26-Sep	*Orion L Cline	M	W		M	Lockhart, Fla		Fla Public Service Co.	Grand View, Ind	Dead When Dr Arrived	Atlanta, Ga
27-Sep	*Geo W Jenkins	M	W		M	721 Hillcrest Ave	16 yrs	Retired	Hadley, N.Y.	Hemorrhage	Hadley, N.Y.
28-Sep	Inf Kelly	M	W			O.G.H.			O.G.H.	Stillborn	St Cloud, Fla
28-Sep	*Mrs Nancy Turner	F	W		W	206 Winter Park Ave	3 yrs	H W	Stewart Co., Ga	Chronic Arteris?	Lumpkin, Ga
20-Aug	Gussie Woods	F	C		W	901 W Holden	5 yrs	Domestic	Ga	Carcinoma cervix	Woodlawn
4-Sep	Mildred Ellis	F	C	5 yrs	S	O.G.H. / 821 W South	5 yrs		Orlando	Primary Acute Broncho-pneumonia	Greenwood
24-Sep	Thos Gardner	M	C	38	M	O.G.H.		Common Labor	Don't Know	Locomotive Ran Over Him	Woodlawn
25-Sep	Cleveland Chatham	M	C	12	S	O.G.H.	4 yrs	School Boy	Fla	Cerebral Tumor	Greenwood
25-Sep	Thelma Harris	F	C	7 hrs	S	808 S McFall	5 yrs		Orlando	Don't Know	Woodlawn
28-Sep	Frank Watts	M	C	58	M	415 W Jackson	17 yrs	Citrus	Ga	Aneurysm of Arch Aorta	Greenwood
28-Sep	John Butt	M	C	29	M	Hilton Sant	12 yrs	Common Labor	Ala	Ruptured Appendical Abscess	Greenwood
29-Sep	Infant of Dave Boyd	F	C	2ds	S	10 R R Ave	2 ds	Infant	Orlando	Don't Know	Woodlawn
30-Sep	Brock J Johnson	M	C	41	M	914 W Livingston	11 yrs	Minister	Fla	Cerebral Hemorrhage	Greenwood
2-Oct	*Wm R Moore	M	W	30	M	Fla Sant	13 ds	Farming	Ocoee	Heart Failure	Ocoee, Fla

1928	Name of Deceased	Sex	Race	Age	Marital	Residence & Place of Death	Orlando Resident	Occupation	Place of Birth	Cause of Death	Place of Burial
4-Oct	*Nellie A Honeywell	F	W	65	M	Fla San	14 yrs	Mission-ary Work	Wisconsin	Lobar Pneumonia	Greenwood
4-Oct	Georgia Ford	F	C	42	M	O.G.H.	6 yrs	Maid	Ga	General Peritonitis	Seaville, Fla
6-Oct	Ambrose E Rankin	M	W	83	W	O.G.H. / St Cloud, Fla	12 yrs	Soldier	Not Known	Cancer of Bladder	St Cloud, Fla
7-Oct	Sallie Margurite Ellison	F	W	65	M	Gore & KY	1 yr 6 mos	H W	Ga	Cerebral Hemorrhage	Anthony, Fla
7-Oct	*Mrs Eliza J Nay	F	W	79	M	1504 S Mills St	4 mos	H W	WVa	Heart Trouble	Pine Grove, WVa
7-Oct	*James B Price	M	W	39	M	South Hughey	2 yrs	Laborer	Miss	Abscess of Brain	Greenwood
7-Oct	*David Henry Kemp	M	W	75	W	O.G.H.	7 ds	Retired	Ind	Myocarditis	Tipton, Ind
11-Oct	Infant of Mr & Mrs A R Pruett	F	W	4 ds	S	Howell Sanit / RFD #4	4 ds		Orlando	Hereditary Syphilis	Greenwood
12-Oct	Cora M Fowler	F	W	69	W		3 yrs	H W	Ga	Carcinoma	Quitman, Ga
13-Oct	*Joyce Ward	F	W		S	Winter Park, Fla			Orlando	Sarcoma of Kidney	Winter Park, Fla
13-Oct	*Lenora Hammond	F	W		W		28 yrs	H W	Brunswick N.C.	Shock From Fall	Greenwood
16-Oct	*Infant of Mr & Mrs David Beck	M	W		S	Orlando, Fla			O.G.H.	Atelectasis	Greenwood
13-Oct	Sinnie Mitchell	F	C	85	S	Orlando		Nurse	Fla	Died Suddenly	Maitland, Fla
12-Oct	Infant of C Norplete	M	C		S	Orlando			Orlando	Stillborn	Woodlawn
15-Oct	*Alice Belle Holmes	F	W	67	W	Wilmore, Ky	4 ds	At Home	Orlando	Pulmonary Tuberculosis	Apopka
17-Oct	*Peter Mach	M	W	82	W	W Pine St	48 yrs	Retired	Germany	Senility	Jacksonville, Fla
18-Oct	*Infant of Mr & Mrs Harry Voorhis	M	W	1		936 Lake Adair Blvd	1 da		Orlando, Fla	Failure Right Lung to Expand	Greenwood
20-Oct	Alex Demps	M	C	51	M	Orlando	5 yrs	Laborer	Madison, Fla	Influenza	Pine Mont, Fla
21-Oct	*Infant of Mr & Mrs John Gossett	M	W	21 d	S	Orlando	21 ds		Orlando	Stillborn	Greenwood
21-Oct	Samuel Thompson	M	C	51	W	Orlando	3 yrs	Laborer	Fla	Chronic Nephritis	Greenwood
22-Oct	*Mrs Eugenie Wentzel	F	W	68	M		3 yrs	H W	France	Chronic Mania	Greenwood
22-Oct	*William H Crocker	M	W	72	M	Clermont, Fla	4 ds	Retired	New York City	Cerebral Hemorrhage	Cremation
23-Oct	*Infant of Mr & Mrs Henry T Norris	M	W	4 ds		Windermere, Fla				Stillborn	Greenwood
23-Oct	*Emma Lovett East	F	W		S	Haines City, Fla	7 ds	H W	Dothan, Ala	Abscess Left Side	Greenwood
24-Oct	*Mrs Lucy C Bailey	F	W	45	W	Fair Villa, Fla	9 yrs	Secty	Knoxville, Tenn	Angina Pectoris	Knoxville, Tenn
24-Oct	Infant of Walter Williams	M	C	SB							Memorial Park
25-Oct	*Ducan [Duane] Nidy	M	W	9	S	Winter Park, Fla	5 yrs		Winter Park	Chronic Tuber_ppal?	Winter Park
28-Oct	*Eva M Comltan [Comptan]	F	W	76	M	Orlando, Fla	5 yrs		Erie Co, Penn	Senility	Cremation
29-Oct	*Infant of Mr & Mrs Ernest Wilfore	F	W	SB							Greenwood
29-Oct	*Frank A Foster	M	W	56	M	Orlando	1 mo	Retired	Portland, Maine	Valvular	Portland, Maine

1928	Name of Deceased	Sex	Race	Age	Marital	Residence & Place of Death	Orlando Resident	Occupation	Place of Birth	Cause of Death	Place of Burial
30-Oct	*Infant of Mr & Mrs H A Burns					1415 E Col Dr				Infancy	Greenwood
1-Nov	Nelson Hill	M	C	52	W	315		Laborer	Fla	Paralysis	Greenwood
3-Nov	Bell Black	F	C	39	M	2 Jackson Ct	15 yrs	Domestic	Fla	Mitral Regurgitation	Quincy, Fla
26-Oct	———	M	C	8 ds		1033 West Holden			Fla	Contusions of Scalp	Woodlawn
29-Oct	*Mrs Nell Stuart	F	W	84	W	County Home	8 yrs			Chronic Nephritis	Greenwood
1-Nov	Mr Walker Brown	M	C	70	M	315 S Parium St	35 yrs	Merchant	Miss	Chronic Nephritis	Memorial Park
2-Nov	Fred Rutherford	M	C	65	M	239 Tampa Ave	40 yrs	Fruit Grower	S.C.	Hemiplegia	Greenwood
2-Nov	*Frank Dease	M	W	43	M	East Washington	15 yrs	Day Laborer	Orange Co., Fla	Crushed Chest, Accident	Conway Cemetery
2-Nov	*Charles W Wood	M	W	85	W	417 East Anderson	10 yrs	Retired	Mass	Hernia	Greenwood
3-Nov	*Louise Hyde	F	W	1	Inf	Evans St	1 yr	Infant	Barwick, Ga	Bronchial Pneumonia	Greenwood
4-Nov	*Mrs Eva Gore Robinson	F	W	60		Orlando	48 yrs	Home Work	Iowa	Cancer	Greenwood
4-Nov	*Infant of Mr & Mrs McDaniel	M	W		Inf	Orlando			Orlando	Stillborn	Greenwood
6-Nov	Mrs D Sessions	F	W	90	W	Orlando	10 yrs	Teacher	West Va.	Morbis Cardis	Greenwood
3-Nov	Robert L Rouse	M	C	8 hr		733 West Robinson			Orlando, Fla	Lack of Care	Greenwood
3-Nov	Rosa Lee Rouse	F	C	8 hr		733 West Robinson			Orlando, Fla	Lack of Care	Greenwood
3-Nov	Robert Taylor	M	C	24	a S	Orlando, Fla				Acute Milliary Tuberculosis	County Home
3-Nov	*George Thomas	M	W	89	W	Orlando, Fla	7 yrs	Retired	Easton, Pa	Chronic Trouble	Huntington, Pa
5-Nov	*Edith Toleyne Webb	F	W	2		Winter Garden, Fla	abt 1 da		Winter Garden, Fla	Poisoned by Tablets	Beulah Cemetery
7-Nov	*Alonzo D Symonds	M	W	84	M	Orlando, Peel Ave	21 yrs	Retired	Elmira, N.Y.	Senility	Elmira, New York
1-Nov	*Infant of Mr & Mrs L M Judge	F	W			Holopaw, Fla	< 8 hrs	Infant	Orlando	Stillborn	Cremation
13-Nov	*Mrs Annie Lou Judge	F	W	34	M	Holopaw, Fla	7 ds	Home Work	Europa, Miss	Postpartum Hemorrhage	Mobile, Ala
1-Nov	Ruth Davis	F	C	16 d	S	Washington Park	16 ds	Infant	Washington Park, Fla	Prematurity	Woodlawn
8-Nov	Richard Talton	M	C	26	M	736 S Lee, Orlando	6 yrs	Common Laborer	Penn	Hemorrhage	Woodlawn
10-Nov	Jerimah Stuard	M	C	5 ds		1022 Federal, Orlando	5 ds	Infant	Fla	Lack of Care	Colored Memorial
7-Nov	Lee B Wright	M	W	67	M	DeLand, Fla	8 ds	Day Work	Georgia	Hernia	Bay Ridge Cemetery
10-Nov	*Thomas B Lanier	M	W	75	W	Orlando, Smith St	1 yr	Retired	Ala	Apoplexy	Tavares, Fla
11-Nov	*Infant of Mr & Mrs N A Prescott	M	W	2 ds		1210 West Rob Ave		Infant	Orlando	Atelectasis	Greenwood
13-Nov	*Milton H. Dunaway	F	W	36	M	Sanford, Fla	7 ds	At Home	Norton, Va	Malignant Endocarditis	Apopka
13-Nov	*Mrs Melissa E Rush	F	W	81	W	522 Daniels St	5 yrs	At Home	Chautauqua, N.Y.	Pulmonary Edema	Greenwood

1928	Name of Deceased	Sex	Race	Age	Marital	Residence & Place of Death	Orlando Resident	Occupation	Place of Birth	Cause of Death	Place of Burial
14-Nov	*Mrs Carrie Way	F	W	74	W	419 E South St	17 yrs	At Home	Vermont	Nephritis	Green [Glyn] Elyn, Ill
14-Nov	John Steward	M	C	9 ds		1022 Federal		Infant	Fla	Lack of Care	Colored Memorial Park
15-Nov	*Frank Reynolds	M	W	47	M	O.G.H.	7 ds	Barber	Ohio	Fracture of Skull	Cremated
15-Nov	*Wm R Durkee	F	W	70	S	206 E Amelia	8 yrs	Retired	Ill	Gastric Carcinoma	Hammond, Pa [La]
15-Nov	*Erkine McCulloch	M	W	50	M	2020 Elizabeth	6 yrs	Book-keeper	Kan	Acute Jaundice	Greenwood
16-Nov	Dennis Eddington	M	C	56	M	W Long St	20 yrs	Laborer	N.C.	Acute Toxic	Col Memorial Park
17-Nov	*Harry Stalberg	M	W	44	M	430 Cathcart St	18 yrs	Merchant	Russia	Carbon Monoxide Poisioning due to Fuel Gas - Suicide	Miami, Fla
17-Nov	Ernest Dixon	M	C	20	S	O.G.H.		Laborer	Ga	Gunshot Wound In Abdomen	Vidalia, Ga
17-Nov	John Pane Burn [Burns]	M	W	51	M	O.G.H.	6 yrs	Engraver	Charleston S.C.	Carcinoma Liver	Greenwood
17-Nov	*Dr Elihu L Sawyer	M	W	73	M	Fla Sant	10 ds	MD	Vermont	Pervalxtix? Illness	In Vault
17-Nov	*Mrs Pholmen St Jean	F	W	73	M	Orlando	4 yrs	At Home	Canada	Oedema	Greenwood
16-Nov	*Thos D Foran	M	W	73	M	231 E Jackson St	11 yrs	Retired	Canada	Hernia Following a 20 year Period Emaceating	Hamilton, Ont., Canada
17-Nov	Herbert H Willis	M	C	11 d		801 South Long St	5 ds	Infamy	Orlando	Congenital Syphilis	Woodlawn
18-Nov	Julia Mae Checkley	F	C	13	S	Lockhart	4 yrs	School Girl	Ga	Tubercolis [sic]	ForrestCity
19-Nov	Lenard J Petterson	M	W	42	M	O.G.H.	43 yrs	Clerk in PO	Fla	Hernia	St Cloud, Fla
21-Nov	Andrew Thomas	M	C	3 mo s		603 Lee St	6 ds	Infant	Orlando	Pneumonia	Greenwood
21-Nov	Johnnie Cunningham	M	C	38	M	419 West	10 yrs	Laborer	Fla	Pneumonia	Apopka
18-Nov	*Will Allen	M	C	50		O.G.H. / Lakeland, Fla	21 ds	Day Laborer		Chronic Nephritis	County Home
25-Nov	Mrs Drake	F	W	86	W	Magnolia Home				Pernicious Anemia	Shelby, Ohio
25-Nov	Doris Hill	F	W	35	D	33 N Garland		House-wife	Chicago, Ill	Spinal Trounble of the Cord	Greenwood Cemetery
30-Nov	Comilla Washington	F	C	50	M	411 Quincy	2 yrs	Laun-dress	Ga	Acute Indigestion	Sparta, Ga
2-Dec	Fred Autrvilet [Autenrieb?]	M	W		M	Cocoa, Fla			Germany	Broncho Pneumonia	Sturgio, Mich
22-Nov	*Charles H Merrill	M	W	82	M	322 Anderson St	22 ds	Retired	Bangour, Maine	Ugosinditis? Following Auto Trip	Bangor, Maine
22-Nov	*Mrs Haddash Howe	F	W	88	W	118 East Central Ave	45 yrs	At Home	Miss	Carcinoma	Greenwood
22-Nov	*Willie Hammond	M	W	12	S	Lake Formosa	12 yrs	In School	Orlando	Accidental Drowned	Greenwood
22-Nov	*Infant of Mr & Mrs Ray Caldwell	F	W			21 Angibelt Add			Orlando, Fla	Stillborn	Cremation
24-Nov	*Philo S Felter	M	W		W	Conway Section	16 yrs		New York	Myocarditis	Woodmere, N.Y.
24-Nov	*Robert Buchan	M	W	80	W	Shady Lane	7 yrs	Retired	Canada	Apoplexy	Greenwood

1928	Name of Deceased	Sex	Race	Age	Marital	Residence & Place of Death	Orlando Resident	Occupation	Place of Birth	Cause of Death	Place of Burial
25-Nov	Charles Daniels	M	W	65	M	O.G.H.	5 ds	Retired	Heyworth, Ill	Mesenteric Carcinoma	Sag? Brook, Ill
28-Nov	*Chas Robt Davidson	M	W		M	419 W Colonial	8 yrs	?	Mt Vernon, Ill	Bladder	Greenwood
27-Nov	Willie Gibson	M	C		Inf	218 S Parramore	4 yrs		Orlando	No Physician Attended Case	Woodlawn
29-Nov	*Henry A Halverson	M	W	76	M	Sanford, Fla	2 mos	Retired	Norway	Nephritis	Greenwood
30-Nov	*Lewis Harris	M	C	65		County Home	4 mos		Don't Know	Cerebral Hemorrhage	County Home
30-Nov	Kate P Kooser?	F	W	76	M	1011 E Colonial		H W	Pittsburgh	Pneumonia	Greenwood
1-Dec	*Martin A Hecht	M	W	49	M	1352 N Mills St	7 yrs	Real Estate	St Louis, Mo	Broncho Pneumonia	Greenwood
5-Dec	George McCloud	M	C	29	M	O.G.H.	1 da	Laborer	Va	Intertural?	Titusville, Fla
5-Dec	Annie P Soloman	F	C		Inf	607 So Parramore	2 yrs		Orlando, Fla	Broncho Pneumonia	Woodlawn
6-Dec	Robert L. Johnson	M	C			1008 Edna St			Orlando	Satoties Lymphotes	Woodlawn
7-Dec	*Nona [Norma?] M Brown	F	W			2023 Harrison St	23 ds		Orlando	Acute Periitonitis	Cremated
4-Dec	*Emma L. Jackson	F	W			113 N Hyer St	3 mos			A__t testum?	Palmetto, Fla
4-Dec	*Andrew Cariss [Carris]	M	C	55	M	County Home	3 mos			Chronic Tuberculosis	County Home
2-Dec	Clark Ford	F	C	24	M	Lucerne Park	10 ds	Domestic	Monticello, Fla	Pilore? Peritonitis	Monticello, Fla
9-Dec	Herbert Webb Lawrence	M	C	5 m 14 d	Infant	O.G.H.	3 ds	Infant	Ala	Retrophareal? Abscess	Oakland, Fla
12-Dec	Lucy Burmett	F	W	76	W	Magnolia Home	4 mos		Nashville Ind	Apoplexy	Magnolia Home Cemetery
12-Dec	Zenobie Brooke	F	W	22	S	Fla Sant / Titusville, Fla	1 mo	Unk	Unknown	Abscessed Teeth	Titusville, Fla
17-Dec	Mrs Eugene F Slayton	F	W	47	M	525 Harvard Ave	3 yrs	Housewife	Azelia, Mich	Carcinoma Right Breast	Dundee, Mich
22-Dec	Mrs Flossie E Wilkins	F	C	28	M	432 S Terry	7 yrs	Housewife	Florida	Lymphangitis Tuberculosis	Gainesville, Fla
11-Dec	*Mrs Dessie Hall	F	W	33	M	407 America	16 yrs	Housewife	Ala	Abscess of Liver	Greenwood
12-Dec	*Mrs Daniel J Shirer	F	W	69	M		5 yrs	Housewife	Penn	Acute Myocarditis	Greenwood
13-Dec	Noomi Smith	F	C		Inf	1041 America	15 ds		Orlando	No Physician	Woodlawn
14-Dec	Elizah Hogan	F	C	58	M	229 N Parramore	13 yrs	Laundry	Fla	Caradoc [sic]	Woodlawn
14-Dec	*John Dickson Burden	M	W	67	M	South of City	43 yrs	Clerical Work	Iowa	Chronic Nephritis	Greenwood
15-Dec	*Jonas C Overholt	M	W	78	W	212 South Hughey	14 ds	Retired	Ohio	Pneumonia	Dutton, Mich
15-Dec	*Mary F. Hutchinson	F	W		S	O.G.H.	2 ds		Haines City, Fla	Acute Peritonitis	Haines City, Fla
16-Dec	John W Alexander	M	C	19	S	O.G.H.		Common Laborer	Ga	Ulcer	Apopka
16-Dec	*Julia S Pomeroy	F	W	73	S	215 E Jackson	30 yrs	At Home	Amherst, Mass	Cerebral Hemorrhage	Greenwood
16-Dec	*Sarah Phelps Arms	F	W	91	W	441 Park Lake Circle	9 yrs	H W	Mass	Chronic ?	In Vault Till Spring
16-Dec	*Carolyn V Carlson	F	W	43	M	Fla Sant	1 yr	H W	Sweden	Severe Anemia	Cremation

155

1928	Name of Deceased	Sex	Race	Age	Marital	Residence & Place of Death	Orlando Resident	Occupation	Place of Birth	Cause of Death	Place of Burial
17-Dec	*Elizabeth Parkhill	F	W	55	M	Orla Vista	8 yrs	H W	Tenn	Tuberculosis	Greenwood
17-Dec	*Mrs Sarah Dickerson	F	W	98	W	Ill Ave	14 yrs	H W	Water-town, NY	Pulmary [sic] Overlum?	Greenwood
23-Dec	John Block	M	C	48	M	514 W Pine St	11 ds		N.C.	Mitral Regurgitation	Memorial Park
23-Dec	Warren Hunter	M	C	80	S	126 E Livingston	20 yrs	Common Laborer	Ga	Hemorrhage	Greenwood
22-Dec	Frank E Williams	M	W			311 Orlando Ave			Orlando, Fla	Stillborn	Retained at Fla Sant
18-Dec	*Henry W Buechner	M	W	72	M	210 Shine St	2 mos	Retired		Dead When I Arrived-Cerebral Hemorrhage	Kalamazoo, Mich
17-Dec	*Francis Mary Lewis	F	W	64	W	West Gore St	6 yrs	At Home	Americus, Ga	Apoplexy	Hartesfield, Ga
20-Dec	Martha Braxvill	F	C	22	S	805 Carter St	3 mos	Day Work	Ga	Acute Pleurisy	Woodlawn
20-Dec	*Earl LeRoy Remington	M	W	16	S	Howell Sant	1 yr	Laborer	N.Y.	Lymphatitis	In Vault
21-Dec	*Mrs Belle D Roe	F	W	60	M	Fla Sant & Hosp	17 ds	H W	Vermont	Chronic Valvular	Clermont, Fla
21-Dec	*Jim Warrick	M	W	36	M	O.G.H.	3 mos	Laborer	Ala	Calculus Anuria?	Greenwood
20-Dec	*Ben Moore	M	W	50	M	O.G.H.	1 da	Day Laborer	Dodge Co., Ga	Pneumonia	Chauncey,
21-Dec	*Infant of Mr & Mrs T T Talley, Jr	M	W			O.G.H.			Orlando	Stillborn	Greenwood
21-Dec	*Infant of Mr & Mrs Jas Lavender	F	W			927 Golf View Ave				Stillborn	Cremated
22-Dec	*Infant of Mr & Mrs Henry C Morgan	F	W			Fla San			Fla San	Stillborn	Titusville, Fla
22-Dec	*Hack Ruffin	M	C	70	W	County Home		Laborer	Ala	Chronic Nephritis	County Home
23-Dec	*Patrica Ann Gillson	F	W	11	S	612 Daniels St	11 mos		Orlando, Fla	Acidosis	Greenwood
25-Dec	*Michel [Michael] Edmond Doyle	F	W	74	M	12 S Terry	9 mos	Retired	Ind	Pneumonia	Park Hill
25-Dec	Williams James	M	C							Stillborn	Memorial Park
27-Dec	*Francis McClain	M	W	56	M	O.G.H.	7 yrs	Laborer	Ind	Syphilis	Greenwood
29-Dec	*Edgar E Engler	M	W	53	M	1218 Green-wood Ave	3 yrs	Laborer	Penn	Angina Pectoris	Bethlehem, Penn
28-Dec	*James T Moore	M	W	88	M	O.G.H.	20 ds	Retired	Ind	Pou-?	Lafayette, Ind
29-Dec	*Anne M Ryan	F	W	23	M	O.G.H.	1 da	At Home	Thomas-ville, Ga	Pueperal Eclampsia	Tallahassee, Fla
29-Dec	*Infant of John Childers	F	W			O.G.H.			Orlando, Fla	Prematurity (6 Months)	Greenwood
29-Dec	*Infant of Mr & Mrs Mark Ryan	M	W			O.G.H.			Orlando, Fla	Stillborn	Tallahassee, Fla
29-Dec	*David Henry Kindig	M	W	83	W	241 Ridgewood Ave	7 ds	Retired	Va	Senility	In Vault Till Spring
31-Dec	Peter E Akaham [Ahearn]	M	W	77	W	1313 Catherine	5 mos	Jewelry Business	Ohio	Angina Pectoris	Sanford, Fla

156

1929	Name of Deceased	Sex	Race	Age	Marital	Residence & Place of Death	Orlando Resident	Occupation	Place of Birth	Cause of Death	Place of Burial
1-Jan	*Sophia E Wettstein	F	W	72	M	O.G.H./Merritt Park	3 yrs	At Home	Brooklyn, N.Y.	Intestinal Obstruction	Greenwood
2-Jan	*Thomas S. Hays	M	W	38	M	O.G.H./ DeLand	4 ds	Real Estate	DeLand, Fla	Anaphelitis lithargilis	DeLand, Fla
2-Jan	*Hattie L Larkin	F	W	7	W	O.G.H./Winter Park	1 yr	Unknown-House Nurse	Unknown	Chronic Purulent Cholecystitis	Willimantis?, Conn
3-Jan	John T. Effinger	M	W	79	W	Pinelock Ave	1 yr	Retired	Evansville, Ind	Mital Regurgitation	Greenwood Cemetery
5-Jan	Harry Bailey	M	W	63	S	O.G.H./ Clermont, Fla	2 ds	Artist	N Y City	Chron Arterio-sclerotic Nephritis	Clermont, Fla
5-Jan	Jessie Keiser	M	W	25	S	O.G.H./ Titusville, Fla	3 ds	Unknown	Unknown	Lobar Pneumonia	Titusville, Fla
2-Jan	Emmer Stewart	F	C	35	M	1022 Federal	4 mos	Housewife	Fla	Pericarditis	Serrento, Fla
9-Jan	Amanda Smith	F	W	63	W	I J Hertz San/Sanford, Fla	13 ds	Housewife	Ga	Chronic Nephritis	Longwood, Fla
28-Dec-28	Lucille McPherson	F	C	28	M	1033 Washington St	6 yrs	Housewife	Ga	Pneumonia	Woodlawn
28-Dec-28	Willie Vance	M	C	28	M	523 Holden	3 yrs	Day Work	Fla	Acute Nephritis	Woodlawn
29-Dec-28	Richard Smith	M	C	50	W	12 Ossie	5 yrs	Day Work	Fla	Chronic Nephritis	Greenwood
1-Jan	*Dr. John C Stephenson	M	W	65	W	Rt # 1, Orlando, Fla	4 yrs	Retired	Boone Co., Ind	Broncho Pneumonia	Indianapolis, Ind
1-Jan	Matttie Davis	F	C	55	W	Taft, Fla	9 mos	At Home	S.C.	Tuberculosis	Taft, Fla
4-Jan	*Cecil L Grier	M	W	8		Winter Garden, Fla			Banks Co., Ga	Gun Shot Wound	Winter Garden, Fla
4-Jan	*Alice A Batterson [Battersby]	F	W	90	W	County Home	16 yrs	At Home	England	Bronchial Asthma	Greenwood
4-Jan	*Miss Rose Flood	F	W	60	S	Fla Sant & Hosp	3 mos	Retired	Hudson Falls, N.Y.	Acute Nephritis	Hudson Falls, N.Y.
5-Jan	*John W Brickey	M	W	72	W	210 Winter Park Ave	2 yrs	Retired	Clark Co., Mo	Asthma	Greenwood
7-Jan	Dorthy Singleton	F	C	2		O.G.H.		Infant	J-Ville, Fla	Acute Nephritis	Greenwood
7-Jan	Pinkey Dallas	F	C	48	M	639 Holden	39 yrs	At Home	Ga	Acute Nephritis	Woodlawn
7-Jan	*John L. Stadler	M	W	65	M	O.G.H.	3 ds	Retired	Cleveland, Ohio	Myocarditis	In Vault Till Spring
8-Jan	*Van Clair McCrory	M	W	32	M	Ridgewood, N.J	17 ds	Vice Pres of McCrory Stores	Johnstown, N.J.	Gunshot Wound	Johnstown, Pa
9-Jan	*Chas Moore	M	W	80	W	Orlando/ O.G.H.	12 yrs	Day Labor	No relatives to obtain any of his history	Myocarditis	County Home
9-Jan	Mrs Isabel Young	F	W	70	W	614 South Division	37 yrs	At Home	W Sulphur Springs, Ga	Pneumonia	Greenwood
10-Jan	Gene Johnson	M	C	18 ds		1831 South	18 ds		Fla	Spinal Meningitis	Greenwood
10-Jan	Leola Jones	F	C	17	S	O.G.H.		At Home	Fla	Arthritis	Oakland, Fla
11-Jan	*Vivian Martin	F	W	8	S	O.G.H.	5 yrs		Geneva, Ala	Pneumonia	Hartford, Ala

1929	Name of Deceased	Sex	Race	Age	Marital	Residence & Place of Death	Orlando Resident	Occupation	Place of Birth	Cause of Death	Place of Burial
11-Jan	*Horace W Tompkins	M	W	62	M	27th St/Angebilt Add	2 mos	Retired	Don't Know	Cancer of Bladder	Micanopby, Ala [FL]
11-Jan	*Ernestine Simmons	F	W			639 W Church St.	9 ds	Infant	Orlando	?	Greenwood
12-Jan	L Smith	M	W	28	M	Winter Haven, Fla	4 ds	Plasterer	Ga	Ulcer of Omentum	Winter Haven, Fla
30-Dec-28	Infant of Charley Collins	M	C			O.G.H.			Orlando	Stillborn	Woodlawn
4-Jan	Josephine Collins	F	C	32	M	O.G.H.		Housewife	Ga	Pneumonia	Oakland
9-Jan	*Gus Williams	M	C	45	unk	O.G.H.	2 yrs	Day Labor	Ga	Pneumonia	County Home
11-Jan	*M Chas. Wright	M	W	79	M	310 W Colonial Dr	21 ds	Retired	Columbus, N.J.	Purulent Emphysema	Columbus, N.J.
10-Jan	*Albert Degler	M	W	44	M	S E of City	5 yrs	Labor	Seatdale, Penn	Cerebral Hemorrhage	Greenwood
12-Jan	*Herman F Krumrey	M	W	41	M	O.G.H.	3 yrs	Contractor	N Hampton, Iowa	Broncho Pneumonia	Greenwood
14-Jan	Roscoe Blackman	M	C	27	S	1041 America	1 mo	Labor	S.C.	Pernicious Anemia	Clearmont, Fla
15-Jan	*Jas M Dominick	M	W	78	M	127 N Mills	20 yrs	Retired	Newberry, S.C.	Myocarditis	Greenwood
15-Jan	*Carrie Hadley	F	W	78	W	Maitland, Fla		At Home	Boston, Mass	Pneumonia, Mitrial	Enfield, N.H.
16-Jan	Cornelous Thomas	M	C	68	M	739 Bentley St	5 yrs	Carpenter		Regurgitis?	Woodlawn
16-Jan	Henry Wilson	M	C	49	W	918 Edna St	3 mos	Laborer	S.C.	General Edema	Greenwood
17-Jan	*Mrs Merle Stone	F	W	36	M	109 Westmoreland	3 yrs	At Home	Huntington, WVa	Lobar Pneumonia	Huntington, Wva
17-Jan	*Ora Madge Abestin [Abstein]	F	W	17	S	1618 E Col Dr	7 mos	At Home	Lockloosa, Fla	Pneumonia	Lockloosa, Fla
17-Jan	*George W Manley	M	W	66	W	Lockhart, Fla	1 yr	Retired	Rush, Ill	Apoplexy	In Vault
19-Jan	*Van Evo B. Martin	F	W	41	M	Hartland, Wis/Orlando, Fla	22 ds	Office Building	Wis	Mechmly?	Milwaukee, Wis
19-Jan	*Charlie F Floyd	M	W	70	W	Mich Ave	15 yrs	Retired	Ga	Uremia	Conway
19-Jan	*Eugean D Garrett	M	W	34	D	O.G.H./Jacksonville, Fla	3 yrs	Salesman	J-Ville, Fla	Pneumonia	Jacksonville, Fla
20-Dec-28	Lance Ringo	M	W	1		Orlando, Fla	1 mo		Cocoa, Fla	Acute Encephalitis	Cocoa, Fla
3-Dec-28	Infant of Mr & Mrs Hugh L McKenney	M	W			517 Macy St			Orlando, Fla	Infanteum?	Family took care of same
15-Jan	Rosa Lee Marsh	F	W	40	W	Kissimmee, Fla	1 da	At Home	St Augustine, Fla	Hemorrhage	Beulah Cemetery
16-Jan	Elevellya Taylor	F	W	16	S	Taft, Fla	5 ds		Fairfield, Maine	Automobile & RR Wreck	Greenwood
17-Jan	John W Grior	M	Col	39	M	722 America	8 yrs	Laborer	Batesville, Ala	Acute Pulmonary	Greenwood

1929	Name of Deceased	Sex	Race	Age	Marital	Residence & Place of Death	Orlando Resident	Occupation	Place of Birth	Cause of Death	Place of Burial
17-Jan	Robert E Holliday	M	W	76	M	1409 E Gore	6 yrs	Laborer	WVa	Cerebral Hemorrhage	Greenwood
19-Jan	*Infant of Mr & Mrs J P Sappington	M	W		S	Fla San & Hosp	6 yrs		Orlando, Fla	Head Locked in Pelvis Labor	Cremation
21-Jan	*Infant of Mr & Mrs F Lazarus	F	W			O.G.H.			Orlando, Fla	Prematurity (6 Months)	Cremation
21-Jan	*Fred Meusse	M	W	67	W	O.G.H.	1 da	Laborer	Germany	Tetanus	Greenwood
21-Jan	Baby Allen	M	C			O.G.H.			Orlando, Fla	Stillborn	Kissimmee, Fla
21-Jan	Infant of Mr & Mrs Al-len Thomas	F	C			1200 Conley St			Orlando, Fla	Stillborn	Woodlawn
22-Jan	Hattie Thomas	F	C		M	1200 Conley St	4 yrs	Laborer	Fla	Childbirth	Woodlawn
21-Jan	*Mrs Addie Moore	F	W	81	W	538 Clayton St	10 yrs	At Home	Ga	Endocardeth (Endocarditis?)	Ocoee Cemetery
23-Jan	*Mrs Sophia Cook	F	W	82	W	1922 Gerda Terr	8 yrs	At Home	South Beach, England	Pneumonia	Syracuse, N.Y.
24-Jan	*Mrs Vergie J Mikell	F	W	30	M	48 W Amelia	5 yrs	At Home	Metter, Ga	Pneumonia	Metter, Ga
25-Jan	Oliva Allen	F	C	23	M	O.G.H.	5 ds	H W	Fla	Carcinoma	Narcoossee, Fla
29-Jan	Fannie H Harwood	F	W	71	W	820 N Summerlin	6 mos	Retired	Joliet, Ill	Apoplexy	Joliet, Ill
25-Jan	*Ralph J. Seeds	M	W	48	M	O.G.H./Jackson Heights, N.Y.		Traveling Salesman	N.Y.	Double Bron-chopneumonia	Greenwood
24-Jan	*Frank W Fairwell	M	W	78	M	303 Shine	2 mos	Retired	Mespotania,	Prostatis Hypertrophy	Greenwood
25-Jan	*Maggie Gentry	F	W	43	M	O.G.H.	1 mo	At Home	Hudson Co., Ala	Myocarditis	Ocoee, Fla
25-Jan	*Evelyn Chapman	F	W	3		O.G.H.	6 ds		Orlando, Fla	Peritonitis	Greenwood
26-Jan	*Wm H Overmyer	M	W	64	W	Fla Sant	3 mos	Retired	Sandusky, Ohio	Nephritis	Indianapolis, Ind
26-Jan	*Charles W Wilde	M	W	73	M	14 N Mt Vernon Ave	3 mos	Retired	Wright Twp, Mich	Auto Intoxication	In Vault
27-Jan	*Jimmie Ann Stewart	F	W	70	W	O.G.H.	14 ds	At Home	Stockton, Ga	Senile Dementia	Apopka, Fla
31-Jan	Andrew Thomas	M	C	35	W	512 W Church	5 mos	Laborer	Quincy, Fla	Nephritis	Sanford, Fla
30-Jan	*Myra G Lane	F	W	59	W	400 E Concord	17 yrs	At Home	Ky	Myocarditis	Greenwood
31-Jan	Joseph Cooper	M	Col	52	W	O.G.H.	a 7 ds	Laborer	Ga	Myocarditis	County Home
31-Jan	Marie Williams	F	Col	28	M	1029 Reynolds	9 yrs	Laborer	Ga	Peritonitis	Rincon Ga
1-Feb	*Willie L Daughtery	M	W	61	M	O.G.H.	18 yrs	ACL Employee	Bainbridge Ga	Septic Gall Bladder	Greenwood
1-Feb	Patrick Hawkins	M	Col	62	M	416 W Jefferson		Laborer	Fla	Sarcoma of Neck	Greenwood
1-Feb	Hubert J Duck? [Duah?]	M	W	79	W	Magnolia Home	2 yrs	Retired	Vermont	Old Age	Magnolia Home Cemetery

159

1929	Name of Deceased	Sex	Race	Age	Marital	Residence & Place of Death	Orlando Resident	Occupation	Place of Birth	Cause of Death	Place of Burial
2-Feb	*Patrick W McKeever	M	W	61	M	900 E Con	14 yrs	Real Estate	Dixon, Ill	Pneumonia	In Vault
4-Feb	*Henry Grader	M	W	64	M	O.G.H.	10 ds	Retired	Hamburg, Germany	Auto Collision	Columbus, Ga
7-Feb	John Freeman	M	W	72	M	Winter Garden Road	2 yrs	Retired	Marksdale, Ont	Apoplexy	Evanston, Ill
6-Feb	*Mrs R Julia Johnson	F	W	83	W	648 Park Lake	4 ds	At Home	N.C.	Senility	Hendersonville, N.C.
15-Jan	*Bertha R Stryker	F	W	55	M	O.G.H.	11 yrs	At Home	N.Y.	Myocarditis	Portland, N.Y.
5-Feb	Moses Bolls	M	C	40	S	O.G.H.	4 yrs	Laborer	Ga	Gangrene	Memorial Park
Feb	Katie Williams	F	C	51		O.G.H.		Domestic	Ga	Secondary Anemia	Greenwood
9-Feb	Hubert Higgins	M	C	1		1203 Conley St	6 mos		Ocala	Don't Know No Dr	Greenwood
10-Feb	*Harley W Cox	M	W	34	M	Fla Sant & Hosp	2 ds	Farming	Ft Christmas, Fla	Pistol Shot Wound	Ft Christmas, Fla
11-Feb	*Daniel B Downey	M	W	71		Fla San	a 1 mo	Retired	Butler Co., Iowa	Acute Nephritis	Allison, Iowa
11-Feb	Barton Pardee	M	W	73	S	O.G.H	3 mos	Retired	Hazeltown, Pa	Myocarditis	Hazeltown, Pa
11-Feb	Mrs Carrie Perkins	F	W	68	W	O.G.H.	1 da	Housewife	Hinsdale, Mass	Ruptured Appendix	Mt Dora, Fla
13-Feb	*Mrs Violet Y Reynolds	F	W	48	M	O.G.H.	9 yrs	At Home	N.Y. City, N.Y.	Pneumonia	Westerly, R.I.
8-Jan	Infant of K J Faith	?	W	?	S	Fla Sant & Hosp			Orlando	Miscarriage	
11-Jan	William Albert Hill	M	W	73	M	N Kissimmee	7 yrs	?	Ga	Intestinal Obstruction	Rose Hill, Kissimmee
14-Feb	*James H. Barton	M	W	52	M	Heitz Sant/417 E Jackson	50 yrs	Collector	Orange Co.	Apoplexy	Lake Hill
15-Feb	Alvin Hill, Jr	M	Col	25	M	916 W South	7 mos	Fruit Picker	Fla	Acute Lobar Pneumonia	Memorial Park
16-Feb	*Mrs Helen A White	M	W	66	W	RFD # 3	15 yrs	At Home	Ind	Apoplexy	Lake Hill
16-Feb	Hattie C Peddycoart	F	W	58	M	615 Lexington	10 yrs	Housewife	Iowa	Organic Heart Disease	Vault
17-Feb	*Mrs Alice B Coney	F	W	57	S	Fla Sant/ Cincinnati, Ohio	1 da	Home	Ohio	Auto Accident	Vault
18-Feb	Infant of T A & Roberta Stewart	F	W	20 min	S	706 N Mills			Orlando, Fla	Prematurity	Greenwood
20-Feb	Infant of T A & R Stewart	F	W	1	S	706 N Mills	1 da		Orlando	Prematurity	Greenwood
19-Feb	*Joe Evans	M	W	45	M	220 Conley	20 ds	Labor	Don't Know	Luetic Myocarditis	County Home
20-Feb	John Way	M	W	57	M	O.G.H./Lawnsdown, Penn	5 ds	VP Prov Met Life Ins	Pa	Acute Pancreatitis	Philadelphia, Pa
20-Feb	James Franklin Stockhouse	M	C	29	S	O.G.H.		Labor	Fla	Auto Accident	Sanford, Fla
20-Feb	*Wm H Handy	M	W	82	W	41 N. Garland	3 mos	Retired	Ohio	Chr Myocarditis	Wauseon,
21-Feb	*Francis W Sloan	F	W	51	M	Fla Sant	14 ds	Home	N.J.	Sterptococcus Septicemia	Manasquan,

1929	Name of Deceased	Sex	Race	Age	Marital	Residence & Place of Death	Orlando Resident	Occupation	Place of Birth	Cause of Death	Place of Burial
21-Feb	*Infant of Mr & Mrs C B Dubose	M	W		S	518 ½ N Summerlin			Orlando	Atelectasis	Cremated
22-Feb	*Nelson H Carroll	M	W	58	M	Rio Grande Ave	58 yrs	City of Orlando	Orlando	Found Dead	Greenwood
23-Feb	D R Young	M	Col	29	M	503 S Lee	7 yrs	Brick Mason	Ga	Lobar Pneumonia	Memorial Park
23-Feb	Gary Turner	M	Col	32	M	Conway	4 yrs	Common Labor	Ga	Pulmonary Hemorrhage	Washington, Ga
23-Feb	*Mrs Elizabeth A Bradley	F	W	62	W	Fla Sant	4 ds	Home	N.Y.	Diabetes Mellitus	Hampton, Va
24-Feb	Flora H Donayer	F	W	52	M	O.G.H./ Chicago, Ill	5 ds	Housewife	Iowa	Double Pneumonia	Chicago, Ill
24-Feb	*Jeannette Inez Hart	F	W	79	W	414 Magnolia Ave	43 yrs	Home	N.Y.	Cerebral Hemorrhage	Greenwood
24-Feb	*Frank M. Ebert	M	W	58	M	Fla Sanit/219 Ridgewood	68 yrs	Retired	Ind	Shock from Auto Accident	Cambridge City, Ind
24-Feb	*John D. Kelly	M	W	1 d	S	Fla Sanit / 913 Osceola ,WP, Fla	1 da		Orlando	Atelectasis	Winter Park
26-Feb	Arthur Hodges	M	W	88	W	1278 E Livingston	1 yr	Retired Civil Engineer	Mass	Senile Myocarditis	Newberry, N.H.
1-Mar	*Frederick W Van Duyn	M	W	61	M	O.G.H./ Ridgewood, NJ	1 mo.	Retired	N.J.	Angina Pectoris	Ridgewood, N.J.
20-Jan	Infant of Jessie Mae Merrett	M	Col		S	414 Parramore	2 yrs		Orlando	Stillborn	Woodlawn
25-Feb	Emanuel Bruton Jr?	M	C	2 mo	S	745 Oakwood	10 yrs [sic]		Orlando	Marasmus	Woodlawn
21-Feb	Rebecca Jackson	F	Col	100 a	W	1201 W Washington	18 yrs	Domestic	Ga	Pulmonary Congestion of Lungs	Woodlawn
26-Feb	*Homer E. D. Newton	M	W	81	W	O.G.H./ 319 Church	20 mos	Retired	Omar, N.J.	Chronic Arterio-sclerotic nephritis	Syracuse, N.Y.
20-Feb	*Geo. G Myers	M	W	78	W	Orla Vista	5 yrs	Retired	Germany	Acute Nephritis	Greenwood
27-Feb	*John W. F. Bray	M	W	77	M	O.G.H./ Winter Garden	15 ds	Citrus Grower	Ga	Coronary Embolism	Oakland
28-Feb	*John H. Ledford	M	W	16	S	Orla Vista	1 mo	Labor	KY	Bronchal Asthma	County Home
1-Mar	Dan Harvy, Jr	M	Col		S	111 Lincoln	4 yrs		Orlando	Stillborn	Woodlawn
2-Mar	Infant of Elizah Demps	F	Col		S	215 Garden			Orlando	Stillborn	Woodlawn
2-Mar	*Mrs Ida Rachell Newell	F	W	62	D	221 South Garland	abt 5 yrs	At Home	Anderson Co., S.C.	Apoplexy	Greenwood
3-Mar	*Eugene J. Hope	M	W	70	M	1634 E Hillcrest / Brooklyn, NY	3 yrs	Retired	Mass	Cerebral Apoplexy	Thornburg, Contario
3-Mar	*Andrew J. Mathews	M	W	71	M	1809 E Colonial	3 yrs	Retired	N.Y.	Angina Pectoris	Greenwood
4-Mar	*Mrs Charlotte M. Ricker	F	W	70	W	403 S. Roslind	4 ds	At Home	Pittsburgh, Pa	Fracture	Washington, D.C.
5-Mar	*George North	M	Col	a65	W	636 Long /O.G.H.	Don't know	Labor	Don't Know	Chronic Myocarditis	County Home

161

1929	Name of Deceased	Sex	Race	Age	Marital	Residence & Place of Death	Orlando Resident	Occupation	Place of Birth	Cause of Death	Place of Burial
5-Mar	*Maryana Gladys Hook	F	W	10d	S	Fla Sanit/ Apopka	10 ds		Orlando	Acute Bronchial Pneumonia	Apopka
5-Mar	*Mrs Etta M Primrose	M [sic]	W	62	W	681 N Orange	3 Yrs	At Home	Ohio	Acute Gastritis	Vault
6-Mar	Bessie Owens Lee	F	C	25	W	206 Quincy	5 yrs	Laundress	Ga	Acute Lobar Pneumonia	Greenwood
6-Mar	John Fray Dixon	M	W	35	M	1 mo	1 mo	Detective Work	WVa	Cirrhosis of Liver	Clarksburg, WVa
7-Mar	Mrs Annie Williams	F	C	33	M	O.G.H./524 W Jackson	8 yrs	Maid	S.C.	Pulmonary Embolism	Arcadia, Fla
7-Mar	*Mrs Daisy Westberry	F	W	a63	W	216 S. Hughey	7 yrs	At Home	Ga	Pneumonia	Jessup, Ga
8-Mar	Corene Clay	F	C	42	S	476 Garfield Ave, W.P.	2 yrs	House-keeper	Ga	Apoplexy	Asheville, Ga
11-Mar	Emma Lane	F	C	36	M	114 N. Terry	18 yrs	Domestic	Ala	Lobar Pneumonia	Wood Lane
13-Mar	*Lester J. Douglass	M	W	29	M	Orange Gen / Winter Park, Fla	6 ds	Lumber Business	Marion Co., Ga	Septicemia Slafblacoge?	Winter Park
14-Mar	Horrace Harold	M	C	57	S	1912 E South	20 yrs	Laborer	Ga	Right Side Paralysis	Greenwood
13-Mar	*Dr. Charles Wattenscheidt	M	W	62	M	Ft Gatlin Hotel	17 yrs	Retired	Baltimore, MD	Angina Pectoris	Vault
13-Mar	*Infant of Mr & Mrs Hazen Carroll	M	W		S	Orange Gen			Orlando	Prematurity, Parental Eclampsia, Toxemia	Greenwood
13-Mar	*Mrs Achrah L. Lucius	F	W	72	M	630 S Division	a 39 yrs	At Home	Ga	Chronic Myo-carditis, Chronic Nephritis	Greenwood
13-Mar	*Margaret Ewing	F	W	10	S	Ocoee, Fla/ Orange Gen	24 days		Ocoee, Fla	Acute Miliary Tuberculosis	Ocoee
13-Mar	*Mildred Lowell	F	W	50	M	4941 Cuylan Ave, Chicago, Ill /Fla Sanit	1 mo	At Home	Chicago, Ill	Probably Double Lobar Pneumonia	Chicago, Ill
12-Mar	Louisa Grant	F	C	76	W	11419 E South	6 yrs	At Home	S.C.	Diabetes	Duzell, S.C.
13-Mar	*Edward Cox	M	W	70	M	Whitney, N.Y. / Lockhart, Fla	4 mos	Retired	Ontario, Canada	Typhoid Fever, Organic Heart Disease	Caldonia, Ont. Canada
15-Mar	Wm M Wells	M	W	86	M	St Cloud/ Fla Sanit	2 wks	Retired (Farmer)	Ohio	Cerebral Hemorrhage, Hemiplegia, Left Side	Ft Dodge, Iowa
16-Mar	*Mrs Mary B. Alban	F	W	50	M	8082 Mich Ave	7 yrs	At Home	WVa	Cancer of the Cervix	Oviedo
15-Mar	*Infant of Mr & Mrs Holloway	M	W			E Washington			Orlando, Fla	Premature	Patrick Cemetery
17-Mar	John Brannon	M	W	42	S	Lake Underhill	4 yrs	Laborer	Ga	TB	Washington, D.C.
18-Mar	Sam Winn	M	C	50		County Home		Laborer	Ga	Chronic Nephritis	County Home
20-Mar	*Joseph [Jasper] B Ozment	M	W	68	M	1864 Cornell Ave	1 yr	Retired	Tenn	Apoplexy	Greenwood

162

1929	Name of Deceased	Sex	Race	Age	Marital	Residence & Place of Death	Orlando Resident	Occupation	Place of Birth	Cause of Death	Place of Burial
21-Mar	August F Freywork	M	W	88	W	401 W Concord	5 yrs	Retired	Germany	Broncho-pneumonia	Greenwood
21-Mar	*Mrs Hattie Davis	F	W	62	W	550 W Piedmont	3 yrs	At Home	Sandersville Ga	Myocarditis	Greenwood
21-Mar	*Christopher Christ	M	W	68	M	Woodron Blvd	5 yrs	Carpenter	N.J.	Myocarditis	Jersey City
21-Mar	*Mrs Ellen Frances Woodman	F	W	86	W	Lockhart, Fla	2 yrs	At Home	R.I.	Paralysis	Apopka, Fla
22-Mar	Sophronia Brooks	F	C	40	M	1501 E South	40 yrs	H.W.	Fla	Lobar Pneumonia	Greenwood
22-Mar	Nathan Bishop	M	C	65	M	626 W Robinson	5 yrs	Painter	N.C.	Acute Nephritis	Greenwood
22-Mar	*Coy M Richardson	M	W	3		O.G.H.	2 yrs		S.C.	Acute gastro ---?	Fair Place, S.C.
24-Mar	*Albert J. Gardner	M	W	80	W	714 S Mills	7 yrs	Retired	N.Y.	Probably Acute Dilation of Heart	Jacksonville, Fla
22-Mar	*Harry L. Beeman	M	W	65	W	22 Gore St	30 yrs	Retired	Ohio	Acute Dilation of Heart	Greenwood
22-Mar	Ruth Louise Haire	F	W	7	S	O.G.H.	7 mos		Orlando, Fla	Pneumonia	Greenwood
10-Mar	Ida Sirmons	F	?	56	W	1049 W Washington	9 yrs	H.W.	Fla	Gastric Colitis	Greenwood
22-Mar	*Leonard G. Brainard	M	W	76	M	RFD 2 B1002	1 mo	Retired	N.Y.P	Endocarditis	Ellington, N.Y.
22-Mar	*Claudio? W Warren	M	W	25	M	O.G.H.	1 mo	Tree Surgeon	N.C.	Collision Auto and Motor Cycle	Greenwood
23-Mar	*John A Dreggars	M	W	46	M	O.G.H.	6 mos	Carpenter	Fla	Carcinoma of Liver	Greenwood
23-Mar	*Verna M. Harris	F	W	9	S	O.G.H.	4 ds		Holopaw, Fla	Acute Broncho Pneumonia	Lake Wales, Fla
24-Mar	*John N Huntsman	M	W	71	M	O.G.H.	14 ds	Retired	Bull Gap, Tenn	Chr Myocarditis	Bristol, Va
25-Mar	*Charles R. Meeker	M	W	28	M	San Juan	1 mo	Baseball Player	Mo	Acute Cardiac Syncope	Kansas City, Kas
25-Mar	*M Harry Kinsey	M	W	64	M	Orlando, Fla Rt #3 Box 86	2 yrs	Retired	Ohio	Hodgkins Disease	Cremation
25-Mar	*Mrs Mary Virginia Wofford	F	W	60	W	Orlando Rt #3	40 yrs	At Home	Miss	Angina	Lake Hill
25-Mar	*Frank Brew [Beev]	M	W	67	S	1124 Kuhl Ave	1 mo	Retired	N.Y.	Apoplexy	Ogdenburg, N.Y.
25-Mar	*Martha E Converse	F	W	79	W	409 Park Lake	6 mos	At Home	Ohio	Angina Pectoris	Mt Vernon, Ohio
27-Mar	Hester Moore	F	W	22	M	O.G.H.	3 mos	H Maid	Ky	Intestinal Obstruction	Garrard, KY
26-Mar	*Anna B Collins	F	W	24	S	Lake 5 miles East of Orlando	2 yrs	At Home	S.C.	Accidentally Drowned	Seneca, S.C.
26-Mar	Clarence Burton Brown [Lee]	M	W	12	S	Lake 5 miles East of Orlando	2 yrs		N.Y	Accidentally Drowned	Greenwood
18-Mar	Till Born	M	C			1229 W Carter St	20 yrs	Laborer	Orlando, Fl	No Physician	Woodlawn

163

1929	Name of Deceased	Sex	Race	Age	Marital	Residence & Place of Death	Orlando Resident	Occupation	Place of Birth	Cause of Death	Place of Burial
29-Mar	Infant of Heywood Rigsbdy & Wife					231 W Moreland	10 yrs		Orlando	Stillborn	Woodlawn
29-Mar	Robert Holt	M	C	1	S	213 N Division St	4 yrs		Orlando	Ascares?	Woodlawn
1-Apr	Aldonia Lee	F	C	22	M	745 Livingston	3 yrs		Fla	Pellagra	Woodlawn
2-Apr	Robert L. Smithwick	M	W	42	M	O.G.H.		Town Marshall	Whitman, Ga	Gun Shot Wound	Groveland, Fla
28-Mar	Louis Bradshaw	F	C			528 W Holden			528 W Holden	Stillborn	Memorial Park
1-Apr	*Lewis Felton	M	C	65	W	County Home	6 mos	Labor	Ga	Chronic Nephritis	County Home
1-Apr	Leland J. Collins	M	W	16d		1305 Catherine			Orlando	Premature	Greenwood
2-Apr	*Dr. J. E. Elligood [Ellegood]	M	W	68	M	O.G.H.	4 mos	Retired	Concord, Del	Chr Myocarditis	Wilmington, Del
4-Apr	B. J. Johnson	M	C	36	M	709 Thomas	9 yrs	Cook	Fla	TB	Woodlawn
5-Apr	*Hattie Helenski	F	W	63	M	1220 E Livingston	4 ds	At Home	Europe	Chronic Nephritis	Chicago, Ill
5-Apr	*George Chandler	M	C	65	W	County Home	2 yrs	Laborer	Ga	Heart Disease	County Home
5-Apr	*Francis L Skelly	M	W	52	M	800 Lucerne Terrace	10 yrs	Mgr, Fruit Growers Assn	Housdale, Pa	Pneumonia	Greenwood
6-Apr	*Albert L. Bentley	M	W	80	M	1816 Cornell	19 yrs	Retired	Casnovia, Grand Rapids, Mich	Myocarditis	Cremation
6-Apr	Dorothy Harding	F	W	19	S	642 West Amelia	18 yrs	Student	Grand Rapids, Mich	Acute Endocarditis	Vault
6-Apr	Elizabeth J. Hall	F	W	66	M	O.G.H.	4? mos	H.W.	N.Y.	Myocarditis	Glen Falls, N.Y.
7-Apr	Jerry L. Jackson	F	C	29	M	208 Bryant	4 yrs	H.W.	Ga	Pulmonary Hemorrhage	Woodlawn
7-Feb	*Mrs John H. Gaskins	F	W	36	W	Fla San and Hosp	3 yrs	At Home	Ga	Following Operation	Nashville, Ga
9-Mar	Harry John Smith	M	W	66	W	Penn Ave	5 mos	Carpenter	England	Cerebral Hemorrhage	Painsville, Ohio
18-Mar	Ollie Cayson	F	W	82	M	Sunny St.		Housewife	Fla	Acute Cardiac Dilitation	Rose Hill Cemetery
4-Apr	*Melvin V Hayes	M	W	20d	S	E Marion			Orlando, Fla	Prematurity	Powell Cemetery
6-Apr	Mrs Tonnie Anne Green	F	W	29	M	O.G.H./ Eustis, Fla	5 ds	Housewife	Carterville, Ga	Peritonitis	Eustis, Fla
8-Apr	*Mrs Emma Florence Johnson	F	W	52	W	438 Macy	52 yrs	At Home	Orlando, Fla	Pulmonary Tuberculosis	Greenwood
8-Apr	Isaac Thomas	M	C	1	S	1216 Polk Ave	4 yrs	Infant	Orlando	Broncho Pneumonia	Greenwood
9-Apr	*Mrs Ella Barwick	F	W	83	W	438 E Kaley	3 yrs	Home	Amands	Arterio-sclerosis	Swainsboro, Ga
9-Apr	*Harriett Louise Horn	F	W	86	W	Fla San/ N Garland	47 yrs	At Home	Cincinnati, Ohio	Broncho Pneumonia	Greenwood
10-Apr	Josie Minnie Lee Hain [see below]	F	W	21	M	O.G.H./ Ocoee	22 ds	Housewife	Miss	Typhoid Fever	Ocoee, Fla

164

1929	Name of Deceased	Sex	Race	Age	Marital	Residence & Place of Death	Orlando Resident	Occupation	Place of Birth	Cause of Death	Place of Burial
10-Apr	Dorethea Watts	F	C	17	S	O.G.H./DeLand, Fla	3 1/2 hrs	School Girl	DeLand, Fla	Peritonitis	DeLand, Fla
10-Apr	Mary Jane Segroves	F	W	21	S	RFD 4	2 ½ yrs	At Home	Tenn	Chronic Pulmonary Tuberculosis	
10-Apr	*Mrs Jocie Haines [see above]	F	W	19	M	O.G.H./Ocoee, Fla	1 mo	At Home	Miss	Typhoid	Ocoee, Fla
10-Apr	*Mary K Dura	F	W	54	M	Fla San/Twesburg, Ohio	1 mo	At Home	Bohemia	Myocarditis	Cleveland, Ohio
10-Apr	*Mrs Louise M Huff	F	W	84	W	Lockhart, Fla	3 yrs	Home	Wrentham, Mass	Heart Trouble	Apopka
11-Apr	*May M Watson	F	W	70	W a	210 E South Ave	15 yrs		Youngstown, Ohio	Endocarditis	Greenwood
12-Apr	*Infant of Mr & Mrs W H Green	F	W	18h	S	O.G.H./Box 2			Orlando, Fla	Premature Birth	Cremation
13-Apr	*Anna Johnson	F	W	70	W a	RFD 4	4 yrs	At Home	Sweden	Cerebral Hemorrahge	Greenwood
13-Apr	*Alice H. Wheless	F	W	72	W	1607 E Jefferson	6 mos	At Home	Talbot Co., Ga	Result of Fracture of Left Hipbone	Phenix City, Ala
13-Apr	Emmit Mitchell Weir [Nair]	M	W	1	S	O.G.H./Groveland, Fla	10 hrs	Infant	Sebring, Fla	Chr Broncho Pneumonia	Groveland, Fla
14-Apr	W T Adams	M	C	66	M	410 W Jefferson	28 yrs	Barber	Ga	Apoplexy	Greenwood
14-Apr	*Richard Wolfe	M	W	68	M	O.G.H./Conway	6 mos	Retired	Mass	Acute Dilation of Heart	Selma, Ohio
14-Apr	*Mable Rice Lane	F	W	51	W	90 E Central	4 mos	At Home	Lisman, KY	Chronic Myocarditis	Lisman, Ohio
16-Apr	James M Kelley	M	W	43	M	644 Hillcrest	4 mos	Allied Contractor	Macedonia Iowa	Aortic Regurgitation	Omaha, Neb
16-Apr	*Infant of Mr & Mrs Ralph Byrd	F	W			Fla Sant/1610 E Marks			Orlando, Fla	Stillborn	Greenwood
19-Apr	*Russell S. Moore	M	W	50	M	417 S Eola Drive	6 yrs	District Mgr Otis Elevator	Me	Cerebral Hemorrhage	Greenwood
19-Apr	*Robert M Webeking	M	W	17	S	O.G.H./405 E Concord	11 yrs	Office Real Estate	Gotha, Fla	Acute Streptococci	Greenwood
19-Apr	Zack Turk	M	C	75	S	O.G.H./Apopka, Fla	12 ds	Labor	Ala	Hypertrophic Prostate	Apopka, Fla
20-Apr	Alonzo W Mickle	M	W	47	M	Minneola, Fla	3 wks	Lather	Mich	Carcinoma of Lung	Minneola
20-Apr	Infant of D H Hanes	M	W	12 hrs	S	O.G.H./Pine Castle	1/2 da	Infant	Fla	Failure of Lungs to Expand	Greenwood
20-Apr	Loyd Detwyler	M	C	81	M	609 W South	43 yrs	Laborer	Ga	Influenzal Pneumonia	Memorial Park
21-Apr	*Rev John D. Martin	M	W	75	W	Fla Sant/525 E Church	2 yrs	Retired	Penn	Cerebral Hemorrahge	Philadelphia, Pa
21-Apr	Oliver T. Green	M	C	9	S	115 N Biggs	9 yrs	School Boy	Orlando	Ptomaine Poisoning	Woodlawn
23-Apr	Aubray L Adkins	M	W	24	S	O.G.H./Lake Jem	4 mos	Telegraph Operator	Vienna, Ga	Fracture of Spine	Vienna, Ga

1929	Name of Deceased	Sex	Race	Age	Marital	Residence & Place of Death	Orlando Resident	Occupation	Place of Birth	Cause of Death	Place of Burial
27 Apr 14	W. R. Frary	M	W	77	M	Tremont Hotel/ Eustis, Fla	2 ds	Retired Plumber	Not known Maine		Eustis, Fla
19-Apr	*Mrs Dr Jennie M Covert	F	W	80	W	1919 S Kuhl Ave	4 mos	Retired	Mass	Acute Dilitation of Heart	Clinton, Wis
23-Apr	*Nichelos Van Polan [Polen]	M	W	64	D	O.G.H./ Fairvilla	2 ds	Farming	Germany	Pernicious Anemia	Greenwood
24-Apr	*Delbert A Routh	M	W	52	M	132 E Muriel	20 yrs	Sheet Metal Worker	Maine	Aneurism of Thoreac Aorta	Greenwood
25-Apr	*Mrs Josephine Yates	F	W	86	M	Yates Ave	8 yrs	At Home	N.Y.	Chr Myocarditis	Madelia, Minn
25-Apr	*Robert L. Bunch	M	W	57	M	1115 W Central	30 yrs	Retired	S.C.	Cerebral Hemorrhage	Greenwood
26-Apr	*Mrs Aggie Winn	F	W	37	M	Heitz Sant	20 ds	At Home	Pine Castle, Fla	Chronic Nephritis	Greenwood
28-Apr	*Mrs Fannie Kerns	F	W	43	M	538 Virginia Dr	3 yrs 4 mos	At Home	Streeter, Ill	Buncular? Fibrillation Heart Block	
28-Apr	*Harry M Slaymaker	M	W	56	M	O.G.H./ 1867 Miller Ave	1 da	Employee of O Morning Sentinel	Penn	Hemophlegia, Cerebral Hemorrhage	Winter Park
29-Apr	*Edward P Shannon	M	W	25	S	O.G.H./ Trenton, Ont	7 mos		Trenton, Ont	General Tuberculosis	Trenton, Ont, Canada
29-Apr	J M Holt	M	W	60	M	109 S Osceola	2 yrs	Real Estate Agt	Mass	Angina Pectoris	Richmond, Va
30-Apr	*Lee M Marble	M	W	40	M	O.G.H./20 N. Eola Dr	10 yrs	Horticulturist	Perry, Mich	Gunshot Wound of Head	Bowling Green, Ohio